Domesticating International Criminal Law

This book provides an essential and critical overview of the most significant issues concerning the domestication of international criminal law, in particular with regard to the implementation of the ICC Statute. It discusses the most recent proposals for reform of the German Code of Crimes under International Law, the "*Völkerstrafgesetzbuch*", 20 years after its entering into force, and introduces the project for an Italian code of international crimes drafted by the Commission established in 2022 by the Ministry of Justice.

Following the adoption of the ICC Statute, many States, including Germany with the "*Völkerstrafgesetzbuch*", introduced specific legislation to incorporate international criminal law into their domestic legal systems, and a considerable number of them have been investigating and prosecuting war crimes, crimes against humanity, genocide and even aggression ever since. Twenty-five years later, however, the process is not completed as other countries, like Italy, are still working on adopting provisions on international crimes. This book opens with a broad overview of the different approaches of the domestication of international criminal law, with a specific focus on the German and the Italian systems. After an assessment of the prerequisites for the domestic implementation of international criminal law, also from a constitutional law perspective, each chapter offers an in-depth analysis of a specific issue, such as: the definition of international crimes (genocide and crimes against humanity, war crimes and aggression); the applicability of and exceptions to the general principles of domestic criminal law; the regulation of individual criminal responsibility; sanctions and sentencing; as well as procedural aspects related to immunities, jurisdiction and prosecutorial discretion. The strong academic perspective of many authors is complemented by an equally strong practitioner perspective of the others, provided by legal scholars in the highest positions in international and national judicial institutions, resulting in a well-informed and critical appraisal of the most recent developments overall in the international criminal justice system.

Domesticating International Criminal Law will be of great interest to legal scholars and students, as well as practitioners with an interest in comparative and international law, international criminal law and international relations.

Florian Jeßberger is Professor of Criminal Law at Humboldt-Universität zu Berlin where he holds the Chair in Criminal Law, Criminal Procedure, International Criminal Law and Modern Legal History and serves as the Director of the Franz von Liszt Institute for International Criminal Justice. He is a Co-Editor of the Journal of International Criminal Justice and published several books and academic articles on international and transnational criminal law, including *Principles of International Criminal Law* (2020, with G Werle) and *Histories of Transnational Criminal Law* (2021, ed with N Boister and S Gless).

Chantal Meloni is Associate Professor of Criminal Law at the Law Faculty of Università degli Studi di Milano where she teaches international criminal law. She is a criminal lawyer admitted to the Italian bar and serves as Senior Legal Advisor to the European Center for Constitutional and Human Rights in Berlin. She also represents victims in proceedings before the ICC and was a member of the Commission established in 2022 by the Ministry of Justice to draft an Italian Code of International Crimes. She is the author of numerous academic articles, book chapters and papers on a variety of issues regarding international justice, including the book *Command Responsibility in International Criminal Law* (2010).

Maria Crippa holds a PhD in 'Juridical Sciences Cesare Beccaria' from Università degli Studi di Milano, with a doctoral thesis on the Italian implementation of the Rome Statute of the International Criminal Court. In 2020 she was Visiting Researcher at Humboldt-Universität zu Berlin. Her research interests cover the domestic prosecution of international crimes; on these topics she published in various law journals. In 2016 she worked at the International Criminal Court in The Hague as a trainee in the Appeals Chamber and she is a qualified lawyer in Italy.

Directions and Developments in Criminal Justice and Law

www.routledge.com/Directions-and-Developments-in-Criminal-Justice-and-Law/book-series/DDCJL

The ways in which crime is constructed in society is of time-honoured interest to criminologists across the globe. The ever-changing landscape of what is criminal and what is not affects scholars and policymakers in their approach to the body of law defining prohibited conduct, how that law evolves and the modes by which it is administered. Rule of law cannot exist without a transparent legal system, strong enforcement structures and an independent judiciary to protect against the arbitrary use of power. Critical consideration of the mechanisms through which societies attempt to make the rule of law a reality is essential to understanding and developing effectual criminal justice systems. The *Directions and Developments in Criminal Justice and Law* series offers the best research on criminal justice and law around the world, offering original insights on a broadly defined range of socio-legal topics in law, criminal procedure, courts, justice, legislation and jurisprudence. With an eye towards using innovative and advanced methodologies, series monographs offer solid social science scholarship illuminating issues and trends in law, crime and justice. Books in this series will appeal to criminologists, sociologists and other social scientists, as well as policymakers, legal researchers and practitioners.

8. **Black Iconography and Colonial (re)production at the ICC**
   (In)dependence Cha Cha Cha?
   Stanley Mwangi Wanjiru

9. **Criminal Justice Responses to Domestic Abuse in Northern Ireland**
   Ronagh J.A. McQuigg

10. **Prison Segregation: The Limits of Law**
    Eleanor Brown

11. **Domesticating International Criminal Law**
    Reflections on the Italian and German Experiences
    Florian Jeßberger, Chantal Meloni and Maria Crippa

Domesticating International Criminal Law

Reflections on the Italian and German Experiences

Edited by Florian Jeßberger, Chantal Meloni and Maria Crippa

Routledge
Taylor & Francis Group
LONDON AND NEW YORK

First published 2023
by Routledge
4 Park Square, Milton Park, Abingdon, Oxon OX14 4RN

and by Routledge
605 Third Avenue, New York, NY 10158

Routledge is an imprint of the Taylor & Francis Group, an informa business

British Library Cataloguing-in-Publication Data
A catalogue record for this book is available from the British Library

ISBN: 978-1-032-34195-8 (hbk)
ISBN: 978-1-032-34196-5 (pbk)
ISBN: 978-1-003-32095-1 (ebk)

DOI: 10.4324/9781003320951

Typeset in Times New Roman
by Newgen Publishing UK

Contents

Contributors

Rosario Aitala is Judge of the International Criminal Court and Professor of International Criminal Law at Libera Università Internazionale degli Studi Sociali (LUISS) "Guido Carli" of Rome. Previously, he has worked as judge and prosecutor in Milano, Trapani and Rome and has served as Senior Adviser on International Crime and Crisis Areas to the Italian Foreign Minister and as Senior Adviser on International and Legal Affairs to the President of the Italian Senate. He has worked in Albania, Afghanistan, the Balkans and Latin America dealing with mafia, terrorism, international crime and institutional building. He is author and scientific counsellor of the *Italian Review of Geopolitics Limes* and has published the books *Il Metodo della Paura* (2018) and *Diritto Internazionale Penale* (2021). He was a member of the Commission established in 2022 by the Ministry of Justice to draft an Italian Code of International Crimes.

Alessandra Annoni is Associate Professor for International Law at the Law Faculty of Università degli Studi di Ferrara where she teaches international military criminal law. She is Deputy Director of the Centre for European Legal Studies on Macro-Crime and co-coordinator of its core crimes cluster. She has published extensively on international humanitarian law, international human rights law and international criminal law, including the books *L'occupazione 'ostile' nel diritto internazionale contemporaneo* (2012) and *La tutela internazionale della persona umana nei conflitti armati* (2019, co-authored with Francesco Salerno).

Giulio Bartolini is Associate Professor of International Law at Università degli Studi Roma Tre where he also directs the International Humanitarian Law Legal Clinic and a Lecturer at the Geneva Academy of International Humanitarian Law and Human Rights. He is Member of the National IHL Commission established by the Italian Ministry of Foreign Affairs and President of the IHL Committee of Experts of the Italian Red Cross. He is Editor-in-Chief of the *Yearbook of International Disaster Law* and Managing Editor of the journal *Questions of International Law*.

Boris Burghardt is Visiting Professor of Criminal Law at the Leuphana Universität Lüneburg, He is the author of numerous academic articles, book chapters and papers on a variety of issues regarding international criminal justice, including a monograph on command responsibility (*Die Vorgesetztenverantwortlichkeit im völkerrechtlichen Straftatsystem*, 2008). Together with Florian Knauer (Friedrich-Schiller-Universität Jena), he is currently a Principal Investigator in a research project funded by the German Research Foundation on the sentence enforcement for international crimes in the aftermath of the Second World War.

Marta Cartabia is Professor of Constitutional Law at Università Commerciale "Luigi Bocconi" di Milano. From 2021 to 2022 she was the Italian Minister of Justice. She was also Judge and President Emeritus of the Italian Constitutional Court. She previously taught Public and Constitutional Law at Università degli Studi di Milano-Bicocca. Since 2017 she has been Substitute Member for Italy in the European Union Venice Commission for Democracy through Law; previously she was a Senior Expert for the European Union Fundamental Rights Agency Network of Legal Experts (FRALEX).

Antonio Coco is Lecturer in Law at the Law School, University of Essex, and a Research Fellow at the Oxford Institute for Ethics, Law and Armed Conflict, at the Blavatnik School of Government, University of Oxford. He holds a PhD in Law from Université de Genève, and he is admitted to practice law in Italy. Antonio's research interests include general international law, international law applicable to new technologies, and international criminal law. He is the author of the monograph *The Defence of Mistake of Law in International Criminal Law: a Study on Ignorance and Blame* (2022).

Maria Crippa holds a PhD in 'Juridical Sciences Cesare Beccaria' from Università degli Studi di Milano, with a doctoral thesis on the Italian implementation of the Rome Statute of the International Criminal Court. In 2020 she was Visiting Researcher at Humboldt-Universität zu Berlin. Her research interests cover the domestic prosecution of international crimes; on these topics she has published in various law journals. In 2016 she worked at the International Criminal Court in The Hague as a trainee in the Appeals Chamber and she is a qualified lawyer in Italy.

Aziz Epik is Assistant Professor of Criminal Law and Criminology (Tenure Track) at Universität Hamburg where he teaches, among others, German and international criminal law. He studied law and received his PhD in Law from Humboldt-Universität zu Berlin with a dissertation on sentencing under the German Code of Crimes Under International Law ('Die Strafzumessung bei Taten nach dem Völkerstrafgesetzbuch', 2017), for which he was awarded the faculty prize for the best dissertation in criminal law. He holds an LLM from the University of Cambridge (2017) with a specialisation in International Law.

Florian Jeßberger is Professor of Criminal Law at Humboldt-Universität zu Berlin where he holds the Chair in Criminal Law, Criminal Procedure, International Criminal Law and Modern Legal History and serves as the Director of the Franz von Liszt Institute for International Criminal Justice. He is a Co-Editor of the Journal of International Criminal Justice and has published several books and academic articles on international and transnational criminal law, including *Principles of International Criminal Law* (4th edn, 2020, with G Werle) and *Histories of Transnational Criminal Law* (2021, ed with N Boister and S Gless).

Annegret Hartig holds a Dr iur from Universität Hamburg with a dissertation in international criminal law ('Making Aggression a Crime Under Domestic Law', 2023). She serves as Program Director of the Global Institute for the Prevention of Aggression. As a research assistant to Professor Jeßberger, she worked on the latest editions of his textbooks *Principles of International Criminal Law* (2020) and *Völkerstrafrecht* (2020).

Marco Longobardo is a Senior Lecturer in International Law at the University of Westminster. He undertook his doctoral studies at Università degli Studi di Roma "La Sapienza" and previously lectured at Università degli Studi di Messina and in the context of international humanitarian law courses for the personnel of the Italian armed forces. He has published extensively on public international law issues and he is the author of *The Use of Armed Force in Occupied Territory* (2018), for which he received the 2021 Paul Reuter Prize. Marco is on the editorial boards of the *Journal of International Humanitarian Legal Studies* and of the *International Community Law Review*.

Triestino Mariniello is Reader in Law (Associate Professor) at Liverpool John Moores University. Currently he is Alexander von Humboldt Research Fellow at Humboldt-Universität zu Berlin.

Kalika Mehta is a human rights lawyer and a Research Coordinator at the Centre for British Studies, Humboldt-Universität zu Berlin. She holds a PhD from Universität Hamburg and an LLM from the Geneva Academy of International Humanitarian Law and Human Rights. She is qualified to practice law in India. Her broad research interests include Third World Approaches to International Law, particularly international criminal law, corporate accountability and legal history.

Chantal Meloni is Associate Professor of Criminal Law at the Law Faculty of Università degli Studi di Milano where she teaches international criminal law. She is a criminal lawyer admitted to the Italian bar and serves as Senior Legal Advisor to the European Center for Constitutional and Human Rights in Berlin. She also represents victims in proceedings before the ICC and was a member of the Commission established in 2022 by the Ministry of Justice to draft an Italian Code of International Crimes.. She is the author of numerous academic articles, book chapters and papers on a variety of issues regarding international justice, including the book *Command Responsibility in International Criminal Law* (2010).

Volker Nerlich is Judge at the Appeals Chamber of the Special Criminal Court in Bangui. He is also Honorary Professor of international criminal justice at the Faculty of Law of Humboldt-Universität zu Berlin and Lecturer at the Ecole Nationale de l'Administration et de la Magistrature of the Central African Republic. He is the author of numerous academic publications in the field of international criminal law and procedure, humanitarian law and transitional justice.

Marco Pedrazzi is Professor of International Law at the Department of International, Legal, Historical and Political Studies of Università degli Studi di Milano, where he teaches international law and international law of armed conflict. He is the author and editor of numerous publications dealing, inter alia, with issues of international criminal law, international humanitarian law and international human rights law. He was a member of the Commission established in 2022 by the Ministry of Justice to draft an Italian Code of International Crimes.

Fausto Pocar is Professor Emeritus of International Law at Università degli Studi di Milano. He holds honorary doctorates from the Universities of Antwerp and Buenos Aires, and serves as a Member of the Institut de droit international. He was a Member and President of the Human Rights Committee under the ICCPR (1985–2000), as well as a Judge and President of the ICTY and of the Appeals Chamber of the ICTR (2000–2017). He is now an ad hoc Judge of the International Court of Justice. He was the co-president of the Commission established in 2022 by the Ministry of Justice to draft an Italian Code of International Crimes.

Luigi Prosperi is an Assistant Professor in International Criminal Law at the Law School of the University of Amsterdam, where he teaches in the LLM program on international and transnational criminal law. He is a former Associate Legal Officer at the ICTY. He is the author of several articles, book chapters and papers, including on crimes against humanity and on the exercise of the ICC's jurisdiction in situations involving non-States Parties. Luigi is also a member of the editorial board of the *Rivista Ordine internazionale e diritti umani*.

Chiara Ragni is Associate Professor of International Law at the Faculty of Political Science of Università degli Studi di Milano, where she teaches international law and international human rights law. Throughout her career, Chiara has been involved in national and international research projects, conferences, courses and lectures on international criminal law, a field on which she has focused her research activities being also the author of articles in journals, book chapters that address different aspects of the topic, and of a volume on the internationalised criminal tribunals.

Alice Riccardi is Associate Professor of International Law at the Department of Law of Università degli Studi Roma Tre, where she directs the International Protection of Human Rights Legal Clinic. She has appeared as amicus curiae, third intervener or legal counsel before the International Criminal Court, the European Court of Human Rights, the UN CEDAW and the Ombudsperson of the ISIL (Da'esh) and Al-Qaida UNSC Sanctions Committee. She is the author of the book *Sentencing at the International Criminal Court: From Nuremberg to The Hague* (2016).

John Schabedoth is a Research Associate at the Chair of Professor Zimmermann at Universität Potsdam. Before that, he was a trainee lawyer (Referendar) at the Berlin Court of Appeal, with positions at the German Ministry of Foreign Affairs, the Council of Europe and a GIZ project in Beijing. In addition to professional stays at the Institute of Peace and Conflict Studies in Delhi and at a law firm in investment protection law in Brussels, he studied law with a focus on international law at the Fletcher School in Medford and at the Universities of Frankfurt, Helsinki, Lyon II and Marburg.

Nicola Selvaggi is Associate Professor of Criminal Law at Università degli Studi "Mediterranea" di Reggio Calabria and Senior Fellow at the Carol and Lawrence Zicklin Center for Business Ethics Research, Wharton School (University of Pennsylvania). He was also Hauser Global Fellow at the New York University Law School and, in the same University, Senior Fellow of the Program on Corporate Compliance and Enforcement. He is member of the AIDP (Association Internationale de Droit Pénal) and one of the founders of the Italian Chapter of the International Society of Public Law and member of its General Council. He was a member of the Commission established in 2022 by the Ministry of Justice to draft an Italian Code of International Crimes.

Leonie Steinl is a Professor of Criminal Law, International Criminal Law and Interdisciplinary Legal Studies at Münster Universität. Her research interests lie in international criminal law and German criminal law, with a particular focus on critical perspectives and gender-based and sexual violence. She has published widely on these issues, including the monograph *Child Soldiers as Agents of War and Peace* (2017) and the volume *International Criminal Law – A Counter-Hegemonic Project?* (2022, ed with F Jeßberger and K Mehta).

Valeria Vegh Weis teaches criminology and transitional justice at Universidad de Buenos Aires and Universidad Nacional de Quilmes. She is currently a Research Fellow at Universität Konstanz Zukunftskolleg, where she researches on the role of human rights and victims' organisations in the confrontation of State crimes. From 2019 to 2021, Vegh Weis was an Alexander von Humboldt Post-Doctoral Researcher at Freie Universität Berlin, where she still teaches State crime criminology. She has held different fellowships including the Fulbright and the Hauser Global Scholarships. Her book *Marxism and Criminology: a History of Criminal Selectivity* (2017, 2018) was awarded the Choice Award by the American Library Association and the Outstanding Book Award by the Academy of Criminal Justice Sciences.

Francesco Viganò is Judge of the Italian Constitutional Court and Professor of Criminal Law at Università Commerciale "Luigi Bocconi" di Milano and, previously, at Università degli Studi di Milano. He was co-founder and director of the law journals *Diritto penale contemporaneo* and *Diritto penale contemporaneo – Rivista trimestrale*. He is Co-Director of Legal Studies in International, European and Comparative Criminal Law, Studi di diritto penale costituzionale ed europeo and Scienze penalistiche e criminologia. He has published widely on criminal law and European/international cooperation in criminal matters, including the books *La proporzionalità della pena: profili di diritto penale e costituzionale* (2021) and *Diritto penale. Una conversazione* (2018, with F Palazzo).

Andreas Zimmermann is Professor of Public, Public International and European Union Law at Universität Potsdam and Director of the Potsdam Centre of Human Rights. He has taught at, inter alia, the University of Michigan, the University of Johannesburg, Hebrew University of Jerusalem, and Birzeit University of Palestine. He was adviser to the German delegation during the Diplomatic Conference on the Establishment of an International Criminal Court, and serves as a member of the Permanent Court of Arbitration, as well as of the Human Rights Committee. He acted as counsel in various cases before international courts, including the International Court of Justice, the Iran–US Claims Tribunal and the European Court of Justice. He is a member of the advisory board on public international law of the German Ministry of Foreign Affairs and has been ad hoc Judge at the ECtHR.

Foreword

This volume presents papers from the conference entitled 'Domesticating International Criminal Justice – Current Challenges'. It was attended by, among others, Raffaele Piccirillo and Nicola Selvaggi, who had, as early as the summer of 2021, presented to me the need to fill a gap in the legal system, thus completing after 20 years the implementation of the Rome Statute.

At first it was decided to wait, because of the urgencies of the government's programme that were pressing, in particular reforms drawn up in the framework of the National Plan for Complementary Investments ("*Piano Nazionale di Ripresa e Resilienza*", PNRR). However, the conflict that broke out in Ukraine immediately rekindled the need and urgency to start again from that reflection, in order to make our possible contribution available to the parliament and the country. The drafting of a code of international crimes seemed to us an act of civilisation of law, essential to respond to the most sensational event in our recent history.

Thus, alongside a series of important cooperation activities with other international bodies (in particular, with the International Criminal Court and Eurojust), the Ministry of Justice began its work by setting up a Commission of experts, chaired by Professors Francesco Palazzo and Fausto Pocar. The results of the Commission's intense and fruitful work led to draft articles, accompanied by a valuable explanatory report, which are published on the Ministry of Justice website,[1] and whose English translation is presented in this volume.[2]

The conclusion of the work by the Commission was followed in July by the illustration to the then-Prime Minister Draghi of our intention to legally adopt the project for a code of international crimes. It was, however, not possible to go any further. As is known, the former government continued to operate until the day the new one sworn in but only within the perimeter of current affairs, which does not allow the outgoing government to commit to new policy choices.

The adaptation of our legal system to the Rome Statute is not a mere symbolic fact. It is the dutiful fulfilment of commitments undertaken at the international level, giving concrete expression to the aspiration that law may take the place of arms as the sole instrument to resolve conflicts. Providing ourselves with a code of international crimes would also mean, for our country, not remaining on the side lines in the face of a conflict taking place on our doorstep. While it is true that there has never been a shortage of conflicts, the war is today so close to our doorstep that it also produces effects affecting us closely in our daily lives.

It should be added that a redefinition of jurisdiction will allow our magistrates to have all the necessary tools to achieve full and effective protection of the goods at stake. In other European Union countries, moreover, national judges are already investigating and prosecuting crimes against humanity that are being committed. We have contributed by supporting the work of the International Criminal Court and Eurojust, but our judges have not yet been able to act because of the missing legislation that would allow them to exercise their jurisdiction fully and clearly.

It has been observed that one of the reasons beyond the difficulty in adopting a code of international crimes may be the fear of jeopardising the system of guarantees safeguarding our criminal justice. In this regard, the Palazzo–Pocar Commission has cautiously taken care to draft this body of legislation in full respect of constitutional principles; caution also used in adjusting the sanctioning part.

Our Constitution calls for justice. And it calls for justice to be done with full respect for guarantees. There is a hendiadys that we cannot fail to emphasise in these times of ours: there is no peace without justice, peace and justice are two words that must go together. Not only because justice guarantees peace, but also because there can be no true peace process that does not pass through a correct enforcement of justice.

Of course, there is justice and justice. It does not help peace if justice is understood as mere revenge or as a "trial against the enemy". This is precisely why we need justice that is celebrated in courtrooms. There is nothing easier than war calling for war, than revenge being the most instinctive response to events of extraordinary gravity. This conception of justice must break out of semantic declinations.

Justice taking place in courts is the first act that is incumbent on those who have suffered acts of unprecedented gravity, such as those acts characterising every armed conflict. Victims demand a word of justice, a public acknowledgement of the full gravity of what happened. And our courts must be allowed to pronounce that word of justice. We owe it to all those women and men who have had their lives shattered, devastated, to those who are missing and cannot be reunited with their families, to the victims of torture, rape and violence of all kinds, to those who, in short, have been trapped in this episode of our history that we never wanted to see again.

Marta Cartabia
Professor of Constitutional Law and Constitutional Justice at Università Commerciale "Luigi Bocconi" di Milano
Former Minister of Justice

Notes

1 www.giustizia.it/giustizia/it/mg_1_36_0.page?contentId=COS372730 See also https://www.sistemapenale.it/it/documenti/codice-dei-crimini-internazionali-pubblicata-la-relazione-della-commissione-palazzo-pocar

2 See The Italian Ministry of Justice Proposal for a Code of International Crimes of 2022 ("Palazzo-Pocar Draft") (EN), p 273.

Preface

Never has international criminal justice attracted as much attention, from practitioners, scholars and the general public alike, as in the past troubled months. The conflict in Europe has subverted the international order, acting as the detonator of pre-existing fault lines and degenerative phenomena of a political nature which have been poisoning the international community for a long time. Any "shot in Sarajevo" has prodromes and antecedents.

Two political factors are particularly worth being pondered upon in the discrete context of international criminal justice. Multilateral political fora, first and foremost the United Nations Security Council, have steadily declined in relevance, failing to prevent and address most, if not all, armed conflicts, political crises and situations of mass abuse of fundamental rights. The costs in human lives and well-being, economic development, environmental security, political stability and democracy have been immense, notably in the Middle East and Africa. Parallelly, the acquiescence with which the international community has frequently tolerated or ignored mass atrocities, and the arrogant disregard and even ridiculing of international law and justice by autocrats and liberal democracies alike, has lowered the legal, political, ethical and moral principles which had been painfully erected on the ruins of the world wars. Today, as a "piecemeal third world war" has unfolded, according to the farsighted formula first pronounced by Pope Francis in 2014, the inevitable condition for human civilisation to outlast the circumstances is the preservation of international law and justice, especially justice of atrocity crimes. Whether this acknowledgement will eventually emerge among States from the traumas of the conflict remains to be seen.

The 2021 Milan conference "Domesticating International Criminal Justice – Current Challenges" revolved around one of the most crucial questions of international criminal justice, namely the relationship between national jurisdictions and international criminal tribunals. The International Criminal Court was conceived as complementary to national jurisdictions, to the effect that a case before the Court is to be declared inadmissible if it is or has been investigated or prosecuted by the courts of the State having ordinary jurisdiction, unless the concerned State is genuinely unable or unwilling to proceed. The primary aim of the statutory system is urging States to investigate and prosecute atrocity crimes. Theoretically, the Court will have fully accomplished its mandate the very moment it proves superfluous. Suicide is the Court's eventual objective.

One of the consequences of the Court being inherently residual – *ie*, a jurisdiction of last resort – and of national courts enjoying primacy, is that State Parties to the treaty conventionally referred to as the "Rome Statute" are duty bound to prosecute international crimes falling within the Court's jurisdiction. For these purposes, they have to implement domestically the Statute, both providing for the categories and classes of crimes set forth therein and establishing grounds of criminal jurisdiction: territoriality, active nationality, passive nationality, universality or a combination of them.

The Statute implicitly refers to these obligations in the Preamble, where it recalls the duty of State Parties to exercise criminal jurisdiction over international crimes and to adopt measures at domestic level to ensure effective prosecution of the most serious crimes of concern to the international community as a whole; as well as, in Articles 1, 17 and 18, envisaging the principle of complementarity and preliminary rulings on admissibility.

On the other hand, the main corollary of the general obligation of State Parties to cooperate fully with the Court in investigations and prosecutions, set forth in Article 86 of the Statute, is the duty under Article 88 to ensure that procedures are available in national laws for all the forms of cooperation specified in Part 9 of the Statute. Italy has partially abided by these duties with Law no 237 of 23 December 2012, which establishes the procedures for the Italian authorities to provide the Court with assistance. For instance, they can take the testimony or a statement from a witness or collect another evidence on the Court's request. However, there is another and at times even more important form of cooperation with the Court or with national judicial authorities who are investigating atrocities, that is securing evidence on atrocity crimes *proprio motu*, particularly when it may not be available subsequently due to armed conflicts or other security emergencies. Recent circumstances have highlighted the value of proactive attitudes of States who, for instance, can take statements from refugees who have fled armed conflicts and have witnessed international crimes. At the time being, Italy lacks legal grounds to do so.

Finally, the inherent limitedness of the Court's space for action, and inevitable selectivity of the crimes it is in the position to prosecute, also makes it an ethical obligation for State Parties to be legally equipped to contribute to the cause of international criminal justice, by adopting universality as one of the jurisdictional grounds.

Italy lacks a legal basis to prosecute the crimes in the Court's jurisdiction.[1] Aggression and crimes against humanity are unknown to Italian legislation, save a reference to the latter category in the offences of instigation to commit international crimes and of dissemination of propaganda based on the denial of international crimes. While the underlying acts of most crimes against humanity under Article 7(1) of the Rome Statute are covered by

Italian criminal law as ordinary offences, albeit sometimes carrying low penalties, others of importance are not or are only indirectly criminalised: extermination, deportation and forcible transfer, forced pregnancy, persecution, enforced disappearance of persons, apartheid and so forth. Either way, the absence of the contextual element as an ingredient of the offences plainly makes the existing provisions inadequate for the criteria of inadmissibility under Article 17 of the Statute to be met. For the purposes of the Statute and international customary law alike, an act only qualifies as a crime against humanity when committed as part of a widespread or systematic attack directed against a civilian population. There lies the disvalue of this category of international crimes.

Many war crimes are not covered by the Italian Wartime Military Criminal Code and many others are criminalised through the "legislation by reference" technique, which is at odds with the requirement of specificity of criminal law. The contextual element requires armed conflicts to involve Italy, including in theory non-international conflicts, although the provisions, dating back to 1941, are plainly aligned with international conflicts and it would be challenging to apply them meaningfully also to non-international conflicts.

The 1967 law criminalising genocide has several problems and needs revision. There are serious problems with the grounds for criminal jurisdiction, too. Italian jurisdiction only covers certain offences committed abroad either on the basis of the active or the passive nationality principles. This list of offences does not coincide with the acts underlying international crimes in the Court's jurisdiction.

In Italy, obligations arising from the Statute have constitutional strength pursuant to Article 117(1) of the Constitution, according to which the legislative power must comply with international obligations.

It has further been argued that States are duty bound to protect fundamental human rights by holding the perpetrators criminally liable.[2] This view usefully applies to the case of violations of rules of international law amounting to international crimes. However, in international criminal law, this duty to prosecute is grounded on international law and only subordinately on human rights law. International criminal law primarily protects collective legal interests coinciding with values of concern to the international community as a whole, aimed at preserving the international legal and political order, namely peace, international security and the well-being of the world. Individual legal interests coinciding with fundamental rights are safeguarded insofar as they are instrumental to protecting those collective values. Criminal repression within the international legal framework is exceptional in nature and implies crucial derogations from ordinary principles of general criminal law, such as irrelevance of immunity, duties of cooperation, universal jurisdiction, non-application of statutory limitations and so forth. Individual criminal liability in international law can only be resorted to when serious violations of international customary and treaty rules intended to protect primary international values occur. Grave breaches of fundamental rights trigger international criminal liability when they have an international dimension, reflected in one of the ingredients of international crimes, namely the contextual element, which sets them apart from ordinary domestic offences. There lies the legitimacy of international criminal law.[3] For instance, an act amounting to murder qualifies as a war crime, crime against humanity or genocide when committed in the context of and in connection with an armed conflict, or as part of a widespread or systematic attack against a civilian population or with the intent to destroy in whole or in part a protected group. In those cases, the act of murdering not only violates the fundamental right to life of the victim, but it also harms or endangers peace and international security. Therefore, it deserves to be punished within the international legal framework.

Adopting a code of international crimes is in the interest of Italy's sovereignty too. Should Italy request a deferral to its investigations and the Prosecutor apply in response to the Pre-Trial Chamber under Article 18(2) of the Statute, the Chamber most likely would rule that Italy is either genuinely unwilling or unable to prosecute the case. Be that as it may, since the Court is tasked to consider whether the domestic investigations cover substantially the same conduct of the investigations before it (ICC, PTC II, Situation in the Islamic Republic of Afghanistan, 31 October 2022), the Chamber would probably conclude in the negative, inasmuch as Italy would be investigating or prosecuting ordinary offences rather than international crimes. Even if the conduct were deemed to substantially coincide with the *actus reus* of an international crime, it would still lack the contextual element, the most defining legal ingredient of international crimes.

From this perspective, the Milan conference contributed to paving the way for the establishment, by former Minister of Justice Marta Cartabia, of an experts' Commission responsible for drafting an Italian code of international crimes. A remarkable achievement.

The Commission pursued clarity and simplicity and has arguably achieved a thoughtful balance between the faithful implementation of the Rome Statute, the preservation of coherence in the criminal justice system, and consistency with stringent constitutional constraints, ensuring where necessary greater protection than the Statute.[4] In certain instances, it made significantly progressive choices. It has provided for universal jurisdiction with the only condition being that the suspect must be in the territory of the State, except for the crime of aggression for which the request of the Minister of Justice was required as well as a condition of admissibility. It has meaningfully expanded the crime of genocide, encompassing linguistic Commission among protected groups, introducing coercion in sexual acts among the prohibited conduct and adding a provision on cultural genocide. In defining penalties, the Commission sought coherence with the Italian criminal justice system while carefully grading the gravity of the different classes of crimes, a particularly challenging task.

The Italian Republic must endow itself with a code of international crimes. Not only would this implement an international obligation and serve Italy's interest to protect its judicial sovereignty but it would further a longstanding policy fostering international law, fundamental human rights and the primacy of human dignity in international relations. There lies a gentle, yet mighty, power that binds together the Italian people with the cause of humanity.

The Hague, November 2022

Rosario Aitala
International Criminal Court
Libera Università Internazionale degli Studi Sociali (LUISS) "Guido Carli" of Rome

Notes

1 M Mancini, 'Italy's Implementation of the Rome Statute of the International Criminal Court and Its Amendments: Unresolved Issues' (2022) 31 Italian Yearbook of International Law.
2 F Viganò, 'L'arbitrio del non punire. Sugli obblighi di tutela penale dei diritti fondamentali', in *Studi in onore di Mario Romano* (Jovene 2011).
3 RS Aitala, *Diritto Internazionale penale* (Le Monnier 2021).
4 S Manacorda, 'Obblighi di adeguamento e coerenza di sistema nel progetto di Codice dei crimini internazionali', in *Quaderni costituzionali* (Il Mulino 2022).

Part I

Introduction

1.1 Obligations, Options and Obstacles

Implementing the Rome Statute Revisited

Chantal Meloni and Florian Jeßberger

With the adoption of the Rome Statute in 1998, the vast majority of States have called for a global criminal justice system determined to put an end to impunity for the perpetrators of international crimes. Within this system, with the International Criminal Court (ICC) playing just a complementary role, adequate legislation at the States' level that reflects the substantive provisions of the Rome Statute is a precondition for compliance. And indeed, over the past 20 years, many States have adopted specific legislation to incorporate international criminal law into their domestic legal systems and, more specifically, made genocide, crimes against humanity, war crimes and the crime of aggression offences under their domestic law. In addition, a growing number of States have set up specialised investigating units and dedicated departments within their prosecution offices to deal with the complexities of such investigations. Against this background, the topic of this volume, "domesticating international criminal law", may appear outdated at first sight. And indeed, also academically this area has already been widely investigated by a number of comparative studies.[1] So, why come back to the issue 20 years after the entering into force of the Rome Statute?

There are several reasons why we consider it useful and even necessary to revisit the issue. First, States' willingness and capacity to deal with the commission of international crimes varies greatly, not only across continents, but also within Europe itself, end even between countries coming from the same legal tradition. This became clear to us by observing the reality of our respective countries: Germany and Italy, which have a common legal tradition and a long history of dialogue and exchange among legal scholars (in particular in the criminal law field), nevertheless are currently at the antipodes with regard to the implementation and enforcement of international criminal law. On the one hand, Germany adopted a Code of Crimes against International Law (the *Völkerstrafgesetzbuch* – VStGB) in 2002, in parallel with the entry into force of the Rome Statute, and has, on this basis, been conducting investigations and proceedings on international crimes committed abroad ever since. Italy, on the other hand, still lacks provisions defining international crimes. For this reason, Italian prosecutors cannot investigate crimes against humanity or war crimes as international crimes and, in the absence of

DOI: 10.4324/9781003320951-2

substantial legislation following up procedural Law no 237/2012 to implement the Rome Statute, Italy is not even in the position to fully cooperate with the ICC. Thus, while the current debate in States like Germany, Belgium, France, Spain, Switzerland or The Netherlands focuses on practical issues related to the exercise of universal criminal jurisdiction, in other countries, like Italy, the discussion remains at a very preliminary stage. However, beyond the rather specific aspect of the "case of Italy", we believe that there are further reasons to revisit the issue: one reason is that, even after the establishment of the ICC and other international tribunals, the indirect enforcement of international criminal law through national courts remains the backbone of international criminal justice in terms of actual numbers, not only as a theoretical point. Moreover, when we look at what happened during the past 20 years at the domestic level, we see, after an initial euphoric phase, a backlash and then, in recent years, again a certain increase of domestic proceedings on international crimes in some countries, in particular in Europe. The growing number of investigations and prosecutions under the principle of universal jurisdiction needs, in our view, to be better investigated. Finally, we believe that we are now in the position to critically reflect upon the experiences of those States where substantive international criminal law has been implemented for the past two decades or so. There are still considerable challenges which cannot be underestimated at the domestic level, in Germany as well in the other countries. It is important to take stock and revisit the issue of domestication in the light of these experiences, and perhaps to identify their trends and gaps, and the common debates we see not only in Germany but also in many other domestic jurisdictions.

These considerations show that this volume is not only topical, but also very timely.

To begin with, it may be helpful to briefly outline which obligations, options and obstacles have been or could have been shaping the implementation processes. As to the obligations to provide for the domestication of international criminal law, a taxonomy should at least distinguish by direction (positive obligations, negative obligations), by source (international law obligations, obligations under domestic criminal and constitutional law) and by content (obligations to prosecute, obligations to criminalize, obligations to establish jurisdiction). Contrary to other international treaties, the Rome Statute – according to the majority opinion – does not explicitly establish any obligation regarding the incorporation of the Statute's substantive criminal law. Thus, State Parties are not obliged to enact criminal legislation or even copy the Rome Statute; rather, they retain their autonomy in this regard. The same consideration also applies for the adoption and exercise of the principle of universal jurisdiction for international crimes. While there is an *authority* under international law to exercise universal jurisdiction with regard to certain crimes, there is, according to most observers, no *duty* to proceed in this sense, at least in the absence of direct links with the domestic system. What is relevant from the international law perspective is that, even though there may not be a strict obligation, the exercise of universal jurisdiction is in line with the spirit and the idea on which the Rome Statute and the whole system of international criminal justice are based. The "division of labour" between States and the ICC has the clear objective of ending impunity and providing for accountability for the gravest crimes; it calls for the adaptation of domestic substantive criminal law. States who want to contribute to this system of international justice are, in fact, *encouraged* in this sense to implement substantive international criminal law into their domestic legal order.

As to the available options, States enjoy wide discretion in deciding not only *if* but also *how* to adopt substantive provisions, in light of international, constitutional and criminal law limits shaping the domesticating process. Among them, a relevant role is played, for instance, by the principle of legality, which is similarly strictly understood in Italy and Germany. There are indeed different options on how to domesticate international criminal law as regards the format and the mechanism of implementation. There may be a complete incorporation, or even a copying of the Rome Statute, as we see in some jurisdictions. There may also be non-adoption at all or a modified incorporation, which takes up the substantive provisions of the Rome Statute and modifies them according to domestic legal constraints and criminal policy needs. States thus enjoy broad discretion as to the contents and modalities of domestication of international criminal law. Regarding the definition of crimes for instance, which is at the core of any implementing legislation, the national legislator can go beyond the Rome Statute by taking into account customary international law which may have emerged after 1998. Other issues regard the relevance and extent of general criminal law principles and of specific procedural rules in the implementation effort.

Finally, many and diverse challenges and even obstacles to the prosecution of crimes under international law before domestic courts may emerge at the level of substantive law, for instance in defining specific crimes, or from procedural bars. One example concerns the ongoing debate within the International Law Commission on the reach of functional immunity, which to many working in the area of international criminal law in the domestic systems came as quite a surprise. Obstacles may obviously result from a lack of political will to prosecute certain crimes, and crimes of the powerful in particular – powerful States or powerful corporations. Other more practical obstacles to domestic prosecutions relate to the issue of capacity building, as well as to the lack of necessary resources, of knowledge and also of technical capacity to apply this specialised implementing legislation.

This volume originates from a three-day international conference, an *Alexander von Humboldt Kolleg*, that we had organised at the University of Milan from 29 September to 1 October 2021. The conference provided a forum for exchange among experts coming from several countries and backgrounds and for discussion of key developments in relation to the implementation of international criminal law into the domestic systems. Besides scholars, the conference included leading practitioners, prosecutors and judges, both at national and international institutions, as well as civil society representatives, which helped to enrich the discussion by bringing in their valuable practical experiences in this field.

The idea of co-organising a conference to analyse the most current and controversial issues concerning the domestic implementation of the Rome Statute started by observing the reality of our respective countries, Italy and Germany, which currently find themselves far apart with regard to their respective roles in the implementation and enforcement of international criminal law. The Italian "delay" is remarkable and regrettable given the leading role Italy played in the context of the emergence of international criminal justice, having not only hosted the Rome conference in 1998, but also playing a key role in the Statute negotiations. Since then, several legislative projects have been presented, focusing on the substantive part of international criminal law, including the so-called Cariplo Project, a private initiative led by international law professor and former ICTY President Fausto Pocar. One – not so secret – aim behind the 2021 Milan conference was, therefore, also to revitalise the debate and inflate new life specifically to Italian unfinished projects of implementation. In this sense, in following up on past projects to finally adopt an Italian legislation on international crimes, the example of Germany and other States that had long since implemented specific legislation and taken measures to deal with such crimes seemed to us of the outmost significance. Given the accumulated delay, Italy could even benefit from the experience gained by other countries and try to anticipate the obstacles that others had faced, thus avoiding their mistakes.

At the same time, this volume, as well as the conference on which it is based, was never intended as a simple comparison between Italy and Germany. It is rather a broad and thorough reflection on what can be learned from the experience accumulated in other countries regarding the domestication of international criminal law. We believe that the experiences arising from Germany and other domestic systems here considered may be useful to inform the debate which we aimed to revitalise. We are happy to note that the conference achieved this aim: at the closing roundtable, Raffaele Piccirillo, the Chef de Cabinet of the then-Minister of Justice, announced that a decision had been made to start works for the elaboration of Italian legislation on international crimes. In fact, a few months later, on 22 March 2022, the then-Minister of Justice Marta Cartabia, who authored the Foreword to this volume, appointed a Commission tasked with the drafting of an Italian "*Codice dei crimini internazionali*" (code of international crimes). The Commission was presided by criminal law professor Francesco Palazzo and international law professor Fausto Pocar, and included a number of jurists, both academics and practitioners with relevant expertise in the field.[2] The very tight timeline given to the Commission was contingent to the dramatic events of 2022 following the Russian aggression against Ukraine, which exposed the urgency for Italy to fully implement the Rome Statute and introduce international crimes in the domestic legal order. Indeed, the Commission had already completed its mandate by 31 May 2022, delivering the Draft Code to the Minister of Justice for final technical adjustments and to initiate the legislative process for the adoption of the law. The Draft Articles and accompanying commentary (*Relazione*) have been recently made publicly available.[3] We are glad to seize this opportunity to publish for the first time the English version of the Draft Code itself (Annex).

The volume first starts with an overview of different approaches on the domestication of international criminal law, with a specific focus on the German and the Italian systems. The first five chapters included in Part 2 discuss the Italian perspectives on the adoption of a code of crimes under international law, including an assessment of prerequisites for the domestic implementation of international criminal law from a constitutional law perspective (see the chapters by Alessandra Annoni and Francesco Viganò). Previous initiatives on Italian implementation, including private initiatives, are also discussed here (see the chapters by Fausto Pocar and Marco Pedrazzi). While this volume, which was designed before the appointment of the Commission, is not intended to be a comment on the very recent Italian draft, the chapter by Nicola Selvaggi (the deputy Chef de Cabinet at the then-Ministry of Justice) will give an overview of the content for the Draft Italian Code of International Crimes, and the methodology followed by the Commission.

The following part includes five chapters on the adoption of domestic laws in other countries (see the chapter by Kalika Metha), with a particular focus on the German Code of Crimes Against International Law (see the chapters by Boris Burghardt and Leonie Steinl) and a global perspective on the issue (see the chapter by Antonio Coco) and the challenges ahead for international justice (see the chapter by Andreas Zimmermann and John Schabedoth).

The chapters in the subsequent three parts are dedicated to the in-depth analysis of specific issues. Part 4 deals with genocide and crimes against humanity (see the chapters by Maria Crippa and Luigi Prosperi); war crimes (see the chapter by Giulio Bartolini and Marco Longobardo) and aggression (see the chapter by Annegret Hartig). Part 5 deals with modes of liability, including command responsibility (see the chapters by Chantal Meloni and Volker Nerlich), sanctions and sentencing (see the chapters by Aziz Epik and Alice Riccardi). Finally, Part 6 includes a discussion on immunities (see the chapters by Chiara Ragni and Valeria Vegh Weis) and prosecutorial discretion (see the chapter by Triestino Mariniello).

Notes

1 See, inter alia, the two volumes co-edited by Professor Lattanzi, *Rome Statute and Domestic Legal Orders* (2000), and a series of books by the Max Planck Institute in Freiburg on the national prosecution of international crimes, published between 2003 and 2006.

2 The documentation on the Commission and its work can be consulted on the MoJ website: www.giustizia.it/giustizia/it/mg_1_36_0.page?contentId=COS372730# See also https://www.sistemapenale.it/it/documenti/codice-dei-crimini-internazionali-pubblicata-la-relazione-della-commissione-palazzo-pocar

3 www.giustizia.it/cmsresources/cms/documents/commissione_PALAZZO_POCAR_relazione_finale_31mag22.pdf

Part II

Italian Perspectives on the Domestic Implementation of International Criminal Law

2.1 The Domestic Codification of International Crimes

The Private Initiative "Cariplo Project"

Fausto Pocar

1 The Domestic Implementation of International Criminal Law

The ability of national jurisdictions to thoroughly implement the international rules providing for the prosecution and punishment of war crimes and crimes against humanity constituting serious violation of international law – either conventional or customary law – is at the centre of legal and political discussions as of the end of the Second World War, after the experience of the Nuremberg and the Far East International Military Tribunals. States have been frequently reluctant to adopt implementation legislation to this effect. Let me recall that a quarter of a century ago, in 1997, at a conference on "War Crimes and the Competence of National Jurisdiction", organised at the University of Milan by the Faculty of Political Sciences,[1] there was a lively and interesting debate on the implementation in Italy of the Geneva Conventions of 12 August 1949 under which each State Party was obliged to adopt domestic legislation necessary to provide effective penal sanctions for persons committing, or ordering to be committed, any of the grave breaches of the conventions as defined in the relevant provisions of the same conventions, to search for persons allegedly responsible for such grave breaches, and to bring them, regardless of their nationality, before its own courts. As Italy had not yet implemented the Geneva Conventions, the general and natural conclusion of the participants in the conference was that, after almost half a century, it was high time to revise the domestic legislation, including with respect to the crimes existing in the military code, with a view to giving full effect to the international obligations. It was further underlined that it was momentous to do so, bearing in mind that an initiative was on the way to convening a United Nations conference to establish, besides the two recently established ad hoc criminal tribunals for the Former Yugoslavia and for Rwanda, a permanent international criminal court.

In presenting the final conclusions of the meeting, one of my observations was that the efficiency of the future permanent court could depend not only on the provision of the necessary resources for its functioning but also on the domestic implementation of the international rules concerning the prosecution of the crimes over which the court would be given jurisdiction. As Italy

DOI: 10.4324/9781003320951-4

was in the front line for the establishment of the future permanent court, its contribution could not simply be to offer hosting and organising the upcoming Rome conference, but should also be to ensure that the domestic legislation would be put in line with the provisions defining the jurisdiction of the court.[2] If that consideration was appropriate before the adoption of the principle of complementarity in the Rome Statute, it is even more warranted now that such a principle is the essential criterion for the coordination between the international and the domestic jurisdiction for the prosecution of international crimes.

In light of the foregoing considerations, it looks striking that – after the success of the Rome conference in July 1998, the early ratification of the Statute of the International Criminal Court ("ICC") and its early entry into force in 2002 – only a law providing for Italy's cooperation with the Court has been adopted, with some delay, in 2012,[3] while legislation enabling domestic courts to prosecute the crimes listed in the Statute and described in the Elements of Crimes adopted by the Assembly of States Parties is still missing.

As the Rome conference and the immediate ratification of the ICC Statute had raised expectations of a timely implementation at the domestic level, it is not surprising that an academic initiative was taken in the University of Milan – in 2009, even before the enactment of the cooperation law of 2012 – of drafting privately a code of international crimes with a view to offering an example of how domestic legislation could set forth a coherent legal framework for the implementation of the Rome Statute and its coordination with existing national provisions on the matter, without prejudice to any improvement that might appear relevant and opportune. Following that academic initiative, which was co-financed by the Foundation Cariplo in Milan, a group of researchers elaborated a Draft Code of International Crimes, commonly known as the "Cariplo Project",[4] that was discussed in several workshops and has become a tool for future reference in the implementation of the Statute of the ICC.[5]

2 The Sources of a Domestic Codification of International Crimes

It is not my intention here to go through the entire proposed Draft Code of International Crimes ("Code"), which classifies the crimes according to the traditional categories that have characterised international criminal law since the 1945 London Agreement instituting the International Military Tribunal to prosecute the main responsible leaders of the European Axis, as revisited by the statutes of the ad hoc tribunals: genocide, crimes against humanity and war crimes.[6] I will rather discuss briefly some of the criteria that have been followed in the elaboration of the Code, bearing in mind the opportunity that its drafting offered to introduce a systematic and progressive approach to international criminal law.

As to the legal sources on which to rely for drafting new domestic provisions on international crimes, the ICC Statute and the Elements of Crimes were necessarily the first reference. Although the ICC Statute does not expressly impose on State Parties the obligation to align their domestic legislation with the international provisions, one of the intended purposes of the Code was to do so in order to provide for a general application of the principle of complementarity and allow that in any concrete case the domestic courts may have priority over the ICC's jurisdiction. However, a mere reference to the ICC legal framework as a source would have resulted in an unnecessary limitation of the domain of the competence of the Italian legislator. It could indeed be anticipated that in defining the scope of the jurisdiction of the ICC, its statute might have omitted some crimes which were to be regarded as international crimes under customary international law, simply because their inclusion had not been proposed or, if proposed, no agreement on their inclusion could be reached at the Rome conference. In such a case it would have been appropriate for a domestic law to comprise these crimes to fully implement customary international law. Hence there was a need to consider customary international law, too, besides the ICC Statute.

In this connection it must be noted that more frequently, rather than omitting an existing international crime, the ICC Statute provides a definition of a given crime, or of a group of crimes, which does not entirely reflect customary international law, either because of a different or wrong assessment of customary law or because the States that negotiated the Statute intended to restrict the scope of or derogate from customary law. While indeed such restrictions or derogations may not be legitimate when a provision of the Statute merely codifies *jus cogens*, nothing prevented States Parties derogating by treaty from customary international law for the purposes of defining the jurisdiction of an international court, thus leaving the adjudication of possible cases concerning the aspects left out to other courts, especially to domestic courts having a broader jurisdiction. Hence, the discussion arose as to whether to retain in the Code the more restricted notion of a given crime as described in the ICC Statute or to conform with the broader notion of that crime as accepted in international customary law.

3 Codifying Genocide

A few examples may better clarify the above considerations. Starting from what has been called "the crime of crimes", the crime of genocide, it must be recalled that Article 2 of the 1948 Convention on the Prevention and Punishment of the Crime of Genocide requires the commission of certain acts with the special intent "to destroy, in whole or in part, a national, ethnic, racial or religious group, as such". In this respect, Article 6 of the ICC Statute reproduces literally the wording of Article 2 of the Convention, which is generally regarded as reflecting customary international law.[7] If there is no doubt that in doing so the ICC Statute, like the Convention, conforms to customary law, it can be argued whether the accepted definition of the crime also exhausts the scope of the crime in international customary law, in particular as far as the qualification of the targeted groups is concerned.

The issue is twofold. On one hand, did the 1948 Convention refer to all the groups which at that time should have been considered for an exhaustive codification of the crime of genocide? On the other, even if it did, could a mere reproduction of the assessment of customary law made in 1948 still fully codify customary international law after half a century, when the ICC Statute was adopted? Furthermore, is that assessment still correct today, when more than 70 years have elapsed? These are burning questions, especially with respect to the inclusion of groups other than the ones mentioned in the 1948 Convention, among them, in particular, cultural groups, where the destruction of a culture and cultural heritage may lead to the extinction of a group as such. The proposal was indeed submitted, during the elaboration of the 1948 Convention, to refer to cultural groups as well, but it was rejected by a vote,[8] which was perhaps justified because of the still limited protection that human rights, including cultural rights of groups under colonial domination, enjoyed at that time under international law. However, it should be considered that the cultural dimension of human rights has progressively acquired such a recognition that the intent to destroy cultural heritage suggests that it now constitutes genocide under customary international law.[9] While it is true that the already codified notion of genocide may cover many cultural groups as ethnic groups, there are situations that would be better captured by including a specific reference to cultural groups in the definition of the crime.[10] It has been deemed more appropriate, therefore, to provide in the Code a more complete implementation of international law concerning the crime of genocide that would have taken into account the progressive development of customary international law. Consequently, the Cariplo Project had added cultural groups to the groups mentioned in the ICC Statute. Other groups had also been added in the Code's definition, which will not be discussed here where the intention is to give only a glaring example of the existence of an unfortunate gap in the ICC Statute.

4 Codifying War Crimes

A similar opportunity to rely on customary international law rather than on the ICC Statute concerned war crimes. It is well known that the category of war crimes was initially identified as referring to international armed conflicts, as shown not only by the 1945 London Agreement but also by the 1949 Geneva Conventions, as well as by the 1977 Additional Protocols thereto. The scope of the "grave breaches" regime of the Geneva Conventions is limited to the violation of provisions applicable in international armed conflicts and this undesirable restriction is not remedied by the protocols, since Additional Protocol II does not contain any reference to grave breaches. Later, however, the distinction between war crimes committed in international and non-international armed conflicts has become obsolete following the seminal International Criminal Tribunal for the former Yugoslavia (ICTY) *Tadic* Jurisdiction decision,[11] which in substance extended the grave breaches regime to non-international armed conflicts, largely relying on common Article 3 of the Geneva Conventions and on customary international law. Notwithstanding that decision, three years later the Rome Statute kept the traditional distinction and dealt separately with war crimes depending on the international or domestic context in which their commission occurred, probably because negotiating States were reluctant to entirely set aside what may have resulted in a limitation of their sovereign prerogatives in addressing criminal conduct carried out on their own territories.

However, in drafting a domestic code of international crimes it appeared inappropriate and unnecessary to adopt different rules applicable in those two contexts and more practical to unify the regime of war crimes thus also simplifying the kind of evidence required to prove their occurrence. The proposed Code therefore adopted the solution to merely have the list of war crimes preceded by a provision stating that "the conducts described in this section constitute war crimes if committed in the context of an armed conflict", and to omit any reference to the qualification – international or domestic – of the conflict.[12] This proposal has the advantage both of avoiding repetitions of the same crimes and of extending to non-international conflicts all the crimes established with respect to international conflicts.

5 Codifying Crimes Against Humanity

Moving on now to crimes against humanity, there were more reasons for following a progressive approach grounded on customary international law rather than following one grounded on the ICC Statute for the purposes of drafting a domestic code of international crimes. First, the ICC Statute has provided for a general restriction of the notion itself of crimes against humanity. These ones are defined, both in the Statute and in customary international law, as a list of acts committed "as part of a widespread or systematic attack directed against any civilian population, with knowledge of the attack".[13] However, in defining the meaning of "attack", the Statute specifies that the course of conduct involving a multiple commission of the prohibited acts should be carried out "pursuant to or in furtherance of a State or organizational policy to commit such attack",[14] thus adding a requirement that does not exist in customary international law, as has been clarified by the jurisprudence of international criminal tribunals since the beginning of their activity. In particular as far as a State policy is concerned, the ICTY has affirmed that although, traditionally, reference to a State policy may have been made, this is not a requirement for crimes against humanity simply because they are not "isolated, random acts of individuals but rather result from a deliberate attempt to target a civilian population".[15] Consequently, the Cariplo Project omitted any reference to a policy in defining the elements of crimes against humanity.[16]

A similar problem arose with respect to the crime of persecution that the ICC Statute defines as "the intentional and severe deprivation of fundamental rights contrary to international law by reason of the identity of a group or collectivity",[17] a definition which is in full conformity with customary international law.[18] There are, however, some aspects which are distinguished, in addition to the policy element discussed above. First, the discriminatory grounds in the Statute's definition are not limited to those reflected in customary international law as assessed in the 1996 Draft Code of Crimes of the International Law Commission[19] and as applied by the ad hoc international criminal tribunals, but also encompass national, cultural, gender and other grounds that are universally recognised as impermissible under international law. Whether this expansion of the law reflected customary international law or is the result of a conventional provision does not need to be discussed; it was in any event welcomed because of its more protective scope. There is, however, a further departure from customary international law that cannot be equally welcomed. The ICC Statute limits the scope of the crime by establishing that it must be committed in connection with any other crime against humanity or any other crime within the jurisdiction of the ICC.[20] There is here a clear deviation from customary international law that appears to go back to a requirement that was retained in the 1945 Charter establishing the International Military Tribunal[21] but was later abandoned in favour of an autonomous notion of the crime of persecution under customary international law.[22] The Cariplo Project had therefore accepted the expansion of the discriminatory grounds made by the ICC Statute but had set aside the restriction requiring a connection with another crime.

6 Identity of Conducts and Different Characterization of Crimes

It may be finally worth mentioning a couple of other issues that were considered by the authors of the Cariplo Project in drafting the provisions of the proposed code of international crimes.

On one hand it was noted that many of the conducts proscribed as international crimes could also be prosecuted as domestic crimes because they were criminalised in the Italian Penal Code. Strictly speaking, the ICC Statute does not require that domestic crimes be transformed into international crimes when the conduct is the same. Indeed, according to the principle of *ne bis in idem* no person who has been tried by another court – including by a domestic court – for conduct also proscribed under the Statute shall be tried by the ICC with respect to the same conduct, unless the proceedings in the other court were held for the purpose of shielding the person concerned from criminal responsibility or were not conducted independently and impartially in accordance with the norms of due process internationally recognised and in a manner which was inconsistent with an intent to bring that person to justice.[23] Therefore, except for these last conditions, a person who is tried by a domestic court for a conduct characterised as an ordinary crime cannot be tried again by the ICC for the same conduct characterised as an international crime. Unlike with respect to the ad hoc international criminal tribunals,[24] the mere qualification of the crime as domestic does not play any role in favour of a retrial under the ICC Statute. However, the consideration that the stigma inherent in the characterisation of a conduct as a violation of international law rather than of domestic law is more significant, as well as the desirability to avoid litigation on the above-mentioned exceptions from the principle of *ne bis in idem*, have led the drafters of the Code to add to the description of such conducts the *chapeau* elements that make them international rather than domestic crimes.

On the other hand, several prohibited conducts that constitute war crimes are identical to conducts that are also proscribed as crimes against humanity. The appropriate qualification of the unlawful conduct in a concrete case will therefore depend on the so-called *chapeau* element of each of the mentioned categories of international crimes, namely the connection with an armed conflict or with a widespread or systematic attack against a civilian population with knowledge of the attack. However, these two *chapeau* elements may coexist, and frequently coexist in a given situation, in particular when an attack against a civilian population, which in principle does not need to be an armed attack, occurs in connection with an armed conflict. Should, in this case, one qualification prevail over the other and the alleged perpetrator be prosecuted accordingly? Or should the two characterisations of the conduct be regarded as independent and prosecution follow under two counts in the indictment, with the possible cumulative conviction for two distinct crimes? The international jurisprudence has clearly favoured the second option since the first cases were brought before the ICTY and the ICTR (International Criminal Tribunal for Rwanda).[25] According to this jurisprudence, when two crimes have common elements and one of them has an additional element, the principle of speciality will prevail in favour of the crime presenting this additional element. By contrast, if under the law both crimes have an additional non-common element, they must be regarded as different crimes and their prosecution may end up in cumulative convictions for the same conduct. This is precisely the case of conduct which meets at the same time the conditions in the *chapeau* element characterising war crimes and crimes against humanity.[26] In the light of this jurisprudence the Cariplo Project has listed crimes based on the same conduct both in the chapter concerning war crimes and crimes against humanity.

7 Conclusions

The foregoing considerations reflect some of the issues that arise out of a domestic implementation of the international rules concerning criminal conducts qualified as international crimes. Such an implementation is a complex operation because of the different sources – customary and conventional – of international law that have to be taken into account and because of the need to coordinate the crimes set forth by international law with the criminal provisions set forth in the domestic legislation with a view to avoiding, as far as possible, a fragmentation of the domestic system by introducing a duplication of criminal provisions concerning the same conduct. In this context there is merit in adopting a special, distinct criminal code of international crimes as the Cariplo Project and the recent Italian Minister of Justice initiative have proposed to adopt.

Notes

1 The proceedings of the conference are published in Pierluigi Lamberti Zanardi and Gabriella Venturini (eds), *Crimini di guerra e competenza delle giurisdizioni nazionali* (Atti del convegno, Milano, 15–17 May 1997) (Giuffrè 1998).
2 See Fausto Pocar, in P Lamberti Zanardi and G Venturini (eds), ibid, 274ff, at 281.
3 Law 23 December 2012 no 237, 'Norme per l'adeguamento alle disposizioni dello Statuto istitutivo della Corte penale internazionale', *Gazzetta Ufficiale*, no 6, 8 January 2013.
4 The Cariplo Project, adopted under the denomination 'International Crimes, Italian Law-Making Policy, and Prospective Legislation', was carried out in the Department of International and Political Studies of the University of Milan and was coordinated by Fausto Pocar and later by Marco Pedrazzi, with the contribution of Milena Costas Trascasas, Sara Gradilone, Chantal Meloni, Laura Paredi, Christian Ponti, and Chiara Ragni, as well as, as a revisor, Gabriella Venturini.
5 Indeed, the finalising of this paper for publication occurred when the Italian Minister of Justice, Marta Cartabia, adopted, on 22 March 2022, a Decree appointing a Commission of Experts comprising academics, judges and practicing lawyers co-presided by professors Francesco Palazzo and Fausto Pocar, tasked with the consideration of former initiatives proposed for the implementation of the Rome Statute and with the elaboration of a Draft Code of International Crimes, which should therefore be the object of a special Act rather than being incorporated into the Italian Penal Code. The Commission is currently working on this official initiative that should give full implementation to the Rome Statute, in the light of previous existing legislation and other documents, including the Cariplo Project.
6 Article 6(a) of the Charter of the International Military Tribunal (annexed to the London Agreement for the Prosecution and Punishment of the Major War Criminals of the European Axis, 8 August 1945, UNTS 82, 279) also provided for the crime of "aggression" as a violation of the *jus ad bellum*. That crime is mentioned in Art 5(1)(d) of the ICC Statute but the jurisdiction of the Court over it was postponed until the adoption of a provision containing its definition. The crime has not been included in the Cariplo Project, which was submitted and approved before the Kampala conference that defined the crime and the conditions under which the Court could start to exercise its jurisdiction over it.
7 As confirmed by the International Court of Justice, which characterised the principles underlying the Convention as "principles which are recognized by civilised nations as binding on States, even without any conventional obligation": see ICJ, *Reservations to the Convention on the Prevention and Punishment of the Crime of Genocide*, Advisory Opinion, 28 May1951, *Reports*, 1951, 23.
8 Hirad Abtahi and Philippa Webb, *The Genocide Convention* (Brill 2008), 731.

9 See among others recently Elisa Novic, *The Concept of Cultural Genocide: An International Law Perspective* (OUP 2016); Leora Bilsky and Rachel Klagsburn, 'The Return of Cultural Genocide' (2018) 29 European Journal International Law 373.

10 An example may concern a linguistic group which is characterised by a specific cultural connotation but does not necessarily meet the requirements for being at the same time an ethnic or national group. It is worth recalling that linguistic minorities are regarded as groups entitled to the same recognition and protection as national or ethnic and religious groups: see Art 27 of the International Covenant on Civil and Political Rights, 18 December 1966, and Art 1(1) of the UN Declaration on the Rights of Persons Belonging to National or Ethnic, Religious and Linguistic Minorities (A/RES/47/135), which underlines the duty of States to protect the identity of those minorities. See also the Universal Declaration on Cultural Diversity adopted by UNESCO on 2 November 2001 which stresses the groups' cultural identity as part of the common heritage of humankind to be preserved and handed on to future generations.

11 See *Prosecutor v Tadić*, ICTY Case no IT-94-1-AR72, Decision on the Defense Motion for Interlocutory Appeal on Jurisdiction, 2 October 1995, paras 74, 88, 143–144.

12 See Cariplo Project, Art 18.

13 ICC Statute, Art 7(1).

14 ICC Statute, Art 7(2)(a).

15 *Prosecutor v Tadić*, ICTY Case no IT-94-1-T, Judgment, 7 May 1997, paras 653–654. See also *Prosecutor v Kupreskić et al*, ICTY Case no IT-95-16-T, Judgment, 14 January 2000, paras 551–555.

16 Cariplo Project, Art 6(1).

17 ICC Statute and Elements of Crimes, Art 7(1)(h).

18 See *Prosecutor* v *Kupreskić et al* (n 12), para 621.

19 'Draft Code of Crimes against Peace and Security of Mankind', *Yearbook of the International Law Commission 1996*, vol II (part two) 17.

20 ICC Statute, Art 7(1)(h).

21 Art 6(c) (n 6).

22 See *Prosecutor v Kupreskić et al* (n 12), para 621; *Prosecutor v Kvočka*, ICTY Case no IT-98-30/1-A, Appeal Judgment, 28 February 2005, para 323.

23 ICC Statute, Art 20(3).

24 See ICTY Statute, Art 10(2)(a) and ICTR Statute, Art 9(2)(a).

25 See especially *Prosecutor v Delalić et al*, ICTY Case no IT-96-21-A, Appeal Judgment, 20 February 2021, para 401.

26 *Prosecutor v Kunarać et al*, ICTY Case IT-96-23-T & IY-96-23/1-T, Trial Judgment, 22 February 2001, para 556; see however *Prosecutor* v *Ongwen*, Case ICC-02/04-01/15, Motion for Immediate Ruling on Standard to Assess Multiple Charging and Convictions, 9 December 2019, para 42.

Selected Bibliography

Abtahi H and Webb P, *The Genocide Convention* (Brill 2008)

Charney JI, 'International Criminal Law and the Role of Domestic Courts' [2001] 95 *American Journal of International Law* 120

Lamberti Zanardi P and Venturini G (eds), *Crimini di guerra e competenza delle giurisdizioni nazionali* (Atti del convegno, Milano, 15–17 May 1997) (Giuffrè 2008)

Novic E, *The Concept of Cultural Genocide: an International Law Perspective* (OUP 2016)

Pocar F, 'Completion or Continuation Strategy?' [2008] 8 *Journal of International Criminal Justice* 655

Pocar F, 'Giustizia internazionale e modelli giuridici nazionali', in P Mania (ed), *Due Lezioni Magistrali* (Sette Città 2022)

2.2 Previous Italian legislative drafts

Marco Pedrazzi

1 The need to incorporate international crimes into the Italian legal system

States must seek to prevent and prosecute international crimes committed by individuals, ie, serious breaches of values deemed fundamental by the international community as a whole, especially those related to the protection of basic human rights or the prohibition of the use of force in international relations – actions that are criminalised in international law. Criminal investigation, prosecution and punishment are certainly among the main tools States can employ to prevent and counter crime. It goes without saying that criminal investigation, prosecution and punishment require the conduct in question to have been criminalised in domestic law (in criminal law, the mere existence of criminalising international norms is not usually deemed sufficient even in the so-called monist systems[1]).

As we know, the criminalisation, criminal investigation, prosecution and punishment of international crimes are, to different degrees and with varying levels of efficacy, also subject to precise legal obligations on the part of States, and Italy in particular. These requirements explicitly derive from international conventions, such as the 1948 Genocide Convention, the four 1949 Geneva Conventions on the protection of victims of armed conflict, 1977 Additional Protocol 1, the 1984 Convention Against Torture, the 1954 Cultural Property Convention, and its 2nd Protocol of 1999. They derive implicitly from international human rights treaties such as, in particular, the 1950 ECHR and the 1966 ICCPR.[2] These obligations are fairly extensive, especially if we include the human rights treaties. Still, they do not necessarily cover the whole list of international crimes (or "core crimes"), including genocide, war crimes, crimes against humanity and the crime of aggression.

The existence of specific customary international law obligations of this kind, encompassing crimes not covered by treaty law, is subject to debate. However, I would claim that there is a clear tendency for customary international law to impose the obligation to criminalise, investigate, prosecute and punish all international crimes as testified, as far as crimes against humanity are concerned, by the 2019 Draft Articles on Crimes against

DOI: 10.4324/9781003320951-5

Humanity adopted by the International Law Commission (ILC) (see Articles 3, 6 and ff.).[3]

As for the Statute of the ICC, on the one hand it affirms in its Preamble that "the most serious crimes of concern to the international community as a whole must not go unpunished and that their effective prosecution must be ensured by taking measures at the national level", and it "recalls" that "it is the duty of every State to exercise its criminal jurisdiction over those responsible for international crimes". On the other hand, it establishes that the Court is complementary to national criminal jurisdictions (Article 1) and thus provides that a case which is already being or has already been investigated or prosecuted by a State with jurisdiction is inadmissible before the Court unless the national proceedings reveal the unwillingness or inability of that State to genuinely carry out the investigation or prosecution (Article 17).

With regard to the principle of complementarity, it is evident that, while there is no formal obligation to introduce the crimes listed in the Statute into national legal systems, only actual implementation of the Statute – which criminalises the Rome crimes within domestic systems – can prevent a State Party from being considered "unable" to prosecute when the national legal system makes no provision for the crime at issue, even as an ordinary offence. Conversely, inadequate or incorrect incorporation of the crimes could lead to the State in question being unable to adequately fulfil its obligations to cooperate with the ICC. There may, for example, be legal obstacles relating to the double criminality rule, preventing an individual charged with a crime not found in a State's domestic criminal code from being surrendered to the Court.[4] Therefore, only correct transposal into national law of the crimes listed in the Rome Statute will permit a complementarity-based international crime-fighting system to work efficiently.[5]

2 International crimes in the Italian legal system: the current state of affairs

Excepting the crime of aggression, concerning which it has only very recently ratified the Kampala amendment,[6] Italy has complied with its obligations to introduce the crime of genocide into its legal system. However, some problems may arise even in this case.[7] It is widely known that Italy's situation vis-à-vis the incorporation of war crimes is somewhat complex. Without going into detail, I will merely recall that this incorporation, mainly centred on the provisions of the 1941 Wartime Military Criminal Code, which has been amended over the years, albeit with other pieces of legislation modifying the overall picture, is incomplete and problematic in several ways.[8] Lastly, Italy has never introduced crimes against humanity into its legal order. Of course, a good number of these are punishable as ordinary crimes, but some of those regulated by the Rome Statute relate to conduct not specifically criminalised in Italy (eg, persecution or apartheid).

There can be no doubt that this situation needs to be remedied through the correct implementation of the Rome Statute as far as the provisions on crimes are concerned.

3 Implementing the Rome Statute in Italy: previous legislative drafts

It is well known that the Rome Statute was initially implemented in the Italian legal system through a law authorising its ratification and execution in the Italian legal order (Law no 232 of 12 July 1999[9]). Clearly, this "incorporation" did not implement the Statute's non-self-executing provisions, such as those imposing obligations on the States Parties regarding judicial cooperation with the Court and the execution of its measures or those containing the list of crimes and regulating other substantial aspects of international criminal law which the ICC must apply.

During the first decade of the 21st century, the government therefore set up various commissions to make proposals for implementing the Rome Statute. These proposals, such as those of the Commissione Conforti (established by the Ministerial Decree of the Minister of Justice of 27 June 2002), provided for the incorporation of international crimes and procedural measures, which allowed judicial cooperation between the Italian authorities and the ICC. However, the parliament's efforts were fruitless. In 2012, parliament was able, under pressure to address a contingent situation, to adopt Law no 237 of 20 December 2012, but this only contains procedural rules regulating and allowing judicial cooperation activities with the ICC and the execution of the Court's measures; it also introduces "delicts against the ICC", implementing the Statute's Article 70 provision on "offences against the administration of justice".[10] This legislation was based on the draft law introduced by Melchiorre and others,[11] deriving in turn from Conforti's procedural project, while his other project concerning the crimes was ignored.

Therefore, we may say that the Rome Statute has only been partially implemented in Italian legislation, also taking into account that failure to fully adapt our criminal legislation to cover the crimes included in the Rome Statute could have negative repercussions even on Italy's cooperation with the Court.

It is impossible to examine here the details of the many draft laws presented in parliament over the years. However, it is worth making some general observations. The interesting aspect of the various drafts concerns what is still lacking, ie, proposals concerning changes harmonising the Italian legal system with the crimes listed in the Rome Statute. As for how the Italian legal system could be adapted to the international crimes included in the Statute, the Commission headed by Benedetto Conforti envisaged the introduction of amendments to the existing legislation, but the prevailing choice, found in the Kessler, Iovene, Pianetta, Gozi and Maritati draft laws, among others, was to adopt a specific code for international crimes. This solution would make it possible to reformulate the definitions of the Rome Statute crimes, as well as incorporating other general principles of international criminal law. At the same time, it would include rules and principles from our Criminal Code, the Wartime Military Criminal Code, and the Peacetime Military Criminal Code, in addition to other special laws.[12]

The scope of the various drafts differs, however. On the one hand, the Pianetta draft only included genocide and crimes against humanity, delegating the government to adopt legislative decrees to modify and integrate the existing rules on war crimes. Conversely, the Kessler, Iovene, Gozi and Maritati drafts included three categories: genocide, crimes against humanity and war crimes.

There is some debate whether the best solution, in terms of legislative technique, would be to have a wholly separate law or code, such as we find in the drafts we are examining, or to add a new section in the existing Penal Code. In my view, a special law or code dealing with international crimes, such as those found in other countries, including Germany,[13] would be commendable, at least from the international law point of view. This would enable international crimes to be classified as special crimes with their own characteristics, even when the underlying acts are identical to those constituting ordinary crimes. Another commendable choice, in my view, would be to bring all international crimes (although aggression was not included in the draft laws) together in one piece of legislation, thereby underling their shared features. This would also make it possible to identify certain norms, such as those regarding the statute of limitations, command responsibility, superior orders and jurisdiction, which apply to all these crimes. And it would obviously be necessary to coordinate these with the shared principles of ordinary criminal law.

I will simply recall some specific problems concerning war crimes, where a number of issues arise in relation to: the amendments to the Wartime Military Criminal Code (WMCC); coordination between the new code or section, the WMCC, the Peacetime MCC, and other special laws; and the identification of the courts competent to try military personnel in times of armed conflict.[14] The ideal solution, in my view, both from the point of view of compliance with the principle of equality under Article 3 of the Italian Constitution[15] and considering the need for a consistent framework regarding the prosecution and punishment of international crimes, would be to subject all suspects – civilian or military – to the jurisdiction of ordinary courts.[16] This solution has thus far encountered tenacious resistance, however.

A further general issue concerns how the separate code or law or section is to be drafted in terms of establishing which crimes to include. It would be preferable, if not necessary, to reword the definitions of the crimes based on the requirements of the legality principle. One solution would be simply to reformulate the definitions of the crimes listed in the Rome Statute in Italian translation, which is basically the situation in the drafts under examination (namely Kessler, Iovene, Pianetta, Gozi and Maritati). They are all somewhat similar, except the significant divergence of the Pianetta draft with regard to war crimes. The drafts essentially reproduce the crimes listed in the Rome Statute, adopting their definitions with minor changes or additions. They all add a reference to the Statute and to the Elements of Crimes adopted by the Assembly of States Parties in the article concerning the interpretation of the law. However, these articles, and the drafts in general, contain broader references to international criminal law and the case law of international tribunals,[17] which would open the door to other possible influences in the interpretive process.

One must note, however, that, concerning war crimes, the rewording mainly consists of bringing the crimes applicable in times of international and non-international armed conflict together in single provisions, but the way this was done, such as by referring to "persons protected by the Geneva Conventions of 1949 and their additional protocols", may give rise to problems, as technically speaking there are no protected persons in non-international armed conflicts. Furthermore, the definition of non-international armed conflicts found in the drafts is not all-encompassing, as it refers to "protracted armed conflicts between government forces and organized armed groups",[18] thereby excluding conflicts involving only organised armed groups.

A different path has been followed, for example, in the German law, which basically reproduces the definitions of the Rome Statute but broadens their application here and there, where to do so has been considered more in line with international customary law.[19]

The status of international customary law in relation to the various crimes is much debated, as is the role that the Rome Statute is playing or will be playing in the near future with regard to customary law. Whatever the solution to this issue, the Cariplo Project made the bold choice, on the one hand, to accept the results achieved by the Rome Statute, even where the Statute goes further than customary law (concerning, for example, the crime of apartheid). On the other hand, it expands some of the notions accepted in Rome when they appear too limited in comparison with customary law or when (and this is clearly a political choice) it seems desirable to support emerging trends in the evolution of customary law (such as to broaden the range of protected groups in the definition of genocide).[20]

The decision expressed in the drafts to provide for the non-applicability of statutes of limitation in relation to these crimes is totally commendable, although not strictly imposed by international law, as it would serve to equate the treatment of these crimes before the ICC and national courts, contributing to the fight against impunity.

Regarding the national jurisdiction to prescribe and adjudicate, the best, albeit convoluted, formulation we can cite is Article 15.3 of the Gozi and Maritati drafts, which states that in the event of a crime being committed abroad that does not involve Italian citizens either as alleged offenders or victims, the crime is to be punished according to Italian law if criminal proceedings have not been initiated before the ICC or a State Party, thus respecting the complementarity principle in accordance with Article 17 of the Statute.

On the contrary, Pianetta's draft provision (Article 14.3), according to which the exercise of universal jurisdiction should also be subject to the request of the Minister of Justice, would require the unacceptable involvement of the political sphere. We should bear in mind that universal jurisdiction (at least in its conditional form), coupled with the "prosecute or extradite" (rather than "extradite or prosecute") rule, is a requirement of international treaties vis-à-vis some of the crimes included in the drafts.[21] Both rules (no statute of limitations and conditional universal jurisdiction coupled with the "prosecute or extradite" rule) are also included in the Draft Articles on Crimes against Humanity adopted by the ILC.[22]

4 A concluding remark

To conclude, a bold step, entailing a special law including a comprehensive codification of international crimes, would, in my view, be the best option. This is the line that the Minister of Justice has recently taken by appointing, on 22 March 2022, a Commission of experts, chaired by Professors Francesco Palazzo and Fausto Pocar, to draw up a Draft Code of International Crimes. This plan was adopted before the outbreak of the war in Ukraine but has become even more urgent in the light of the news concerning the multiple horrific crimes being committed in the course of this conflict.[23]

It is my ardent hope that the entire Italian political system will finally – and quickly – be able to demonstrate its *willingness* and *ability* to genuinely complete the implementation of the Rome Statute in our domestic legal order in the best possible way.

Notes

1 See, inter alia, Olympia Bekou and Katerina Katsimardou Miariti, *Implementing the Rome Statute of the International Criminal Court* (Case Matrix Network, Centre for International Law Research and Policy 2017). On the different possible ways of introducing international crimes into the domestic legal system, see Gerhard Werle and Florian Jeßberger, *Principles of International Criminal Law* (4th edn, OUP 2020) 182ff.

2 See, among others, Francesco Bestagno, *Diritti umani e impunità. Obblighi positivi degli Stati in materia penale* (Vita e Pensiero 2003) 27ff; Francesco Viganò, 'L'arbitrio del non punire: sugli obblighi di tutela penale dei diritti fondamentali', in *Studi in onore di Mario Romano* (Jovene 2011) 2645ff; Noelle Higgins and Michael O'Flaherty, 'International Human Rights Law and "Criminalization"' [2015] Japanese Yearbook of International Law 45ff; Marco Longobardo, 'The Italian Legislature and International and EU Obligations of Domestic Criminalisation' [2021] International Criminal Law Review 1, 6ff.

3 International Law Commission (ILC), *Draft articles on Prevention and Punishment of Crimes Against Humanity, with commentaries* (2019) UN Doc A/74/10, 22ff.

4 On the much-debated applicability of the rule – not included in Law no 237 of 20 December 2012 (regarding which see below) – to Italy's cooperation with the ICC, see, inter alia, Chiara Amalfitano, 'Un primo parziale adeguamento allo Statuto della Corte penale internazionale' [2013] Legislazione penale 723ff, at 730. On other possible constitutional obstacles to Italy's cooperation with the ICC see, in particular, Chiara Ragni, 'Obblighi di cooperazione con la Corte penale internazionale e principi fondamentali dell'ordinamento giuridico italiano' [2013] Legislazione penale 732ff. See also Luigi Prosperi, '"With or Without You": Why Italy Should Incorporate Crimes Against Humanity and Genocide Into Its National Legal System' [2021] International Criminal Law Review 1, 15ff.

5 As recalled in Bekou and Katsimardou Miariti, *Implementing the Rome Statute* (n 1) 7, "(t)he dual purpose of enacting national implementing legislation is (1) to empower States to cooperate with the Court; and (2) to enable States to exercise primary jurisdiction over the core international crimes, thereby giving meaning to complementarity". For a broad overview of the reasons for adopting implementing legislation relating to the Rome Statute, see also Maria Crippa, 'Sulla (perdurante?) necessità di un adeguamento della legislazione interna in materia di crimini internazionali ai sensi dello Statuto della Corte penale internazionale' [2016] Diritto penale contemporaneo 2ff.

6 See Law no 202 of 10 November 2021, *Gazzetta Ufficiale della Repubblica italiana* Serie Generale No 287 of 2 December 2021.

7 See Law no 962 of 9 October 1967, *Gazzetta Ufficiale della Repubblica Italiana* No 272 of 30 October 1967. It is also worth recalling that under Constitutional Law no 1 of 21 June 1967 (*Gazzetta Ufficiale della Repubblica Italiana* No 164 of 3 July 1967), the provisions of Articles 10, last sentence, and 26, last sentence of the Constitution, making it unlawful to extradite foreigners and nationals for political crimes, were declared non-applicable in cases of the crime of genocide. See Michela Miraglia, 'Genocide: The Italian Perspective' [2005] International Criminal Law Review 351ff, and, for some critical remarks, Luigi Prosperi (n 4) 13ff.

8 For a broad analysis, see Giulio Bartolini, 'The Criminalization of War Crimes in Italy and the Shortcomings of the Domestic Legal Framework' [2021] International Criminal Law Review 1ff.

9 *Gazzetta Ufficiale della Repubblica italiana* No 167 of 19 July 1999, *Supplemento ordinario* No 135.

10 *Gazzetta Ufficiale della Repubblica italiana* No 6 of 8 January 2013. For a detailed commentary on this law, see Chiara Amalfitano and others, 'L. 20.12.2012 n. 237 – Norme per l'adeguamento alle disposizioni dello statuto istitutivo della Corte penale internazionale (*G.U.* 8.1.2013 n. 6)' [2013] Legislazione penale 723ff. See also, among others, Flavia Lattanzi, 'Un piccolo passo sulla via dell'adeguamento allo Statuto della Corte penale internazionale' [2013] Rivista di diritto internazionale 492ff, and Chantal Meloni, 'Il lento adeguamento dell'Italia allo Statuto della Corte penale internazionale: pubblicata la legge sulla cooperazione giudiziaria con la Corte e sull'esecuzione dei suoi provvedimenti' [2013] Diritto penale contemporaneo.

11 Camera dei deputati, XVI legislatura, Proposta di legge di iniziativa dei deputati Melchiorre, Brugger, Nucara, Tanoni, No 1439, introduced on 2 July 2008.

12 See Camera dei deputati, XIV legislatura, Proposta di legge d'iniziativa dei deputati Kessler, Violante, Calzolaio, Finocchiaro, Melandri, Minniti, Buemi, Carboni, No 2724, introduced on 9 May 2002; Senato della Repubblica, XIV

legislatura, Disegno di legge d'iniziativa dei senatori Iovene, De Zulueta, Battisti, Bedin, Boco, Bonfietti, Chiusoli, Coviello, Di Siena, Donati, Falomi, Flammia, Liguori, Longhi, Pasquini, Peterlini, Pizzinato, Ripamonti, Zancan, No 1638, introduced on 24 July 2002; Senato della Repubblica, XV legislatura, Disegno di legge d'iniziativa del senatore Pianetta, No 893, introduced on 27 July 2006; Camera dei deputati, XVI legislatura, Proposta di legge d'iniziativa dei deputati Gozi, Zaccaria, Ferranti, No 1695, introduced on 24 September 2008; Senato della Repubblica, XVI legislatura, Disegno di legge d'iniziativa dei senatori Maritati, Marcenaro, No 1112, introduced on 14 October 2008.

13 *Völkerstrafgesetzbuch* (VStGB) of 26 June 2002.

14 See Giulio Bartolini (n 8).

15 Without neglecting Art 103 of the Constitution, which contemplates the existence of military tribunals.

16 Such a solution would also avoid any concerns within the ICC, ill-founded as they may be, about an exercise of criminal jurisdiction by Italy aiming to shield the accused from criminal liability.

17 See, in particular, the Pianetta draft, Art 5.

18 See, for example, the Maritati draft, Art 42.2.

19 See, in particular, Gerhard Werle and Florian Jeßberger, 'International Criminal Justice is Coming Home: The New German Code of Crimes Against International Law' [2002] Criminal Law Forum 191, 209.

20 The Cariplo Project was not a legislative draft: rather, it was an academic effort, headed by Professor Fausto Pocar, and was based in the Department of International Studies of Milan University and financed by the Cariplo Foundation (Fausto Pocar and others, *Progetto Cariplo: International Crimes, Italian Law-Making Policy, and Prospective Legislation*, *Commento al Codice di crimini internazionali per l'adeguamento della legislazione italiana allo Statuto della Corte penale internazionale*, presented at the international seminar 'Un codice dei crimini internazionali – Proposta per l'adeguamento dell'ordinamento italiano allo Statuto della Corte penale internazionale', Milan University, 26 March 2015). The project contained a code of 54 articles encompassing the crimes of genocide, crimes against humanity and war crimes, and a commentary.

21 In particular, the four Geneva Conventions of 12 August 1949 and Additional Protocol I of 8 June 1977 in relation to "grave breaches", and the UN Convention against torture of 10 December 1984.

22 See in particular Arts 6.6, 7.2 and 10, and their respective commentaries.

23 The final report of the Commission was presented to the Minister on 31 May 2022 and subsequently published on the Ministry's website, together with the text of the proposed code. See also "Codice dei Crimini internazionali: pubblicata la relazione della Commissione Palazzo-Pocar", Sistema penale, 24 June 2022 (www.sistemapenale.it/it/documenti/codice-dei-crimini-internazionali-pubblicata-la-relazione-della-commissione-palazzo-pocar).

Selected bibliography

Additional Protocol I to the Geneva Conventions of 12 August 1949, relating to the protection of victims of international armed conflicts, 8 June 1977

Amalfitano C and others, 'L. 20.12.2012 n. 237 – Norme per l'adeguamento alle disposizioni dello statuto istitutivo della Corte penale internazionale (G.U. 8.1.2013 n. 6)' [2013] *Legislazione penale* 723 ff

Amalfitano C, 'Un primo parziale adeguamento allo Statuto della Corte penale internazionale' [2013] *Legislazione penale* 723 ff

Bartolini G, 'The Criminalization of War Crimes in Italy and the Shortcomings of the Domestic Legal Framework' [2021] *International Criminal Law Review* 1 ff

Bekou O and Katsimardou Miariti K, *Implementing the Rome Statute of the International Criminal Court* (Case Matrix Network, Centre for International Law Research and Policy 2017) www.legal-tools.org/doc/e05157/

Bestagno F, *Diritti umani e impunità. Obblighi positivi degli Stati in materia penale* (Vita e Pensiero 2003)

Camera dei deputati, XIV legislatura, Proposta di legge d'iniziativa dei deputati Kessler, Violante, Calzolaio, Finocchiaro, Melandri, Minniti, Buemi, Carboni, no 2724, introduced on 9 May 2002

Camera dei deputati, XVI legislatura, Proposta di legge d'iniziativa dei deputati Gozi, Zaccaria, Ferranti, no 1695, introduced on 24 September 2008

Camera dei deputati, XVI legislatura, Proposta di legge di iniziativa dei deputati Melchiorre, Brugger, Nucara, Tanoni, no 1439, introduced on 2 July 2008

"Codice dei Crimini internazionali: pubblicata la relazione della Commissione Palazzo-Pocar", Sistema penale, 24 June 2022

Commissione crimini internazionali Palazzo-Pocar, *Relazione*, 2022, www.gnewsonline.it/codice-dei-crimini-internazionali-ecco-la-proposta-della-commissione-ministeriale/

Convention for the Protection of Human Rights and Fundamental Freedoms (ECHR), Rome, 4 November 1950

Costituzione della Repubblica italiana, 27 December 1947

Crippa M, 'Sulla (perdurante?) necessità di un adeguamento della legislazione interna in materia di crimini internazionali ai sensi dello Statuto della Corte penale internazionale' [2016] *Diritto penale contemporaneo* 2 ff

Geneva Conventions I, II, III and IV of 12 August 1949 relating to the protection of victims of armed conflicts

Higgins N and O'Flaherty M, 'International Human Rights Law and "Criminalization"' [2015] *Japanese Yearbook of International Law* 45 ff

International Covenant on Civil and Political Rights (ICCPR), New York, 16 December 1966

International Law Commission (ILC), *Draft articles on Prevention and Punishment of Crimes Against Humanity, with commentaries* (2019) UN Doc A/74/10, 22 ff

Lattanzi F, 'Un piccolo passo sulla via dell'adeguamento allo Statuto della Corte penale internazionale' [2013] *Rivista di diritto internazionale* 492 ff

Legge costituzionale 21 giugno 1967 no 1, *Gazzetta Ufficiale della Repubblica Italiana* no 164 of 3 July 1967

Legge 9 ottobre 1967 no 962, *Gazzetta Ufficiale della Repubblica Italiana* no 272 of 30 October 1967

Legge 10 novembre 2021 no 202, *Gazzetta Ufficiale della Repubblica Italiana* Serie Generale no 287 of 2 December 2021

Legge 12 luglio 1999 no 232, *Gazzetta Ufficiale della Repubblica Italiana* no 167 of 19 July 1999, *Supplemento ordinario* no 135

Legge 20 dicembre 2012 no 237, *Gazzetta Ufficiale della Repubblica Italiana* no 6 of 8 January 2013

Longobardo M, 'The Italian Legislature and International and EU Obligations of Domestic Criminalisation' [2021] *International Criminal Law Review* 1 ff

Meloni C, 'Il lento adeguamento dell'Italia allo Statuto della Corte penale internazionale: pubblicata la legge sulla cooperazione giudiziaria con la Corte e sull'esecuzione dei suoi provvedimenti' [2013] *Diritto penale contemporaneo*

Miraglia M, 'Genocide: the Italian Perspective' [2005] *International Criminal Law Review* 351 ff

Pocar F and others, *Progetto Cariplo: International Crimes, Italian Law-Making Policy, and Prospective Legislation, Commento al Codice di crimini internazionali per l'adeguamento della legislazione italiana allo Statuto della Corte penale internazionale,* presented at the international seminar "Un codice dei crimini internazionali – Proposta per l'adeguamento dell'ordinamento italiano allo Statuto della Corte penale internazionale", Milan University, 26 March 2015

Prosperi L, '"With or Without You"': Why Italy Should Incorporate Crimes Against Humanity and Genocide Into Its National Legal System' [2021] *International Criminal Law Review* 1 ff

Ragni C, 'Obblighi di cooperazione con la Corte penale internazionale e principi fondamentali dell'ordinamento giuridico italiano' [2013] *Legislazione penale* 732 ff

Senato della Repubblica, XIV legislatura, Disegno di legge d'iniziativa dei senatori Iovene, De Zulueta, Battisti, Bedin, Boco, Bonfietti, Chiusoli, Coviello, Di Siena, Donati, Falomi, Flammia, Liguori, Longhi, Pasquini, Peterlini, Pizzinato, Ripamonti e Zancan, no 1638, introduced on 24 July 2002

Senato della Repubblica, XV legislatura, Disegno di legge d'iniziativa del senatore Pianetta, no 893, introduced on 27 July 2006

Senato della Repubblica, XVI legislatura, Disegno di legge d'iniziativa dei senatori Maritati e Marcenaro, no 1112, introduced on 14 October 2008

Viganò F, 'L'arbitrio del non punire: sugli obblighi di tutela penale dei diritti fondamentali', in *Studi in onore di Mario Romano* (Jovene, 2011) 2645 ff

Völkerstrafgesetzbuch (VStGB), 26 June 2002

Werle G and Jessberger F, 'International Criminal Justice is Coming Home: the New German Code of Crimes Against International Law' [2002] *Criminal Law Forum* 191 ff

Werle G and Jessberger F, *Principles of International Criminal Law* (4th edn, OUP 2020)

2.3 Implementation of substantive rules of international criminal law in Italy

Between international obligations and constitutional law principles

Alessandra Annoni

1 Introduction

Italy ratified the Rome Statute of the International Criminal Court (ICC) in 1999.[1] The authorisation Law no 232 of 12 July 1999 included the enforcement order, which brought the Statute into force domestically.[2] A further step towards implementing the Statute was taken by adopting Law no 237 of 23 December 2012, which, however, only dealt with procedural issues, regulating judicial cooperation between Italian authorities and the ICC. Since 1999, several legislative proposals have been put forward to implement the substantive part of the Statute and to introduce the crimes defined under its Articles 6–8*bis* into the Italian legal system. A recent effort in this direction was the elaboration of a Draft Code of International Crimes by a Commission of Experts established by the Ministry of Justice.[3]

This chapter will firstly try to clarify whether, and to what extent, the Italian Parliament is required under international law to introduce substantive norms on international crimes. After identifying the sources and content of international obligations in this field, it will assess their impact on the domestic legal system, before (and beyond) the adoption of specific legislation criminalising conducts under Articles 6–8*bis* of the Rome Statute, taking into account Italy's constitutional restraints (ie the principles of legality and certainty), as well as its constitutional guarantees for the respect of international obligations, set out in Articles 10(2), 11 and 117(1) of the Italian Constitution.

2 Obligation to prosecute international crimes

Past and present projects aiming for a code of crimes under international law rest on the premise that the implementation of statutory offences at the domestic level is a requirement under the Rome Statute.[4] However, the Statute does not expressly oblige States Parties to incorporate crimes under Articles 6–8*bis* into domestic law, nor does it explicitly mandate them to prosecute these crimes internally. Nevertheless, States Parties which fail to implement

DOI: 10.4324/9781003320951-6

the substantive provisions of the Statute domestically may not be in a position to effectively prosecute individuals accused of core crimes and, therefore, they risk the ICC exercising its complementary jurisdiction.[5] From this perspective, complementarity serves as a strong incentive for national implementation.[6] Complementarity, however, is much more than that: as a broader principle that allocates authority among concurrently empowered institutions,[7] it is the mechanism which informs the entire structure of the international criminal justice system.[8] The Rome Statute entrusts primary responsibility for the prosecution of international crimes to national criminal jurisdictions, assigning the ICC a purely supplementary role. In this framework, even though the Statute does not incorporate an express obligation to implement international crimes into domestic law, States Parties are still required to do so in order to comply with the spirit of the Rome Treaty.[9]

On the other hand, as the Preamble itself recalls, the Statute is not the only source of international obligations in this field.[10] All States (including those which have not ratified the Statute) have a duty to exercise their criminal jurisdiction in respect of crimes under customary international law, at least those perpetrated on their territory.[11] Further, Italy is a party to a number of international treaties – including the four 1949 Geneva Conventions and the Genocide Convention – which stipulate the prosecution of international crimes.[12] Additionally, the obligation to criminalise international crimes which involve heinous human rights violations stems from the duty to ensure respect for human rights, as defined in the various human rights conventions which Italy has ratified.[13] From this perspective, the implementation of the Rome Statute's substantive provisions into domestic law can be seen as an opportunity to fulfil international obligations to which our country is bound, irrespective of the Statute.

3 Domestic implementation of the obligation to prosecute international crimes

Implementation of substantive international criminal law provisions may take different forms: with the obligation to prosecute international crimes being an obligation of result (and not an obligation of means),[14] States enjoy a wide margin of discretion in deciding how to proceed.[15] Insofar as existing domestic legislation ensures full criminalisation of conduct punishable under international law, no further legislative action is required. However, a number of international crimes remain unspecified in the Italian penal system and they cannot adequately be covered by "ordinary" criminal law provisions, either because the elements of the crimes do not match, or because the sanction foreseen is not commensurate with the gravity of the international crime, or because statutes of limitations apply.

In principle, an international rule could also be implemented by a simple referral (or renvoi). In the Italian legal system, this can happen through the adoption of an enforcement order (in the case of treaties), or by means of

Article 10(1) of the Constitution[16] (in the case of international customary rules).[17] The ICC Statute and other relevant international criminal law conventions have all been the object of formal enforcement orders in Italian law, which have ordered their full domestic implementation. Provided that they respect the Constitution, they now enjoy supra-legislative status under Article 117(1) of the Constitution,[18] barring the adoption of ordinary legislation inconsistent with their provisions. The Rome Statute may have even higher status within the Italian legal system if it were considered as falling under the scope of Article 11 of the Constitution.[19] In fact, according to the Constitutional Court, treaties which are covered by the latter provision are purely bound by the fundamental principles of the Italian Constitution.

Insofar as substantive provisions of international criminal law have acquired the status of customary rules, implementation by renvoi is granted by Article 10(1) of the Italian Constitution. The latter provision operates as a "permanent transformer", which automatically introduces into the domestic legal system the provisions necessary for implementing international customary rules, as soon as the latter come into existence at the international level and as long as they respect the fundamental principles of the Constitution.

Implementation by renvoi, be it through an enforcement order or Article 10(1) of the Constitution, can, however, only fully operate in respect of international self-executing rules, which can be directly applied by domestic courts. In order to be fully enforceable at the domestic level, the relevant international criminal rules need to comply with the principle of legality of crimes and penalties, as established under Article 25(2) of the Italian Constitution, which is considered a fundamental principle of the Italian Constitution.[20] Then again, substantive rules of the "special part"[21] of international criminal law seem unable to meet this standard:[22] their formulation is often too open-ended to satisfy the requirement of determinacy and foreseeability, and they fail to specify which penalties are to be applied to perpetrators. Therefore, the adoption of new substantive criminal rules seems indispensable to complement implementation by renvoi, in order to ensure that these provisions are fully enforceable at the domestic level.

4 Relevance of non-self-executing substantive rules of international criminal law before (and beyond) their incorporation into domestic law

Substantive provisions of international criminal law are largely non-self-executing, which makes implementation by renvoi insufficient, but not irrelevant. The enforcement orders of pertinent treaties and Article 10(1) of the Constitution (covering crimes under customary law) still operate and allow the international rules to have an impact on the domestic system. Albeit not immediately effective, international criminal rules "circulate" within the Italian legal system and must be coordinated with the other rules which constitute the system.[23]

Implementation by renvoi makes the principle of consistent interpretation fully applicable: existing domestic rules should always be interpreted with the aim of fulfilling the State's international obligations.[24] This applies to criminal rules of the "special part",[25] and also to the rules of the "general part" when they are applied to conduct which amounts to an international crime. The Italian Supreme Court of Cassation may have been inspired by this principle when it interpreted the domestic rules on co-perpetration (Articles 110–119 of the Italian Penal Code; hereinafter: *Codice penale*) relatively extensively in the Condor case,[26] concerning the enforced disappearance of a number of Italian citizens in Latin American States during the 1970s and 1980s. Since the crime of enforced disappearance is not specifically provided for under Italian criminal law, the defendants were charged with aggravated multiple murder, kidnapping and other minor offences, where murder was the only crime which was not statute barred. Unlike the court of first instance, the Supreme Court of Cassation deemed the defendants – including those who had kidnapped the victims and taken them to a designated secret detention centre, but who had not directly taken part in their subsequent murder – as co-perpetrators of the crime. This allowed the Supreme Court of Cassation to convict all of the individuals who would have qualified as co-perpetrators of the crime of enforced disappearance under Articles 7(1)(*i*) and 25(3)(*a*) of the Rome Statute.

From a different perspective, the international customary obligation to prosecute core crimes, to which the Italian legal order has automatically conformed owing to Article 10(1) of the Constitution, should be taken into account by State authorities when they consider granting a pardon or commuting sentences. The General Prosecution Office at the *Corte d'appello di Milano* actually did so when it expressed its opinion against the granting of a presidential pardon to Colonel Joseph Romano III, who was implicated in "extremely serious crimes against international humanitarian law".[27]

5 Non-applicability of statutes of limitations to international crimes: an example of a self-executing provision of international criminal law?

Substantive rules of the special part of international criminal law may not be fully enforceable at the domestic level without further specification by the legislature; but would this also apply to all of the general part's rules? Take for instance, the principle of non-applicability of statutes of limitations to international crimes: the rule is provided in two different treaties (which Italy never ratified)[28] and in Article 29 of the Rome Statute; it has been codified in the Draft articles on Prevention and Punishment of Crimes Against Humanity, adopted in 2019 by the International Law Commission (ILC);[29] it can now be found in the legislation of many States and has already been considered as a rule of customary international law by domestic courts.[30] All these factors militate towards its recognition as a general rule of international law.[31]

The rule – to which the Italian legal order has automatically adapted, owing to Article 10(1) of the Constitution – is clear and unconditional, but partly runs counter to Article 157 of the *Codice penale*, which imposes statutes of limitations on all crimes, except those bearing life-imprisonment sentences. Should prescription ever be invoked during ongoing criminal proceedings concerning facts which amount to an international crime,[32] the ordinary court would be prevented from setting aside the rule on statutory limitations but could be expected to raise the issue of its constitutionality before the Constitutional Court.[33] The latter would then have to assess: a) whether the inapplicability of statutes of limitations to international crimes is indeed prescribed by a customary rule of international law; and b) whether this rule can be directly applied within the Italian legal order, or whether it necessitates intervention by the legislative branch in order to be fully enforceable.

The answer to the latter question largely depends on how Article 25(2) of the Italian Constitution is interpreted.[34] The Constitutional Court has long clarified that the principle of legality also applies to the setting of statutes of limitations, which is an essential factor in parliament's decision on the punitive response to any given individual conduct.[35] The result has been a refusal by the Court to address issues of constitutionality concerning Article 157 of the *Codice penale*. Had the Court decided on the merit, and declared Article 157 of the *Codice penale* partially unconstitutional, it would have ended up impinging on choices in the criminal field which Article 25(2) reserves for the legislative branch.[36] However, none of the cases so far examined by the Constitutional Court concerned the compatibility of Article 157 of the *Codice penale* with international rules.

An opportunity to rule on such an issue emerged in the framework of the criminal proceedings concerning violent acts perpetrated by law-enforcement officials during the 2001 G8 summit in Genoa. The forms of criminal conduct at stake met the definition of torture under international law, but were qualified as ordinary offences because the crime of torture was not, at the time, provided for under Italian law. Pending the proceedings, the time limitation had expired for most of these crimes, but the Prosecutor questioned the constitutionality of Article 157 of the *Codice penale* in the light of Article 117(1) of the Constitution: they pointed out that the application of statutes of limitations to criminal acts which amount to torture runs counters to Article 3 of the European Convention of Human Rights, as interpreted by the Strasbourg Court. However, the Supreme Court of Cassation refused to bring the issue before the Constitutional Court, recalling the latter's previous case law on Article 25(2) of the Constitution and statutes of limitations.[37]

As emphasised by some scholars,[38] however, this case is different to any other the Constitutional Court has ever addressed. In respect of criminal acts which amount to torture under international law, the margin of discretion which parliament normally enjoys when setting time limitations is already limited by a clear and unconditional rule of international law which occupies a supra-legislative rank under Article 117(1) of the Constitution. Since the international rule leaves no choice but to set prescription aside, by declaring Article 157 of the *Codice penale* constitutionally illegitimate insofar as it subjects to time limitations the prosecution of criminal acts which amount to torture, the Constitutional Court would adopt the only solution compatible with the State's international obligations; therefore, its decision would stay within the *rime obbligate*, the "verses prescribed"[39] by the Constitution, thereby leaving the division of power between the Constitutional Court and parliament unaffected.[40]

A similar argument could, *a fortiori*,[41] be used to challenge the constitutionality of Article 157 of the *Codice penale* in light of Article 10(1) of the Constitution, insofar as that criminal provision allows time limitations to apply to criminal acts which amount to crimes under customary international law.

In my opinion, these considerations retain their validity even in light of the Constitutional Court's recent practice concerning the potential impact of EU law on statutes of limitations. On this, two cases deserve consideration. The first[42] originated from a request by the *Tribunale di Roma*, which raised a question of constitutionality regarding Article 6(1), (4) and (5) of Law no 251 of 5 December 2005, by reference to Articles 11[43] and 117(1) of the Constitution, read in conjunction with the EU Council Framework Decision 2004/68/JHA of 22 December 2003 on combating the sexual exploitation of children and child pornography. According to the *a quo* judge, by introducing a more favourable regime on statutory limitations, without excluding its application to sexual crimes against minors, the newly enacted domestic act prevented Italy from achieving the result required by Article 8(6) of the Framework Decision, according to which Member States must "take the necessary measures to enable the prosecution, in accordance with national law, of at least the most serious of the offences referred to in Article 2 after the victim has reached the age of majority". In dismissing the case, the Constitutional Court referred to Article 25(2) of the Constitution; it pointed out that Article 8(6) of the Framework Decision fails to clearly identify the crimes it refers to (merely mentioning "the most serious of the offences" covered by Article 2) and does not specify what would be the minimum acceptable time of prescription for these crimes. Clearly, the reason why the case was dismissed had little to do with the alleged inability of *any* international (or EU) law to directly affect rules on statutory limitations. What led the Court to conclude that it did not have the power to impinge, *in malam partem,* on the punitive choice made by parliament was rather the indeterminacy of the international (or rather, EU) rule invoked in the specific case: the result required by Article 8(6) of the Framework Decision could indeed be achieved in many different ways, and not necessarily by affecting the regime of statute of limitations.[44]

The second judgement of the Constitutional Court deserving consideration is the one which ended the (in)famous Taricco saga.[45] The latter started with a preliminary ruling delivered on 8 September 2015 by the European Court of Justice (ECJ) upon a reference by the *Tribunale di Cuneo*, concerning the compatibility of national legislation on statutory limitations with Article 325 of the Treaty on the Functioning of the European Union (TFEU), which requires Member States to adopt effective measures to counter fraud which affects the Union's financial interests, and to take the same measures to counter fraud affecting the Union's financial interests as they take to counter fraud affecting their own. The ECJ held that a national rule (as provided for in Articles 160 and 161 of the *Codice penale* – which stipulated that the interruption of criminal proceedings concerning serious fraud in relation to value added tax had the effect of extending the limitation period by only a quarter of its initial duration) was liable to jeopardise the fulfilment of the Member States' obligations under Article 325(1) and (2) of the TFEU,

> if that national rule prevents the imposition of effective and dissuasive penalties *in a significant number of cases* of *serious fraud* affecting the financial interests of the European Union, or provides for longer limitation periods in respect of cases of fraud affecting the financial interests of the Member State concerned than in respect of those affecting the financial interests of the European Union.[46]

The ECJ also clarified that domestic courts must give full effect to Article 325(1) and (2) of the TFEU, if necessary by disapplying the conflicting provisions of national law.

The decision prompted the *Corte d'appello di Milano* and the Supreme Court of Cassation to challenge the compatibility of Article 325 of the TFEU, as interpreted by the ECJ (hereinafter: the Taricco rule) with the principle of legality in criminal matters, as protected under the Italian Constitution.[47] In an attempt to avoid a direct clash with the Luxembourg Court, the Italian Constitutional Court solicited a new preliminary ruling asking the ECJ to better clarify the scope of Article 325(1) and (2) of the TFEU.[48] This gave the ECJ the opportunity to introduce a *caveat* in the Taricco rule which clarifies that national courts are not required to disapply rules on statutes of limitations when such disapplication would entail a breach of the principle that offences and penalties must be defined by law, because of the lack of precision of the applicable law or because of the retroactive application of legislation imposing conditions of criminal liability stricter than those in force at the time the infringement was committed.[49]

This solution satisfied the Constitutional Court. Ruling on the original requests by the *Corte d'appello di Milano* and the Supreme Court of Cassation, the *Consulta* maintained that the Taricco rule could not be applied to facts committed prior to the date of publication of the judgement establishing the rule (8 September 2015). The Court also pointed out that Article 325 of the TFEU (as interpreted by the ECJ) was marked by "an evident lack of certainty", in that the definition of the "considerable number of cases" that trigger the application of the Taricco rule is irreparably vague. Nevertheless, the questions raised by both referring Courts were considered as unfounded because, in light of the interpretative clarification provided by the ECJ itself, the Taricco rule did not in fact require disapplication of domestic rules on statutory limitations in pending proceedings.[50]

In my opinion, it is impossible to infer from the *Taricco* judgement a general rule to the effect that Article 25(2) of the Constitution prevents any international (or EU) law impinging on statutes of limitations from producing direct effects *in malam partem*. Article 325 of the TFEU (as interpreted by the ECJ) was considered as incapable of producing such effects because of its indeterminacy and insofar as it produced retroactive effects. None of these arguments would hold in respect of the customary rule on the non-applicability of statutes of limitations to international crimes, which is a clear-cut and longstanding rule[51] and which provides an unambiguous and immediate answer as to whether conduct may be prosecuted or not.

6 Conclusion

When it comes to ensuring the possibility of prosecuting international crimes at the domestic level, the shortcomings of the Italian legal system are self-evident. Nevertheless, some of these deficiencies could be overcome by relying on an "internationally oriented" interpretation of the relevant domestic rules and, elsewhere, by recognising that at least some substantive international criminal law provisions do fulfil the requirements for them to produce direct effects in the Italian legal system without impinging on the fundamental principle of legality laid down in Article 25(2) of the Constitution. However, this should not be an excuse for parliament to postpone the adoption of specific legislation in this field any longer.

Notes

1 Rome Statute of the International Criminal Court (adopted 17 July 1998, entered into force 1 July 2002) 2187 UNTS 900 (Rome Statute).
2 Law no 202 of 10 November 2021, which authorised the President of the Republic to ratify the Kampala amendments, also includes the relevant enforcement order.
3 The text of the draft code was submitted to the Ministry on 31 May 2022 and is available at: www.giustizia.it/cmsresources/cms/documents/commissione_PALAZZO_POCAR_articolato_31mag22.pdf
4 See, for instance, AC 1695 (XVI Leg), Disposizioni per l'adeguamento dell'ordinamento interno allo Statuto della Corte penale internazionale. Relazione alla proposta di legge di iniziativa dei deputati Gozi, Zaccaria, Ferranti, 24 September 2008, 1, at http://documenti.camera.it/apps/commonServices/getDocumento.ashx?sezione=lavori&tipoDoc=testo_pdl_pdf&idlegislatura=16&codice=16PDL0027030: "La proposta di legge nasce dall'esigenza di adattare il nostro ordinamento alle prescrizioni contenute nello Statuto della Corte penale internazionale" ("the proposal arises from the need to adapt the Italian legal system to the provisions of the ICC Statute").

5 A State whose domestic legislation cannot ensure full criminalisation of conduct punishable before the ICC is likely to be considered "unable" to prosecute under Art 17 of the Statute. *See* Luigi Condorelli, 'La Cour pénale internationale: Un pas de géant (pourvu qu'il soit accompli...)' (1999) 103 RGDIP 7, 21.

6 Jean K Kleffner, 'The Impact of Complementarity on National Implementation of Substantive International Criminal Law' (2003) 1 J Int'l Crim Just 86, 87.

7 William W Burke-White, 'Proactive Complementarity: The International Criminal Court and National Courts in the Rome System of International Justice' (2008) 49 Harv Int'l LJ 53, 79.

8 Emanuela Fronza, 'Complementarità, esercizio della giurisdizione e adeguamento a livello interno', in Enrico Amati and others, *Introduzione al diritto penale internazionale* (4th edn, Giappichelli 2020). *See* also Otto Triffterer, 'Legal and Political Implications of Domestic Ratification and Implementation Processes', in Claus Kreß and Flavia Lattanzi (eds), *The Rome Statute and Domestic Legal Orders*, vol 1 (Nomos 2000) 13–24.

9 Gerhard Werle and Florian Jeßberger, *Principles of International Criminal Law* (4th edn, OUP 2020) 183. *See* also Kleffner (n 6) 91–94. According to Marco Roscini, 'Great Expectations. The Implementation of the Rome Statute in Italy' (2007) 5 J Int'l Crim Just 493, 497, States Parties which do not fulfil their responsibility to allow the Court to operate effectively would also breach the customary obligation to perform treaties in good faith.

10 *See* Rome Statute, preamble: "[I]t is the duty of every State to exercise its criminal jurisdiction over those responsible for international crimes" and "[the effective prosecution of the most serious crimes of concern to the international community] must be ensured by taking measures at the national level and by enhancing international cooperation".

11 Werle and Jeßberger (n 9) 104–105. Although nothing prevents a State from prosecuting a core crime perpetrated abroad, even when neither the perpetrator nor the victim are its nationals, the exercise of universal jurisdiction is not at present the object of an obligation under customary international law (*see* Alessandra Annoni, 'International Cooperation for the Repression of Core Crimes: What Role for the UNTOC?', in Serena Forlati (ed), *The Palermo Convention at Twenty: Institutional and Substantive Challenges* (Brill 2020) 69–74). The customary nature of the *aut dedere aut judicare* rule (whereby a State must either prosecute the individuals accused of international crimes who are present on its territory or hand them over to a State which is willing to exercise jurisdiction) is also controversial. *See*, in this respect, Cherif Bassiouni and Edward M Wise, Aut Dedere Aut Judicare*: The Duty to Extradite or Prosecute in International Law* (Martinus Nijhoff Publishers 1995) 3–69; Claire Mitchell, Aut Dedere, Aut Judicare*: The Extradite or Prosecute Clause in International Law* (Graduate Institute Publications 2009). *See* also ILC, 'The Obligation to Extradite or Prosecute (*aut dedere aut judicare*), Final Report on the Topic' (2014) 2(2) ILC Ybk 91, paras 49–55.

12 Paola Gaeta, 'International Criminalization of Prohibited Conduct', in Antonio Cassese (ed), *The Oxford Companion to International Criminal Justice* (OUP 2009).

13 *See* Francesco Viganò, 'L'arbitrio del non punire. Sugli obblighi di tutela penale dei diritti fondamentali', in *Studi in onore di Mario Romano* (Jovene 2011).

14 *See* Marco Longobardo, 'The Italian Legislature and International and EU Obligations of Domestic Criminalisation' (2021) 21 Int'l Crim L Rev 623, 627–632.

15 *See* Matthias Neuner (ed), *National Legislation Incorporating International Crimes. Approaches of Civil and Common Law Countries* (BWV 2003); Julio Bacio Terracino, 'National Implementation of ICC Crimes' (2007) 5 J Int'l Crim Just 421; Morten Bergsmo, Mads Harlem and Nobuo Hayashi (eds), *Importing Core International Crimes into National Law* (2nd edn, Torkel Opsahl Academic EPublisher 2010); Olympia Bekou, 'Crimes at Crossroads: Incorporating International Crimes at the National Level' (2012) 10 J Int'l Crim Just 677.

16 This provision reads: "The Italian legal system conforms to the generally recognised rules of international law".

17 For an overview of the methods of implementation of international law within the Italian legal system *see* Giuseppe Cataldi, 'Italy', in Dinah Shelton (ed), *International Law and Domestic Legal Systems. Incorporation, Transformation, and Persuasion* (OUP 2011).

18 The provision reads as follows: "Legislative powers shall be vested in the State and the Regions in compliance with the Constitution and with the constraints deriving from EU legislation and international obligations".

19 The provision reads: "Italy agrees, on conditions of equality with other States, to the limitations of sovereignty that may be necessary to a world order ensuring peace and justice among the Nations. Italy promotes and encourages international organisations furthering such ends". The Constitutional Court has so far invoked this provision mostly with reference to EU rules (see below, n 43) but some scholars consider it could apply also to the Rome Statute (see, among others, Flavia Lattanzi, 'Un piccolo passo sulla via dell'adeguamento allo Statuto della Corte penale internazionale' (2013) 96 Riv dir int 492, 509).

20 The provision reads: "No punishment may be inflicted except by virtue of a law in force at the time the offence was committed". On the relevance of the national principle of legality as an obstacle to core crimes prosecutions *see* Ward N Ferdinandusse, *Direct Application of International Criminal Law in National Courts* (TMC Asser Institute 2006) 263–267; Thordis Ingadóttir, 'The Implementation of the Rome Statute of the International Criminal Court in the Nordic Countries: A New Comprehensive Criminalization of Serious Crimes', in Astrid Kjeldgaard-Pedersen (ed), *Nordic Approaches to International Law* (Brill 2018) 120–122.

21 In national doctrine, criminal law is usually divided into the "general part", which sets principles of criminal responsibility that apply to all crimes, and the "special part", which defines the elements of criminal offences and the respective penalties.

22 *See* Luigi Condorelli, *Il giudice italiano e i trattati internazionali. Gli accordi* self-executing *e non* self-executing *nell'ottica della giurisprudenza* (CEDAM 1974) 62; Mario Pisani, 'La "penetrazione" del diritto internazionale penale nel diritto penale italiano' (1979) 13 Indice penale 5; Giulio Bartolini, 'The Criminalization of War Crimes in Italy and the Shortcomings of the Domestic Legal Framework' (2021) 21 Int'l Crim L Rev 679, 689; Luigi Prosperi, '"With or Without You": Why Italy Should Incorporate Crimes Against Humanity and Genocide Into Its National Legal System' (2021) 21 Int'l Crim L Rev 698.

23 Francesco Salerno, 'Il limite – non il contro-limite – della riserva di legge all'attuazione diretta della norma internazionale "generalmente riconosciuta" in materia penale', in *Scritti in onore di Giuseppe Tesauro*, vol 4 (Editoriale scientifica 2014) 2887. *See* also Beatrice I Bonafè, 'Constitutional Judicial Review and International Obligations of Criminalization' (2021) 21 Int'l Crim L Rev 660, 668–673.

24 For an overview of the application of the principle of consistent interpretation by Italian criminal courts *see* Daniele Amoroso, 'The Duties of Criminalization under International Law in the Practice of Italian Judges: An Overview' (2021) 21 Int'l Crim L Rev 641, 644–651.

25 Thus, for example, Art 600 of the *Codice penale*: "Riduzione o mantenimento in schiavitù o in servitù" must be interpreted in the light of the definition of slavery and practices similar to slavery provided under the Supplementary Convention on the Abolition of Slavery, the Slave Trade, and Institutions and Practices Similar to Slavery, which Italy ratified in 1958 and whose enforcement order was given with Law no 1304 of 20 December 1957.

26 *See* Cass pen (Italy) 9 July 2021 No 43693.

27 5 April 2013 No 2013-23-14-Vs. n. 31.2-3500.

28 Convention on the Non-Applicability of Statutory Limitations to War Crimes and Crimes against Humanity (adopted 26 November 1968, entered into force 11 November 1970) 754 UNTS 73; European Convention on the Non-Applicability of Statutory Limitation to Crimes against Humanity and War Crimes (adopted 25 January 1974, entered into force 27 June 2003) ETS No 082. Both instruments have been sparsely ratified. This, however, should not be interpreted as a general rejection by States of the principle of non-applicability of statutory limitations to international crimes. The first Convention included a rule whereby the principle was to be applied also to international crimes for which the time limit had already expired, and this was considered by many States to be incompatible with the principle of non-retroactivity of penal law, as affirmed in their respective Constitutions (*see* Robert H Miller, 'The Convention on the Non-Applicability of Statutory Limitations to War Crimes and Crimes against Humanity' (1971) 65 Am J Int'l L 476). The rule was not reproduced in the European Convention, but when the latter was adopted most European States had already enforced domestic norms providing for the non-applicability of statutory limitations to international crimes, which made the ratification of the European Convention somewhat superfluous (*see* Ruth A Kok, *Statutory Limitations in International Criminal Law* (TMC Asser Press 2007) 90–102).

29 ILC, 'Draft articles on Prevention and Punishment of Crimes Against Humanity, with commentaries' (2019) 2(2) ILC Ybk, Art 6(6).

30 *See* Cass pen (France) 26 January 1984, 83-94425 (*Barbie* Supreme Court judgement) and *Tribunale Militare di Roma* 22 July 1997 (*Hass-Priebke* judgment).

31 Kok (n 28) 345–391; ICRC (Advisory Service on International Humanitarian Law), *General principles of international criminal law*, 3/2014. *See* also Sergio Marchisio, 'The *Priebke* case before the Italian Military Tribunals: A Reaffirmation of the Principle of Non-Applicability of Statutory Limitations to War Crimes and Crimes against Humanity' (1998) 1 Yrbk Intl Hum L 344, 345. According to this author, the principle of non-applicability of statutory limitations on war crimes is consolidating as a peremptory norm of general international law.

32 The issue actually arose in the *Hass-Priebke* case. Since the defendant had been charged with a crime punishable with life imprisonment, however, statutes of limitations were inapplicable on the basis of Art 157 of the *Codice penale* itself.

33 *See*, in this respect, ItConstCt 278/1992 and 131/2001. All judgements of the Italian Constitutional Court can be retrieved on the Court's website (www.cortecostituzionale.it); some of them are also published in English. *See* also Francesco

Salerno, 'Le norme di diritto internazionale "generalmente riconosciute" nella prospettiva della Corte costituzionale' (2000) 103 Riv dir int 291.

34 *See* Marco M Scoletta, *Metamorfosi della legalità.* Favor libertatis *e sindacabilità* in malam partem *delle norme penali* (Monboso casa editrice 2012).

35 *See*, among others, ItConstCt 34/2009.

36 See *ex plurimis* ItConstCt 394/2006, para 6.1.

37 Cass pen (Italy) 5 July 2012 No 38085, in Dir pen cont 16 October 2012.

38 Viganò (n 13) 2681–2682; Viviana Zanetti, 'La tortura dalle parti di Bolzaneto e della Diaz. Il legislatore negligente, gli obblighi internazionali e la Corte costituzionale' (2012) 4 Studium Iuris 430; Andrea Pugiotto, 'Repressione penale della tortura e Costituzione: anatomia di un reato che non c'è' (2014) 2 Dir pen cont 129, 149.

39 *See* Franco Ferrari, *Introduction to Italian Public Law* (Giuffrè 2008) 205.

40 On the evolution of the doctrine of "rime obbligate" *see*, among others, Marilisa D'Amico, 'Corte costituzionale e discrezionalità del legislatore in materia penale' (2016) 4 Rivista Aic 1; Dario Martire, 'Giurisprudenza costituzionale e rime obbligate: il fine giustifica i mezzi? Note a margine della sentenza n. 113 del 2020 della Corte costituzionale' (2020) 6 Osservatorio costituzionale 244.

41 As mentioned above (*see* Section 3), under Art 117(1) of the Constitution international treaties duly ratified by Italy set rules which are "interposed" between the Constitution and ordinary law, whereas customary rules of international law are granted by Art 10(1) of the Constitution the status of constitutional law and are subject only to the respect of core constitutional values.

42 ItConstCt 143/2018. See Nicola Canzian, 'La prescrizione dei reati ancora di fronte alla Costituzione: la debolezza del parametro interposto' (2018) 61 Riv it dir proc pen 1775.

43 Above, n 19. In the Constitutional Court's view, the provision serves as the legal basis for the participation of Italy in the European integration process, and to the transfer of some legislative competences from Italian Parliament to EU's institutions. Thus, ordinary judges are entitled to set aside any piece of domestic legislation which falls within the scope of EU law and that is inconsistent with any EU rule enjoying direct effects within the domestic legal order. Nevertheless, the Constitutional Court has reserved the power to rule upon the conformity of EU rules with the fundamental principles of the Italian Constitution (the so-called "counter-limits").

44 *See*, for an identical conclusion based on similar arguments, ItConstCt 234/2018.

45 See Chiara Amalfitano (ed), *Primato del diritto dell'Unione europea e controlimiti alla prova della 'saga* Taricco*'* (Giuffrè 2018); Matteo Bonelli, 'The *Taricco* Saga and the Consolidation of Judicial Dialogue in the European Union' (2018) 25 Maast J Eur & Comp L 357; Giovanni Piccirilli, 'The "*Taricco* Saga": The Italian Constitutional Court Continues Its European Journey' (2018) 14 EuConst 814.

46 ECJ (Grand Chamber) Case C-105/14 *Ivo Taricco and Others* [2015] ECR Court General Reports (emphasis added).

47 Technically, the two referring judges challenged the constitutionality of Art 2 of Law no 130 of 2 August 2008, providing for the ratification and implementation of the Treaty of Lisbon.

48 ItConstCt 24/2017.

49 ECJ (Grand Chamber) Case C-42/17 *MAS and MB* [2017] ECR Court General Reports.

50 ItConstCt 115/2018.
51 According to Kok (n 28) 380–382, the rule consolidated at the beginning of the 21st century.

Selected bibliography

Amalfitano C (ed), *Primato del diritto dell'Unione europea e controlimiti alla prova della 'saga Taricco'* (Giuffrè 2018)

Amoroso D, 'The Duties of Criminalization under International Law in the Practice of Italian Judges: an Overview' (2021) 21 *Int'l Crim L Rev* 641

Annoni A, 'International Cooperation for the Repression of Core Crimes: What Role for the UNTOC?', in Forlati S (ed), *The Palermo Convention at Twenty: Institutional and Substantive Challenges* (Brill 2020)

Bacio Terracino J, 'National Implementation of ICC Crimes' (2007) 5 *J Int'l Crim Just* 421

Bartolini G, 'The Criminalization of War Crimes in Italy and the Shortcomings of the Domestic Legal Framework' (2021) 21 *Int'l Crim L Rev* 679

Bassiouni C and Wise EM, *Aut Dedere Aut Judicare: The Duty to Extradite or Prosecute in International Law* (Martinus Nijhoff Publishers 1995)

Bekou O, 'Crimes at Crossroads: Incorporating International Crimes at the National Level' (2012) 10 *J Int'l Crim Just* 677

Bergsmo M, Harlem M and Hayashi N (eds), *Importing Core International Crimes into National Law* (2nd edn, Torkel Opsahl Academic EPublisher 2010)

Bonafè BI, 'Constitutional Judicial Review and International Obligations of Criminalization' (2021) 21 *Int'l Crim L Rev* 660

Bonelli M, 'The *Taricco* Saga and the Consolidation of Judicial Dialogue in the European Union' (2018) 25 *Maast J Eur & Comp L* 357

Burke-White WW, 'Proactive Complementarity: the International Criminal Court and National Courts in the Rome System of International Justice' (2008) 49 *Harv Int'l LJ* 53

Canzian N, 'La prescrizione dei reati ancora di fronte alla Costituzione: la debolezza del parametro interposto' (2018) 61 *Riv it dir proc pen* 1775

Cataldi G, 'Italy', in Shelton D (ed), *International Law and Domestic Legal Systems. Incorporation, Transformation, and Persuasion* (OUP 2011)

Condorelli L, *Il giudice italiano e i trattati internazionali. Gli accordi self-executing e non self-executing nell'ottica della giurisprudenza* (CEDAM 1974)

Condorelli L, 'La Cour pénale internationale: Un pas de géant (pourvu qu'il soit accompli. . .)' (1999) 103 *RGDIP* 7

D'Amico M, 'Corte costituzionale e discrezionalità del legislatore in materia penale' (2016) 4 *Rivista Aic* 1

Ferdinandusse WN, *Direct Application of International Criminal Law in National Courts* (TMC Asser Institute 2006)

Ferrari F, *Introduction to Italian Public Law* (Giuffrè 2008)

Fronza E, 'Complementarità, esercizio della giurisdizione e adeguamento a livello interno', in Amati E and others, *Introduzione al diritto penale internazionale* (4th edn, Giappichelli 2020)

Gaeta P, 'International Criminalization of Prohibited Conduct', in Cassese A (ed), *The Oxford Companion to International Criminal Justice* (OUP 2009)

Ingadóttir T, 'The Implementation of the Rome Statute of the International Criminal Court in the Nordic Countries: a New Comprehensive Criminalization of Serious Crimes', in Kjeldgaard-Pedersen A (ed), *Nordic Approaches to International Law* (Brill 2018)

Kleffner JK, 'The Impact of Complementarity on National Implementation of Substantive International Criminal Law' (2003) 1 *J Int'l Crim Just* 86

Kok RA, *Statutory Limitations in International Criminal Law* (TMC Asser Press 2007)

Lattanzi F, 'Un piccolo passo sulla via dell'adeguamento allo Statuto della Corte penale internazionale' (2013) 96 *Riv dir int* 492

Longobardo M, 'The Italian Legislature and International and EU Obligations of Domestic Criminalisation' (2021) 21 *Int'l Crim L Rev* 623

Marchisio S, 'The *Priebke* case before the Italian Military Tribunals: a Reaffirmation of the Principle of Non-Applicability of Statutory Limitations to War Crimes and Crimes against Humanity' (1998) 1 *Yrbk Intl Hum L* 344

Martire D, 'Giurisprudenza costituzionale e rime obbligate: il fine giustifica i mezzi? Note a margine della sentenza n. 113 del 2020 della Corte costituzionale' (2020) 6 *Osservatorio costituzionale* 244

Miller RH, 'The Convention on the Non-Applicability of Statutory Limitations to War Crimes and Crimes against Humanity' (1971) 65 *Am J Int'l L* 476

Mitchell C, *Aut Dedere, Aut Judicare: The Extradite or Prosecute Clause in International Law* (Graduate Institute Publications 2009)

Neuner M (ed), *National Legislation Incorporating International Crimes. Approaches of Civil and Common Law Countries* (BWV 2003)

Piccirilli G, 'The "*Taricco* Saga": the Italian Constitutional Court Continues its European Journey' (2018) 14 *EuConst* 814

Pisani M, 'La "penetrazione" del diritto internazionale penale nel diritto penale italiano' (1979) 13 *Indice penale* 5

Prosperi L, '"With or Without You": Why Italy Should Incorporate Crimes Against Humanity and Genocide Into Its National Legal System' (2021) 21 *Int'l Crim L Rev* 698

Pugiotto A, 'Repressione penale della tortura e Costituzione: anatomia di un reato che non c'è' (2014) 2 *Dir pen cont* 129

Roscini M, 'Great Expectations: the Implementation of the Rome Statute in Italy' (2007) 5 *J Int'l Crim Just* 493

Salerno F, 'Le norme di diritto internazionale "generalmente riconosciute" nella prospettiva della Corte costituzionale' (2000) 103 *Riv dir int* 291

Salerno F, 'Il limite – non il contro-limite – della riserva di legge all'attuazione diretta della norma internazionale "generalmente riconosciuta" in materia penale', in *Scritti in onore di Giuseppe Tesauro*, vol 4 (Editoriale scientifica 2014)

Scoletta MM, *Metamorfosi della legalità, Favor libertatis e sindacabilità in malam partem delle norme penali* (Monboso casa editrice 2012)

Triffterer O, 'Legal and Political Implications of Domestic Ratification and Implementation Processes', in Kreß C and Lattanzi F (eds), *The Rome Statute and Domestic Legal Orders*, vol 1 (Nomos 2000)

Viganò F, 'L'arbitrio del non punire. Sugli obblighi di tutela penale dei diritti fondamentali', in *Studi in onore di Mario Romano* (Jovene 2011)

Werle G and Jeßberger F, *Principles of International Criminal Law* (4th edn, OUP 2020)

Zanetti V, 'La tortura dalle parti di Bolzaneto e della Diaz. Il legislatore negligente, gli obblighi internazionali e la Corte costituzionale' (2012) 4 *Studium Iuris* 430

2.4 International criminal law implementation and constitutional law

Francesco Viganò[1]

1 Statutory basis of criminal liability and punishment (Article 25(2) Italian Constitution)

A first obvious issue, while implementing international criminal law in a domestic system, is the principle of *legality in criminal matters* – a principle on which the Italian Constitutional Court (ItConstCt) case law has put a remarkable emphasis, with the effect that its scope is wider in Italy than according to current international standards.

Let us start with the sub-principle of "*riserva di legge*", or "*Gesetzesvorbehalt*", which is familiar to continental scholars, but is not recognised as such in Anglo-Saxon legal systems, nor in the European Convention of Human Rights (ECHR). Every criminal offence must, under Article 25(2) of the Italian Constitution (IC), be established by an *act of legislation* – ie, by an act of parliament, or at least by an act enjoying the same legal force.

There is no provision, in the IC, contemplating a possible role for international law as a legal basis for criminal liability, such as Article 7(2) ECHR. As a consequence, international criminal law – whether customary or treaty law – cannot create criminal offences that are enforceable within the Italian legal system without the necessary mediation of domestic legislation.

To what extent this principle is compatible with existing legislative provisions (such as Article 185*bis* of our Military Criminal Code of Wartime) which rely on international obligations to set forth the single elements of the offence, is a very disputable issue. It is worth noting that the question on the compatibility with the principle of legality in criminal matters of the use of the "blanket references" or "legislation by reference" technique in the definition of an offence was extensively addressed by the European Court for Human Rights (ECtHR) in May 2020, in an advisory opinion delivered following a request by the Armenian Constitutional Court.[2] This opinion arguably sets a minimum standard of protection for the principle of legality in criminal matters, which must be met within any State Party to the Convention, without prejudice to the possibility for a higher standard of protection to be set at a national level, according to Article 53 ECHR. It

DOI: 10.4324/9781003320951-7

is clear, however, that the enactment on provisions with extensive references to international law could well lead to constitutional challenges, whose outcome would be difficult to predict. Therefore, it would probably be a safer choice for the national legislator to directly select the courses of conduct to be penalised, thereby avoiding references to international sources of the law.

The ItConstCt case law also extends the requirement of a statutory basis to any provision that is relevant for the application of substantive criminal law, including – crucially – *limitation rules*, which are often considered in other jurisdictions as part of procedural law, not covered as such by the scope of the *nullum crimen* principle.[3] The ItConstCt went as far as to consider that the requirement of a statutory basis in criminal matters works as a counter-limit against EU obligations,[4] namely those set forth by the EU Court of Justice in its well-known *Taricco* case.[5] The requirement of a (national) legal basis for criminal liability, even in respect of limitation rules, was held by the ItConstCt to be an essential part of the very constitutional identity of the Italian Republic, which must be preserved even against the general limitation of national sovereignty flowing from participation in the EU, according to Article 11 of the Constitution. It is likely, then, that the same principle would also be affirmed in respect of customary international law or treaty international law, which are binding on Italy according, respectively, to Articles 10 and 117 IC, but within the limits marked by the respect for the basic principles of the constitutional order – including the *nullum crimen* principle, to the extent recognised by the domestic constitutional traditions.

It seems, therefore, very unlikely that Italian criminal courts will ever disapply national limitation rules, giving precedence to international rules on the imprescriptibility of (all or some) international crimes, as argued by Prof Annoni in her contribution.[6]

A different question, also raised by Prof Annoni, is whether the ItConstCt could strike down, in an incidental proceeding brought at the public prosecution's request, a domestic law on limitation because of its incompatibility with customary international law.[7] The point, which has never been addressed as such by the ItConstCt, certainly deserves closer scrutiny. I would just mention, here, a possible obstacle, namely the necessity to fill the gap created by a hypothetical decision by the Court to strike down the national limitation rule. If rules on limitation should have a (national) statutory basis, how could the rule applicable to the case at issue – namely, the rule of imprescriptibility for the crime – be itself based on international law? And in any case, since one of the essential components of the principle of legality is the non-retroactivity of criminal law, such a rule could never be applied to the defendant in the very trial where the constitutional question was raised – he should be acquitted in any case.

To avoid all these difficulties, and to ensure their effectiveness in the Italian legal order, the rules on imprescriptibility – which already exist, in Italy, with respect to the offences punishable with life imprisonment – should be explicitly set forth by statutory law, in the awareness that these rules will only work *pro futuro*.

2 *Lex certa* (Article 25(2) Italian Constitution)

A second aspect of the principle of legality – closely related to the former, but conceptually different – which is relevant in our context is the *lex certa* principle: a criminal provision must be worded in a sufficiently precise manner, so as to enable the addressee of the norm to foresee its possible application, including the sanction that might be imposed on him for the crime. Again, in the *Taricco* decisions[8] and in subsequent case law[9] the ItConstCt has highlighted an additional rationale to the principle, namely the separation of powers between legislation and judiciary: a lack of precision in norms empowers courts to draw the line between criminal and non-criminal behaviour, thereby usurping a task which the Constitution only confers on the legislator.

Of course, this constitutional requirement cannot be overstretched, since no provision could be drafted in such a way as to eliminate any doubt about its interpretation. As observed by the ECtHR, the "penumbra of doubt in relation to borderline facts does not in itself make a provision incompatible with Article 7, provided that it proves to be sufficiently clear in the large majority of cases".[10] Yet, the recent ItConstCt case law has made it clear that the addressees of the norm should be able to foresee their possible criminal liability based on the *text* of the criminal provision – this principle being linked, under the ItConstCt's perspective, to the prohibition of analogy at the detriment of the accused, which is also considered as part of the scope of the *nullum crimen* and is infringed whenever a court applies a criminal provision in a case which cannot be reasonably considered to be covered by the very wording of the provision itself.[11] This marks a slightly different approach of the ItConstCt in respect of the ECtHR, which is prepared to recognise the foreseeability of criminal liability when the person concerned can assess, to a degree that is reasonable in the circumstances, the consequences which a given action may entail with the assistance of the relevant case law and, if necessary, by requesting legal advice.[12]

The principles established in the Italian case law make it hard to imagine that vague wording in a provision could withstand constitutional scrutiny based on the argument that the content of general clauses contained in it is clarified by international case law.

Therefore, an effort will be required from the Italian legislator – following the example of the German legislator – to reformulate some admittedly vague provisions contained in the Rome Statute and in the Elements of Crimes in a more precise manner, incorporating into the text of the provision the existing case law on these crimes, such as to give clear guidance to national judges and avoid constitutional challenges.

Suffice it to think of the crime of persecution (Article 7(2)(h) of the Statute), whose *actus reus* is described as "the intentional and severe deprivation of fundamental rights contrary to international law by reason of the identity of the group or collectivity". Such a description leaves a very broad discretion to courts, and should be integrated by the legislator with some more precise guidance to withstand possible constitutional challenges.

Another striking example is Article 7(1)(k) of the Statute, which generically refers to "other inhumane acts *of a similar character* intentionally causing great suffering, or serious injury to body or to mental or physical health". This provision poses the additional problem – from a constitutional point of view – of incorporating in the legislative description an analogy clause, which seems to require courts to use precisely the interpretative technique that is in general terms prohibited by the principle of legality.

3 Other challenges for the principle of legality in the context of international criminal law

Having said all that, it is also clear that the well-established political rationales of the principle of legality in criminal matters are not fully adequate for the context of international criminal law, and need to be adapted to it.

Let us just think of the two basic sub-principles I have just mentioned: the statutory basis of criminal liability, and foreseeability based on the text of the relevant provision. Both of them have been developed from the perspective of a national legal system, where parliament – as the body representing the whole community, to whose composition every citizen concurs through democratic elections – is vested with the unique power to establish sanctions limiting the personal liberty of those same citizens, and where those citizens have a freedom to do everything which is not expressly prohibited by the laws enacted through their democratic involvement.

This model does not make much sense when a parliamentary law shall be equally applied to citizens and non-citizens based on the principle of extraterritorial jurisdiction, which is a cornerstone in the decentralised enforcement of international criminal law. Foreign military officers and commanders have absolutely nothing to do with Italian democratic processes and the enactment of legislation criminalising international offences at that domestic level; and cannot receive any fair warning about the possible consequences of their actions according to the wording of Italian provisions.

The logic of *nullum crimen* should reasonably be confined, here, to a requirement for the foreseeability of their criminal conviction based on the relevant *international law* in force at the time of the commission of the offence; and the task of domestic criminal actors could perhaps be rethought as a contribution to the enforcement of international, rather than national, criminal law, on behalf of the whole international community.

As a consequence, States should be extremely careful, in implementing international criminal law provisions in their domestic legal systems, to *not* unduly expand criminal offences to courses of conduct which are not already clearly covered by international provisions or well-settled international case law. The understandable desire to drive the evolution of international criminal law by widening the scope of existing offences for the sake of a deeper protection of human rights could easily lead to a violation of the human rights of defendants, namely their right to foresee the possible application of (very harsh) criminal sanctions as a consequence of their conduct, insofar as they are entitled to receive fair warnings in this respect by international law, not by the legislative choices of German or Italian legislators – whose criminal provisions are certainly accessible to German and Italian citizens, but not necessarily to Russian or Congolese nationals.

4 Proportionality and rehabilitative purpose of penalties (Articles 3 and 27(3) Italian Constitution)

Another constitutional principle that is worth mentioning here, which is also discussed in Dr Epik's contribution, is proportionality of penalties[13] – or, in terms more familiar to German doctrine, the principle of the "*schuldangemessene Strafe*".

The ItConstCt has developed a wide-ranging case law on the subject, which should obviously be taken into account while legislating in this field. For example, fixed penalties are likely to be considered unconstitutional in Italy, since they cannot be adjusted to the concrete seriousness of the individual offence. Therefore, life imprisonment is in principle compatible with the Constitution (provided that such a penalty is *de iure* and *de facto* reducible, as clarified by both the ItConstCt and ECtHR case laws[14]), but the court should always have the possibility of recognising mitigating circumstances that can lead to the imposition of a lower sentence, even with respect to the most heinous crimes.

A point, here, deserves particular attention. One of the key features of the principle of proportionality of punishment in Italy is the need to adjust punishment to the degree of *mens rea* of the perpetrator, and in general to the degree of his or her culpability.[15] As a consequence, the rules on command responsibility set forth in Article 28 of the Statute should probably be "unpacked", it being necessary to distinguish – for the purpose of establishing different sentencing frameworks – between intentional liability and mere reckless/negligent culpability. Indeed, a common sentencing framework for all these forms of command responsibility would probably not withstand constitutional scrutiny, based on the principles set forth by the case law in 1979 in a case concerning a provision contained in the Military Criminal Code for Peacetime, which established an undifferentiated sentencing framework for offences with different degrees of *mens rea*.[16] A further distinction will also be needed, within the realm of Article 28 offences, based on the different seriousness of the conduct, between failure to *prevent* crimes and failure to *report* already committed crimes. How this differentiation could be carried out in detail – whether following the VStGB model, or in some other way – would then be a matter for legislative discretion.

Moreover, as Article 27(3) ICC makes it clear, punishments must pursue, in the Italian legal system, the offender's rehabilitation. This means not only that life imprisonment should always be reducible, but also that alternative measures during the execution of the sentence should be granted to every prisoner, irrespective of the seriousness of their offence, according to their actual progress towards rehabilitation. Restorative justice mechanisms could also be imagined and implemented.

On the other hand, one has to remember that sanctions for heinous violations of human rights, such as those always implied in international crimes, should, under international human rights law and the ECHR law in particular, be punished in a way that sends a clear deterrent message to potential perpetrators, and fulfils the victims' need for justice.[17] In this respect, the very idea of proportionality of penalties cannot but include a requirement of sufficient severity of the sentence – which, by the way, is also a condition for the judgment to be considered adequate to bar a further prosecution before the ICC or, arguably, other States' jurisdictions.

5 A procedural issue: mandatory prosecution (Article 112 Italian Constitution)

One last word about a further difficult constitutional issue, which is probably peculiar to the Italian legal system.

Article 112 IC sets forth, in explicit terms, the principle of mandatory prosecution: public prosecutors are under a constitutional duty to prosecute every crime whose commission they are aware of.

The stiffness of this mandate has long been questioned among legal scholars, who often point out the practical impossibility of prosecuting every crime – which actually leads the prosecutors' offices to ignore many *notitiae criminis*, and simply let limitation periods expire as to them. But a special difficulty, as far as I can see, will arise as regards "domesticated" international criminal law provisions, which aspire to be enforced everywhere in the world according to the universal jurisdiction principle.

An unconditional obligation to prosecute every international crime, wherever and by whomever committed, would be impossible to enforce. However, Article 112 poses a serious obstacle to any attempt to recognise and regulate prosecutorial discretion in choosing which crimes to investigate upon, and later prosecute. Even a solution such as section 153f of the German criminal procedure code would be, in this respect, open to constitutional challenges.

Objective criteria as to the preconditions for the exercise of extraterritorial jurisdiction, directly set forth by the law, will therefore be needed, following the example of the existing provisions in Articles 7–10 of the Italian Criminal Code. The presence of the suspect in the Italian territory would be, for example, one of the obvious options; but the question should also be clarified whether and, if so, to what extent prosecution offices could or should conduct investigations concerning alleged international crimes, where the suspect is not yet in the Italian territory. Otherwise, Article 112 IC would impose an unconditional obligation for prosecution offices to investigate based on whatever complaint presented to them, without any clear rules as to which territorial office should proceed – a solution which could lead to unreasonable investments in terms of financial and human resources, at least whenever there is no reasonable prospect of arresting the suspect and subsequently bringing him to trial.

Notes

1 Judge of the Italian Constitutional Court and Criminal Law Professor at Bocconi University, Milano. The opinions expressed in this paper are his own and do not necessarily represent the views of the Court.
2 ECtHR, *Advisory opinion concerning the use of the "blanket reference" or "legislation by reference" technique in the definition of an offence and the standards of comparison between the criminal law in force at the time of the commission of the offence and the amended criminal law* (GC), 29 May 2020, para 74.
3 See, most recently, ItConstCt, Judgments No 140/2021, para 12 and No 278/2020, para 9.
4 ItConstCt, Order No 24/2017, paras 4–6 and Judgment No 115/2018, para 5.
5 ECtHR, *Taricco* (GC), 8 September 2015, Case C-105/14.
6 See Alessandra Annoni, Chapter 2.3, Implementation of Substantive Rules of International Criminal Law in Italy: between International Obligations and Constitutional Law Principles.
7 ibid.
8 See, in particular, ItConstCt, Order No 24/2017, para 9.
9 ItConstCt, Judgment No 32/2020, para 4.3.1.
10 ECtHR, *Cantoni v France* App no 17862/91 (11 November 1996) para 32.
11 ItConstCt, Judgment No 98/2021, para 2.4.
12 See, again, *Cantoni* (n 10), para 32: "The role of adjudication vested in the courts is precisely to dissipate such interpretational doubts as remain, taking into account the changes in everyday practice. The Court must accordingly ascertain whether in the present case the text of the statutory rule *read in the light of the accompanying interpretive case-law* satisfied this test at the relevant time" (emphasis added). In the same vein, *Kafkaris v Cyprus* (GC) App no 21906/04 (12 February 2008) para 141; *SW v the United Kingdom* App no 2016692 (22 November 1995) para 36; *Streletz, Kessler and Krenz v Germany* (GC) App no 34044/96 and others (22 March 2001) para 50; *Kononov v Latvia* (GC) App no 36376/04 (17 May 2010) para 185; *Norman v the United Kingdom* (6 July 2021), paras 60 and 66.
13 See Aziz Epik, Chapter 5.3, Domesticating International Criminal Justice: Sanctions and Sentencing. For a comprehensive discussion, on a comparative perspective, see Francesco Viganò, *La proporzionalità della pena* (Giappichelli 2021).
14 As to the former, see in particular ItConstCt, Judgments No 204/1974, No 264/1994 and No 161/1997; as to the latter, ECtHR, *Kafkaris* (n 12) para 98; *Vinter v the United Kingdom* (GC) App no 66069/09 and others (9 July 2013) paras 108, 119.

15 On this aspect see, recently, ItConstCt, Judgments No 73/2020, para 4.2, and No 55/2021, para 8.
16 ItConstCt, Judgment No 16/1979.
17 For a concrete application of this principle with respect of torture, see ECtHR, *Gäfgen v Germany* (GC) App no 22978/05 (1 June 2010) para 124. Extensively on the point referred to in the text, Francesco Viganò, 'L'arbitrio del non punire', in *Studi in onore di Mario Romano*, vol IV (Jovene 2011) 2645–2704.

Selected bibliography

ECtHR, *Advisory opinion concerning the use of the "blanket reference" or "legislation by reference" technique in the definition of an offence and the standards of comparison between the criminal law in force at the time of the commission of the offence and the amended criminal law (GC)*, 29 May 2020

Viganò F, *La proporzionalità della pena* (Giappichelli 2021)

Viganò F, 'L'arbitrio del non punire', in *Studi in onore di Mario Romano, vol IV* (Jovene 2011)

Relevant case law

ECtHR, *S. W. v the United Kingdom* App no 2016692 (22 November 1995)
ECtHR, *Cantoni v France* App no 17862/91 (11 November 1996)
ECtHR, *Streletz, Kessler and Krenz v Germany* (GC) App no 34044/96 and others (22 March 2001)
ECtHR, *Kafkaris v Cyprus* (GC) App no 21906/04 (12 February 2008)
ECtHR, *Kononov v Latvia* (GC) App no 36376/04 (17 May 2010)
ECtHR, *Gäfgen v Germany* (GC) App no 22978/05 (1 June 2010)
ECtHR, *Taricco* (GC) case C-105/14 (8 September 2015)
ECtHR, *Norman v the United Kingdom* (6 July 2021)
ItConstCt, Judgment No 16/1979
ItConstCt, Order No 24/2017
ItConstCt, Judgment No 115/2018
ItConstCt, Judgment No 32/2020
ItConstCt, Judgment No 73/2020
ItConstCt, Judgment No 278/2020
ItConstCt, Judgment No 55/2021
ItConstCt, Judgment No 98/2021
ItConstCt, Judgment No 140/2021

2.5 The way forward

An overview on the draft "Palazzo-Pocar" of 2022

Nicola Selvaggi

1 Premise

This chapter is intended to outline some of the main issues in adapting the substantive provisions of the Rome Statute to domestic law, while at the same time recalling the most significant steps that have been taken to ensure its complete domestication. I will make special reference to the latest work of the Commission established within the Italian Ministry of Justice, chaired by Professors Palazzo and Pocar, in which I participated as deputy head of Cabinet.[1]

It goes without saying that domestic legislation is still far from a comprehensive implementation of all aspects relating to international criminal law as required by the Rome Statute. As a matter of fact, Law no 237 of 20 December 2012 has only made partial adjustments, introducing procedural rules in the Italian legal system aimed at cooperation with the International Criminal Court.

As regards substantive criminal law, domestic provisions still lack the contextual elements, now widely investigated by international jurisprudence and doctrine, which define the dimension of crimes and which are the reference for the construction of international crimes, including the *actus reus* and the *mens rea* as well as aggravating and mitigating circumstances.

While some crimes against humanity may correspond to domestic offences (eg, reduction in slavery, deportation or forced transfer of population), in many other cases regulation is only partial and may require more complete definitions (as in the case of deprivations of liberty in violation of the rules of international law and sexual violence, in view of Articles 600 and 609*bis* of the Criminal Code).

With a view to fully implementing the Rome Statute and international criminal law, several legislative attempts have been initiated, without ever being adopted. These include the project drawn up by the "Conforti Commission", established by Ministerial Decree on 27 June 2002, which was also involved in the drafting of substantive norms; the proposed law for an "International Criminal Code" or "Kessler Project" presented by AC no 2724 of 9 May 2002 ("Norms for the adaptation of the internal system

DOI: 10.4324/9781003320951-8

to the Statute of the International Criminal Court"); the proposal in 2015 for a "Code of International Crimes", specifically limited to the special part (known as the "Cariplo Project", as it resulted from research co-financed by the Cariplo Foundation); a project developed by a working group operating within the framework of research promoted by the Association of Criminal Law Professors; and, finally, a Commission appointed on 22 March 2022 by the Italian Minister of Justice, charged with the elaboration of a "*Codice dei crimini internazionali*".

A combination of reasons has made this march towards a full implementation of the Rome Statute, and, more generally speaking, of international criminal law, a longstanding and as yet unaccomplished path.

The fundamental clarifications provided in the statutes establishing *ad hoc* tribunals, in relevant case law and finally in the consolidated sets of rules in the Rome Statute make it possible to highlight legal traditions and values in a single framework and thus constitute the stepping-stone to conceive a universal grammar of criminal law.

Nevertheless, domesticating international criminal law requires diverse experience and expertise to sort through a complex subject matter consisting of a multi-layered normative dimension: the Rome Statute; the unifying framework of principles on criminal responsibility – ie, the Criminal Code, where relevant provisions can also be located; the military criminal codes, especially with regard to war crimes; and finally the Constitution, the European Convention on Human Rights and the Charter of Fundamental Rights of the EU, where we find the fundamental values that international criminal justice must help safeguard and the general criteria under whose presidium criminal protection itself must operate (legality, proportionality, offensiveness, culpability, humanity and the re-educative purpose of punishment).

2 Criminal code or code of international crimes? Choosing the regulatory framework

Domesticating requires, in the first place, choosing between providing a specific title in the Criminal Code or drafting a separate normative body.

The first option would undoubtedly enrich the Criminal Code through the introduction of an autonomous section thereof, as a valid implementation of the Rome Statute. For example, an interesting aspect of the draft prepared by the working group of the Criminal Law Professors Association may be found in the attempt to gather, within the same set of rules, not only provisions for the domestication of the Rome Statute but also other offences, particularly those intended to strengthen the protection of human dignity.

On the other hand, finding an appropriate place within the Criminal Code does not seem like an easy task. Things would change in an ideal perspective aimed at re-founding the special part of the Code as a direct expression of an authentically constitutional and oriented vision of the relationship between the individual and the State, and thus essentially and primarily focused on the protection of the human being. This would clearly entail a complete departure from the so-called "descending progression" characteristic of the "Codice Rocco" of 1930, based instead on the pivotal role of the State-person.

Another problem that domestication within the Criminal Code may raise is the coexistence of international crimes and a very traditional normative environment.

Therefore, it seems preferable to focus on a code of international crimes that also includes provisions of a general nature such as those on the obligations to prevent the commission of crimes, on the "non-political" nature of crimes (particularly for the purposes of extradition), on interpretation, on the responsibility of legal persons and on the statute of limitations.

This was, indeed, the draft delivered by the Commission "Palazzo–Pocar". I will briefly sketch out some of its choices.

3 The good symbolism

Scholars engaged in examining the most significant trends in criminal justice reforms in recent years often observe that they are marked by the recurring presence of merely symbolic provisions. While in general this is certainly a negative trait of any criminal justice system, there may be exceptions. One of these is the choice of the Commission "Palazzo–Pocar" to retain, for offences under the Code, the designation of "*crimini*", which does not appear in Italian criminal law. In the draft prepared by the Commission, however, it is well clarified that this choice does not imply the introduction of a new type of crime in the Italian system and that the rules provided by the Criminal Code for serious forms of crime apply to international crimes.

4 A principles-based implementation of the Rome Statute: some examples

In many ways, the adaptation of the Rome Statute required the Commission "Palazzo-Pocar" to address a complex alignment with the models of criminal liability provided as a rule by Italian criminal law.

The draft prepared by the Commission has chosen a minimalist approach in this respect, introducing provisions only where necessary. It then relied on the interaction of general principles to solve difficult cases.

4.1 Command responsibility

As far as individual liability is concerned, a fitting example is offered by Article 28 of Rome Statute on command responsibility, a mode of liability that must be evaluated considering the fundamental principles and general rules of the Italian Criminal Code (such as those provided for by Arts 40 and 110).[2]

This provision seems to conceive the failure to adopt measures to prevent and to repress a crime as equivalent; the same can be said for the failure to submit the matter to the competent authorities for investigation and prosecution. Since these are different situations and not comparable in terms of general principles, the draft prepared by the Commission "Palazzo-Pocar" rightly regulates them as distinct forms of liability.[3] A distinction is thus made between failure to comply with the obligation to prevent the crime and failure to punish or report it. The latter in fact does not make the commander responsible for the crime committed. Yet, an interesting issue arises when a commander has tolerated other persons' criminal conduct, which is a situation that lies somewhere between facilitating the commission of an offence by active conduct and the failure to exercise necessary and due supervision. In this regard, some general remarks can be made.

As a matter of fact, it lies in the structure of any criminal justice system to make it possible to hold responsible those who cooperate in, or facilitate, other persons' criminal activity (such cases attract the application of the provisions on participation in an offence, which in any system serve the purpose of charging with a crime also those who have not committed an offence – *actus reus* – in all its elements, but rather only a part thereof), and those who do not hinder the commission of another person's offence when they are under a specific legal obligation to do so (the provisions on omission apply in this case).

With respect to these fundamental liability patterns, questions may arise when a commander, without playing an active or direct role in a single illicit activity, has an ambiguous behaviour that is indeed suitable and even univocally intended to influence an employee's (unlawful) conduct. This situation may occur in different ways; for example, it may be the case for a person holding a prominent position to have a tolerant attitude, by simply staying idle in front of repeated breaches of law by subordinates. In such cases the qualified idleness of a person should not be regarded as criminally irrelevant, even though morally ambiguous, or even blameworthy.

No criminal responsibility system rules out the possibility to highlight any tolerant attitude by those who are in a prominent position towards other persons' criminal activities, specifically through the legal instruments briefly outlined above. From a criminal law perspective, inaction *per se* would not be relevant, but rather a continued failure to take action over time, because such repeated behaviour ends up with facilitating a subordinate's criminality or strengthening his/her criminal intent.

According to the literature, both in Italy and other European countries (see for example France and Germany), quite often in specific contexts typified by peculiar social and linguistic conventions inaction and silence may have a specific meaning in a communication context.

In German case law and doctrine as well, mention has sometimes been made with respect to a wide range of different situations (eg, presence in the place of commission of extortion or in some cases of fraud), to "communicative silence" or "meaningful silence" – ie, also a "naturally neutral" attitude may indeed reflect specific contents if poured into a determinate social reality.

In some cases, Italian courts have established that in organised crime groups, particularly those that are "mafia-based", the most important decisions for a criminal association, such as planning and carrying out attacks against representatives of public institutions (magistrates, politicians, etc.), are made by a collegiate body (in the organisation referred to as Cosa Nostra, the so-called "Cupola") where the persons who intervene, especially if they hold top positions, do not utter a word but are silent. Italian case law has established that such "silence" should be interpreted as decisions or, at least, as acceptance of the general will.

Certainly, there might also be other scenarios, as in the case of someone in a prominent position who is in support of unlawful deviance and who puts in place a system of incentives to encourage the commission of offences or, in general, carries out or contributes to reinforcing a policy for the entity as a whole. Without participating – or rather contributing directly or openly to the commission of any single offence – he/she builds a context or a cradle for illegality.

Nevertheless – although this is a further problem – it may not always be easy to construe the meaning of this type of behaviour and pierce the veil of ambiguity to detect a univocal content that most legal systems, in compliance with the fundamental principles governing the legal structure and ascertainment of a criminal offence, may require.

4.2 The execution of superior's orders

Halfway between justification and excuse are, on the other hand, certain hypotheses that are related to the execution of a superior's order. As a matter of fact, when reference is made to the "condition" of the subordinate agent, different situations may come to the fore: on the one hand, the direct link stemming from the relationship of hierarchy (military or administrative) or the lack of knowledge of the illegitimacy of the order; on the other, certain types of "coercion" that are not related to the binding nature of an illegitimate order.

As to a superior's order and the effect of "coercion" it entails, there are two possibilities: (a) the effect of coercion derives from the order considered in itself; and (b) the effect of coercion derives from a more complex conduct, as when the superior gives an order that the subordinate refuses to execute as it is blatantly illegal, but his superior nevertheless forces the subordinate to execute it. In the latter case, it seems that the superior does not so much leverage his authority as make a threat, because, in excluding any possible alternative approach for the subordinate, the superior tends to create a situation that could be defined as a "lack of choice" for those affected by it.

Here, again, the Commission's approach has been to introduce the minimum necessary adaptation of the Rome Statute, thus allowing the general principles and criteria to operate. Indeed, such a distinction seems to have been the result of the experience of *ad hoc* criminal courts, whose case law has sometimes merged the rule of irrelevance of the criminal order with an accurate evaluation of the criteria of exemption from liability which, *basically*, respond to the logic of the "duress".[4]

Even in light of the general principles of criminal liability in the Italian legal system, the regulatory constraint that would derive from the order (if it were lawful) is replaced by the relevance of a "constraint" of an entirely different content, to be identified in the coercion provoked by the way the order is formulated. This is in view of the assessment of the lack of an authentic and personal "moral adhesion" of the agent to the superior's order.

5 Corporate criminal liability

Collective entities have hardly been considered as a recipient of international criminal law, despite the attempts also made during the preparatory work of the Rome Statute to lay out provisions for corporate liability in the event of an international crime.[5]

Space has traditionally been left for considering other options in those cases where a collective subject – such as a multinational company – commits serious violations of human rights.[6] In this regard, it should be remarked how the application of civil-law regimes – as demonstrated, in particular, by the interesting case law related to the US Alien Tort Claims Act (almost a "clearing house" due to a lack of provisions for corporate liability deriving from international crime[7]) with respect to extraordinarily serious facts that frequently constitute international crimes – has actually enhanced the development of schemes for attributing liability, for carrying out "tests". At the same time, careful attention should also be paid to those aspects that point to the culpable nature of a collective entity's contribution.[8]

The Commission's decision to provide for the criminal liability of companies under the rules of Legislative Decree no 231/2001 (Italian discipline of the *ex crimine* corporate responsibility) is therefore of great importance.[9] Close attention should be devoted to the principles at the basis of the corporate liability scheme. One of the results that may be attributed to the Italian legislator is certainly the introduction of a clear and direct link between the offence and the entity's organisation, by giving relevance to compliance programmes,[10] a key factor that makes it ultimately possible to incorporate the overall attitude of a collective entity towards an individual offence into the contents of (corporate) misconduct.

As has been remarked, the abidance by the principle of personality is primarily connected to the logic of compliance programmes that should allow a collective entity to prove its innocence from an objective and subjective viewpoint.[11] As a matter of fact, the emphasis given by Legislative Decree 231/2001 to the failure to adopt and effectively implement compliance programmes sheds a light on the essential contents of the liability regime, revolving around the acknowledgement of corporate organisational efforts and policies with preventive purposes.[12] Moreover, the relevance given to the failure to adopt and implement compliance programmes would also build a direct connection between the general exercise of the organisational power and the specific offence. Thus, considering both an (objective) defect in the organisation (ie, taking into account the entity's conduct) and the latter's attitude as a whole in a merely subjective perspective that could also be related to a concept of "will", although adjusted to the specific features and peculiarities of an entity.[13]

In emphasising a precise connection to the collective subject, this model of liability then seems particularly suitable when it comes to imputing international crimes to corporations. Also, this set of rules seems to meet the needs of large enterprises (irrespective of the ownership), more exposed than others to the risk of being involved in the commission of international crimes.

6 Genocide

The definitions of crimes mirror other important choices made by the Commission in the drafting process. I will only consider those related to genocide.

First of all, it was decided to provide for different offences and only one crime of genocide. As cleared by the Commission in its "Relazione", the unifying elements of the offences are: (a) the specific intent to destroy the group, provided for in the 1948 Convention; and (b) a contextual element ("the conduct took place in the context of a manifest pattern of similar conduct directed against that group or was conduct that could itself effect such destruction") drafted by adapting the expression of the Elements of Crime of the International Criminal Court, with a view to avoiding any "subjectivisation" of the offences.[14] Furthermore, the language group is introduced as a protected autonomous group. Finally, the draft defines cultural genocide so as to punish acts, recurring in history and today, aimed at destroying the cultural, linguistic or religious characteristics that distinguish a certain group, so that its identity is lost and assimilated into the dominant group.

7 The way forward

These are therefore some of the most interesting contents proposed by the Palazzo-Pocar Commission. With respect to these contents, it is worth noting that the "march" towards the full implementation of the Rome Statute has not stopped.

Recently, a working group was set up within the new Ministry of Justice with the task of conducting an in-depth examination of the text proposed by the Commission and proposing possible additions and necessary coordination.

The group is now concluding its work, thus bringing the likely start of the legislative process ever closer.

Notes

1 The Italian Ministry of Justice Proposal for a Code of International Crimes of 2022 ("Palazzo-Pocar Draft") (EN).

2 Chantal Meloni, *Command Responsibility in International Criminal Law* (TMC Asser 2010) 139ff.

3 See Chantal Meloni, Chapter 5.1, How to domesticate the modes of liability for international crimes in the Italian system.

4 In this respect, the Erdemovic case is quite significant, see Sienho Yee, 'The Erdemovic Sentencing Judgement. A Questionable Milestone for the International Criminal Tribunal for the Former Yugoslavia' [1997] Georgia J Int Comp L, 263ff, 287ff; Jan Christoph Nemitz, 'Aggravating and Mitigating Circumstances in International Humanitarian Law – The Erdemovic-Case' (1997) 10(1) Humanitäres Völkerrecht 7, 22ff.

5 Celia Kay Wells and Elias Juanita, 'Catching the Conscience of the King: Corporate Players on the International Stage', in Philip Alston (ed), *Non-State Actors and Human Rights* (OUP 2005) 141ff.

6 The incorporation, in particular, of transnational and multinational companies into the international system for the protection of human rights, by developing inputs and recommendations (next to the voluntary initiatives taken by those companies in the framework of what is referred to as "corporate social responsibility"), has led to the provision of obligations to be directly imposed on these entities, so much so that some scholars concluded that they would also obtain a legal subjectivity from the viewpoint of international law (sometimes considering this evolution as a *fait accompli*: see David Adedayo Ijalaye, *The Extension of Corporate Personality in International Law* (Cambridge University Press 1978) 245; in general, this issue has long been debated: for a synthesis, see Andrew Clapham, *Human Rights Obligations of Non-State Actors* (OUP 2006) 76ff. In any case, the system of safeguards has been made effective at present by resorting to civil law instruments or, quite rarely, by invoking State responsibility; on these developments, in very extensive literature, a comparison may be made between, inter alia, the following authors: David Whyte and Stefanie Khoury, *Corporate Human Rights Violations, Global Prospects for Legal Action* (Routledge 2017) 77ff, 156ff; August Reinisch, 'The Changing International Legal Framework for Dealing with Non-State Actors', in Philip Alston (ed), *Non-State Actors and Human Rights*, ibid, 37ff; Ralph G Steinhardt, 'Corporate Responsibility and the International Law of Human Rights: The New *Lex Mercatoria*', in Philip Alston (ed), *Non-State Actors and Human Rights*, ibid, 177ff.

7 Claims seeking redress have been made over time, ranging from Second World War facts to the abuses committed at Abu Ghraib prison in Iraq: see, Christoph Kathollnig, *Unternehmensstrafrecht und Menschenrechtsverantwortung* (NWV im Verlag Österreich GmbH 2016) 229ff; Michael D Ramsey, 'International Law Limits on Investor in Human Rights Litigation' (2009) 50 Harvard International Law Journal 9; Sarah Joseph, *Corporations and Transnational Human Rights Litigation* (Hart 2004); Anita Ramasastry, 'Corporate Complicity: From Nuremberg to Rangoon. An Examination of Forced Labor Cases and Their Impact on the Liability of Multinational Corporations' (2002) 20 Berkley JIL 91–159.

8 In this regard, the *Unocal* case is very significant indeed (*John Roe III*; *John Roe VII*; *John Roe VIII*; *John Roe X v Unocal Corp; Union Oil Rswl Co of California* US Court of Appeal for the Ninth Circuit, 18 September 2002), where the following has been remarked with respect to the subjective attribution of liability (§ 13): "A reasonable factfinder could also conclude that Unocal's conduct met the mens rea requirement of aiding and abetting as we define it today, namely, actual or constructive (ie, reasonable) knowledge that accomplice's actions will assist the perpetrator in the commission of the crime. The District Court found that 'the evidence does suggest that Unocal knew that forced labour was being utilized and that Joint Venturers benefitted from the practice'"; it was also added that, as shown by further circumstances, the company, in its capacity as a defendant, knew (or at least could figure out) that, through direct payment or specific directions, it encouraged Myanmar's military to subject actors to, and keep them in, forced labour; for further notes on this case, Andrew Clapham (n 4) 257ff.

9 See Chantal Meloni, Chapter 5.1, How to domesticate the modes of liability for international crimes in the Italian system.

10 See Antonio Fiorella and Nicola Selvaggi, '*Compliance programs* e dominabilità "aggregata" del fatto. Verso una responsabilità da reato dell'ente compiutamente personale' (2014) 3 Diritto penale contemporaneo. Rivista trimestrale 105ff.

11 Without claiming to be exhaustive, Enrica Villani, *La "colpa di organizzazione" nell'illecito dell'ente da reato. Un'indagine di diritto comparato* (Aracne 2013) 200ff; Antonio Fiorella, 'Oggettivo e soggettivo nella definizione dell'efficacia dei c.d. modelli organizzativi. Problemi e linee di sviluppo della ricerca', in Antonio Fiorella and Alfonso Maria Stile (eds), *Corporate Criminal Liability and Compliance Programs. First Colloquium* (Jovene 2012) 53ff; Nicola Selvaggi, 'Compliance Programmes and "Organisational Fault" in Italian Legislation' (2012) 3 Eucrim 127ff; Carlo Piergallini, 'Paradigmatica dell'autocontrollo penale (dalla funzione alla struttura del "modello organizzativo" ex d.lgs. n. 231/2001)', in *Studi in onore di M Romano* (Jovene 2011) 2056ff; Carlo Enrico Paliero and Carlo Piergallini, 'La colpa di organizzazione', in *La responsabilità amministrativa delle società e degli enti* (Zanichelli 2006) 3, 173ff; Giancarlo De Vero, 'La responsabilità penale delle persone giuridiche', in Carlo Federico Grosso, Tullio Padovani and Antonio Pagliaro (eds), *Trattato di diritto penale* (Giuffrè 2008) 164ff; Domenico Pulitanò, 'La responsabilità da reato degli enti: i criteri di imputazione'[2002] Riv It Dir Proc Pen 415.

12 O Paola Severino, 'Guest Editorial' (2012) 1(3) Eucrim 89; it should be borne in mind that, under Decree no 231/2001, compliance programmes may be associated not only with a possible exemption from liability but also a significant mitigation of sanctions in the event that compliance programmes have been adopted *post-factum*.

13 Antonio Fiorella, 'Responsabilità da reato degli enti', in Sabino Cassese (ed), *Dizionario di diritto pubblico* (Giuffrè 2006) 5103.

14 See Maria Crippa, Chapter 4.1, How to Implement Crimes Against Humanity and Genocide in the Italian System.

Selected bibliography

Adedayo Ijalaye D, *The Extension of Corporate Personality in International Law* (Oceania, 1978)

Clapham A, *Human Rights Obligations of Non-State Actors* (OUP 2006)

De Vero G, 'La responsabilità penale delle persone giuridiche', in Grosso C F, Padovani T, and Pagliaro A (eds), *Trattato di diritto penale* (Giuffrè 2008) 164ff

Fiorella A, 'Responsabilità da reato degli enti', in Cassese S (ed), *Dizionario di diritto pubblico* (Giuffrè 2006)

Fiorella A, 'Oggettivo e soggettivo nella definizione dell'efficacia dei c.d. modelli organizzativi. Problemi e linee di sviluppo della ricerca', in Fiorella A and Stile AM (eds), *Corporate Criminal Liability and Compliance Programs: First Colloquium* (Jovene 2012)

Fiorella A and Selvaggi S, '*Compliance programs* e dominabilità "aggregata" del fatto. Verso una responsabilità da reato dell'ente compiutamente personale, Diritto penale contemporaneo' (2014) 3 *Rivista trimestrale* 105ff

Joseph S, *Corporations and Transnational Human Rights Litigation* (Hart Publishing 2004)

Kathollnig C, *Unternehmensstrafrecht und Menschenrechtsverantwortung* (NWV im Verlag Österreich GmbH 2016)

Meloni C, *Command Responsibility in International Criminal Law* (TMC Asser, 2010)

Nemitz J C, 'Aggravating and Mitigating Circumstances in International Humanitarian Law – The Erdemovic-Case' (1997) 10(1) *Humanitäres Völkerrecht*

Piergallini C, 'Paradigmatica dell'autocontrollo penale (dalla funzione alla struttura del "modello organizzativo" ex d.lgs. n. 231/2001)', in *Studi in onore di M Romano* (Jovene 2011) 2056ff

Paliero C E and Piergallini C, 'La colpa di organizzazione' (2006) 3 *La responsabilità amministrativa delle società e degli enti* 173ff

Pulitanò D, 'La responsabilità da reato degli enti: i criteri di imputazione' [2002] *Riv It Dir Proc Pen* 415

Ramasastry A, 'Corporate Complicity: from Nuremberg to Rangoon. An Examination of Forced Labor Cases and Their Impact on the Liability of Multinational Corporations' (2002) 20 *Berkley JIL* 91

Ramsey M D, 'International Law Limits on Investor in Human Rights Litigation' (2009) 50 *Harvard International Law Journal*

Reinisch A, 'The Changing International Legal Framework for Dealing with Non-State Actors', in Alston P (ed), *Non-State Actors and Human Rights* (OUP 2005)

Selvaggi N, 'Compliance Programmes and "Organisational Fault" in Italian Legislation' (2012) 3 *Eucrim* 127ff

Severino P, 'Guest Editorial' (2012) 3 *Eucrim*

Steinhardt R G, 'Corporate Responsibility and the International Law of Human Rights: the New *Lex Mercatoria*', in Alston P (ed), *Non-State Actors and Human Rights* (OUP 2005)

Villani E, *La 'colpa di organizzazione' nell'illecito dell'ente da reato. Un'indagine di diritto comparato* (Aracne 2013)

Wells KC and Juanita E, 'Catching the Conscience of the King: Corporate Players on the International Stage', in Alston P (ed), *Non-State Actors and Human Rights* (OUP 2005)

Whyte D and Khoury S, *Corporate Human Rights Violations. Global Prospects for Legal Action* (Routledge 2017)

Yee S, 'The Erdemovic Sentencing Judgement. A Questionable Milestone for the International Criminal Tribunal for the Former Yugoslavia' [1997] *Georgia J Int Comp L*

Part III

The adoption of domestic laws on international criminal justice

The German code of crimes against international law (*Völkerstrafgesetzbuch*) and the global perspective

3.1 Domestic and international criminal justice

Challenges ahead*

Andreas Zimmermann and John Schabedoth

1 International Criminal Court, quo vadis?

In 2022, 20 years after the entry into force of the Rome Statute creating the International Criminal Court (ICC), the Court stands at a crossroads in view of the meanwhile significantly changed world situation. It has to face multiple challenges.

On the one hand, these challenges are reflected in the stagnating number of States Parties, partially declining support of the existing States Parties to the Statute and a rather mixed track record of the ICC's practical work to date. Furthermore, such challenges are also evident in cases against nationals of non-Member States, and in the dependence of the Court on volatile political developments in States, to which its investigations refer, as well as in a jurisprudence that deviates from general international law in some cases.

On 17 July 1998, at the UN Diplomatic Conference on the Establishment of an International Criminal Court in Rome, 120 States voted to adopt the text of the Rome Statute.[1] In 2022, almost 25 years later, 123 States are parties to the Statute.[2] After an initially impressive rate of ratifications in the first few years, which enabled the Statute to enter into force in 2002 after the 60th ratification document had been deposited, it has become apparent in recent years that the number of States Parties has by now largely stagnated.[3] Since 2015 there have been only three smaller States acceding to the Rome Statute, namely Palestine in 2015, El Salvador in 2016 and Kiribati in 2019,[4] while important States such as the United States, China, the Russian Federation or India are still not among the 123 States Parties. Also, since 2015, two States Parties, namely Burundi in 2016[5] and the Philippines in 2018,[6] have decided to terminate their treaty membership.[7] Two additional withdrawals, namely the ones by South Africa and The Gambia, were reversed before entering into effect, in the case of South Africa for domestic constitutional reasons[8] and in the case of The Gambia due to a change of government.[9]

Furthermore, during the same period, in 2016, the Russian Federation informed the depositary of the Rome Statute that it no longer intended to ratify the Statute and thus "withdrew" its signature to the Rome Statute.[10] As a result, its obligation under Article 18(a) of the Vienna Convention on the

DOI: 10.4324/9781003320951-10

Law of Treaties to refrain from acts which would defeat the object and purpose of the Rome Statute no longer applies. The Russian Federation thereby followed the examples of the United States, Israel and Sudan in this regard.[11] Overall, it seems that the Statute with its current ratification status has at least largely "exhausted" the group of States that can realistically be expected to accede to the Rome Statute in the foreseeable future. Even the other 27 signatory States that have already signed the Statute but not yet ratified it are unlikely to join in the near future, especially since this group includes, besides small States such as São Tomé and Príncipe or the Solomon Islands, States such as Morocco, Syria, Yemen or Zimbabwe, which are currently involved in conflicts in which violations of the Rome Statute by State actors are, if not likely, at least not to be dismissed out of hand.[12]

However, a decline of enthusiasm for international criminal law can also be observed among the current States Parties to the Rome Statute. For example, the various amendments to the Rome Statute adopted from 2010 onwards have, at least so far, not been met with much support by States Parties. Most of the various amendments related to the war crimes provisions of the Rome Statute have so far been ratified by fewer than ten States Parties,[13] the extension of the prohibition of the use of certain weapons (such as asphyxiating, poisonous or other gases and dum-dum bullets) to non-international armed conflicts being the sole exception with 43 ratifications.[14] But even these 43 States are still only roughly a third of the current 123 contracting parties. The same holds true for the deletion of Article 124 of the Rome Statute, the introduction of which had been very controversial during the negotiations[15] and which allows newly acceding States to exempt themselves from the jurisdiction of the ICC for war crimes for a period of seven years. This amendment, too, although only affecting newly acceding States, has only been ratified so far by 18 States Parties[16] and will therefore not enter into force in the foreseeable future, since the approval of seven-eighths of the States Parties is required for the deletion of Article 124 to take effect under Article 121(4) of the Rome Statute. And even the amendment of the Rome Statute to define the crime of aggression will for a long time remain a mere "law on the bookshelf"-provision given the limitations of the Court's jurisdiction under Article 15*bis* of the Rome Statute and the ratification of only 43 States Parties to date,[17] especially since the States that have ratified the amendment so far almost exclusively belong to those that, given their size, will hardly ever be involved in acts of aggression.[18]

The record of the ICC's previous practice is also mixed. Almost 20 years after the entry into force of the Rome Statute and with approximately two billion Euros[19] spent, only nine defendants have been convicted so far, with five convictions relating to offences against the administration of justice committed in former ICC cases.[20] Four people have been acquitted of alleged war crimes and crimes against humanity.[21] Eight other defendants are currently held in ICC custody, either because their main trial is ongoing or has not yet started or because a verdict has been appealed.[22] An arrest warrant was issued against another 14 people who remain at large.[23] In nine cases the charges were unconfirmed, vacated or withdrawn.[24] In another case, the Court declared that it lacked jurisdiction.[25] Six suspects died while proceedings against them were ongoing.[26] Overall, after almost 20 years in the ICC, only 50 defendants have been involved in proceedings, resulting in only nine convictions.[27] Notwithstanding the obvious complexities of the cases and situations involved, and the poor record of cooperation on the part of both States Parties and third States, these case numbers, also in comparison with earlier ad hoc tribunals, at the very least do not provide any evidence of a clear success story.[28]

Structurally complicating the Court's work, it has recently been dealing with an increasing number of situations involving nationals of non-States Parties which are politically delicate. According to Article 12(2) of the Rome Statute, the ICC may exercise its jurisdiction against nationals of non-States Parties if they are suspected to have committed a crime under international law on the territory of a State Party. So far, such gatherings before the ICC have concerned nationals of the United States with regard to the situation in Afghanistan,[29] Israel with regard to the situation in Palestine,[30] Myanmar with regard to the situation in Bangladesh[31] and the Russian Federation with regard to the situation in Georgia[32] and Ukraine.[33] In addition, the ICC exercises its jurisdiction over nationals of Sudan[34] and Libya[35] on the basis of resolutions of the UN Security Council, which provide for the Court's jurisdiction by virtue of Article 13(b) of the Rome Statute. To state the obvious, non-States Parties are not obliged to cooperate with the ICC in proceedings against their nationals, except the just-mentioned case of a referral to the ICC by the UN Security Council under Chapter VII of the UN Charter. Many of the non-States Parties therefore do not cooperate with the ICC in relation to their own nationals, which makes it difficult to conduct such cases. In these gatherings, identifying the facts, accessing evidence and also accessing the accused are more difficult, if at all possible.

At the same time, however, some of the non-States Parties affected by or politically affiliated with them, and even some States Parties, sometimes exercise significant political pressure to get the ICC to discontinue such proceedings. This applies not least to the United States. It is true that the current US government under President Biden (fortunately) revoked the sanctions previously imposed by the Trump administration against the then ICC Prosecutor Fatou Bensouda and some of her staff in April 2021.[36] Nevertheless, the new US administration also expects that the new ICC Prosecutor, Karim Khan, will "refocus" his efforts on cases and situations not involving third States' nationals, although the pressure exerted is now more subtle compared to the previous administration. For example, in his April 2021 press release on the ending of the sanctions against ICC staff, the new US Secretary of State, Anthony Blinken, reconfirmed the United States' longstanding but incorrect objection to the Court's efforts to assert jurisdiction over personnel of non-States Parties such as the United States and Israel.[37] It is problematic that the

United States is thereby implying that the ICC should apply the same policy of not exercising jurisdiction over non-party nationals vis-à-vis nationals of Myanmar in the context of the Rohingya crisis and nationals of Russia in the context of the war in Ukraine, as well as the earlier conflict in Georgia.

However, there is much to be said for assuming that the message behind this statement did not remain without effect on the new ICC Prosecutor. In his 27 September 2021 press release regarding his request to resume investigations concerning the Afghanistan situation, he indicated that he would focus his Office's investigations in Afghanistan on crimes allegedly committed by the Taliban and the Islamic State, while at the same time deprioritising "other aspects of this investigation".[38] Background to this is the fact that, in the context of the situation in Afghanistan, the Prosecutor initially also looked at possible crimes within the jurisdiction of the ICC that might have been committed by US nationals in Afghanistan. Since the ICC Prosecutor thereby effectively held out the prospect of a suspension of investigations into possible crimes under international law committed by US citizens in connection with the situation in Afghanistan, this message has likely been taken by the US State Department as a confirmation of its own position. This reaction of the ICC Prosecutor to the attempts of the USA to exert political influence appears to be quite alarming. The acts for which the Taliban and the Islamic State are responsible undoubtedly constitute core crimes under international law worthy of investigation. However, it would not have been necessary to announce at the same time the at least de facto end to the investigation of such crimes committed by US nationals and members of the former Afghan armed forces, especially since the likelihood that alleged offenders will be caught is equally low under the given circumstances for all groups of offenders.

But the ICC is also under pressure from some European States Parties. European States are still perceived to be the most important political supporters of the ICC. However, it remains to be seen how they will react once the Prosecutor focuses on Israeli nationals as possible defendants. As a matter of fact, it is worth noting that the UK Prime Minister Boris Johnson published a statement in April 2021, after the Court's finding that it had jurisdiction over any war crimes committed on the territory of Palestine (including the crime of transferring its own civilian population into occupied territories),[39] that the United Kingdom does not "accept that the ICC has jurisdiction in this instance, given that Israel is not a party to the Statute of Rome".[40] This statement was issued even though the United Kingdom, with its ratification of the Rome Statute, has accepted such an extension of jurisdiction to third State nationals inherent in Article 12 of the Statute. In February 2021, the then German Minister of Foreign Affairs, Heiko Maas, also explicitly objected to the finding of the Pre-Trial Chamber I of the ICC on the jurisdiction in these cases and took the position that Germany's "legal view on jurisdiction of the International Criminal Court regarding alleged crimes committed in the Palestine territories remains unchanged" because "the court has no jurisdiction".[41] What is striking here is that in other parallel constellations, such as in the dispute between the Philippines and China regarding claims over maritime areas in the South China Sea[42] and in the dispute between Slovenia and Croatia regarding their sea border in the Gulf of Piran,[43] in which China[44] and Croatia[45] respectively disputed the jurisdiction of the court seized, the German government had correctly argued that an international court is able to make binding decisions on its own jurisdiction within the framework of its *competence de la competence.*[46]

Overall, these statements do not augur very well for the actual political support of the Court when it comes to future politically sensitive cases. However, as one of the current judges at the ICC, Bertram Schmitt, once aptly put it, the Court was never meant to be a comfort zone,[47] which must have also been apparent to the contracting parties. Rather it was clear that the principle of territoriality underlying Article 12 of the Rome Statute, almost inevitably, would lead to political conflicts with third States.

Given these political and practical hurdles with reference to third States, it remains to be seen whether the new Prosecutor, as he has already indicated, will change course by henceforth focusing exclusively, or at least primarily, on somewhat "easier" and politically less sensitive cases. Such a focus in turn might then, however, incite allegations of the Court being one-sided and politically and/or region-wise biased in the selection of cases. At least so far, the Court itself seems to remain unimpressed by the challenges involved in cases against nationals of third States. This is confirmed by the 2020 decision of the Appeals Chamber regarding the situation in Afghanistan,[48] as well as the decision of the Pre-Trial Chamber I concerning the situation in Palestine,[49] in each of which the Court correctly confirmed its jurisdiction.

The Russian invasion of Ukraine on 24 February 2022 then marked a significant and eventually decisive turning point in the work of the International Criminal Court. Just four days after the invasion, the ICC Prosecutor announced that he intended to proceed with opening an investigation into the new situation in Ukraine.[50] At the same time, he subtly requested States Parties to refer the situation to him according to Articles 13(a) and 14 of the Rome Statute,[51] since that would mean the further requirements of a *proprio motu* investigation according to Articles 13(c) and 15 of the Rome Statute – in particular the requirement for a prior permission to be granted by the Pre-Trial Chamber – do not have to be fulfilled. Following a response from Lithuania on that very day,[52] 39 parties had complied with the request by 3 March 2022 and jointly referred the situation in Ukraine to the Office of the Prosecutor, whereupon the Prosecutor announced that he would investigate all allegations of war crimes, crimes against humanity and genocide committed during the ongoing armed conflict in Ukraine.[53] While Ukraine is not a party to the Rome Statute, it has, in 2014 and 2015 respectively, submitted two ad hoc declarations under Article 12(2) and (3) of the Rome Statute, allowing the ICC to exercise its jurisdiction over crimes committed on the territory of the declaring State or by its nationals, while the second declaration prolonged the duration of this effect indefinitely.[54]

Yet, while the ICC thus has jurisdiction as to possible war crimes, crimes against humanity and acts of genocide committed on Ukrainian soil, it cannot examine the obvious allegation of the crime of aggression having been committed by the Russian leadership according to Article 8*bis* of the Rome Statute. This is due to the fact that Russia is not a party to the Rome Statute and that, according to Article 15*bis*(5) of the Rome Statute, the ICC cannot exercise its treaty-based jurisdiction over the crime of aggression if the crime was committed by nationals of, or on the territory of a State which is not party to the Statute. The status as a non-State Party would only be irrelevant if the UN Security Council, acting under Chapter VII of the Charter, were to refer the situation in Ukraine under Articles 13(b) and 15*ter* of the ICC Statute to the ICC. Yet, it is obvious that this is, given Russia's veto power in the Security Council, completely out of the question.

This unsatisfactory situation has led to the proposal by Ukraine to set up an ad hoc special tribunal whose jurisdiction should include the crime of aggression committed by the Russian leadership against Ukraine.[55] This proposal has, however, so far met with rather little enthusiasm by the international community at large.[56] In any case, it is safe to assume that Russia will not transfer members of its political leadership to such a tribunal either (nor will it cooperate with the ICC), which therefore, apart from the political symbolism of the creation of such a special tribunal, raises the question of what additional benefit such a tribunal would have compared to the ICC. This example, for the first time ever, confirms that the specific jurisdictional regime for the crime of aggression, as currently contained in Article 15*bis* of the Rome Statute, reduces the Court's role when it comes to the prosecution of the crime of aggression in most relevant cases and situations to a largely symbolic and theoretical one.

It is nevertheless safe to state that the armed conflict launched by the Russian Federation against Ukraine tends to strengthen the role of the International Criminal Court in world politics. Notably, many contracting parties have quite significantly increased their financial support for the ICC Office of the Prosecutor, even though the ICC Prosecutor made it clear that he would not accept voluntary donations exclusively linked to the situation in Ukraine, but would spend the funds received according to self-defined priorities.[57] Nevertheless, it should be noted that these priorities might not be too different from the priorities of the supporting States given that the Office of the Prosecutor has never before conducted investigations on such a scale as in relation to the situation in Ukraine.[58] The support the ICC has received since the start of the war in Ukraine is not just limited to its States Parties, among them those such as the UK, which, as mentioned before, had opposed investigations against nationals of non-States Parties just a year earlier. Remarkably, even the US is now supporting the ICC's investigation into the situation in Ukraine, despite the fact that the US had in the past taken the position that third party nationals ought not be subject to the ICC's jurisdiction. In March 2022, it was even the US Senate which, with bipartisan support, passed a resolution supporting the referral of the situation in Ukraine by States Parties of the Rome Statute to the ICC.[59]

Some challenges to international criminal law also emerged from the Court's jurisprudence. When studying the jurisprudence of the ICC, it is striking that on several occasions its chambers, including the Appeals Chamber, have attempted to "progressively" further develop international criminal law and, by the same token, the rules of international humanitarian law and general international law, on which it is partly based. This development raises the question of whether international criminal law is beginning to detach itself too much from humanitarian and general international law, these branches of international law thereby eventually becoming more and more "alienated" from one another. This would call into question the effectiveness of international law at large. Two cases, the Ntaganda case and the Al-Bashir case, show particularly clearly how the ICC, when interpreting the war crimes provisions of the Rome Statute, which are rooted in and based on international humanitarian law and must therefore also be interpreted in the light and in accordance with it, breaks away from these very roots.

On the one hand, in June 2017 the ICC Appeals Chamber confirmed the decision of Trial Chamber VI on the jurisdiction of the ICC in the Ntaganda case from January of the same year, in which it had found that the Rome Statute does not exclude members of an armed group from protection against acts committed by members of the very same armed group.[60] The ICC's chambers thus deviated without convincing justification from the opposite view that had previously prevailed in the field of international humanitarian law, which, in the light of its protective scope, assumed that only members of the respective enemy in an armed conflict were protected by the rules of international humanitarian law.[61] According to these decisions, as under general human rights law, the nationality of the victims or their affiliation with an enemy party in the armed conflict is apparently no longer relevant. In contrast, the Special Court for Sierra Leone, for example, had still correctly assumed that the limitation of the protective scope of international humanitarian law to enemy parties was a fundamental rule of this branch of law that should not be called into question.[62] With such an extended interpretation of war crimes to also include acts against one's own combatants, the ICC's interpretation goes beyond the original protective purpose of this norm, namely to ensure the protection of the members of the other party to the armed conflict. To put it another way, the ICC converts these rules originally specifically developed for armed conflicts into quasi-human rights norms, which also apply regardless of the nationality of the victims. At the same time, such an interpretation leads to the fact that violations of international humanitarian law, ie war crimes, almost gain the character of crimes against humanity, though without the other requirements of this crime, such as in particular the existence of a widespread or systematic attack against a civilian population, having to be met at the same time.

Also, in the Ntaganda case, the ICC Appeals Chamber gave the term "attack", as used in Article 8(2)(e)(iv) of the Rome Statute, a significantly broader meaning divorced from international humanitarian law, although the drafters of the Rome Statute obviously wanted to use the term "attack" to refer to its meaning in international humanitarian law, where it had a long tradition and has been developed in detail.[63] As is well known, international humanitarian law has traditionally distinguished between the protection of individuals from the conduct of hostilities, known as Hague law, and the protection of certain groups of people who are in the hands of a belligerent party, known as Geneva law. So far, this has meant that war crimes in the context of "attacks" have, in accordance with the relevant provisions of international humanitarian law, required the attack to take place as a part of conduct of hostilities as a mandatory requirement, in addition to the general requirement for all types of war crimes that the relevant act needs to be related to the armed conflict.[64] The ICC has now detached itself from this former requirement and has assumed that the looting of a hospital after the end of current hostilities could also constitute a prohibited "attack" on a civilian target.[65] This broader interpretation of the term prohibited "attack", divorced from international humanitarian law, is of far-reaching importance, since the term is used on 11 occasions in Article 8 of the Rome Statute alone.[66] Again, the Appeals Chamber is thereby breaking away from the dogmatic roots of the war crimes provisions of the Rome Statute to extend the scope of criminal liability.[67]

All in all, these and other recent decisions of the ICC[68] show an ever-increasing divergence between international criminal law on the one hand and international humanitarian law on the other, which in the long term could lead to a further, unfortunately conflict-prone, disentanglement of these two branches of international law. Apart from that, this would also involve the danger that the two epistemic communities, namely international criminal lawyers on the one hand and those applying international humanitarian law as such (eg as legal advisers to armed forces or the International Committee of the Red Cross) on the other, would also diverge even further from each other than they are already doing.

But the ICC is also setting a new tone in general international law, more specifically with regard to the immunity of heads of State. For example, in its 2019 decision on Jordan's possible extradition obligation regarding the longstanding former Sudanese President, Al-Bashir (who was still in office at the time of the possible extradition obligation, and against whom an arrest warrant from the ICC had been issued for genocide, crimes against humanity and war crimes in the context of the Darfur conflict), the Court not only took the opportunity to address the question of whether, in the case of a Security Council referral according to Article 13(b) of the Rome Statute, the immunity of a current head of State of a non-State Party is set aside – to which question the Appeals Chamber, and rightly so, replied in the affirmative.[69] Rather, the Appeals Chamber also addressed the more general, yet more controversial and difficult, question of whether under customary international law a current head of State of a non-State Party enjoys immunity before a domestic court when such court is asked to take this head of State into custody to surrender him or her to the ICC – which the court ultimately denied.[70] In fact, in this case there was no need for the Appeals Chamber to decide this issue, given that, as mentioned, it had already previously found that the UN Security Council resolution referring the Al-Bashir case to the ICC had set aside President Al-Bashir's immunity anyhow. Thus, as a matter of judicial policy, especially in the light of the current challenges for the ICC, it might have been more wise to leave the second question aside and unanswered for the time being, and to wait for another occasion where this question would indeed arise – namely where the ICC's jurisdiction is not based on a referral of the UN Security Council, but on the fact that the head of State or government, or minister of foreign affairs, of a non-State Party is accused of having committed crimes within the territory of a party which falls within the jurisdiction of the ICC.

The recent history of the ICC shows that volatile domestic political developments in States Parties or States that are otherwise obliged to cooperate with the ICC, especially by an UN Security resolution, have a decisive influence on the functioning of the ICC. In addition to the above-mentioned domestically motivated revocations of the declarations of withdrawal from the Rome Statute by Gambia and South Africa,[71] a change in the domestic situation in Sudan could also have led to decisive progress for the work of the ICC. In August 2021, the Sudanese interim government, which had come to power in the wake of the protests in 2019, announced its intention to surrender Al-Bashir to the Court.[72] In addition, the transitional government in power at the time stated that Sudan wanted to accede to the Rome Statute.[73] The military coup in October 2021, which brought back allies of former President Al-Bashir into the government, shows, however, that at least at present there is little chance of these earlier announcements being implemented. In addition, the Security Council, on whose referral the ICC's jurisdiction in Sudan rests, has not taken any steps whatsoever since that referral to bring Sudan into compliance with its UN Charter obligation to cooperate with the ICC. In this context, it may be helpful to recall that in Serbia, too, it was a fundamental political change that led, albeit after some time, to the extradition of former President Slobodan Milošević and, even later, to the extradition of Radovan Karadžić and Ratko Mladić to the United Nations Yugoslavia Tribunal.[74]

2 Domestic international criminal law, quo vadis?

Domestic international criminal law, too, has played a major role in the further development of international criminal law in recent years. Domestic international criminal law became more relevant notably when a significant number of States Parties of the Rome Statute, although not all, have, when they respectively acceded to the Statute, *mutatis mutandis* replicated in their domestic criminal law the provisions of the Rome Statute.[75] There are several reasons for such a replication. On the one hand, the priority of the exercise of jurisdiction by domestic criminal courts vis-à-vis that of the ICC, i.e. the so-called principle of complementarity, is explicitly laid down in the Rome Statute. By introducing domestic international criminal law, a State can thus ensure that it can itself exercise criminal jurisdiction over its own nationals once they allegedly commit crimes under international law. In addition, some States have enacted such domestic statutes to also fulfil other pre-existing international obligations. An example for such an obligation is the obligation of States Parties to the four Geneva Conventions of 1949 relating to the protection of victims of international armed conflicts to punish persons that have committed or ordered to commit grave breaches of the Conventions and its Additional Protocol I, such as torture.[76]

However, not infrequently States have gone beyond these existing obligations and the implementation of the principle of complementarity when transposing international criminal law into domestic law. Many States have, at least to a certain extent, established universal jurisdiction for their courts when it comes to genocide, crimes against humanity and war crimes, even when committed in non-international armed conflicts, meaning that the exercise of jurisdiction is independent of any specific link to the State exercising jurisdiction.[77] As a matter of fact, it is safe to assume that the exercise of such universal jurisdiction by domestic courts for the mentioned crimes under international law, committed in both international and non-international armed conflict, is permissible under international law, at least from today's perspective.[78]

In addition to the work of the ICC, the implementation of universal jurisdiction in domestic legal systems as well as convictions of those accused of crimes under international law can make an important contribution to the effective enforcement of international criminal law. After all, according to Article 12 of the Rome Statute, the jurisdiction of the ICC is already as a matter of principle limited to crimes committed on the territory of States Parties or by their nationals. Furthermore, the Court is, as a matter of practical limitations, de facto not in a position to address all crimes that come within its jurisdiction *ratione loci* and *ratione personae.*

At the same time it should also be noted that, at least so far, such domestic proceedings relating to crimes under international law have mainly, if not almost exclusively, been undertaken by Western States, and here again mainly by European States.[79] Those States should therefore be careful to avoid any impression that such domestic criminal proceedings are aiming exclusively at potential defendants from States who are not politically close to the respective forum State, or, *vice versa,* that defendants from States that are politically affiliated with the forum State are not subject to prosecution. Hence, there is much to be said for structuring the national judiciary, at least in the field of international criminal law, in such a way that the triggering of an investigation is not subject to a requirement of governmental authorisation, and thus possibly depending on political considerations, but is to be decided, depending on the judicial system of the forum State, by either an independent prosecutor or by a *juge d'instruction*.

Also, the substance of international criminal law can be effectively further developed through domestic implementation of the Rome Statute since the States can deviate from the provisions of the Rome Statute when implementing substantive legal norms. The wording of the Rome Statute is mostly based on compromises that were made to reach the widest possible consensus among the negotiating parties during the negotiations that led to the adoption of the Rome Statute.[80] The national legislators, who are freed from such constraints, can, if they wish, formulate broader provisions and thus better reflect the current status of customary international law or advance its further development. That way, domestic statutes may also be closer to the current state of customary international law as compared to the Rome Statute, which for the just-mentioned political reasons had remained below the threshold that may safely be considered to form part of customary international law. It is therefore sometimes the case that the domestic implementation of international criminal law norms anticipates possible future amendments to the Rome Statute, as seen in the following two examples from the German Code of Crimes Against International Law (*Völkerstrafgesetzbuch*).

While the Rome Statute initially only classified the use of certain prohibited weapons, such as poison and dum-dum bullets, to constitute a war crime in international armed conflicts as per Article 8(2)(b)(xvii)–(xix) of the Rome Statute, the German Code of Crimes Against International Law had from the very outset (for almost 20 years) already made it a crime under German domestic criminal law to use such weapons in both international *and non-international* armed conflicts.[81] It was, however, only in 2010 that the Rome Statute by way of an amendment provided that the use of such weapons in non-international armed conflicts did amount to a war crime as per the newly introduced Article 8(2)(e).[82] *Mutatis mutandis,* the same holds true with regard to the crime of starvation of civilians as a method of warfare, which is punishable under section 11(1)(5) of the German Code of Crimes Against International Law regardless of the character, international or non-international, of the underlying armed conflict, while as far as the Rome Statute is concerned, a parallel norm for non-international armed conflicts was only adopted in December 2019 as per Article 8(2)(e)(xix) of the Rome Statute.[83]

Domestic extensions of the scope of norms of international criminal law, such as the two examples mentioned, can therefore pave the way for similar extensions at the international level. In this way, further developments in international criminal law reinforce each other at both levels of the legal system. Likewise, if an already existing norm of international criminal law is replicated at the domestic level, this leads to a further consolidation of the validity of these norms under customary international law.

In addition, the implementation of international criminal law at the domestic level and any decisions by domestic courts in this area can provide new impetus to classic debates about the scope of customary international law as far as international criminal law is concerned. By way of example, the debate on immunity *ratione personae* (personal immunity) and immunity *ratione materiae* (functional immunity) in proceedings for violations of international criminal law will be discussed in more detail here.

For international criminal courts such as the ICC, the legal situation has been largely clarified by the above-mentioned judgement of the ICC Appeals Chamber in the Al-Bashir case.[84] However, with regard to domestic criminal proceedings initiated for crimes that may have been committed under international law, the issue of the personal immunity of high-ranking officials (such as heads of State and government or foreign ministers), and of the functional immunity of State officials acting on behalf of their respective States, is less clear.

As far as immunity *ratione personae* is concerned, it is probably safe to state that the 2002 judgement by the International Court of Justice (ICJ) in the *Arrest Warrant of 11 April 2000 (Democratic Republic of the Congo v. Belgium)* case – according to which under customary international law the so-called "big three", ie heads of State, heads of government and ministers of foreign affairs, are not subject to the criminal jurisdiction of foreign States as long as they hold on to their positions – still reflects the current state of customary international law.[85] This is also confirmed by the more recent work of the International Law Commission (ILC) on the immunity of State officials from foreign criminal jurisdiction.[86] Article 3 of the ILC's 2013 draft articles on the matter also provides that "Heads of State, Heads of Government and Ministers for Foreign Affairs enjoy immunity *ratione personae* from the exercise of foreign criminal jurisdiction".[87] Unlike Article 7 of the draft articles, which regulates exceptions to immunity *ratione personae*, this norm was largely uncontroversial in the ILC[88] and was supported by a significant number of States in the 6th Committee of the General Assembly.[89]

With regard to *lower-ranking* State officials, where obviously only the issue of functional immunity arises, the situation is less clear-cut under customary international law. In that regard, in addition to the just-mentioned work of the ILC, a recent judgment by the German Federal Court of Justice comes into play. In a case involving a former Afghan officer who was tried in Germany for committing war crimes during the non-international armed conflict in Afghanistan, the German Federal Court of Justice in early 2021 found that State officials who hold subordinate positions do not enjoy functional immunity under customary international law in foreign criminal proceedings when having allegedly committed war crimes.[90] The Court also held that, since the issue of whether such a rule of customary international law curtailing immunity does exist or not was so "clear-cut" and obvious, it was not obliged to submit the question to the German Constitutional Court[91] (given that the Court would have been obliged to submit such a submission in case of doubts about the existence of such a rule of customary international law under Article 100(2) German Basic Law). In reaching its conclusion, the Court notably attached considerable weight to the Statute of the International Military Tribunal (London Charter), the Nuremberg principles developed by the ILC on behalf of the UN General Assembly following the Nuremberg trials, and the jurisprudence of the International Criminal Tribunal for the former Yugoslavia (ICTY).[92] The result reached by the Court, ie that low-ranking officials cannot claim immunity when it comes to acts of war crimes even before domestic courts and tribunals, is convincing. However, it is questionable whether the solution found was actually so obvious that the Court would not have had to submit the question to the Constitutional Court under Article 100(2) German Basic Law. According to the case law of the Constitutional Court, the German Federal Court of Justice must do so, as the Federal Court of Justice itself explained in the decision, when the deciding court does not have doubts itself but, when examining the question, it encounters serious doubts of "third parties" and additionally that the deciding court's result deviates from the opinion of a constitutional body or from the decisions of high German, foreign or international courts or from the teachings of recognised authors of international law.[93] Such contrary views would, however, have been easy to find, at least among international law scholars.[94]

In addition, the methodological approach chosen by the Court to determine the current state of customary international law warrants some remarks. The Federal Court of Justice refers inter alia to the case law of the ICTY and the ICC.[95] However, directly transposing the practice involving *international* criminal courts and tribunals to domestic courts disregards the structural differences that exist between the two levels. This is particularly true where the respective tribunal, such as the ICTY or the ICC in case of a Security Council referral, is exercising delegated Chapter VII powers[96] because, in that case, the UN Security Council could have set aside an otherwise existing immunity anyhow. This is confirmed by the already mentioned 2002 judgement of the ICJ in the *Arrest Warrant* case where the Court was very strictly distinguishing between proceedings before domestic courts and those before international courts.[97]

Besides, when looking for evidence of an exception under customary international law to the functional immunity of State officials, the Court referred to the judgements of the military courts of the four Allied occupying powers in their respective zones of occupation against German war criminals after World War II.[98] However, after the unconditional surrender of Germany, by virtue of the Berlin Declaration of 5 June 1945, the Allied powers had "assume[d] supreme authority with respect to Germany, including all the powers possessed by the German Government".[99] The Allied powers thus acted on behalf of the German State as a whole, even when exercising criminal jurisdiction over German nationals, so that the question of functional immunity in those cases did not play a role from the outset.

Otherwise, apart from referring to the above-mentioned international sources, the German Federal Court of Justice cited as further evidence for its result the more recent practice of German, Israeli, Dutch, Spanish, Italian,

Swiss, French and Belgian court decisions denying functional immunity in proceedings for war crimes, crimes against humanity and genocide.[100] The lack of geographical diversity in this evidence, however, puts into question the required *generalised* and universal character of the State practice, which is needed to bring about a new rule of customary international law denying functional immunity.

Hence, as pointed out by Sean D Murphy (one of the members of the ILC who, during the debates on the customary international law position on functional immunity, advocated in favour of upholding functional immunity even in the case of allegations of war crimes and crimes against humanity), one can at least ask the question of where State practice in support of exceptions to immunity *ratione materiae* of State officials from foreign criminal jurisdiction can actually be found.[101]

Moreover, it is also worth noting that, somewhat akin to the approach chosen by the ICC's Appeals Chamber in the Al-Bashir case,[102] the German Federal Court of Justice also found that the debate within the ILC, on whether trials for crimes under international law are subject to an exception to functional immunity under customary international law, could not have set aside a pre-existing rule of customary international law providing for an exception to functional immunity in these cases.[103] However, the Court should have, and could have, examined whether a new rule of customary international law has positively developed as a result of the ILC's activity with this question, or whether, as the ILC's Special Rapporteur had put it, there exists at least a "clear trend" towards recognising such exception as a matter of customary international law.[104]

It remains to be seen whether other States, when implementing the Rome Statute at domestic level, will in the future expressively and unequivocally confirm that they share the view of the German Federal Court of Justice on the customary international law exception to functional immunity in cases of crimes under international law. In particular, it would be helpful for demonstrating a general practice under international law if States outside the European context were to take a position on the issue of exceptions to functional immunity. For the sake of completeness, it has to be underlined that the sensitive issue of any such exception to the functional immunity from foreign criminal jurisdiction has to be clearly distinguished from matters of State immunity in civil proceedings.[105] This form of immunity concerns a fundamentally different issue and, since it plays an essential role for peaceful interstate relations, cannot be restricted.

3 Concluding remarks

Overall, these developments, as just outlined, may lead one to apply and paraphrase the by now well-known and famous paradigm by the German legal scholar and constitutional judge Ernst-Wolfgang Böckenförde that the ICC, too, lives by basic prerequisites which it cannot guarantee itself, since it depends on the support of a large number of States Parties that have an interest in a rules-based international legal order to carry out its task effectively. Though, compared to the years in which the Rome Statute was negotiated, not only have times changed, as Bob Dylan once put it, but there are increasing indications that the relative importance of the various States within the international community is also changing. In particular, the political weight of those States favouring and supporting a rules-based legal order, within which international criminal law plays an important part, might be perceived as diminishing.

Hence, it seems as if the honeymoon in the relationship between the international community of States at large and international criminal law might be over. This means that the ICC finds itself increasingly in turbulent waters. The same holds true for the relationship between international criminal law and general international law. One cannot but hope, however, that just like in a long-lasting marriage, while the vows of love might eventually be a thing of the past, the aging couples will not divorce but will get along, even if one from time to time one might be surprised by the other's approach and understanding of how to regulate international relations. Against this background, it seems appropriate to adhere to a strict exercise of its jurisdiction not guided by political influence, especially when dealing with third States nationals who are subject to its jurisdiction. On the other hand, however, an attempt should also be made to interpret and apply the provisions of the Rome Statute within the framework of other existing rules of international law, whether those of international humanitarian law or those of general international law, to avoid friction between international criminal law and the ICC on the one hand and the surrounding international legal order on the other.

Notes

* Revised and enlarged version of an article published in German, Andreas Zimmermann, 'Internationaler Strafgerichtshof am Scheideweg' (2022) 77 Juristenzeitung 261.

1 United Nations Press Release L/2889, 'UN Diplomatic Conference Concludes in Rome with Decision to Establish Permanent International Criminal Court', 20 July 1998, available online at www.un.org/press/en/1998/19980720.l2889.html (visited 22 September 2022).

2 List of States Parties available online at https://asp.icc-cpi.int/en_menus/asp/states%20parties/Pages/states%20parties%20_%20chronological%20list.aspx (visited 22 September 2022).

3 For a comprehensive graphic overview of the development of the number of States Parties, see Andreas Zimmermann, 'Finally… Or Would Rather Less Have Been More? The Recent Amendment on the Deletion of Article 124 of the Rome Statute and the Continued Quest for the Universality of the International Criminal Court' (2016) 14 Journal of International Criminal Justice 505, 512.

4 List of acceding States with accession date available online at https://treaties.un.org/pages/ViewDetails.aspx?src=IND&mtdsg_no=XVIII-10&chapter=18&clang=_en (visited 22 September 2022).

5 Depositary Notification available online at https://treaties.un.org/doc/Publication/CN/2016/CN.805.2016-Eng.pdf (visited 22 September 2022).

6 Depositary Notification available online at https://treaties.un.org/doc/Publication/CN/2018/CN.138.2018-Eng.pdf (visited 22 September 2022).

7 For details on Burundi's withdrawal, see Manisuli Ssenyonjo, 'State Withdrawal Notifications from the Rome Statute of the International Criminal Court: South Africa, Burundi and the Gambia' (2018) 29 Criminal Law Forum 63.

8 For details, see Niko Pavlopoulos, 'South Africa's Withdrawal: A Lesson Learned?', EJIL: Talk! Blog of the European Journal of International Law, 6 December 2016, available online at www.ejiltalk.org/south-africas-withdrawal-a-lesson-learned/ (visited 22 September 2022); the underlying decision of the North Gauteng High Court (Pretoria) is available online at www.saflii.org/za/cases/ZAGPPHC/2017/53.html (visited 22 September 2022).

9 Depositary Notification available online at https://treaties.un.org/doc/Publication/CN/2017/CN.62.2017-Eng.pdf (visited 22 September 2022).

10 Communication available online at https://treaties.un.org/pages/ViewDetails.aspx?src=IND&mtdsg_no=XVIII-10&chapter=18&clang=_en#4, fn 9 (visited 22 September 2022); for more details, see Sergey Sayapin, 'Russia's Withdrawal of Signature from the Rome Statute Would not Shield its Nationals from Potential Prosecution at the ICC', EJIL: Talk! Blog of the European Journal of International Law, 21 November 2016, available online at www.ejiltalk.org/russias-withdrawal-of-signature-from-the-rome-statute-would-not-shield-its-nationals-from-potential-prosecution-at-the-icc/ (visited 22 September 2022).

11 Communication available online at https://treaties.un.org/pages/ViewDetails.aspx?src=IND&mtdsg_no=XVIII-10&chapter=18&clang=_en#4, note 4 (Israel), note 10 (Sudan) and note 12 (USA) (visited 22 September 2022).

12 Other States that have signed but have not yet ratified the Statute are: Algeria, Angola, Armenia, Bahamas, Bahrain, Cameroon, Egypt, Eritrea, Guinea-Bissau, Haiti, Iran, Jamaica, Kuwait, Kyrgyzstan, Monaco, Mozambique, Oman, Thailand, the United Arab Emirates, Ukraine and Uzbekistan; a list of States having signed but not yet ratified the Statute is available online at https://treaties.un.org/pages/ViewDetails.aspx?src=IND&mtdsg_no=XVIII-10&chapter=18&clang=_en (visited 22 September 2022).

13 Overview of the States Parties that have ratified amendments to the Rome Statute is available online at https://asp.icc-cpi.int/en_menus/asp/RomeStatute/pages/default.aspx (visited 22 September 2022).

14 List of States Parties having ratified the amendment is available online at https://treaties.un.org/pages/ViewDetails.aspx?src=IND&mtdsg_no=XVIII-10-a&chapter=18&clang=_en (visited 22 September 2022).

15 For details on the drafting history, see Andreas Zimmermann, 'Finally…' (n 3).

16 List of States Parties having ratified the amendment is available online at https://treaties.un.org/pages/ViewDetails.aspx?src=IND&mtdsg_no=XVIII-10-c&chapter=18&clang=_en (visited 22 September 2022).

17 List of States Parties having ratified the amendment is available online at https://treaties.un.org/pages/ViewDetails.aspx?src=TREATY&mtdsg_no=XVIII-10-b&chapter=18&clang=_en (visited 22 September 2022).

18 For details, see Andreas Zimmermann, '*Alea Iacta Est*: The Kampala Amendment on the Crime of Aggression Post-2017: A Response to Koh and Buchwald' (2015) 109 American Journal of International Law Unbound 240; Andreas Zimmermann,

'A Victory for International Rule of Law? Or: All's Well that Ends Well? The 2017 ASP Decision to Amend the Kampala Amendment on the Crime of Aggression' (2018) 16 Journal of International Criminal Justice 19; Andreas Zimmermann and E Freiburg-Braun, *Aggression under the Rome Statute* (Bloomsbury 2019) *passim*.

19 An overview of the respective yearly budget of the ICC is available online at https://asp.icc-cpi.int/en_menus/asp/bureau/WorkingGroups/budget/Pages/default.aspx (visited 22 September 2022).

20 The defendants Bemba, Kilolo Musamba, Mangenda Kabongo, Babala Wandu and Arido have been convicted for offences against the administration of justice; the other defendants are Al-Mahdi, Katanga, Lubanga and Ntaganda. A list of defendants and the status of their trials is available online at www.icc-cpi.int/defendants (visited 22 September 2022).

21 The (former) defendants L Gbagbo, Blé Goudé, Ngudjolo Chui and Bemba, although the latter was convicted of offences against the administration of justice under Article 70 Rome Statute, ibid; for details in regard to the latter case see Hannah K Brodersen and Lysandre Papadopoulos, 'Guilty but Free: The ICC Renders its First Contempt Case Judgement', EJIL: Talk! Blog of the European Journal of International Law, 1 November 2016, available online at www.ejiltalk.org/guilty-but-free-the-icc-renders-its-first-contempt-case-judgment/ (visited 22 September 2022).

22 The defendants Abd-Al-Rahman, Al Hassan, Gicheru, Mokom, Ngaissona, Ongwen, Said and Yekatom (n 20).

23 The defendants Al-Bashir, Banda, Barasa, Bett, Saif Al-Islam Gaddafi, Georgiyevich Sanakoev, Guchmazov, Harun, Hussein, Kony, Mayramovich Mindzaev, Mudacumura, Nouradine Adam and Otti (n 20).

24 The defendants Abu Garda, Ali, S Gbagbo, Kenyatta, Kosgey, Mbarushimana, Muthaura, Ruto and Sang (n 20).

25 The defendant Al-Senussi (n 20).

26 The defendants Al-Werfalli, M Gaddafi, Jerbo Jamus, Khaled, Lukwiya and Odhiambo (n 20).

27 ibid.

28 For instance, during the comparable 22-year period, the International Criminal Tribunal for the former Yugoslavia managed to indict 161 people, 90 of whom were convicted and 19 acquitted, while 13 cases were referred to domestic courts, 2 were in retrial before the MICT and 37 proceedings were terminated, or the indictments withdrawn. Case statistics are available online at www.icty.org/node/9590 (visited 22 September 2022).

29 Judgment on the appeal against the decision on the authorisation of an investigation into the situation in the Islamic Republic of Afghanistan, *Situation in the Islamic Republic of Afghanistan* (ICC-02/17 OA4), Appeals Chamber, 5 March 2020.

30 Decision on the Prosecution request pursuant to article 19(3) for a ruling on the Court's territorial jurisdiction in Palestine, *Situation in the State of Palestine* (ICC-01/18), Pre-Trial Chamber I, 5 February 2021.

31 Decision on the Prosecution's Request for a Ruling on Jurisdiction under Article 19(3) of the Statute, *Request under Regulation 46 (3) of the Regulations of the Court* (ICC-RoC46(3)-01/18), Pre-Trial Chamber I, 6 September 2018.

32 Decision on the Prosecutor's request for authorization of an investigation, *Situation in Georgia*, (ICC-01/15) Pre-Trial Chamber I, 27 January 2016.

33 'Statement of the Prosecutor, Fatou Bensouda, on the conclusion of the preliminary examination in the situation in Ukraine', 11 December 2020, available online at www.icc-cpi.int/Pages/item.aspx?name=201211-otp-statement-ukraine (visited 22 September 2022); 'Statement of ICC Prosecutor, Karim AA Khan QC, on the Situation in Ukraine: Receipt of Referrals from 39 States Parties and the Opening of an Investigation', 2 March 2022, available online at www.icc-cpi.int/news/statement-icc-prosecutor-karim-aa-khan-qc-situation-ukraine-receipt-referrals-39-states (visited 22 September 2022).

34 UNSC Res 1593 (31 March 2005) UN Doc S/RES/1593.

35 UNSC Res 1970 (26 February 2011) UN Doc S/RES/1970.

36 Exec Order 14,022, 86 Fed Reg 17,895 (1 April 2021); cf Antony J Blinken, 'Ending Sanctions and Visa Restrictions against Personnel of the International Criminal Court – Press Statement', available online at www.state.gov/ending-sanctions-and-visa-restrictions-against-personnel-of-the-international-criminal-court/ (visited 22 September 2022); For details, see Kristen Eichensehr, 'Biden Administration Rescinds Sanctions Against International Criminal Court Officials' (2021) 115 American Journal of International Law 729.

37 ibid.

38 'Statement of the Prosecutor of the International Criminal Court, Karim AA Khan QC, following the application for an expedited order under article 18(2) seeking authorization to resume investigations in the Situation in Afghanistan', 27 September 2021, available online at www.icc-cpi.int/Pages/item.aspx?name=2021-09-27-otp-statement-afghanistan (visited 22 September 2022).

39 Decision on the Prosecution request pursuant to article 19(3) for a ruling on the Court's territorial jurisdiction in Palestine (n 30).

40 Boris Johnson, Letter to Stephen Crabb, 9 April 2021, available online at https://static.jewishnews.co.uk/jewishndev/uploads/2021/04/Ey4IcKOXMAcGiwf.jpeg (visited 22 September 2022).

41 Heiko Maas, Twitter post, 9 February 2021, available online at https://twitter.com/heikomaas/status/1359215215913623564 (visited 22 September 2022).

42 Award in the Matter of the South China Sea Arbitration, *The Republic of the Philippines v The People's Republic of China* (PCA Case no 2013-19), An Arbitral Tribunal Constituted under Annex VII to the 1982 United Nations Convention on the Law of the Sea, 12 July 2016.

43 Final Award in the Matter of an Arbitration under the Arbitration Agreement between the Government of the Republic of Croatia and the Government of the Republic of Slovenia, signed on 4 November 2009, *Arbitration Between the Republic of Croatia and the Republic of Slovenia* (PCA Case no 2012-04), 29 June 2017.

44 'Position Paper of the Government of the People's Republic of China on the Matter of Jurisdiction in the South China Sea Arbitration Initiated by the Republic of the Philippines', 7 December 2014, available online at www.fmprc.gov.cn/nanhai/eng/snhwtlcwj_1/201606/t20160602_8527277.htm (visited 22 September 2022).

45 Partial Award in the Matter of an Arbitration under the Arbitration Agreement between the Government of the Republic of Croatia and the Government of the Republic of Slovenia, signed on 4 November 2009, *Arbitration Between the Republic of Croatia and the Republic of Slovenia* (PCA Case no 2012-04), 30 June 2016. The Permanent Court of Arbitration, 'In the matter of an arbitration under the arbitration agreement between the government of the republic of Croatia and

the government of the Republic of Slovenia, signed on 4 November 2009 – Partial Award 30 June 2016', § 88 et seq.

46 cf Stefan Talmon, 'Arbitration between Croatia and Slovenia', German Practice in International Law, 1 October 2017, available online at https://gpil.jura.uni-bonn.de/2017/10/arbitration-croatia-slovenia/ (visited 22 September 2022); Stefan Talmon, 'Germany Takes a More Outspoken and Active Position on the South China Sea Disputes', German Practice in International Law, 30 March 2021, available online at https://gpil.jura.uni-bonn.de/2021/03/germany-takes-a-more-outspoken-and-active-position-on-the-south-china-sea-disputes/ (visited 22 September 2022).

47 Bertram Schmitt, 'ICC Judge Schmitt Counsels Resilience to Preserve International Justice', Just Security, 13 February 2019, available online at www.justsecurity.org/62577/icc-judge-schmitt-counsels-resilience-preserve-international-justice/ (visited 22 September 2022).

48 Judgment on the appeal against the decision on the authorisation of an investigation into the situation in the Islamic Republic of Afghanistan (n 29).

49 Decision on the Prosecution request pursuant to article 19(3) for a ruling on the Court's territorial jurisdiction in Palestine (n 30).

50 'Statement of ICC Prosecutor, Karim AA Khan QC, on the Situation in Ukraine: "I have decided to proceed with opening an investigation."', 28 February 2022, available online at www.icc-cpi.int/news/statement-icc-prosecutor-karim-aa-khan-qc-situation-ukraine-i-have-decided-proceed-opening (visited 22 September 2022).

51 ibid.

52 Andrius Sytas and others, 'Lithuania Asks International Criminal Court to Investigate War Crimes in Ukraine', Reuters, 28 February 2022, available online at www.reuters.com/world/europe/lithuania-asks-international-criminal-court-investigate-war-crimes-ukraine-2022-02-28/ (visited 28 September 2022).

53 'Statement of ICC Prosecutor, Karim AA Khan QC, on the Situation in Ukraine: Receipt of Referrals from 39 States Parties and the Opening of an Investigation', 2 March 2022, available online at www.icc-cpi.int/news/statement-icc-prosecutor-karim-aa-khan-qc-situation-ukraine-receipt-referrals-39-states (visited 22 September 2022); by the beginning of April 2022, Chile, Japan, Montenegro and Northern Macedonia had also referred the situation to the Prosecutor.

54 Declaration No 61219/35-673-384 of the Embassy of Ukraine to the Kingdom of the Netherlands to the Registrar of the International Criminal Court, 9 April 2014, available online at www.icc-cpi.int/itemsDocuments/997/declarationRecognitionJuristiction09-04-2014.pdf; Declaration of the Minister for Foreign Affairs of Ukraine to the Registrar of the International Criminal Court, 8 September 2015, available online at www.icc-cpi.int/iccdocs/other/Ukraine_Art_12-3_declaration_08092015.pdf.

55 The Foreign Minister of Ukraine, Dmytro Kuleba, approved a proposal calling for the Creation of a Special Tribunal for the Punishment of the Crime of Aggression against Ukraine, available at https://gordonandsarahbrown.com/wp-content/uploads/2022/03/Combined-Statement-and-Declaration.pdf in his official capacity, at an event at Chatham House, for which a video is available at www.chathamhouse.org/events/all/research-event/criminal-tribunal-aggression-ukraine

56 cf Isobel Koshiw and Patrick Wintour, 'West Reluctant to Put Putin on Trial, Say Ukrainian Officials', The Guardian, 6 September 2022, available online at

www.theguardian.com/world/2022/sep/06/west-reluctant-to-put-putin-on-trial-say-ukrainian-officials (visited 28 September 2022).

57 'Statement of ICC Prosecutor, Karim AA Khan QC: Contributions and support from States Parties will accelerate action across our investigations', 28 March 2022, available online at www.icc-cpi.int/news/statement-icc-prosecutor-karim-aa-khan-qc-contributions-and-support-states-parties-will-0 (visited 22 September 2022).

58 'ICC Prosecutor Karim AA Khan QC Announces Deployment of Forensics and Investigative Team to Ukraine, Welcomes Strong Cooperation with the Government of the Netherlands', 17 May 2022, available online at www.icc-cpi.int/news/icc-prosecutor-karim-aa-khan-qc-announces-deployment-forensics-and-investigative-team-ukraine (visited 22 September 2022).

59 117th Congress, S Res 531, 3 March 2022, 'A resolution expressing the sense of the Senate condemning the Russian Federation, President Vladimir Putin, members of the Russian Security Council, the Russian Armed Forces, and Russian military commanders for committing flagrant acts of aggression and other atrocities rising to the level of crimes against humanity and war crimes against the people of Ukraine and others', available online at www.congress.gov/bill/117th-congress/senate-resolution/531.

60 Judgment on the appeal of Mr Ntaganda against the "Second decision on the Defence's challenge to the jurisdiction of the Court in respect of Counts 6 and 9", *Situation in the Democratic Republic of Congo in the Case of the Prosecutor v Bosco Ntaganda* (ICC-01/04-02/06 OA5), Appeals Chamber, 15 June 2017, § 2, 46ff; Second decision on the Defence's challenge to the jurisdiction of the Court in respect of Counts 6 and 9, *Situation in the Democratic Republic of Congo in the Case of the Prosecutor v Bosco Ntaganda* (ICC-01/04-02/06), Trial Chamber VI, 4 January 2017, § 38 et seq.

61 See inter alia Antonio Cassese, *Cassese's International Criminal Law* (3rd edn, OUP 2013) 78; for a differing view on this, see inter alia C Kenny and Y McDermott, 'The Expanding Protection of Members of a Party's own Armed Forces under International Criminal Law' (2019) 68 International & Comparative Law Quarterly 943.

62 Judgement, *Prosecutor v Issa Sesay, Morris Kallon and Augustine Gbao* (SCSL-04-15-T), Trial Chamber I of the Special Court for Sierra Leone, 2 March 2009, § 1453.

63 Regarding the background of that term, see inter alia Michael Bothe, Karl Josef Partsch and Waldemar Solf, 'Art. 49', in Michael Bothe, Karl Josef Partsch and Waldemar Solf, *New Rules for Victims of Armed Conflicts: Commentary on the Two 1977 Additional Protocols to the Geneva Conventions of 1949* (Brill 2013) 329ff.

64 See inter alia, Claude Pilloud and Jean De Preux, 'Art. 124', in Claude Pilloud and others (eds), *Commentary on the Additional Protocols of 8 June 1977 to the Geneva Conventions of 12 August 1949* (International Committee of the Red Cross: Martinus Nijhoff Publishers; Distributors for the United States and Canada: Kluwer Academic Publishers 1987) mn 1880.

65 Judgment on the appeals of Mr Bosco Ntaganda and the Prosecutor against the decision of Trial Chamber VI of 8 July 2019 entitled 'Judgment', *Situation in the Democratic Republic of Congo in the Case of the Prosecutor v Bosco Ntaganda* (ICC-01/04-02/06 A A2), Appeals Chamber, 30 March 2021, § 1164 et seq.

66 Rome Statute, Art 8(2)(b)(i), (ii), (iii), (iv), (v), (ix), (xxiv) and 8(2)(e)(i), (ii), (iii), (iv).

67 For a critical assessment of the judgement, see Abhimanyu George Jain, 'The Ntaganda Appeal Judgement and the Meaning of "Attack" in Conduct of Hostilities War Crimes', EJIL: Talk! Blog of the European Journal of International Law, 2 April 2021, available online at www.ejiltalk.org/the-ntaganda-appeal-judgment-and-the-meaning-of-attack-in-conduct-of-hostilities-war-crimes/ (visited 22 September 2022); for a more approving assessment of the judgement, see Pearce Clancy, 'Ntaganda and the "Conduct of Hostilities Crimes"', EJIL: Talk! Blog of the European Journal of International Law, 20 August 2021, available online at www.ejiltalk.org/ntaganda-and-the-conduct-of-hostilities-crimes/(visited 22 September 2022).

68 For other decisions of the ICC in this regard, see Fernanda Garcia Pinto, 'The International Committee of the Red Cross and the International Criminal Court: Turning International Humanitarian Law Into a Two-Headed Snake?' *International Review of the Red Cross* 102 (2020), 745ff; more generally in this regard, see Volker Nerlich, 'The International Criminal Court and Substantive Criminal Law: Progressive Development or Cautious Reluctance?', in Gerhard Werle and Andreas Zimmermann (eds), *The International Court in Turbulent Times*, 145ff; regarding earlier developments, see Andreas Zimmermann, 'Das Völkerstrafgesetzbuch im Spiegel des Völkerrechts und seiner Anwendungspraxis', in Florian Jeßberger and Julia Geneuss (eds), *Zehn Jahre Völkerstrafgesetzbuch – Bilanz und Perspektiven* (Stämpfli 2013) 231 et seq.

69 Judgment in the Jordan Referral re Al-Bashir Appeal, *Situation in Darfur, Sudan in the Case of the Prosecutor v Omar Hassan Ahmad Al-Bashir* (ICC-02/05-01/09 OA2), Appeals Chamber, 6 May 2019, § 133 et seq.

70 ibid § 100 et seq.

71 Ssenyonjo (n 8) and Pavlopoulos (n 9).

72 cf Kara Elsadig and others, 'Sudan Cabinet: "Unanimous decision" to Hand Darfur War Crimes Accused to ICC', Dabanga, 27 June 2022, available online at www.dabangasudan.org/en/all-news/article/sudan-cabinet-unanimous-decision-to-hand-darfur-war-crimes-accused-to-icc (visited 22 September 2022); see also 'Press Release – The Prosecutor of the International Criminal Court, Mr Karim AA Khan QC, Concludes His First Visit to Sudan with the Signing of a New Memorandum of Understanding Ensuring Greater Cooperation', 17 August 2021, available online at www.icc-cpi.int/Pages/item.aspx?name=PR1607 (visited 22 September 2022).

73 cf Kara Elsadig and others, 'Sudan Cabinet Unanimous on Bill to Join Rome Statute of ICC', 3 August 2021, available online at www.dabangasudan.org/en/all-news/article/sudan-cabinet-unanimous-on-bill-to-join-rome-statute-of-icc (visited 22 September 2022).

74 cf A Rusbridger and others, 'Milosevic extradited', The Guardian, 29 June 2001, available online at www.theguardian.com/world/2001/jun/29/warcrimes.guardianleaders (visited 22 September 2022).

75 In 2012, 166 States have defined one or more of the four crimes under international law for universal jurisdiction over one or more crimes under international law (although, given the number, not all of those States did this due to their accession to the Rome Statute) according to Amnesty International, 'Universal Jurisdiction – A preliminary Survey of Legislation around the World – 2012 Update', 9 October 2012, available online at www.amnesty.org/en/documents/ior53/019/2012/en/ (visited 22 September 2022), 1 et seq., 23 et seq.; for more details, see also Jann K

Kleffner, *Complementarity in the Rome Statute and National Criminal Jurisdictions* (OUP 2008) 31 et seq.

76 Articles 49 and 50 of Convention (I) for the Amelioration of the Condition of the Wounded and Sick in Armed Forces in the Field, Geneva, 12 August 1949; Arts 50 and 51 of Convention (II) for the Amelioration of the Condition of Wounded Sick and Shipwrecked Members of Armed Forces at Sea, Geneva, 12 August 1949; Arts 129 and 130 of Convention (III) relative to the Treatment of Prisoners of War, Geneva, 12 August 1949; Arts 146 and 147 of Convention (IV) relative to the Protection of Civilian Persons in Time of War, Geneva, 12 August 1949.

77 In 2012, 147 States have provided for universal jurisdiction over one or more crimes under international law, according to Amnesty International, 'Universal Jurisdiction – A preliminary Survey of Legislation around the World – 2012 Update', available online at www.amnesty.org/en/documents/ior53/019/2012/en/ (visited 22 September 2022), 2, 23 et seq.

78 See inter alia Gerhard Werle and Florian Jeßberger, *Principles of International Criminal Law* (4th edn, OUP 2020) mn 218 et seq.

79 For an overview as of 2011, see Máximo Langer, 'The Diplomacy of Universal Jurisdiction: The Political Branches and the Transnational Prosecution of International Crimes' (2011) 105 American Journal of International Law 1, 44.

80 See Karine Fanny Bonneau and John L Washburn, *Negotiating the International Criminal Court* (Brill Nijhoff, 2014).

81 German Code of Crimes Against International Law, s 12(1).

82 Amendment to the Rome Statute of the International Criminal Court, Kampala, 10 June 2010, Adoption of Amendment to Article 8, C.N.533.2010.TREATIES-6.

83 Amendment to Article 8 of the Rome Statute of the International Criminal Court (Intentionally using starvation of civilians), The Hague, 6 December 2019, Adoption of Amendment to Article 8, C.N.394.2020.TREATIES-XVIII.10.g.

84 Judgment in the Jordan Referral re Al-Bashir Appeal (n 69) § 46 et seq.

85 ICJ, Case concerning the arrest warrant of 11 April 2000 (Democratic Republic of the Congo v Belgium), Judgment of 14 February 2002, § 51 et seq.

86 The ILC's work in this field is available online at https://legal.un.org/ilc/guide/4_2.shtml (visited 22 September 2022).

87 International Law Commission, *Immunity of State officials from foreign criminal jurisdiction Text of draft articles 1, 3 and 4 provisionally adopted by the Drafting Committee at the sixty-fifth session of the International Law Commission* (2013) UN Doc A/CN.4/L.814.

88 cf International Law Commission, *Report of the International Law Commission, Sixty-fifth session* (6 May to 7 June and 8 July to 9 August 2013) UN Doc A/68/10, 43 et seq.

89 Statements of the States at the sixty-eighth session of the Sixth Committee, UN General Assembly (2013) available online at www.un.org/en/ga/sixth/68/ILC.shtm (visited 22 September 2022).

90 German Federal Court of Justice (Bundesgerichtshof), Judgement of 28 January 2021, 3 StR 564/19, § 22 et seq.

91 ibid § 60.

92 ibid § 24 et seq.

93 ibid § 54; The order that the German Federal Court of Justice is referring to is German Constitutional Court (Bundesverfassungsgericht), Order of 12 October 2011, 2 BvR 2984/09, § 27.

94 cf inter alia H Fox and P Webb, *The Law of State Immunity* (The Oxford International Law Library, 2015) 570ff; S Murphy, 'Immunity *Ratione Materiae* of State Officials from Foreign Criminal Jurisdiction: Where is the State Practice in Support of Exceptions?' (2018) 112 American Journal of International Law Unbound 4.

95 German Federal Court of Justice (n 90) § 25.

96 cf UNSC Res 827 (25 May 1993) UN Doc S/RES/827.

97 ICJ (n 85), § 58 and 61.

98 German Federal Court of Justice (n 90) § 20.

99 Declaration regarding the defeat of Germany and the assumption of supreme authority with respect to Germany by the Governments of the United States of America, the Union of Soviet Socialist Republics, the United Kingdom and the Provisional Government of the French Republic, 5 June 1945, available online at https://avalon.law.yale.edu/wwii/ger01.asp (visited 22 September 2022).

100 German Federal Court of Justice (n 90) § 26 et seq.

101 Murphy (n 94).

102 Judgment in the Jordan Referral re Al-Bashir Appeal (n 69) § 116.

103 German Federal Court of Justice (n 90) § 35 et seq.

104 International Law Commission, *Fifth report on immunity of State officials from foreign criminal jurisdiction by Concepcion Escobar Hernandez, Special reporter* (2016) UN Doc A/CN.4/701, § 179 and 188.

105 Concerning the latter, see inter alia P-T Stoll, 'State Immunity', in *The Max Planck Encyclopedia of Public International Law*, available online at https://opil.ouplaw.com/view/10.1093/law:epil/9780199231690/law-9780199231690-e1106 (visited 22 September 2022).

Selected bibliography

Benedetti F, Bonneau K and Washburn JL, *Negotiating the International Criminal Court* (Brill Nijhoff 2014)

Bothe M, Partsch KJ and Solf W (eds), *New Rules for Victims of Armed Conflicts: Commentary on the two 1977 Additional Protocols to the Geneva Conventions of 1949 (*Martinus Nijhoff Publishers 2013)

Brodersen K H and Papadopoulos L, 'Guilty but Free: the ICC Renders its First Contempt Case Judgement', EJIL: Talk! Blog of the European Journal of International Law, 1 November 2016, www.ejiltalk.org/guilty-but-free-the-icc-renders-its-first-contempt-case-judgment/

Cassese A, *Cassese's International Criminal Law* (Oxford University Press 2013)

Clancy P, 'Ntaganda and the Conduct of Hostilities Crimes', *EJIL: Talk! Blog of the European Journal of International Law,* 20 August 2021 www.ejiltalk.org/ntaganda-and-the-conduct-of-hostilities-crimes/

Eichensehr KE, 'Biden Administration Rescinds Sanctions Against International Criminal Court Officials' (2021) 115(4) *American Journal of International Law* 729

Fox H and Webb P, *The Law of State Immunity* (The Oxford International Law Library 2015)

Jain AG, 'The Ntaganda Appeal Judgement and the Meaning of "Attack" in Conduct of Hostilities War Crimes', EJIL: Talk! Blog of the European Journal of International Law, 2 April 2021, www.ejiltalk.org/the-ntaganda-appeal-judgment-and-the-meaning-of-attack-in-conduct-of-hostilities-war-crimes/

Kenny C and McDermott Y, 'The Expanding Protection of Members of a Party's Own Armed Forces Under International Criminal Law' (2019) 68(4) *International & Comparative Law Quarterly* 943

Kleffner JK, *Complementarity in the Rome Statute and National Criminal Jurisdictions* (Oxford University Press 2008)

Langer M, 'The Diplomacy of Universal Jurisdiction: the Political Branches and the Transnational Prosecution of International Crimes' (2011) 105(1) *American Journal of International Law* 1

Murphy SD, 'Immunity *Ratione Materiae* of State Officials from Foreign Criminal Jurisdiction: Where is the State Practice in Support of Exceptions?' (2018) 112 *American Journal of International Law Unbound* 4

Nerlich V, 'The International Criminal Court and Substantive Criminal Law: Progressive Development or Cautious Reluctance?', in Gerhard Werle and Andreas Zimmermann (eds), *The International Court in Turbulent Times* (TMC Asser Press 2019) 145

Pavlopoulos N, 'South Africa's Withdrawal: a Lesson Learned?' EJIL: Talk! Blog of the European Journal of International Law, 6 December 2016, www.ejiltalk.org/south-africas-withdrawal-a-lesson-learned/

Pilloud C and others (eds), *Commentary on the Additional Protocols of 8 June 1977 to the Geneva Conventions of 12 August 1949* (Martinus Nijhoff Publishers 1987)

Pinto FG, 'The International Committee of the Red Cross and the International Criminal Court: Turning International Humanitarian Law Into a Two-Headed Snake?' (2020) 102(914) *International Review of the Red Cross* 745

Sayapin S, 'Russia's Withdrawal of Signature from the Rome Statute Would not Shield its Nationals from Potential Prosecution at the ICC', EJIL: Talk! Blog of the European Journal of International Law, 21 November 2016, www.ejiltalk.org/russias-withdrawal-of-signature-from-the-rome-statute-would-not-shield-its-nationals-from-potential-prosecution-at-the-icc/

Schmitt B, 'ICC Judge Schmitt Counsels Resilience to Preserve International Justice', Just Security, 13 February 2019, www.justsecurity.org/62577/icc-judge-schmitt-counsels-resilience-preserve-international-justice/

Ssenyonjo M, 'State Withdrawal Notifications from the Rome Statute of the International Criminal Court: South Africa, Burundi and the Gambia' (2018) 29(1) *Criminal Law Forum* 63

Stoll P-T, 'State Immunity', in *The Max Planck Encyclopedia of Public International Law* (Oxford University Press 2019), https://opil.ouplaw.com/view/10.1093/law:epil/9780199231690/law-9780199231690-e1106

Talmon S, 'Arbitration between Croatia and Slovenia', *German Practice in International Law*, 1 October 2017, https://gpil.jura.uni-bonn.de/2017/10/arbitration-croatia-slovenia/

Talmon S, 'Germany Takes a More Outspoken and Active Position on the South China Sea Disputes', *German Practice in International Law*, 30 March 2021, https://gpil.jura.uni-bonn.de/2021/03/germany-takes-a-more-outspoken-and-active-position-on-the-south-china-sea-disputes/

Werle G and Jeßberger F, *Principles of International Criminal Law* (Oxford University Press 2020)

Zimmermann A and Freiburg-Braun E, *Aggression under the Rome Statute* (Nomos, 2019)

Zimmermann A, '*Alea Iacta Est*: the Kampala Amendment on the Crime of Aggression Post-2017: a Response to Koh and Buchwald' (2015) 109 *American Journal of International Law Unbound* 240

Zimmermann A, 'Finally… Or Would Rather Less Have Been More? The Recent Amendment on the Deletion of Article 124 of the Rome Statute and the Continued Quest for the Universality of the International Criminal Court' (2016) 14(3) *Journal of International Criminal Justice* 505

Zimmermann A, 'A Victory for International Rule of Law? Or: All's Well that Ends Well? The 2017 ASP Decision to Amend the Kampala Amendment on the Crime of Aggression' (2018) 16(1) *Journal of International Criminal Justice* 19

Zimmermann A, 'Das Völkerstrafgesetzbuch im Spiegel des Völkerrechts und seiner Anwendungspraxis', in Jeßberger F and Geneuss J (eds), *Zehn Jahre Völkerstrafgesetzbuch – Bilanz und Perspektiven* (Nomos 2013)

3.2 Between international solidarity and "no safe haven"

The German *Völkerstrafgesetzbuch* 20 years on

Boris Burghardt[1]

1 Concept and aims of the VStGB

The VStGB is part of a larger set of laws, meant to implement the material law of the Rome Statute into German criminal law. For this purpose, the Federal Ministry of Justice established an expert working group in October 1999, which submitted a "Working Draft of a Law for the Introduction of a Code of Crimes Against International Law" in May 2001. As all political parties supported the project, it was passed unanimously in the German parliament in March of 2002 without substantial divergence from the Draft of the Special Working Group.[2]

According to the Official Explanatory Memorandum,[3] the VStGB intends to achieve four aims.

1 Firstly, the code aims at expressing the "specific wrong of crimes under international law". Essentially, the VStGB meant to tackle the lack of implementation of the Nuremberg law into domestic law: The German Criminal Code had previously contained no provisions on war crimes or crimes against humanity.[4] This lack of implementation was the result of the Federal Republic's long-lasting rejection of the "legacy of Nuremberg". It was only after the end of the Cold War that this scepticism was replaced by a quintessentially international criminal law-friendly attitude.[5] Only then was the inappropriateness of the so-called "ordinary crimes approach" fully recognised within the German legal and political discourse.
2 The second aim of the VStGB is to promote "legal clarity and practical application" by providing a unified code of international criminal law for the German judiciary. Smaller modifications to the law of the ICC Statute were supposed to be necessary in order for it to adhere to constitutional principles of German criminal law such as the principle of legal certainty and the principle of culpability. Other adaptations of the law of the Rome Statute seemed necessary to avoid contradictions and

DOI: 10.4324/9781003320951-11

inconsistencies with systematic structures of German criminal law. Two of the most notable deviations of the VStGB from the ICC Statute may exemplify this approach.

The first regards the implementation of Article 28 of the ICC Statute. According to the expert group, the doctrine of command responsibility under Article 28 of the ICC Statute was an example of "rough justice" that unduly meshed different forms of a superior's omission without taking into account the varying degrees of his or her guilt.[6] Therefore, in the German implementation, Article 28 was split into three separate provisions.

Secondly, section 2 mandates the application of ordinary German criminal law when no special rules are created by the VStGB. Consequently, the German legislator refrained from implementing the general principles of the ICC Statute on the subjective element, mistake, self-defence or modes of participation, but rather relied on the existing rules and principles in German criminal law regarding these matters.[7]

These adaptations to basic structures of German criminal law have been a wise decision, as they helped to ensure the acceptance of the VStGB amongst the German judiciary. Even though the crimes of the VStGB were new and partly deviated from the law that German prosecutors, judges and criminal law scholars were familiar with, it was not "too far off". German lawyers could make sense of it. From a historical perspective, this is a key difference to the failed implementation of international criminal law within German criminal law in the aftermath of WWII. Back then, Control Council Law no 10 was met with widespread rejection, amongst other reasons due to it appearing as a foreign body of law. Contemporary statements in fact dismissed it as not "deutschrechtlich", a wording that, apart from carrying a decidedly nationalistic undertone, may also be read as meaning "alien to German legal thinking".[8]

3 The third aim of the VStGB is to ensure that Germany was "always in a position to prosecute crimes over which the ICC has jurisdiction". Germany was to fulfil all the requisites under the principle of complementarity in order to secure that no German citizen would ever end up before the ICC.[9]

4 The fourth aim is to contribute to the promotion and proliferation of international criminal law. The VStGB is carried by the idea that blending the substantive law of the ICC Statute with the principled and systematic approach of German criminal law doctrine would make for a better version of the Rome Statute, and could thus serve as a model code for the implementation process in other States.[10] An example is the law of war crimes for which systematic concerns set the impetus for a complete restructuring. War crimes in the VStGB are classified primarily with regard to the target of the attack, not with regard to the international or non-international nature of the armed conflict.[11]

To enable the prosecution of international crimes under the VStGB, some adaptations within the institutional structure of the German criminal justice system were necessary. The competent authority to investigate and prosecute crimes under the VStGB is the Federal Public Prosecutor (Generalbundesanwalt, GBA), not the Regional Public Prosecutor offices (cf § 142a(1) with § 120(1) no 8 Gerichtsverfassungsgesetz, GVG). In consequence, there is one central office to prosecute all cases within which crimes under the VStGB are investigated. Should the GBA decide to press charges in a certain case, those charges are brought before the Higher Regional Courts (Oberlandesgerichte, OLG) – more precisely, before the "Staatsschutzsenate", special panels that normally deal with crimes against State security, mostly terrorism cases (§ 120 I no 8 GVG). Additionally, a special investigation unit for investigating war crimes and other crimes under the VStGB was established within the German Federal Criminal Police.[12]

2 Which role for Germany in a multi-level system of prosecution of international crimes?

Neither the four official aims of the VStGB nor the institutional structures set in place for the prosecution of international crimes provide a clear answer to the actual core question that arises in the context of the practical application of the VStGB: Which role should the Federal Republic of Germany play in prosecuting crimes under international law?

Generally, the adjudication of international crimes by domestic criminal justice systems is evaluated along the lines of two different ideal types distinguished by Máximo Langer: the "global enforcer" approach and the "no safe haven" approach.[13]

The "global enforcer" label, however, does not frame its underlying rationale accurately. It should rather be called "the international solidarity" approach being built upon the idea that international criminal justice, in order to fulfil its function, needs to be administered on a multitude of levels simultaneously. This approach recognises that third States supporting the general idea of international criminal law have to play an active role in the enforcement of it and cannot defer to the ICC or other international(ised) criminal tribunals. It is simply not enough for third States to merely adjudicate cases with a link to their territory, nationals or residents. This understanding is to be distinguished from the claim that a single State could step in and globally ensure the enforcement of international criminal law on its own, as the "global enforcer" label suggests.

As regards Germany's role in a multi-level system of international criminal justice, the most important regulations may be found in section 1 of the VStGB as well as section 153(f) of the German Code of Criminal Procedure. Section 1, sentence 1 of the VStGB mandates the universality principle and applies to war crimes, crimes against humanity, and genocide.[14] Thus, in these cases, German courts have jurisdiction "even when the offence was committed abroad and bears no relation to Germany". The German legislator hereby embraced the "international solidarity" approach. Indeed, the explanatory memorandum to the law explicitly states: "Since the primary aims is to prevent the impunity of perpetrators of crimes under international law through international solidarity in prosecution, the *duty* to investigate and prosecute is not limited to acts that have a point of connection to Germany."[15] In the same vein, the then Parliamentary State Secretary in the Federal Ministry of Justice, Eckhart Pick, stated in his speech on the occasion of the first reading of the draft law in the Bundestag: "The message of the Rome Statute, that the perpetrators and torturers of this world may no longer feel safe anywhere and at any time, will in future be given quasi legal status in Germany through the VStGB."[16]

Section 153f of the Code of Criminal Procedure, however, scales back this commitment, albeit it is unclear to what precise extent. At least in those cases without a domestic link to the alleged crime a certain level of discretion is opened to abstain from investigating and prosecuting these crimes. In sum, section 1 paves the way for an ambitious practice of prosecuting atrocity crimes worldwide by the German judiciary while the procedural rule section 153(f) allowed for boiling down this prosecutorial practice to a self-serving, "not in my backyard" approach.[17]

3 The VStGB in practice

Within the last 20 years of prosecutorial activity with regard to the VStGB, three stages can be distinguished.

3.1 Rocky starting years

Some have suggested that the latest stage could be headlined "towards complementary preparedness".[18] If so, the adequate label for the first five to ten years of the VStGB is "complete unpreparedness". After all, until 2009 both the GBA and the special investigation unit within the Federal Criminal Police lacked the personnel and resources to conduct any meaningful investigations.[19] During this time, the only visible activity of the GBA in the realm of international criminal law cases was to dismiss public complaints brought up by NGOs urging him to take on high-profile cases such as Donald Rumsfeld and other high-ranking military officials and civil advisers for the US torture and rendition programme installed after 9/11. During these years, representatives of the GBA gave the impression of being overwhelmed by the public scrutiny and activist critique of their work and maintained constantly a passive-aggressive mode of defending their inactivity.[20]

The most notable result was the ruling of the Higher Regional Court of Stuttgart, confirming that the Federal Public Prosecutor indeed enjoyed a large amount of discretion in deciding whether to investigate and prosecute international crimes with no direct link to Germany. The court also held that the decision of the GBA to abstain from prosecution in line with section 153(f) of the Criminal Code of Procedure was not subject to judicial review.[21] Thus, in an act of self-empowerment against the legislative will – while nonetheless in accordance with the actual political will of the government and political authorities at that time – the judiciary freed itself from the VStGB's ambitious promise to prosecute international crimes in *all* potential cases worldwide. At the same time, criticism regarding the GBA's inactivity continued to increase.

3.2 Only low-cost cases, please

In the second phase, the GBA gained sufficient resources and got equipped with a proper War Crimes Unit and more personnel. Around the same time, the Prosecutor also became more willing and able to better explain his approach. Indeed, it was the head of the department of the GBA's office for the prosecution of crimes under international law who, at a conference on the occasion of the 10th anniversary of the VStGB, summarised the GBA's policy with the label "no safe haven Germany", later taken up by Máximo Langer, thereby largely neglecting the ambitious vision of section 1 of the VStGB.[22]

During the following years, this approach underwent a further development which may be summarised best under the maxim of "only low-cost cases, please". The GBA succeeded in ending all "uncomfortable" investigations in their early stages. These included cases directed against German military personnel for acts committed in the context of foreign missions, most notably the 2009 Kunduz airstrike in Afghanistan.[23] The same was true for cases surrounding the involvement of German security authorities in possible crimes under international law committed by NATO partners, namely the US, eg in the context of drone programmes of targeted killings.[24]

One the other hand, the Federal Public Prosecutor was willing to conduct so-called "structural investigations", that is, broad preliminary investigations not directed against specific suspects but designed to gather evidence related to potential crimes that could be used in future proceedings, be it by the German or any other international or domestic judiciary, even in criminal scenarios with no link to Germany, if only he was confident that no substantial political backlash would result from such investigations.[25]

Consequently, the prosecutorial practice in this second stage was characterised by a very small number of cases that eventually came to trial.[26] A case that exemplifies this phase fairly well and which coincidentally also led to the first conviction on the basis of the VStGB, concerned two leading functionaries, Ignace Murwanashyaka and Straton Musoni, of the Hutu rebel militia Forces Démocratiques de Libération du Rwanda (FDLR). Albeit being resident in Germany at the time of the commission of the crimes they were being charged with, both Murwanashyaka and Musoni had, according to the indictment, participated in massacres perpetrated in the provinces of North and South Kivu/Democratic Republic of Congo, through giving instructions via satellite telephone and by their propagandist activities for the FDLR in Europe.[27] In 2015, the Higher Regional Court of Stuttgart convicted Murwanashyaka for assisting four incidents of war crimes and for membership as a ringleader in a foreign terrorist group and sentenced him to 13 years of imprisonment. Musoni was found guilty of membership as a ringleader in a foreign terrorist group while being acquitted of all charges of war crimes or crimes against humanity, and sentenced to eight years of imprisonment. However, in 2019, Murwanashyaka's conviction was overturned by the German Federal Court of Justice (Bundesgerichtshof, BGH), and the accused died in custody while awaiting the retrial that same year.

3.3 Syria, Afghanistan and the "Islamic State" (IS)

The third phase of prosecutorial activity started around 2015 and is characterised by a significant increase of cases in which crimes under the VStGB were investigated and prosecuted. This stage has to be understood in the context of the civil war in Syria, the activities of the terrorist group Islamic State in Iraq and Syria, the continuing armed conflict in Afghanistan, and, last but not least, the arrival of hundreds of thousands of refugees from these war-torn regions since 2011.

Three kinds of cases can be distinguished in this phase:

1 Men who had participated actively as part of armed groups in these conflicts, mostly as low-rank recruits of the IS or some other Islamist militias. These men were either German citizens, persons that had been resident in Germany before and returned to the country, or refugees who sought shelter in the Federal Republic.
2 Women who travelled from Germany to regions under the (temporary) control of the IS in order to marry IS fighters.
3 Higher-rank personnel involved in the larger-scale organisation and commission of crimes against humanity, including some functionaries of the Assad regime or IS commanders.

These three categories of cases do not carry the same weight in the practice of the German judiciary. Only cases from the first two categories have been brought to trial in larger numbers as of today. Here, the German judiciary has convicted individuals as war criminals even if they could be proven to have done no more than posed with the mutilated bodies of fallen enemy combatants.[28] Women who had voluntarily travelled to IS-held areas in order to marry IS fighters were considered to have participated in the commission of a war crime if the joint household was run in a house appropriated in violation of international law or if enslaved Yezidi women and girls were forced to perform labour services in that same household.[29] Thus, German courts have stretched the scope of the application of war crimes in these cases well beyond the personnel that had been convicted for international crimes before.

A further notable feature of the cases of the first two categories is that the charges brought against the accused oftentimes not only consist of international crimes but also include charges of membership of a foreign terrorist organisation and of illegally carrying military weapons. Thus, a convergence of international criminal law with anti-terrorism law can be observed.[30] This convergence is problematic for a number of reasons, particularly as it further reinforces the already existing selectivity of criminal prosecutions in the context of armed conflicts: in the vast majority of cases, the German judiciary goes after members of groups that are classified as terrorist by the international community. Those who commit crimes in the service of State armed forces or security agencies, on the other hand, are much less likely to become the focus of attention of the German criminal justice system.

It is to be mentioned, however, that the German Federal Court seized the opportunity provided by proceedings against a former officer of the Afghan army, who was charged with war crimes committed against members of the Taliban, to comment on the question of functional immunity of State officials before third State courts. At this occasion, the court did emphasise that an exception to the rule of functional immunity of State officials existed in the case of allegations of crimes under international law. At the same time, however, the Federal Court expressly affirmed such an exception only for lower-ranking functionaries.[31]

The third category of cases has only limited practical relevance so far. There is a small number of undisclosed arrest warrants against high-rank suspects of the Syrian Assad regime. The only disclosed arrest warrant is directed against Jamil Hassan, the head of Syria's Air Force Intelligence.[32] Additionally, three low- to mid-level suspects have been arrested in Germany and charged with having participated in Assad's torture programmes. Two of them have been convicted of assisting crimes against humanity by the Higher Regional Court in Koblenz, while the third is currently at trial before the Higher Regional Court in Frankfurt/Main.[33] The last case that falls into the third category is the one regarding Taha A-J, an Iraqi national and high-rank IS member who was convicted of genocide, crimes against humanity and war crimes against the Yezidi population.[34]

In contrast to the dozens of category I and II proceedings, only those very few cases of the aforementioned third category carry a symbolic significance that extends beyond Germany: for the first time, Assad's systematic crimes of torture against the Syrian civilian population and the genocidal campaign of the IS against the Yezidi population became the subject of criminal trials. This does not, however, change the fact that even these proceedings ultimately are politically low-cost as well.

4 The VStGB under the auspices of the Russian War of Aggression against the Ukraine

Russia's war against the Ukraine has recently changed the political backdrop against which the German judiciary prosecutes international crimes.

Throughout the Western world, calls for criminal investigations and the prosecution of Vladimir Putin and his inner circle have emerged. Impunity for the main political and military leaders responsible for this war of aggression and the crimes committed against the Ukrainian civilian population appears as an intolerable option even to those who have so far been sceptical or even hostile towards the International Criminal Court or the idea of national prosecution of crimes under international law by third States on the basis of the universality principle. The GBA has recognised the signs of the times and quickly opened a structural investigation in order to gather information and evidence on possible crimes under the VStGB in Ukraine while the political branch has agreed to provide more financial resources to the GBA so that two additional units can be established to undertake this investigation.[35] In this context, it is undisputed that, under international law, the political leadership surrounding and including Russian President Vladimir Putin and Foreign Minister Sergei Lavrov cannot become defendants in German criminal proceedings for reasons of immunity, as long as they hold office. Moreover, while the crime of aggression was incorporated into the VStGB in 2016 in order to implement the Kampala Amendments to the Rome Statute, the universality principle does not apply to this crime. Therefore, the German judiciary does not have the authority to prosecute the crime of aggression in this scenario. Once again, it is highlighted to what extent the actual practice of international criminal law is determined by questions of political and military power. It is only of little comfort that the terrible suffering currently caused to the Ukrainian population might provide a boost to the longstanding call for a less selective application of international criminal law and that it has to be enforced, above all, against those in positions of power.

5 Conclusion

German international criminal law has been searching for its role ever since the entry into force of the VStGB. Initially, there was the perhaps too idealistic promise that Germany would play an active role in the global fight against impunity for crimes under international law and would prosecute crimes of this kind everywhere. This promise, however, has never been fulfilled in practice. Instead, the German criminal justice system has chosen a course characterised above all by the avoidance of politically inconvenient proceedings. Surely, since 2015 the number of cases has increased considerably. The prosecutorial efforts of the Federal Public Prosecutor are also no longer exclusively limited to a "no safe haven approach", as there are ongoing structural investigations and occasional investigations and prosecutorial measures taken against individual suspects, even in lack of a link to Germany. Nonetheless, the prosecutorial practice is still far from the ambitious vision sketched out in section 1 of the VStGB. The most influential guiding principle of the Federal Public Prosecutor still appears to be to stick to low-cost cases which, naturally, add little to the larger project of international criminal law: ending the impunity of large-scale atrocities. It remains to be seen whether this will change in light of the currently widespread call for the prosecution of those politically and militarily responsible for crimes committed in the war in Ukraine.

Notes

1 The author thanks Rachel Behring and Henrike Groß for their research and assistance in drafting this chapter.

2 More extensively on the law's origins: Gerhard Werle and Florian Jeßberger, 'International Criminal Justice is Coming Home: The New German Code of Crimes Against International Law' (2002) 13 Criminal Law Forum 199.

3 Bundestagsdrucksache (Parliamentary Document) 14/8524.

4 Bundestagsdrucksache (Parliamentary Document) 14/8524, p 12.

5 See for more details Ronen Steinke, *The Politics of International Criminal Justice: German Perspectives from Nuremberg to The Hague* (Hart Publishing 2012); Gerhard Werle and Florian Jeßberger, *Principles of International Criminal Law* (4th edn, OUP 2020) paras 485ff.

6 Bundestagsdrucksache (Parliamentary Document) 14/8524, pp 18–19. For a different evaluation of Art 28 of the ICC Statute: Boris Burghardt, 'Die Vorgesetztenverantwortlichkeit nach Völkerstrafrecht und deutschem Recht (§ 4 VStGB)' (2010) 5 Zeitschrift für Internationale Strafrechtsdogmatik 695ff.

7 Bundestagsdrucksache (Parliamentary Document) 14/8524, p 14.

8 For a detailed account, see Edith Raim, *Justiz zwischen Diktatur und Demokratie* (De Gruyter 2013) 579ff.

9 Bundestagsdrucksache (Parliamentary Document) 14/8524, p 12.

10 Bundestagsdrucksache (Parliamentary Document) 14/8524, p 12.

11 Bundestagsdrucksache (Parliamentary Document) 14/8524, pp 23–24.

12 See Klaus Zorn, 'Die Zentralstelle für die Bekämpfung von Kriegsverbrechen und weiteren Straftaten nach dem Völkerstrafgesetzbuch' (2017) 12 Zeitschrift für internationale Strafrechtsdogmatik 762.

13 Máximo Langer, 'Universal Jurisdiction is not Disappearing' (2015) 13 Journal of International Criminal Justice 246.

14 A different, much more restricted approach was chosen with regard to jurisdiction over the crime of aggression, see Florian Jeßberger, 'Implementing Kampala: The New Crime of Aggression under the German Code of Crimes against International Law', in Martin Böse and others (eds), *Justice Without Borders, Essays in Honour of Wolfgang Schomburg* (Brill 2018) 180.

15 Bundestagsdrucksache (Parliamentary Document) 14/8254, p 37 (emphasis by the author).

16 Bundestagsplenarprotokoll (Plenary Minute) 14/228, p 22685. See also Bundestagsplenarprotokoll (Plenary Minute) 14/228, p 22682 (Parliamentarian Röttgen), p 22683 (Parliamentarian Grießhaber).

17 Bundestagsdrucksache (Parliamentary Document) 14/8254, p 37; Thomas Beck and Christian Ritscher, 'Do Criminal Complaints Make Sense in (German) International Criminal Law?' (2015) 13 Journal of International Criminal Justice 230; see also Gerhard Werle, 'Völkerstrafrecht und deutsches Völkerstrafgesetzbuch' (2012) 67 JuristenZeitung 376.

18 Florian Jeßberger, 'Towards a "Complementary Preparedness" Approach to Universal Jurisdiction – Recent Trends and Best Practices in the European

Union', in European Parliament, *Universal Jurisdiction and International Crimes: Constraints and Best Practices* (2018) 53.

19 Boris Burghardt, 'Zwischen internationaler Solidarität und "not in my backyard"' (2018) 51 Kritische Justiz 24.

20 Claus Kreß, 'Nationale Umsetzung des Völkerstrafgesetzbuches' (2007) 13 Zeitschrift für Internationale Strafrechtsdogmatik 515, 523–525; see also Kai Ambos, '§ 1 Völkerstrafgesetzbuch', paras 29ff, in Wolfgang Joecks and Klaus Miebach, *Münchener Kommentar zum Strafgesetzbuch* (4th edn, CH Beck 2022).

21 OLG Stuttgart [2006] Neue Zeitschrift für Strafrecht 117. See on this decision Kai Ambos, 'International Core Crimes, Universal Jurisdiction and § 153f of the German Criminal Procedure Code: A Commentary on the Decisions of the Federal Prosecutor General and the Stuttgart Higher Regional Court in the Abu Ghraib/Rumsfeld Case' (2007) 18 Criminal Law Forum 43.

22 See Thomas Beck, 'Das Völkerstrafgesetzbuch in der praktischen Anwendung', in Florian Jeßberger and Julia Geneuss (eds), *Zehn Jahre Völkerstrafgesetzbuch, Bilanz und Perspektiven eines "deutschen Völkerstrafrechts"* (Nomos 2013) 161. Similar for the German Bundesregierung (Government), see for instance Bundestagsdrucksache (Parliamentary Document) 16/11479, p 4.

23 See Generalbundesanwalt, Decision of 16 April 2010 – 3 BJs 6/10-4. For a critical evaluation, see Constantin von der Groeben, 'Criminal Responsibility of German Soldiers in Afghanistan: The Case of Colonel Klein' (2010) 11 German Law Journal 469.

24 Generalbundesanwalt, Decision of 20 June 2013 – 3 BJs 7/12-4 [2013] Neue Zeitschrift für Strafrecht 644ff. For a critical evaluation, see K Ambos, 'Einstellungsverfügung GBA vom 20. 6. 2013 zum Drohneneinsatz in Mir Ali/ Pakistan am 4. 10. 2010 u. Tötung des dt. Staatsangehörigen B.E. – Anmerkung zur "offenen Version" vom 23. 7. 2013' [2013] Neue Zeitschrift für Strafrecht 634.

25 For further information about these investigations see Julia Geneuss, *Völkerrechtsverbrechen und Verfolgungsermessen* (Nomos 2013) 294ff; Wolfgang Kaleck, 'Strafverfolgung nach dem Völkerstrafgesetzbuch: Ein kurzer Blick in die Zukunft – ein Kommentar zum Beitrag von Martin Böse', in Florian Jeßberger and Julia Geneuss (eds), *Zehn Jahre Völkerstrafgesetzbuch, Bilanz und Perspektiven eines "deutschen Völkerstrafrechts"* (Nomos 2013) 177 (179).

26 Thomas Beck, 'Das Völkerstrafgesetzbuch in der praktischen Anwendung', in Florian Jeßberger and Julia Geneuss (eds), ibid, 161; Rolf Hannich, 'Justice in the Name of All' (2007) 13 Zeitschrift für Internationale Strafrechtsdogmatik 507, 513–514.

27 See on this trial: ECCHR, Universal Jurisdiction in Germany?, available at: www.ecchr.eu/fileadmin/Juristische_Dokumente/Report_Executive_Summary_FDLR_EN.pdf (accessed 23 September 2022); Dominic Johnson, Bianca Schmolze and Simone Schlindwein, *Tatort Kongo – Prozess in Deutschland, Die Verbrechen der ruandischen Miliz FDLR und der Versuch einer juristischen Aufarbeitung* (Ch. Links Verlag 2016).

28 See OLG Frankfurt, Judgement of 8 November 2016 – 5 – 2 StE 10/16 – 9 – 2/1; BGH, Decision of 8 September 2016 – StB 27,16; OLG Frankfurt, Judgement of 12 July 2016 – 5 – 3 StE 2/16 – 4 – 1/16; BGH, Judgement of 27 July 2017 – 3 StR 57,17 – BGHSt 62, 272.

29 BGH, Decision of 4 April 2019 – AK 12,19; OLG Düsseldorf, Judgement of 4 December 2019 – 2 StE 2/19.

30 See for example Peter Frank and Holger Schneider-Glockzin, 'Terrorismus und Völkerstraftaten im bewaffneten Konflikt' [2017] Neue Zeitschrift für Strafrecht 6.

31 BGH, 3 StR 564/19. For a detailed account Gerhard Werle, 'Anmerkung' (2021) 76 Juristen Zeitung 732; Florian Jessberger and Aziz Epik, 'Anmerkung' (2022) Juristische Rundschau 10.

32 For further information concerning the arrest warrant see: European Center for Constitutional and Human Rights, 'Deutsche Justiz erlässt Haftbefehl gegen syrischen Geheimdienstchef Jamil Hassan', www.ecchr.eu/fall/deutsche-justiz-erlaesst-haftbefehl-gegen-syrischen-geheimdienstchef-jamil-hassan/#case_case (accessed 20 September 2022).

33 OLG Koblenz, Judgement of 24 February 2021 – 1 StE 3/21; OLG Koblenz, Judgement of 13 January 2022 – 1 StE 9/19; BGH, Decision of 20 April 2022, Az. 3 StR 367/21.

34 OLG Frankfurt am Main, Judgement of 30 November 2021 – 5–3 StE 1/20 – 4 – 1/20.

35 See, eg, Johannes Block, 'Committed in Ukraine, Prosecuted in Germany?', Völkerrechtsblog, 7 April 2022 <https://voelkerrechtsblog.org/de/committed-in-ukraine-prosecuted-in-germany/> (accessed 20 September 2022)

Selected bibliography

Ambos K, '§ 1 Völkerstrafgesetzbuch', in Joecks W and Miebach K, *Münchener Kommentar zum Strafgesetzbuch* (4th edn, CH Beck 2022) paras 29ff

Ambos K, 'Einstellungsverfügung GBA vom 20. 6. 2013 zum Drohneneinsatz in Mir Ali/Pakistan am 4. 10. 2010 u. Tötung des dt. Staatsangehörigen B.E – Anmerkung zur "offenen Version" vom 23. 7. 2013' [2013] *Neue Zeitschrift für Strafrecht*

Ambos K, 'International Core Crimes, Universal Jurisdiction and § 153f of the German Criminal Procedure Code: A Commentary on the Decisions of the Federal Prosecutor General and the Stuttgart Higher Regional Court in the Abu Ghraib/Rumsfeld Case' (2007) 18 *Criminal Law Forum*

Beck T and Ritscher C, 'Do Criminal Complaints Make Sense in (German) International Criminal Law?' (2015) 13 *Journal of International Criminal Justice* 230

Beck T, 'Das Völkerstrafgesetzbuch in der praktischen Anwendung', in Jeßberger F and Geneuss J (eds), *Zehn Jahre Völkerstrafgesetzbuch, Bilanz und Perspektiven eines 'deutschen Völkerstrafrechts'* (Nomos 2013)

Block J, 'Committed in Ukraine, Prosecuted in Germany?', Völkerrechtsblog, 7 April 2022, <https://voelkerrechtsblog.org/de/committed-in-ukraine-prosecuted-in-germany/> (accessed 20 September 2022)

Burghardt B, 'Die Vorgesetztenverantwortlichkeit nach Völkerstrafrecht und deutschem Recht (§ 4 VStGB)' (2010) 5 *Zeitschrift für Internationale Strafrechtsdogmatik*

Burghardt B, 'Zwischen internationaler Solidarität und "not in my backyard"' (2018) 51 *Kritische Justiz*

European Center for Constitutional and Human Rights, 'Deutsche Justiz erlässt Haftbefehl gegen syrischen Geheimdienstchef Jamil Hassan', www.ecchr.eu/fall/deutsche-justiz-erlaesst-haftbefehl-gegen-syrischen-geheimdienstchef-jamil-hassan/#case_case (accessed 20 September 2022)

European Center for Constitutional and Human Rights, *Universal Jurisdiction in Germany?*, www.ecchr.eu/fileadmin/Juristische_Dokumente/Report_Executive_Summary_FDLR_EN.pdf (accessed 23 September 2022)

Frank P and Schneider-Glockzin H, 'Terrorismus und Völkerstraftaten im bewaffneten Konflikt' [2017] *Neue Zeitschrift für Strafrecht* 6
Geneuss J, *Völkerrechtsverbrechen und Verfolgungsermessen* (Nomos 2013)
Hannich R, 'Justice in the Name of All' (2007) 13 *Zeitschrift für Internationale Strafrechtsdogmatik* 507
Jeßberger F, 'Implementing Kampala: The New Crime of Aggression under the German Code of Crimes against International Law', in Böse M and others (eds), *Justice Without Borders, Essays in Honour of Wolfgang Schomburg* (Brill 2018)
Jeßberger F, 'Towards a "Complementary Preparedness" Approach to Universal Jurisdiction – Recent Trends and Best Practices in the European Union', in European Parliament, *Universal Jurisdiction and International Crimes: Constraints and Best Practices* (2018)
Jessberger F and Epik A, 'Anmerkung' [2022] *Juristische Rundschau* 10
Johnson D, Schmolze B and Schlindwein S, *Tatort Kongo – Prozess in Deutschland, Die Verbrechen der ruandischen Miliz FDLR und der Versuch einer juristischen Aufarbeitung* (Ch Links Verlag 2016)
Kaleck W, 'Strafverfolgung nach dem Völkerstrafgesetzbuch: Ein kurzer Blick in die Zukunft – ein Kommentar zum Beitrag von Martin Böse', in Jeßberger F and Geneuss J (eds), *Zehn Jahre Völkerstrafgesetzbuch, Bilanz und Perspektiven eines "deutschen Völkerstrafrechts"* (Nomos 2013)
Kreß C, 'Nationale Umsetzung des Völkerstrafgesetzbuches' (2007) 13 *Zeitschrift für Internationale Strafrechtsdogmatik* 523
Langer M, 'Universal Jurisdiction is not Disappearing' (2015) 13 *Journal of International Criminal Justice* 246
Raim E, *Justiz zwischen Diktatur und Demokratie* (De Gruyter 2013)
Steinke R, *The Politics of International Criminal Justice: German Perspectives from Nuremberg to The Hague* (Hart Publishing 2012)
Von der Groeben C, 'Criminal Responsibility of German Soldiers in Afghanistan: The Case of Colonel Klein' (2010) 11 *German Law Journal*
Werle G, 'Völkerstrafrecht und deutsches Völkerstrafgesetzbuch' (2012) 67 *JuristenZeitung*
Werle G and Jeßberger F, 'International Criminal Justice is Coming Home: The New German Code of Crimes Against International Law' (2002) 13 *Criminal Law Forum*
Werle G and Jeßberger F, *Principles of International Criminal Law* (4th edn, OUP 2020)
Zorn K, 'Die Zentralstelle für die Bekämpfung von Kriegsverbrechen und weiteren Straftaten nach dem Völkerstrafgesetzbuch' (2017) 12 *Zeitschrift für internationale Strafrechtsdogmatik*

3.3 Shortcomings and Proposals for Reform of the *Völkerstrafgesetzbuch*

Leonie Steinl

1 Introduction

20 years after the entry into force of the *Völkerstrafgesetzbuch* (German Code of Crimes Against International Law), Germany is increasingly viewed as a champion of international criminal justice. The conviction of an ISIS-member for genocide against the Yazidi by the Higher Regional Court of Frankfurt in November 2021[1] and the conviction of two Syrian intelligence officers for crimes against humanity by the Higher Regional Court of Koblenz in January 2022[2] were celebrated worldwide as important steps towards justice for victims of the Syrian war. With a trial currently underway against a member of a Gambian paramilitary unit charged with crimes against humanity before the Higher Regional Court of Celle[3] and the German Federal Prosecutor's recent announcement of a structural investigation into crimes under international law committed in the war in Ukraine,[4] Germany seems to be nothing short of a model student of international criminal law.

Looking back at the development and enforcement of the *Völkerstrafgesetzbuch* over the past decades, the status quo seems to call for a (birthday) celebration. It is now clear that the Code is in fact not just a paper tiger. The initial state of "complete unpreparedness"[5] has passed and the number of investigations and trials has increased significantly over the past few years.[6] Yet, despite these successes, the 20th anniversary of the *Völkerstrafgesetzbuch* also presents an apt opportunity to reflect critically on the Code as well as its enforcement. The aim of this chapter is to highlight some of the shortcomings and proposals for reform that have been identified by the German international criminal law discourse with regard to the *Völkerstrafgesetzbuch* and its application.[7]

2 German International Criminal Law – A Modest Success Story

The German international criminal law project can be described as a path from high hopes to grim realities and, in its latest phase, modest successes. Modest successes because despite the increasing number of trials and convictions, German international criminal law is still being applied asymmetrically.

DOI: 10.4324/9781003320951-12

As Boris Burghardt has sketched out in his chapter, trials tend to focus on "smaller fish", often non-State actors, in many cases from the Global South, and invariably only cases with low political follow-up costs.[8] Hence, the familiar criticism of this particular form of selectivity in international criminal justice – previously voiced in particular from the perspective of post-colonial and TWAIL scholars[9] – applies not only to the ICC but also to German international criminal law.[10]

Scholars and practitioners have, however, not only criticised who is prosecuted for crimes under international law in Germany (and more importantly, who is not)[11] but also how these proceedings are conducted. The following section will give an overview of the critiques and corresponding reform proposals. These concern inter alia procedural questions (2.1), such as the lack of effective control of non-prosecution decisions (a) and the lack of documentation and communication about these proceedings (b). Further points of discussion relate to the effective exercise of victims' rights to participation and support (c) and the question of the need for a specialisation of the judiciary (d). A distinct and less prominent point of critique relates to the substantive side and calls for a reform of the crimes of sexual and reproductive violence in the *Völkerstrafgesetzbuch* (2.2).[12]

2.1 Shortcomings and Proposals for Reform from a Procedural Perspective

a Effective Control of Non-Prosecution Decisions

De lege lata, an effective control of non-prosecution decisions is only possible to a limited extent in Germany. Decisions under section 153f *Strafprozessordnung* (Code of Criminal Procedure) are subject to judicial review only with regard to the existence of the discretionary prerequisites for the facts and the questions of either non-use of discretion or exceeding the limit to arbitrariness in the exercise of discretion. The actual discretionary decision is, however, non-justiciable.

Scholars and practitioners have long criticised the lack of effective control of the Federal Prosecutor's discretionary decisions to abstain from prosecution.[13] Proposals for reform include subjecting the decision not to prosecute to judicial review through an expansion of the proceedings aimed at forcing the initiation of preliminary proceedings (so-called *Klageerzwingungsverfahren* regulated in section 172 of the *Strafprozessordnung*).[14] Another option would be to stipulate a judicial approval requirement as contained in section 153a/b of the *Strafprozessordnung*.[15]

The latter solution is preferable as it is modelled on the provisions of Article 53(3)(b) of the Rome Statute of the International Criminal Court. According to this provision, a non-investigation or non-prosecution decision by the Prosecutor of the ICC, which is not based on the jurisdiction or other considerations of admissibility but solely on the exercise of the Prosecutor's discretion, is only validated effective upon confirmation by the Pre-Trial

Chamber. Judicial approval is thus a prerequisite for refraining from criminal investigations and prosecutions on discretionary grounds.

Ensuring the effective control of non-prosecution decisions would hence not only be in line with the Rome Statute regulations, but it could also serve as an important means of making the asymmetrical application visible and possibly even counteracting it.

b Documentation and Communication

Documentation and communication both play a key role in international criminal justice proceedings. They not only do justice to the specific acknowledgement and truth-seeking function of international criminal trials but also contribute to the broader transitional justice objective of facilitating lasting peace.

Criminal law proceedings before the regional and higher regional courts in Germany, however, generally do not produce any records of the proceedings as regards the substance – be it written or audio-visual. Section 169 of the *Gerichtsverfassungsordnung* (Courts Constitution Act) stipulates that audio and television or radio recordings as well as audio and film recordings for the purpose of public presentation or publication of their contents are not permitted. The law makes an exception "for scientific and historical purposes ... if the proceedings are of outstanding contemporary historical significance for the Federal Republic of Germany".[16] Yet, in the *Al-Khatib* trial concerning crimes under international law in Syrian detention centres, the presiding judge interpreted this provision in a very narrow manner and declined an application to produce such a recording arguing that while the proceedings may be of outstanding contemporary historical significance for the Syrian victims, this was not the case for Germany. Further, the court declined to grant access to existing simultaneous translation into Arabic to the accredited Arabic-speaking journalists.[17] This could be viewed as evidence of a lack of understanding of the function and significance of international criminal justice proceedings.

The documentation of the course and content of the proceedings would not only correspond to the practice of international criminal courts, but also take into account the objectives of international criminal justice as mentioned above. The documentation should take place by means of audio-visual recording in order to make the proceedings as accessible as possible. Further, all press releases and court decisions should be translated into English and the languages spoken by those directly affected by the proceedings.

c Victims' Rights to Participation and Support

International criminal law recognises the importance of victim participation and support in the proceedings.[18] German criminal law allows for a certain mode of victim participation in the form of accessory prosecution (*Nebenklage*). As accessory prosecutors, victims do not merely serve as witnesses but can assert certain procedural rights, such as the right to be present, the right to request evidence, and the right to ask questions.[19] The *Strafprozessordnung* further grants victims access to psychosocial trial support (*Psychosoziale Prozessbegleitung*), which includes qualified support and the provision of information and assistance during the criminal proceedings with the aim of reducing the individual burden on the victims.

Yet, the right to accessory prosecution is only available to victims of certain crimes and the right to a publicly funded lawyer to represent the victim as an accessory Prosecutor is even more limited. This also applies to the right to psychosocial trial support. Further, the applicable provisions in sections 395 and 397a of the *Strafprozessordnung* do not explicitly refer to the provisions in the *Völkerstrafgesetzbuch* but include merely the "ordinary" German criminal law provisions of, eg, rape and assault. It therefore seems appropriate to explicitly include a reference to sections 6, 7 and 8 of the *Völkerstrafgesetzbuch* in the mentioned provisions and accordingly to amend section 406g of the *Strafprozessordnung*, regulating the right to psychosocial trial support, in order to underline their relevance in cases of crimes under international law.[20]

d Specialisation of the Judiciary?

While specialisation on the Prosecutor side has proven essential in ensuring the effective prosecution of crimes under international law,[21] there is no similar degree of specialisation in the judiciary. The *Oberlandesgerichte* (Higher Regional Courts) at the seat of the state level governments are competent to judge cases of crimes under international law according to section 120(1) no 8 *Gerichtsverfassungsgesetz*.

Hence, such proceedings not seldom present the first (and only) time in their careers that judges are confronted with the *Völkerstrafgesetzbuch* and the corresponding realities and difficulties of investigating mass atrocities in foreign macro-criminal contexts and of dealing with severely traumatised victims with different cultural backgrounds. This can render the proceedings challenging in the absence of a learning effect. This raises the question as to whether a more specialised system of jurisdiction for crimes under international law could be a step in the right direction.[22]

2.2 Shortcomings and Proposals for Reform from a Substantive Perspective – Blind Spots with Regard to Sexual and Reproductive Crimes

While the *Völkerstrafgesetzbuch* is often lauded for striking a balance between adhering fully to the provisions in the Rome Statute of the ICC as well as to the principle of legal certainty enshrined in the German Constitution, this is not the case when it comes to sexual and reproductive crimes under international law. The relevant *Völkerstrafgesetzbuch* provisions are in fact not entirely in line with the Rome Statute and respective ICC jurisprudence in this regard.

As such, there is no separate crime of sexual slavery in the *Völkerstrafgesetzbuch*. As a result, the specific harm of this crime is not adequately captured in German international criminal law.[23] Further, there is no offence of "other sexual acts of comparable gravity", potentially leaving gaps for violations such as forced nudity and forced abortion.[24] Moreover, the crime of forced pregnancy exists only in a significantly narrower context than the Rome Statue, requiring the intent to influence the ethnic composition of a population, whereas the Rome Statute also includes the intent to commit other serious violations of international law.[25] As the result, the recent conviction of Dominic Ongwen by the ICC for the crime of forced pregnancy would not meet the requirements of German international criminal law. This leads to considerable gaps, as forced pregnancies have often been documented in contexts of forced "marriages" and sexual slavery without an ethnic dimension. In fact, practically speaking, this seems to be the more relevant constellation.[26]

These findings support calls for a reform of the *Völkerstrafgesetzbuch* in order to ensure the effective prosecution of sexual and reproductive crimes under international law in Germany.[27]

3 Conclusion

The *Völkerstrafgesetzbuch* is coming of age. As a result, German international criminal law – just as international criminal law in general – is increasingly confronted with the expectation to deliver on its promise of accountability for crimes under international law – and with frustration it fails to do so. One of the main and lasting challenges is to ensure the even application of international criminal law. Facing this challenge is necessary if we want to see the (German) international criminal law project succeed. A procedural step in the right direction would be to enable the effective control of non-prosecution decisions in order to ensure that politically costly perpetrators of crimes under international law do not manage to escape responsibility as easily. Further, from a substantive perspective, amending the *Völkerstrafgesetzbuch* to include all crimes of sexual and reproductive violence codified in the ICC Statute would contribute towards facilitating equal access to justice for victims of gender-based violence. With the growing relevance of German international criminal law, there is also a growing demand to grapple with the identified shortcomings and take the corresponding reform proposals seriously. The 20th anniversary of the *Völkerstrafgesetzbuch* might present the perfect opportunity to do so.

Notes

1 See OLG Frankfurt am Main, Press Release (30 November 2021), available at: <https://ordentliche-gerichtsbarkeit.hessen.de/sites/ordentliche-gerichtsbarkeit.hessen.de/files/PI%2053ste1204120%20%28Urteil%20Taha%20Al%20J.%29_0.pdf> (accessed 20 September 2022). The judgment is now final, see Bundesgerichtshof, 30 November 2022, 3 StR 230/22.

2 See OLG Koblenz, Press Release (13 January 2022), available at: <https://olgko.justiz.rlp.de/de/startseite/detail/news/News/detail/lebenslange-haft-ua-wegen-verbrechens-gegen-die-menschlichkeit-und-wegen-mordes-urteil-gegen-ein-1/> (accessed 20 September 2022). The first judgment is final, see Bundesgerichtshof, 20 April 2022, 3 StR 367/21.

3 See OLG Celle, Press Release (24 March 2022), available at: <https://oberlandesgericht-celle.niedersachsen.de/startseite/aktuelles/presseinformationen/staatsschutzverfahren-wegen-des-verdachts-von-verbrechen-gegen-die-menschlichkeit-in-gambia-210231.html> (accessed 20 September 2022).

4 See Tagesschau, 'Bundesanwaltschaft prüft Ermittlungen wegen möglicher Kriegsverbrechen', 8 March 2022, available at: <www.tagesschau.de/inland/gesellschaft/bundesanwalt-ermittlungen-russland-101.html> (accessed 20 September 2022).

5 See the chapter by Boris Burghardt in this volume, Chapter 3.2, Between International Solidarity and "No Safe Haven" – The German Völkerstrafgesetzbuch 20 Years On.

6 See Gerhard Werle and Florian Jeßberger, *Münchener Kommentar zum StGB* (4th edn, Beck 2022) Einleitung VStGB, para 62ff.

7 After completion of this text, the Federal Ministry of Justice announced a "Key Issues Paper on the Further Development of International Criminal Law", containing a number of proposed changes to the Völkerstrafgesetzbuch, such as the expansion of the right to accessory prosecution and the inclusion of sexual slavery, see Bundesministerium der Justiz, 'Eckpunktepapier zur Fortentwicklung des Völkerstrafrechts', 23 February 2023, available at: <www.bmj.de/SharedDocs/Downloads/DE/News/PM/230223_Eckpunkte_VStGB.html;jsessionid=4D43C9BC4E99CA3A275D8BE92FCBAE5B.2_cid334?nn=6705022> (accessed 6 March 2023). It remains to be seen to what extent the suggested changes will be implemented.

8 See the chapter by Boris Burghardt in this volume (n 5).

9 See Leonie Steinl, 'Postkoloniale Kritik am Völkerstrafrecht', in Florian Jeßberger and others (eds), *Strafrecht und Systemunrecht: Festschrift für Gerhard Werle zum 70. Geburtstag* (Mohr Siebeck 2022) 295ff.

10 See Florian Jeßberger, 'Eine kurze Geschichte der Verfolgung von Völkerrechtsverbrechen in Deutschland', in: Wolfgang Kaleck and Patrick Kroker (eds), *Folter in Syrien vor Gericht* (Bundeszentrale für politische Bildung 2023 forthcoming) Florian Jeßberger and Julia Geneuss, 'Zum Stand des "deutschen Völkerstrafrechts" zehn Jahre nach Inkrafttreten des Völkerstrafgesetzbuchs', in Florian Jeßberger and Julia Geneuss (eds), *Zehn Jahre Völkerstrafgesetzbuch: Bilanz und Perspektiven eines "deutschen Völkerstrafrechts"* (Nomos 2013) 293ff; Wolfgang Kaleck, 'Von Doppelstandards im Völkerstrafrecht', in Florian Jeßberger and others (eds), *Strafrecht und Systemunrecht: Festschrift für Gerhard Werle zum 70. Geburtstag* (Mohr Siebeck 2022) 156ff.

11 See Jeßberger (n 9).

12 These critiques and proposals for reform are by no means exhaustive. For additional points of discussion see eg Jeßberger and Geneuss (n 9) 293ff; Gerhard Werle and Moritz Vormbaum, 'Völkerstrafverfahren in Deutschland' (2017) JuristenZeitung 12.

13 See Deutscher Bundestag Ausschuss für Recht und Verbraucherschutz, Wortprotokoll 18/96, available at: <www.bundestag.de/resource/blob/434554/7652b42e0d025e830fa990be110fefda/wortprotokoll-data.pdf>

(accessed 20 September 2022); Julia Geneuss, *Völkerrechtsverbrechen und Verfolgungsermessen: § 153f StPO im System völkerrechtlicher Strafrechtspflege* (Nomos 2013) 312ff, 340; Florian Jeßberger, 'Stellungnahme vor dem Ausschuss für Recht und Verbraucherschutz des Deutschen Bundestages am 25. April 2016', available at: <www.bundestag.de/resource/blob/420308/7cfc61bf4b2602136 5da44c32ae6cc09/jessberger-data.pdf> (accessed 20 September 2022); Gerhard Werle and Moritz Vormbaum, 'Völkerstrafverfahren in Deutschland' (2017) JuristenZeitung 12, 13.

14 See eg Kai Ambos, 'Völkerrechtliche Kernverbrechen, Weltrechtsprinzip und § 153f StPO' [2006] Neue Zeitschrift für Strafrecht 434, 438.

15 See eg Julia Geneuss, *Völkerrechtsverbrechen und Verfolgungsermessen: § 153f StPO im System völkerrechtlicher Strafrechtspflege* (Nomos 2013) 312ff, 340; Jeßberger, 'Stellungnahme vor dem Ausschuss für Recht und Verbraucherschutz des Deutschen Bundestages am 25. April 2016' (n 12); Werle and Vormbaum (n 12) 12, 13.

16 Translation by author.

17 See Susann Aboueldahab and Finn-Jasper Langmack, 'The End of the Al-Khatib Trial: A Historic Verdict and a Trial of Missed Opportunities', *Völkerrechtsblog*, 7 July 2022, available at: <https://voelkerrechtsblog.org/the-end-of-the-al-khatib-trial/> (accessed 20 September 2022).

18 See generally Luke Moffett, *Justice for Victims before the International Criminal Court* (Routledge 2014) passim.

19 See generally Anne-Katrin Wolf and Maja Werner, 'Victims' Rights Looking Good on Paper: How Criminal Prosecution in Germany Fails Victims of Sexual Violence' (2021) German Law Journal 800, 804ff.

20 See also Deutscher Bundestag Ausschuss für Recht und Verbraucherschutz, Wortprotokoll 18/96, available at: <www.bundestag.de/resource/blob/434554/7652b42e0d025e830fa990be110fefda/wortprotokoll-data.pdf> (accessed 20 September 2022).

21 Jeßberger and Geneuss (n 9) 293, 297.

22 Specialised jurisdictions already exist for offences committed abroad at sea and offences committed abroad by soldiers, as regulated in *Strafprozessordnung*, ss 10a and 11a.

23 See Tanja Altunjan and Leonie Steinl, 'Zum Schutz der sexuellen und reproduktiven Selbstbestimmung: Aktuelle Entwicklungen und Reformbedarf im Völkerstrafgesetzbuch' (2021) 12(3) Rechtswissenschaft 335, 361ff. See also Aziz Epik and Leonie Steinl, 'Shortcomings of a Showpiece: Reflections on the Need for Reform of the German Code of Crimes Against International Law and Challenges for Its Application', (2023) *Journal of International Criminal Justice* (forthcoming).

24 See Altunjan and Steinl (n 22) 352ff.

25 See ibid 348ff. See generally Tanja Altunjan, *Reproductive Violence and International Criminal Law* (Springer/Asser 2021) passim.

26 See Altunjan and Steinl (n 22) 349.

27 Furthermore, it should be noted that a recent fundamental reform of the offences of sexual violence in the German Criminal Code already suggest a reform of the *Völkerstrafgesetzbuch* as the central terms and concept on which it relies have changed significantly, raising a number of complex interpretation questions. See ibid 339ff.

Selected Bibliography

Aboueldahab S and Langmack F-J, 'The End of the Al-Khatib Trial: A Historic Verdict and a Trial of Missed Opportunities', Völkerrechtsblog, 7 July 2022, available at: <https://voelkerrechtsblog.org/the-end-of-the-al-khatib-trial/> (accessed 20 September 2022)

Altunjan T and Steinl L, 'Zum Schutz der sexuellen und reproduktiven Selbstbestimmung: Aktuelle Entwicklungen und Reformbedarf im Völkerstrafgesetzbuch' (2021) 12(3) *Rechtswissenschaft* 335

Altunjan T, *Reproductive Violence and International Criminal Law* (Springer/Asser 2021)

Ambos K, 'Völkerrechtliche Kernverbrechen, Weltrechtsprinzip und § 153f StPO' (2006) *Neue Zeitschrift für Strafrecht* 434

Epik A and Steinl L, 'Shortcomings of a Showpiece: Reflections on the Need for Reform of the German Code of Crimes Against International Law and Challenges for Its Application' (2023) *Journal of International Criminal Justice* (forthcoming)

Geneuss J, *Völkerrechtsverbrechen und Verfolgungsermessen: § 153f StPO im System völkerrechtlicher Strafrechtspflege* (Nomos 2013)

Jeßberger F, 'Eine kurze Geschichte der Verfolgung von Völkerrechtsverbrechen in Deutschland', in Wolfgang Kaleck und Patrick Kroker (eds), *Folter in Syrien vor Gericht* (Bundeszentrale für politische Bildung 2023 forthcoming)

Jeßberger F and Geneuss J, 'Zum Stand des "deutschen Völkerstrafrechts" zehn Jahre nach Inkrafttreten des Völkerstrafgesetzbuchs', in Florian Jeßberger and Julia Geneuss (eds), *Zehn Jahre Völkerstrafgesetzbuch: Bilanz und Perspektiven eines "deutschen Völkerstrafrechts"* (Nomos 2013) 293

Jeßberger F, Stellungnahme vor dem Ausschuss für Recht und Verbraucherschutz des Deutschen Bundestages am 25. April 2016, available at: <www.bundestag.de/resource/blob/420308/7cfc61bf4b26021365da44c32ae6cc09/jessberger-data.pdf> (accessed 20 September 2022)

Kaleck W, 'Von Doppelstandards im Völkerstrafrecht', in Florian Jeßberger and others (eds), *Strafrecht und Systemunrecht: Festschrift für Gerhard Werle zum 70. Geburtstag* (Mohr Siebeck 2022) 156

Steinl L, 'Postkoloniale Kritik am Völkerstrafrecht', in Florian Jeßberger and others (eds), *Strafrecht und Systemunrecht: Festschrift für Gerhard Werle zum 70. Geburtstag* (Mohr Siebeck 2022) 295

Werle G and Jeßberger F, 'Einleitung VStGB', in *Münchener Kommentar zum StGB* (4th edn, Beck 2022)

Werle G and Vormbaum M, 'Völkerstrafverfahren in Deutschland' (2017) *JuristenZeitung* 12

3.4 Domesticating the ICC Statute

A global perspective

Antonio Coco

1 Introduction

In early 2022, Italy announced the constitution of an expert Commission in charge of drawing a national "code of international crimes", with the aim of enacting domestic legislation which would ensure the criminal repression of conducts criminalised in international law, like those listed and defined in the Rome Statute of the International Criminal Court (ICC).[1] Italy's move is not a novelty, since several States have engaged in similar initiatives in the past, in different forms.[2] The phenomenon of adopting national criminal legislation which mirrors or implements international legal provisions can be labelled as "domestication".[3] In this short contribution, I aim to clarify whether States are in fact obliged under international law to put in place such domestication initiatives with respect to the ICC Statute specifically, and whether they face any constraints in this effort. In so doing, I will offer examples of ICC Statute "domestication" practices, reflecting on their compatibility with international law, on their strengths and on their weaknesses. It is hoped that such analysis may be of assistance for States and individuals engaged in comparable initiatives currently or in the future.

At the heart of the domestication issue lie the rules on the relationship between international law and domestic law. In this context, one must remember that the ICC Statute does not exist in isolation: States Parties to the ICC are bound not only by the Statute, but also by other applicable rules of treaty and customary international law, which may steer State practice in the implementation of the ICC Statute and international criminal law more in general. The ICC Statute itself, moreover, is an international treaty: thus, rules and principles of international law of treaties may also impact on practices of domestication.

2 The lack of a general obligation to "domesticate" the ICC Statute

There is no general obligation for States Parties to enact domestic legislation which implements or conforms to provisions of the ICC Statute – including those concerning the crimes under ICC jurisdiction.[4] Should States Parties

DOI: 10.4324/9781003320951-13

decide to embark on such initiatives, they would still enjoy a good measure of discretion in deciding how to formulate the relevant legislation.

This is not to say that specific ICC Statute provisions do not demand domestic implementation. If States Parties are to comply with their duty to cooperate fully with the Court (Article 86), pursuant Article 88 of the ICC Statute, they must ensure that national law makes appropriate procedures available under their national law.[5] The ICC Statute also provides that each State Party must make offences against the administration of justice referred to in Article 70 punishable under national law, when committed on that State's territory, or by one of its nationals.[6]

Moreover, all States (not necessarily just States Parties) may want to align certain provisions of national legislation to the standards provided in the ICC Statute, for reasons of convenience. For instance, to ensure that evidence collected by national authorities can be transferred to and used before the ICC, States must ensure that national provisions on rights of suspects during investigations guarantee the same level of protection as those contained in the Statute. This is the avenue followed, inter alia, by the United Kingdom (UK).[7]

And, of course, it is in States' interests to make sure that national criminal law allows for the investigation and prosecution of cases involving conduct which is also under the jurisdiction of the ICC, if they want to be the authority actually exercising jurisdiction over such cases: if not – in the event that the ICC is seeking to exercise its own jurisdiction over the same case – the case may be found to be admissible due to the inability of the State in question to carry out the investigation or prosecution in accordance with Article 17 ICC Statute.[8] One may wonder whether it could be possible to rely on customary international law for national prosecutions in the absence of relevant domestic legislation, without the need to embark into a legislative "domestication" process. However, reliance on customary international law alone may at times be contrary to relevant constitutional and human rights protections, including the principle of legality.[9]

The lack of a general obligation to "domesticate", of course, does not imply that the extent of States Parties' discretion is unfettered. In fact, considering that the ICC Statute is a treaty, rules of international law of treaties must guide States Parties when adopting national legislation in matters of relevance to the Statute. At least three rules come to mind in this respect. First – pursuant to the rule enshrined in Article 18 of the Vienna Convention on the Law of Treaties (VCLT), which according to some has achieved customary status and would, thus, apply to the ICC Statute[10] – until the Statute enters into force for a particular State who has signed it or otherwise expressed its consent to be bound, such State is obliged not to defeat the treaty's object and purpose with its own conduct. Secondly, States Parties to the ICC Statute must behave in good faith in the performance of the treaty, in accordance with a rule of customary nature reflected in Article 26 VLCT.[11] Thirdly, even at the stage of domestic implementation, a treaty must be interpreted in good faith in accordance with the ordinary meaning to be given to the terms of the treaty in their context and in the light of its object and purpose, in line with customary rules on treaty interpretation contained in Article 31 VCLT.[12] Considering these three rules together, it appears that any domestication initiative must be carried out in good faith and be compatible with the object and purpose of the ICC Statute. Whilst being conscious that it would be an extreme case, of which luckily I could find no example in practice, it could be a violation of these rules if a State Party adopted a crime definition that manifestly abuses the labels used in the Statute to the point that it may actually favour the commission of "unimaginable atrocities".[13] For instance, this could happen if the definition of crimes against humanity is maliciously extended to include forms of non-violent political dissent and abused to effectively deprive certain groups of their rights in a discriminatory way – what could effectively amount to the crime against humanity of persecution.

Moreover, any domestication effort must be consistent with at least two other sets of rules of international law. First, the grounds upon which the relevant State establishes and will exercise its own national criminal jurisdiction need to be consistent with applicable rules of treaty and customary law, for instance those allowing for the exercise of jurisdiction over persons who are not nationals of the proceeding State and who did not commit a crime on the territory of such State.[14] Second, national criminal provisions must abide by the principle of legality as recognised under international human rights law[15] and must, thus and inter alia, be non-retroactive, accessible and foreseeable.[16]

3 Duties to adopt domestic legislation to ensure the repression of international crimes, beyond the ICC Statute

Even though the ICC Statute itself does not provide for an obligation to enact implementing domestic legislation, obligations to enact such legislation for crimes under the jurisdiction of the ICC may derive from other international treaties.

With respect to the crime of genocide, listed and defined in Article 6 of the ICC Statute, such obligation descends from the 1948 Genocide Convention, Article V, establishing that "The Contracting Parties undertake to enact, in accordance with their respective Constitutions, the necessary legislation to give effect to the provisions of the present Convention, and, in particular, to provide effective penalties for persons guilty of genocide or any of the other acts enumerated in article III" – namely: conspiracy to commit genocide; direct and public incitement to commit genocide; attempt to commit genocide; complicity in genocide. Considering the formulation of Article V ("persons guilty of genocide") it appears that domestic legislation is required to maintain the label of genocide for the relevant offence: proscribing the relevant conduct under a different criminal label would not be enough.

States Parties to the ICC also have an obligation to "enact any legislation necessary to provide effective penal sanctions for persons committing, or ordering to be committed, any of the grave breaches"[17] of the 1949 Geneva Conventions, a category of war crimes which is the object of Article 8(2)(a) of the ICC Statute. In this case, unlike for genocide, there seems to be no explicit requirement that the relevant domestic legislation resorts to the crime label of "war crimes" or "grave breaches": what matters is that "effective penal sanctions" are stipulated in domestic legislation.[18] Of note, Article 8 ICC Statute provides a list of war crimes which is much longer than those amounting to grave breaches of the 1949 Geneva Conventions, for which technically there is thus no treaty obligation to adopt domestic legislation. Nonetheless, domestic legislation covering *all* war crimes may be necessary as a matter of customary international law. According to the study of customary international humanitarian law authored by the International Committee of the Red Cross (ICRC), Rule 158, states must indeed "investigate war crimes allegedly committed by their nationals or armed forces, or on their territory, and, if appropriate, prosecute the suspects. They must also investigate other war crimes over which they have jurisdiction and, if appropriate, prosecute the suspects."[19] The only way for States to comply with such customary obligations is to equip themselves with adequate national law. Furthermore, it must be noted that the obligation to enact *effective* penal sanctions arguably entails the need to ensure that applicable domestic legislation excludes statutes of limitations, the defence of superior orders and amnesties for grave breaches of the Geneva Conventions.[20]

Crimes against humanity, as is well known, are not the subject of any comprehensive treaty regime at the time of writing. Should such a treaty be adopted and enter into force, an obligation to enact relevant domestic legislation could be included there. For instance, the United Nations International Law Commission's Draft Articles on Crimes against Humanity, which could be the starting point for a comprehensive treaty on the subject, provide that each State "shall take the necessary measures to ensure that crimes against humanity constitute offences under its criminal law".[21] Moreover, despite the lack of a comprehensive treaty, conduct which could amount to specific crimes against humanity – or to other crimes under the ICC jurisdiction – has been the object of specific treaties which establish an obligation to enact relevant domestic criminal legislation. Such is the case, for instance, of the international conventions against apartheid, torture and enforced disappearance.[22]

With respect to the crime of aggression, finally, no discrete obligation to enact domestic legislation appears to exist, even though several States have implemented such legislation.[23]

Of note, the ICC Statute Preamble recalls that "it is the duty of every state to exercise its criminal jurisdiction over those responsible for international crimes",[24] implying the need to adopt relevant national legislation covering conduct which would amount to international crimes,[25] including crimes against humanity and the crime of aggression, even if not necessarily under those criminal labels.

4 Routes towards "domestication" of the ICC Statute

States, in light of the above, must find a balance when it comes to domestication of the ICC Statute: on one side, they have obligations to enact national legislation implementing certain parts of the Statute, and incentives to pass legislation covering a wider amount of issues than they are legally obliged to; on the other, they enjoy a measure of discretion as to how to proceed to domestication, albeit with the constraints posed inter alia by the law of treaties, the rules on jurisdiction, and international human rights law. This may result in different routes leading to "domestication", of which it is possible to identify at least four – often pursued not alternatively to each other but "mixing and matching" between them.

First, an ICC State Party may decide not to adopt specific legislation to incorporate ICC Statute provisions, believing that existing domestic criminal law is already sufficient to deal with the relevant issues. This is the avenue chosen, for instance, by the UK with respect to offences against the administration of justice[26] and to the rules on the general part of criminal law, including modes of liability and defences.[27] The advantage of this approach is that no additional legislation is needed, and the system is simply assessed to be already sufficiently equipped to deal with the issues that may arise in relation to the crimes in question. However, as a disadvantage, some elements of the applicable domestic law may not fully reflect the distinct nature and gravity of the crimes under the ICC jurisdiction. Moreover, certain defences recognised in the ICC Statute (for instance duress as a defence to murder or superior orders) may not be available to defendants in the relevant domestic law, resulting in a disparity of treatment between the ICC and the domestic system in question.[28]

Secondly, an ICC State Party may decide to enact domestic legislation that makes a simple reference, a *renvoi*, to the relevant ICC Statute provisions, as done by the UK with respect to the definition of crimes listed in Article 5 of the ICC Statute.[29] Such form of incorporation has the advantage of being relatively straightforward, and of keeping national legislation automatically up to date with any amendments to the original ICC Statute wording. Nonetheless, it may make it difficult to provide for differentiated penalties for the long list of crimes – often very different from each other in character and gravity – to which reference is made. Moreover, it may engender issues of compatibility with already existing domestic law.[30] Considering how the law of war crimes is intrinsically related to international humanitarian law, furthermore, national courts of States choosing this form of domestication will need to consider the existence of any reservations or declarations made by the State in question to the relevant treaties.[31]

Thirdly, a State Party to the ICC Statute may decide to replicate *verbatim* the relevant provisions of the ICC Statute into its own national legislation, as for instance Switzerland did with respect to crimes against humanity in Article 264a of its own Criminal Code. Such an approach may be seen as one that maximises accessibility and foreseeability for individuals, addressing concerns or the respect of the principle of legality: individuals would be able to consult the relevant legal provisions in *both* national law and the ICC Statute, doubling the chances for them to acquire the relevant knowledge. Nevertheless, it may lead to the introduction, in national law, of language and offence structures which are not commonly used and may, thus, make it more difficult to fully comprehend their meaning.

Fourthly and finally, a State Party to the ICC Statute may domesticate its provisions by adopting legislation which partly reflects the ICC Statute language, but also presents modifications aimed to adapt that language to the specificities of the national legal system, or that are aimed at addressing specific national policies and strategies.[32] Modifications, in this respect, may take many different shapes. For example, the definition of protected groups for the purposes of the crime of genocide may be expanded, inter alia by adding social and political groups[33] or "groups defined by any other arbitrary criterion".[34] Or, as another example, war crimes originally conceived for international armed conflict may be made equally criminal if carried out in a non-international armed conflict.[35] Moreover, new offences related to core international crimes may be created, for instance by extending the offence of incitement not only to genocide but also to crimes against humanity and war crimes,[36] or by punishing the imposition of distinctive signs upon members of a group protected against genocide, especially if such signs are imposed with a view to prepare the partial or total destruction of the group.[37] Of course, it may happen that a modification effectively makes the definition of the crimes in question more demanding: for instance, the United States – even though not a party to the ICC Statute – adopted a definition of genocide which requires mental harm to amount to permanent impairment of mental faculties, arguably more than what would be required by the case law of the ICC and other international criminal tribunals.[38]

The pros of this "tailored implementation" approach include a better chance to coordinate the ICC Statute rules with the peculiarities of the national legal system in which they are transplanted, and an enticing possibility to drive changes in customary international criminal law – which, after all, may well diverge from the ICC Statute. A disadvantage of this approach, on the other side, would be that if crime definitions are made broader, this could result in a dilution of the stigma usually associated with the crime in question (for instance, for genocide). As another weakness of such an approach, issues of judicial cooperation may arise if different definitions of the same crime exist across different national jurisdictions. Modifying crime definitions in domestic law, moreover, may come with certain knock-on effects, as they relate inter alia to the granting of refugee status,[39] or to the eligibility for certain offices, since some vetting processes may exclude personnel who have engaged in international crimes.

Regarding forms by which a domestication initiative is carried out, this can be done by either a single comprehensive legislative act, or by amending existing national legislation gradually. The latter solution could be brought about in different moments, ensuring quicker action on more urgent matters.[40] The former solution, instead, has the advantage of avoiding fragmentation and ensuring consistency.[41]

5 Conclusion

This short contribution has sought to highlight that, whilst the ICC Statute itself does not provide for a general obligation to enact national implementing legislation, such legislation is often demanded by other rules of conventional and customary international law, including rules on war crimes, genocide, and certain forms of conduct which may amount to crimes against humanity. And, whilst States that decide to adopt national legislation to implement the ICC Statute enjoy discretion on the specific avenue to follow, such discretion is limited by the operation of rules of the international law of treaties, of those on the establishment and exercise of jurisdiction, and of international human rights law. The legal framework they create is the basis for assessing the lawfulness of any past initiative of "domestication" of the ICC Statute, and for guiding any present or future such initiatives.

Notes

1 Italy, Ministry of Justice, Decree 22 March 2022, *Commissione per l'elaborazione di un progetto di Codice dei Crimini internazionali* ('Commission on the Elaboration of a Draft Code of International Crimes'), at <www.giustizia.it/giustizia/it/mg_1_8_1.page?contentId=SDC372746&previsiousPage=mg_1_36_0> (visited 2 May 2022).

2 For instance, see Germany, *Völkerstrafgesetzbuch* ('Code of Crimes against International Law'), 26 June 2002 (Federal Law Gazette I, p 2254), as last amended by Art 1 of the Act of 22 December 2016 (Federal Law Gazette I, p 3150); or the relevant provisions in the implementing legislation of, inter alia, the United Kingdom, *International Criminal Court Act 2001* (c 17) ('UK ICC Act 2001'); South Africa, *Implementation of the Rome Statute of the International Criminal Court Act 27 of 2002* (Gazette 23761 of 16 August 2002); Uganda, *The International Criminal Court Act 2010*, Acts Supplement n 6 to the Uganda Gazette n 39, Col CIII, 25 June 2010.

3 As is done, for instance, by Lisa J Laplante, 'The Domestication of International Criminal Law: A Proposal for Expanding the International Criminal Court's Sphere of Influence' (2010) 43 John Marshall Law Review 635.

4 Gerhard Werle and Florian Jeßberger, *Principles of International Criminal Law* (OUP 2020) 181, § 464.

5 See also Olympia Bekou and Katerina Katsimardou Miariti, *Implementing the Rome Statute of the International Criminal Court* (Case Matrix Network, Centre for International Law Research and Policy 2017) 81, 84 <www.legal-tools.org/doc/e05157/>.

6 ICCSt, Art 70(4).

7 UK ICC Act 2001, ss 28, 29 and 30 on questioning and taking or production of evidence. Robert Cryer, 'Implementation of the Criminal Court Statute in England and Wales' (2002) 51 International & Comparative Law Quarterly 733, 735.

8 In this sense, among others, Jann K Kleffner, 'The Impact of Complementarity on National Implementation of Substantive International Criminal Law' (2003) 1 Journal of International Criminal Justice 86, 88–89; Julio Bacio Terracino, 'National Implementation of ICC Crimes: Impact on National Jurisdictions and the ICC' (2007) 5 *Journal of International Criminal Justice* 421, 435–437; Olympia Bekou, 'Crimes at Crossroads: Incorporating International Crimes at the National Level' (2012) 10 Journal of International Criminal Justice 677, 678–679.

9 For instance, resort to customary international law alone was implicitly excluded by the UK House of Lords in *R v Bow Street Stipendiary Magistrate, ex parte Pinochet Ugarte* [No3] [1999] 2 WLR 827. Lord Millet, at 912, refers to this as the opinion of his fellow lord justices. The position is critiqued in Roger O'Keefe, 'Customary International Crimes in English Courts' (2002) 72 British Yearbook of International Law 293. However, in *R v Jones* [2006] UKHL 16, Lord Bingham, whilst rejecting that a crime recognised in customary international law may be automatically assimilated into domestic criminal law (§ 23), considered that such assimilation has already occurred, in the United Kingdom, for war crimes (§ 22). See also the opinion of Lord Hoffmann, § 59. Of relevance, s 65A of the UK ICC Act 2001 provides that war crimes, crimes against humanity, and genocide are, retroactively, offences in the law of England and Wales, and of Northern Ireland, from 1 January 1991. The date was chosen because, signposting the beginning of the temporal jurisdiction of the International Criminal Tribunal for the former Yugoslavia, it gives a strong hint that such offences had already been criminalised in international law. Robert Cryer and Paul David Mora, 'The Coroners and Justice Act 2009 and International Criminal Law: Backing into the Future?' (2010) 59 International & Comparative Law Quarterly 803, 805. However, s 65B also provides that crimes against humanity and war crimes committed in non-international armed conflict before the entry into force of the UK ICC Act 2001 will be considered to be offences in the relevant domestic law only if 'at the time the act constituting that crime was committed, the act amounted in the circumstances to a criminal offence under international law'. Similarly, a reference to customary law has been incorporated in the *Canadian Crimes Against Humanity and War Crimes Act*, SC 2000, c 24, ss 4(3), 6(3) and 7(5).

10 Hinting that the provision possesses customary status, Dino Kritsiotis, 'The Object and Purpose of a Treaty's Object and Purpose', in Michael J Bowman and Dino Kritsiotis (eds), *Conceptual and Contextual Perspectives on the Modern Law of Treaties* (Cambridge University Press 2018) 271–272. See also Laurence Boisson de Chazournes, Anne-Marie La Rosa and Makane Moise Mbengue, 'Article 18 – Obligation Not to Defeat the Object and Purpose of a Treaty Prior to Its Entry into Force', in Olivier Corten and Pierre Klein (eds), *The Vienna Conventions on the Law of Treaties: A Commentary*, vol I (OUP 2011) 372–383. At 382–383, the authors conclude: "Article 18 reflects a principle of international law to which

States consider themselves bound either by an obligation following from the signature of a treaty or by an existing obligation in general international law independently of any signature or ratification of a legal instrument. It is, however, true that the outlines of the principle are not yet well-defined".

11 As convincingly concluded by Jean Salmon, 'Article 26 – Pacta Sunt Servanda', in Corten and Klein (eds), ibid 661–682.

12 On the customary nature of such provision see, inter alia, *Territorial Dispute (Libyan Arab Jamahiriya/Chad)*, Judgment, ICJ Reports 1994, p 6, at pp 21–22, § 41; and Jean-Marc Sorel and Valérie Boré Eveno, 'Article 31 – General Rule of Interpretation', in Corten and Klein (eds), ibid 817–823.

13 ICCSt, Preamble, § 2.

14 For instance, s 68 of UK ICC Act 2001 seems to be a provision of this kind. For an overview of the rules concerning the exercise of jurisdiction based on grounds other than territoriality, see Menno Kamminga, 'Extraterritoriality', *Max Planck Encyclopaedia of Public International Law* (OUP 2020) <https://opil.ouplaw.com/view/10.1093/law:epil/9780199231690/law-9780199231690-e1040> (accessed 3 May 2022).

15 For example International Covenant on Civil and Political Rights, Art 15; European Convention on Human Rights, Art 7; African Charter of Human and Peoples' Rights, Art 7(2); American Convention on Human Rights, Art 9.

16 Kenneth S Gallant, *The Principle of Legality in International and Comparative Criminal Law* (Cambridge University Press 2009) 359; Talita de Souza Dias, 'Accessibility and Foreseeability in the Application of the Principle of Legality under General International Law: A Time for Revision?' (2019) 19 Human Rights Law Review 649. The European Court of Human Rights has stressed this point, inter alia, in *Sunday Times v United Kingdom* App no 6538/74 (26 April 1979) [49]; *Korbely v Hungary* App no 9174/02 (19 September 2008) [70]; *Kononov v Latvia* App no 36376/04 (17 May 2010) [185].

17 Convention (I) for the Amelioration of the Condition of the Wounded and Sick in Armed Forces in the Field, Geneva, 12 August 1949, Art 49; Convention (II) for the Amelioration of the Condition of Wounded, Sick and Shipwrecked Members of Armed Forces at Sea, Geneva, 12 August 1949, Art 50; Convention (III) relative to the Treatment of Prisoners of War, Geneva, 12 August 1949, Art 129; Convention (IV) relative to the Protection of Civilian Persons in Time of War, Geneva, 12 August 1949, Art 146.

18 Often, what matters is not the exact charge under which an internationally criminalised conduct is prosecuted domestically, but the adequacy of domestic law provisions to reflect the nature and gravity of the conduct and to avoid impunity for it. This is the direction chosen by the ICC itself, for instance when making its complementarity assessment. See, eg, Decision on the admissibility of the case against Saif Al-Islam Gaddafi, *Gaddafi* (ICC-01/11-01/11-344-Red), Pre-Trial Chamber I, 31 May 2013, §§ 85–88, explaining that the legal characterisation is not important if the criminal proceedings cover the same conduct. See also Werle and Jeßberger (n 4) 181, § 464, fn 1125. Expressing scepticism on this point, Knut Dörmann and Robin Geiβ, 'The Implementation of Grave Breaches into Domestic Legal Orders' (2009) 7 Journal of International Criminal Justice 703, 710.

19 International Committee of the Red Cross (ICRC), *IHL Database – Customary IHL*, Rule 158, at https://ihl-databases.icrc.org/customary-ihl/eng/docs/v1_rul_rule158 (visited 2 May 2022).

20 ICRC, *Updated Commentary on the Third Geneva Convention* (2020), Art 129, § 5111.

21 'Draft articles on Prevention and Punishment of Crimes Against Humanity', *Yearbook of the International Law Commission 2019*, vol II (part two), Art 6.

22 International Convention on the Suppression and Punishment of the Crime of Apartheid, New York, 30 November 1973, Art 4; Convention against Torture and Other Cruel, Inhuman or Degrading Treatment or Punishment, New York, 10 December 1984, Art 4; International Convention for the Protection of All Persons from Enforced Disappearance, New York, 20 December 2006, Art 4.

23 Some examples, including Luxembourg, are discussed in Bekou and Katsimardou Miariti (n 5) 45–46; Meagan Wong, 'Germany and Botswana Ratify the Kampala Amendments on the Crime of Aggression: 7 Ratifications, 23 More Ratifications to Go!', *EJIL: Talk!*, 10 June 2013, <www.ejiltalk.org/germany-and-botswana-ratify-the-kampala-amendments-on-the-crime-of-aggression-7-ratifications-23-more-ratifications-to-go/> (accessed 3 May 2022).

24 ICCSt, Preamble, § 6.

25 Kleffner (n 8) 92.

26 UK ICC Act, s 54, which, however, clarifies what domestic provisions are applicable.

27 UK ICC Act, s 56, providing that, in determining whether an offence has been committed, the court shall apply the relevant principles of the law of England and Wales. However, new rules are adopted to accommodate the definition provided in the ICC Act of intent for offences (s 66, corresponding to ICC Statute, Art 30) and for superior responsibility (s 65, corresponding to ICC Statute, Art 28).

28 As noted in Robert Cryer and Olympia Bekou, 'International Crimes and ICC Cooperation in England and Wales' (2007) 5 Journal of International Criminal Justice 441, 448–449.

29 UK ICC Act, ss 50–51.

30 For instance, in the United Kingdom, certain war crimes had already been introduced in domestic legislation by effect of the Geneva Conventions Act, s 1(A)(b): how they relate to the war crimes listed and defined in the ICC law is to be seen.

31 For instance, see the UK ICC Act, s 50(4).

32 Werle and Jeßberger (n 4) 184, § 474.

33 Swiss Criminal Code, Art 264.

34 '*groupe déterminé à partir de tout autre critère arbitraire*': French Criminal Code, Art 211-1 (own translation).

35 As done by Switzerland (Criminal Code, Art 264b and Military Criminal Code, Art 110) if the nature of the offence does not exclude it ('*si la nature de l'infraction ne l'exclut pas*').

36 UK ICC Act, s 55(1)(b). Cryer and Bekou (n 28) 446.

37 As done by Italy not when implementing the ICC Statute, but when adopting national legislation enacting the crime of genocide: Law no 962, 9 October 1967, Art 6.

38 18 US Code, § 1091(a)(3). See Bekou (n 9) 682.

39 For instance, in application of the 1951 Refugee Convention, Art 2(F), establishing that the provisions of the convention do not apply to persons for whom there are serious reasons for considering that "they have committed a crime against peace, a war crime, or a crime against humanity, as defined in the international instruments drawn up to make provision in respect of such crimes".

40 For instance, Switzerland first passed legislation on cooperation with ICC (*Loi fédérale sur la coopération avec la Cour pénale internationale*, RO 2002 1493, 22 June 2001), then modified the substantive criminal law about a decade later (*Loi fédérale portant modification de lois fédérales en vue de la mise en œuvre du Statut de Rome de la Cour pénale internationale*, RO 2010 4963, 18 June 2010).

41 A good example being the UK ICC Act 2001.

Selected bibliography

Bacio Terracino J, 'National Implementation of ICC Crimes: Impact on National Jurisdictions and the ICC' (2007) 5 *Journal of International Criminal Justice* 421

Bekou O, 'Crimes at Crossroads: Incorporating International Crimes at the National Level' (2012) 10 *Journal of International Criminal Justice* 677

Bekou O and Katsimardou Miariti K, *Implementing the Rome Statute of the International Criminal Court* (Case Matrix Network, Centre for International Law Research and Policy 2017) <www.legal-tools.org/doc/e05157/>

Boisson de Chazournes L, La Rosa A-M and Mbengue MM, 'Article 18 – Obligation Not to Defeat the Object and Purpose of a Treaty Prior to Its Entry into Force', in Olivier Corten and Pierre Klein (eds), *The Vienna Conventions on the Law of Treaties: A Commentary*, vol I (Oxford University Press 2011)

Cryer R, 'Implementation of the Criminal Court Statute in England and Wales' (2002) 51 *International & Comparative Law Quarterly* 733

Cryer R and Bekou O, 'International Crimes and ICC Cooperation in England and Wales' (2007) 5 *Journal of International Criminal Justice* 441

Cryer R and Mora PD, 'The Coroners and Justice Act 2009 and International Criminal Law: Backing into the Future?' (2010) 59 *International & Comparative Law Quarterly* 803

de Souza Dias T, 'Accessibility and Foreseeability in the Application of the Principle of Legality under General International Law: A Time for Revision?' (2019) 19 *Human Rights Law Review* 649

Dörmann K and Geiβ R, 'The Implementation of Grave Breaches into Domestic Legal Orders' (2009) 7 *Journal of International Criminal Justice* 703

Gallant KS, *The Principle of Legality in International and Comparative Criminal Law* (Cambridge University Press 2009)

Kamminga M, 'Extraterritoriality', *Max Planck Encyclopaedia of Public International Law* (Oxford University Press 2020) <https://opil.ouplaw.com/view/10.1093/law:epil/9780199231690/law-9780199231690-e1040> (accessed 3 May 2022)

Kleffner JK, 'The Impact of Complementarity on National Implementation of Substantive International Criminal Law' (2003) 1 *Journal of International Criminal Justice* 86

Kritsiotis D, 'The Object and Purpose of a Treaty's Object and Purpose', in Michael J Bowman and Dino Kritsiotis (eds), *Conceptual and Contextual Perspectives on the Modern Law of Treaties* (Cambridge University Press 2018)

Laplante LJ, 'The Domestication of International Criminal Law: A Proposal for Expanding the International Criminal Court's Sphere of Influence' (2010) 43 *John Marshall Law Review* 635

O'Keefe R, 'Customary International Crimes in English Courts' (2002) 72 *British Yearbook of International Law* 293

Salmon J, 'Article 26 – Pacta Sunt Servanda', in Olivier Corten and Pierre Klein (eds), *The Vienna Conventions on the Law of Treaties: A Commentary*, vol I (Oxford University Press 2011)

Sorel J-M and Boré Eveno V, 'Article 31 – General Rule of Interpretation', in Olivier Corten and Pierre Klein (eds), *The Vienna Conventions on the Law of Treaties: A Commentary*, vol I (Oxford University Press 2011)

Werle G and Jeßberger F, *Principles of International Criminal Law* (Oxford University Press 2020)

Wong M, 'Germany and Botswana Ratify the Kampala Amendments on the Crime of Aggression: 7 Ratifications, 23 More Ratifications to Go!', *EJIL: Talk!*, 10 June 2013, <www.ejiltalk.org/germany-and-botswana-ratify-the-kampala-amendments-on-the-crime-of-aggression-7-ratifications-23-more-ratifications-to-go/> (accessed 3 May 2022)

3.5 Other Examples of Domestic Implementation of the ICC Statute

Kalika Mehta

1 Introduction

The ICC Statute envisages a decentralised administration of justice where the International Criminal Court (ICC) is complementary to the national criminal jurisdictions, hence referred to as the court of last resort.[1] This preference of indirect (domestic) enforcement of international criminal law makes domestic implementation of the ICC Statute an important element of the international criminal justice system.[2] Given the significance, it is ironic that the ICC Statute does not provide any explicit conditions or obligations concerning its incorporation in domestic law, thus leaving a broad discretion to the States Parties.[3] Although not limited by the Statute itself, this discretion of States Parties is nevertheless subject to their obligations under a) the international law of treaties; b) other applicable international obligations enshrined in specific treaties (eg the Genocide Convention and the 1949 Geneva Conventions); and c) customary international law.

While the States are not obliged to enact a domestic legislation incorporating the Statute, the principle of complementarity and cooperation duties certainly encourage them to do so.[4] Complying with their respective domestic legal system, the States may choose to implement the ICC Statute by way of complete incorporation (either direct replication or by reference); modified incorporation (with amendments); or non-incorporation ie by applying "ordinary" criminal law (referred to as the "zero solution").[5] Each of these varied approaches to domesticate the ICC Statute has its own merits and limitations. This chapter discusses the following examples of domestic implementation to explore how these States have addressed novel and highly complex legal issues[6] that arise in the domestication process: Argentina, Canada, Norway, South Africa and the United Kingdom. Within each of these examples, their respective sections deal with the merits and challenges of their approach to domestication of the ICC Statute, key differences or departures in the definitions of international crimes and modes of liability in the domestic law vis-à-vis the ICC Statute, the scope of extraterritorial jurisdiction, and finally, the practice of laws incorporating the Statute in domestic jurisdiction.

DOI: 10.4324/9781003320951-14

2 Argentina

As a "like-minded" State in favour of establishment of the ICC, Argentina was quick to sign the ICC Statute on 8 January 1999 and deposited its instrument of ratification on 8 February 2001.[7] In order to domesticate the ICC Statute, the Argentine Congress deliberated on the choice whether to draft a special implementation law or to incorporate the elements required by the Statute into pre-existing legislations.[8] Ultimately, it was decided to draft a special implementing legislation to ensure that such law would contain all the elements necessary for the implementation of the ICC Statute.[9] The implementing legislation was passed in December 2006.[10]

The 2006 law incorporates the ICC Statute crimes into domestic law by direct reference to its definitions. The legislation also incorporates Elements of Crime and Rules for Procedure and Evidence making it a part of Argentinian domestic law. On two specific aspects, the legislation deviates from the definitions provided under the ICC Statute: one, the difference in the age limit below which conscription of minors may constitute as a war crime. The domestic law introduces the age limit set forth by the Convention on the Rights of the Child framework, namely prohibition of conscription or enlistment of minors below 18 which is higher than the limit proscribed in the ICC Statute, ie 15 years.[11] Two, the Argentinian law makes the prohibition on "intentionally using starvation of civilians as a method of warfare" applicable also in non-international armed conflicts.[12]

While the Argentinian courts have traditionally exercised only territorial jurisdiction, the 2006 implementing law extends the remit of domestic courts' jurisdiction and includes the principle of universality as a basis for exercising jurisdiction over someone on Argentinian territory who cannot be extradited to a requesting State or handed over to the ICC.[13]

Although the Argentinian domestic law provides that statutes of limitations are not applicable on international crimes, it is unclear whether this rule has retroactive application.[14] However, the domestic courts in Argentina have established the non-applicability of the statutes of limitations to crimes against humanity, because the latter are crimes under international law which, according to both Articles 75 and 118 of the Constitution, are directly enforceable by domestic courts.[15]

In terms of practice, Argentinian courts have been very active in implementation of international criminal law. For instance, in 2010, relying on the 2006 implementing law, two victims of Spanish dictator Franco's regime and several NGOs presented a claim before the Argentinian judicial system for the alleged commission of genocide and/or crimes against humanity (including torture, forced disappearances and kidnapping of children) in Spain from 1936 to 1977. Given they had been denied justice in Spain, a Buenos Aires court ordered initiation of investigation, and issued arrest warrants against alleged torturers while requesting Spain to extradite the alleged perpetrators.[16]

Since then, many other universal jurisdiction claims have been brought before the domestic courts in Argentina regarding violations committed in China against Falun Gong members, in Gaza against Palestinians, in Paraguay against indigenous people and other victims of the Stroessner regime, in Saudi Arabia against female activists and journalists, and in Myanmar against Rohingyas.[17] In keeping with these developments, the National Office of the Prosecutor of Argentina has also created a Working Group on Universal Criminal Jurisdiction within the Crimes Against Humanity Prosecution Unit to support the work of prosecutors on the interpretation and application of universal jurisdiction, among other tasks.[18]

3 Canada

Even before the 1998 Rome negotiations, Canada had initiated several prosecutions against Nazi war criminals in the 1980s and early 1990s.[19] On 29 June 2000, Canada became the first State to adopt a comprehensive legislation incorporating the ICC Statute into domestic law. The Canadian implementing legislation, the Crimes Against Humanity and War Crimes Act (War Crimes Act) combines elements of the reference and the codification models.[20]

Section 4 of the War Crimes Act makes it an offence to commit genocide, crimes against humanity or war crimes in Canada. The definition of these crimes refers to the relevant crimes under conventional, customary international law or under general principles.[21] In this way, the Canadian approach goes beyond the mere implementation of the crimes within the ICC Statute. However, to ensure that the crimes of Articles 6 to 8 of the ICC Statute are included, the Act declares that "for greater certainty, crimes described in Articles 6 and 7 and paragraph 2 of Article 8 of the Rome Statute are, as of 17 July 1998, crimes according to customary international law",[22] thereby including these provisions in the definitions of the crimes under Canadian law. In addition, the Act provides clarity by specifying certain requirements for criminal legal liability indicating elements of the codification model of domestic implementation of the ICC Statute.

The War Crimes Act makes a distinction between crimes committed in Canada and outside Canada. It is only the latter that have retrospective application.[23] As a potential safeguard against violations of the principle of legality resulting from such retrospective application, the law stipulates compliance with the principle of legality, in every case, requiring the trial judge to determine the exact definition of international crimes at the time period specified in the charges.[24] This kind of incorporation based on customary international law keeps the definitions of the crimes flexible and updated as the international definitions evolve, thereby eliminating the need to amend the domestic law as international law changes.

The Canadian implementing legislation also expands the list of offences for which Canada can exercise extraterritorial jurisdiction to include air piracy,[25] offences against cultural property,[26] hostage taking for the purpose of terrorism,[27] and other terrorism-related offences.

Additionally, under Canadian law, breach of military and superior responsibility is added as a separate offence instead of a mode of liability elevating the gravity of such conduct.[28] Furthermore, while it has not been tested in practice yet, the War Crimes Act could potentially be implemented against corporations as well since the jurisdiction clause mentions "persons" taken to include organisations and legal entities as well.

Canadian implementing legislation, while still substantively far-reaching, does not relinquish the requirement of an additional link to Canada. A prosecution under this legislation for a crime committed outside Canada will only be brought if one of several possible links to Canada is present in the case.[29] Section 8(c) provides for a limited universal jurisdiction, as the offender may be prosecuted in Canada even if the crime was committed outside Canada by a non-Canadian citizen against a non-Canadian citizen if only "he [or she] is *present* in Canada" (emphasis added). Additionally, the Attorney General's written consent is required before a prosecution can proceed.[30] Such a condition serves to limit the right of private citizens to invoke the criminal process and allows for considerations of foreign policy to be assessed at the political level.[31] Thus, universal jurisdiction in Canada is subject to both presence and consent requirements. How exactly these requirements will play out in Canada is still unclear, as this law remains severely underused.

Only two cases connected to the genocide in Rwanda have been tried before the Canadian courts, with one leading to conviction.[32] One of the reasons for such underuse of the Act, as has been repeatedly pointed out, is the budgetary constraints of the Canadian War Crimes Program. Also, the Canadian State has preferred denial of visas to war criminals to avoid becoming a safe haven, and imposing administrative sanctions as a strategy, rather than carrying out expensive prosecutions.[33]

4 Norway

In 2001, Norway enacted a national implementation law to incorporate the ICC Statute. The legislation, however, only dealt with cooperation measures while leaving the international crimes to be prosecuted under the existing domestic criminal law.[34] In 2005, Norway created a special prosecutorial post and established a unit within the National Criminal Investigation Service (NCIS) to investigate and potentially extradite or prosecute individuals suspected of involvement in core international crimes.[35] The NCIS identified numerous suspects on its territory, but Norway's desire to prosecute war criminals was frustrated when its attempt to have the trial of Michel Bagaragaza transferred to its jurisdiction was refused by the International Criminal Tribunal for Rwanda (ICTR) on the grounds that Norway lacked appropriate legislation to prosecute him.[36] According to the ICTR, the legal characterisation and protected legal values for the crimes of genocide and homicide under domestic law were different.[37] This led Norway to enact legislation to prohibit international crimes that were not specifically provided under this label in domestic law prior to 2008.[38]

Norway adopted a modified incorporation model and implemented the ICC Statute by introducing a special section by way of an amendment in the Norwegian Penal Code of 2005.[39] Some of the deviations from the ICC Statute include: overcoming the distinction between international and non-international armed conflicts, the description of superior responsibility and incitement, and the non-inclusion of certain offences. Incitement and conspiracy to commit crimes against humanity, war crimes and genocide are separate offences under Norwegian law.[40]

With regard to jurisdiction, the exercise of universal jurisdiction over foreign perpetrators requires additional conditions concerning the perpetrator's or victim's link to Norway. These requirements are: (1) the alleged perpetrator is domiciled in Norway; or (2) the alleged perpetrator is a national of or domiciled in another Nordic country and is present in Norway; or (3) the alleged perpetrator is present in Norway.[41] Additionally, the prosecution must be in the public interest.[42] As a result, the Prosecutor exercises broad discretion on whether to prosecute these crimes or not when they are committed abroad.[43] But unlike a few other jurisdictions, the decision to prosecute a case based on universal jurisdiction is taken by the local prosecutor or police commissioner without any senior political input, thereby potentially minimising critiques of political or foreign policy influence.

Interestingly, under Norwegian criminal law, corporate entities can be prosecuted if a person who has acted on behalf of the enterprise commits a crime.[44] Thus, a corporate entity that is headquartered in Norway can be prosecuted for international crimes.[45]

Since 2008, Norway has regularly engaged with other States and extradited alleged criminals when possible.[46] On two occasions, the attempt to prosecute international crimes committed in former Yugoslavia and Rwanda proved unsuccessful as the Supreme Court disallowed retroactive application of the law, thereby laying down that only crimes committed after 2008 can be prosecuted in Norway under the aforementioned provisions.[47]

5 South Africa

South Africa's post-apartheid transitional period, resulting in the establishment of the Truth and Reconciliation Commission, witnessed an overall renewed interest and commitment to the principles of responsibility, accountability and justice.[48] It led to the adoption of customary international law as part of its Constitution[49] as well as the ratification and incorporation of international treaties, including the ICC Statute. South Africa signed and ratified the Statute in July 1998 and in order to give effect to its complementarity obligations, it passed the Implementation of the Rome Statute of the International Criminal Court Act in 2002.[50]

The Act follows a direct incorporation approach where the definitions of crimes have been included *verbatim* in the domestic law and provides for a full range of measures to cooperate with the ICC.

A few distinct points to be noted in South African domestication of the ICC Statute include the fact that the South African ICC Act does not explicitly provide for reliance on Elements of Crime, thus leaving no clear statutory aids for interpretation of international criminal law by domestic courts.[51] Also, it did not replicate the general principles of criminal law set out in Articles 22–33 of the ICC Statute. The South African ICC Act requires that the consent of the National Director of Public Prosecutions (NDPP) must be obtained before any prosecution is instituted against a person accused of having committed a crime.[52]

While the Act does not provide for "pure" universal jurisdiction, its scope is broader than others, for instance, the United Kingdom's implementing Act which has a specific residence requirement. In addition to traditional bases of jurisdiction, the South African implementing legislation also recognises jurisdiction over any person who, after the commission of the offence, is *present* or in the territory of the State on the basis of principle of universality.[53] In what can be termed as a progressive application of international criminal law by domestic courts, the South African Constitutional Court has interpreted the universal jurisdiction clause to allow investigations in the absence of a suspect as long as such investigations do not offend the Constitution or international law.[54]

While the South African implementing Act has been built on solid theoretical foundations, backed by the constitution and courts, the legislation has not been implemented for lack of political will. The position that the South African government took in the Torture Docket Case, together with the controversial failure to arrest President Omar Al-Bashir during his visit to South Africa, which was later found to be in violation of the Constitution, international obligations and South African law, points to a clear break from the past support for the norms and enforcement mechanisms of international humanitarian and international criminal law.

The South African government also attempted to withdraw from the ICC Statute,[55] albeit without success. Against the backdrop of this internal tension between the government and the courts, and regional developments such as the Malabo Protocol, the future course of this South African domestication model remains unpredictable.

6 The United Kingdom

Acting on its intention to become one of the first 60 States to ratify the Statute and bring it into force,[56] the United Kingdom (UK) ratified the ICC Statute in 2001. As a dualist legal system, the UK had to enact domestic legislation to do so – the International Criminal Court Act 2001. Following the complementarity regime strictly,[57] the implementing Act incorporates definitions of core crimes by reference to Articles 6, 7 and 8(2) of the ICC Statute. *Prima facie,* the Act appears to restrict the UK's jurisdiction only to the crimes defined by the ICC Statute, thus leaving out crimes under customary international law. However, in order to keep up with the developing norms, the Act sets out that the domestic courts shall rely on interpretative aid from Elements of Crimes[58] and relevant judgements of the ICC when interpreting these crimes,[59] and other relevant obligations and reservations of the UK under international treaties/conventions, including customary international law.[60] It must be noted that such incorporation by reference, on the one hand, guarantees complete compliance with the standard under international law. On the other hand, the actual substance of the crime is taken out of the hands of the national legislative organs.

Regarding jurisdiction, the UK ICC Act explicitly limits the principle of pure universal jurisdiction. It grants jurisdiction to domestic courts over international crimes if they are committed in England and Wales or when these offences are committed "outside the United Kingdom by a United Kingdom national, a United Kingdom resident or a person subject to United Kingdom's service jurisdiction".[61] For crimes committed outside of the UK, the Act explicitly provides for a "residence requirement". Proceedings may be brought against "a person who commits. . .[ICC crimes]. . . outside the United Kingdom . . . and who subsequently becomes a resident in the United Kingdom" so long as the person is a resident of the UK when the proceedings are brought and the acts would have been an offence had they occurred in the UK.[62] It must be noted that the residence requirement is different and narrower than the presence requirement as provided in some other jurisdictions discussed above. However, to make up for the narrow jurisdiction, the implementing Act waived the dual-criminality extradition rule so that States which have a broader criminal jurisdiction can seek extradition of a suspect from the UK and that request will not be subject to residence requirement either.[63]

With regard to modes of liability, as a general rule the national laws of the UK are applicable to international crimes. However, the ICC Act expressly incorporates the principle of command responsibility, which is not present in the British criminal law, into the domestic law,[64] arguably viewing it as a form of secondary liability.[65] Similarly, crimes concerning administration of justice are also the same as existing British law and not the ICC Statute.

In practice, however, the required permission of the Attorney General before beginning a prosecution and narrow scope of jurisdiction have resulted in a limited use of the ICC Act in UK. There has been only one prosecution of armed forces personnel in relation to war crimes committed during the Iraq war from 2003 to 2008 under the ICC Act, which resulted in the conviction of Colonel Payne.[66] The attempts made by the UK worked in favour of the State in terms of complimentarity regime as the Office of the Prosecutor of the ICC (OTP) opened a preliminary examination into the situation of war crimes committed in Iraq by the UK armed forces in 2006 and again in 2014.

The examination was finally closed as the OTP concluded that, although there was a reasonable basis to believe that members of UK armed forces committed war crimes, the UK was not unwilling to carry out relevant investigative inquiries and/or prosecutions.[67]

7 Conclusion

The discussion reflects how each of these States situate their own national criminal law regimes within the overall international criminal law system and translate as well as transform the international law norms into domestic norms. To a large extent, each State's implementing legislation is a response to their distinct domestic political and legal concerns. While most of the implementing legislations discussed here were enacted relatively early after the ICC Statute came into force, the States Parties yet to enact their implementing legislation have a particular advantage to not only learn from the lessons of other States that incorporated the ICC Statute into their domestic jurisdictions, but to also keep in consideration and aim to address the concerns and critiques expressed against the practice of the ICC. New implementing legislation provides an opportunity to address concerns on account of, inter alia, selectivity, neocolonialism and structural racism that may further the legitimacy of the international criminal justice system at large.

Notes

1 Gerhard Werle and Florian Jeßberger, 'Domestic Implementation', in *Principles of International Criminal Law* (OUP 2020) 180.
2 William W Burke-White, 'Proactive Complementarity: The International Criminal Court and National Courts in the Rome System of International Justice' (2008) 49 Harvard International Law Journal 53.
3 Article 70(4) of the ICC Statute is an exception. See generally, ICC Statute, Pt 9.
4 ICC Statute, Arts 1, 17 (Complementarity), 86 and 88 (Cooperation duties). See Claus Kreß and others (eds), *The Rome Statute and Domestic Legal Orders: Constitutional Issues, Cooperation and Enforcement*, vol 2 (Nomos 2005).
5 Werle and Jeßberger (n 1) 184–185.
6 Julio Bacio Terracino, 'National Implementation of ICC Crimes: Impact on National Jurisdictions and the ICC' (2007) 5(2) Journal of International Criminal Justice 421.
7 Argentina, Assembly of State Parties to the ICC Statute available at <https://asp.icc-cpi.int/states-parties/latin-american-and-caribbean-states/argentina>.
8 By virtue of Article 118 of the Argentine Constitution (part of the Constitution since 1853), the courts have argued that Argentina has always recognised international criminal law and the existence of certain offences that breach the international order as a part of it. See Natalia Luterstein, 'A Historical Approach to International Criminal Law through the Lenses of Domestic Prosecutions: Judging Massive Human Rights Violations in Argentina', in Morten Bergsmo and others (eds), *Historical Origins of International Criminal Law*, vol 4 (Torkel Opsahl Academic EPublisher 2015).

9 Alejandro Alvarez, 'The Implementation of the ICC Statute in Argentina' (2007) 5(2) Journal of International Criminal Justice 480.

10 Ley de Implementación del Estatuto de Roma, aprobado por la Ley No 25390 y ratificado el 16 de enero de 2001, de la Corte Penal Internacional. Ley 26.200 (Law on the Implementation of the Rome Statute, Law 26.200 of 13 December 2006).

11 Compare Arts 8(2)(b)(xxvi) and 8(2)(e)(vii) of the Statute with Art 10 of the Law 26.200.

12 ICCSt, Art 8(2)(b)(xxv) and Law 26.200, Art 10.

13 Law 26.200, Art 4.

14 Alvarez (n 9) 480–492, 487.

15 See Pablo Parenti, 'The Prosecution of International Crimes in Argentina' (2010) 10 International Criminal Law Review 491.

16 AL Garcia, 'Overview of the Argentine Lawsuit against the Crimes of the Franco Regime: Outcomes and Challenges' (2021) 9 Journal of Political Sciences & Public Affairs 110.

17 Máximo Langer and Mackenzie Eason, 'The Quiet Expansion of Universal Jurisdiction' (2019) 30(3) European Journal of International Law 779, 803; Thun Khin and Tomás Ojea Quintana, 'Symposium on the Current Crisis in Myanmar: Inching Closer to a Historic Universal Jurisdiction Case in Argentina on the Rohingya Genocide', Opinio Juris, 30 September 2021, available at <http://opiniojuris.org/2021/09/30/symposium-on-the-current-crisis-in-myanmar-inching-closer-to-a-historic-universal-jurisdiction-case-in-argentina-on-the-rohingya-genocide/>

18 Langer and Eason (n 17) 779–817, 803.

19 See *R v Finta*, 1 SCR 701 Supreme Court of Canada, 1994; *R v Pawlowski*, OJ No 2499, Ont Ct J (Gen Div), 1991. See Fannie Lafontaine, *Prosecuting Genocide, Crimes Against Humanity and War Crimes in Canadian Courts* (Carswell 2012); Robert Hage, 'Implementing the Rome Statute: Canada's Experience', in Thomas Lee, *States' Responses to Issues Arising from the ICC Statute* (Brill Nijhoff 2005) 47–55.

20 Crimes Against Humanity and War Crimes Act (SC 2000, c 24).

21 The crimes are defined in s 4(3). The wording of the ICC Statute serves as a starting point, but each category is widened to include "any further specified act, that, at the time and in the place of its commission, constitutes crimes against humanity or genocide according to customary international law or conventional international law or by virtue of its being criminal according to the general principles of law recognized by the community of nations, whether or not it constitutes a contravention of the law in force at the time and in the place of its commission". War Crimes are also defined in s 4(3), namely, as "an act or omission committed during an armed conflict that, at the time and in the place of its commission, constitutes a war crime according to customary international law or conventional international law applicable to armed conflicts, whether or not it constitutes a contravention of the law in force at the time and in the place of its commission".

22 Crimes Against Humanity and War Crimes Act 2000, s 4(4).

23 Compare ss 6(1) and 4(1) of the Crimes Against Humanity and War Crimes Act. The reasons for such distinctions are unclear, but concerns about potential prosecutions for core crimes committed against Indigenous Peoples could serve to partly explain this otherwise unexplainable dichotomy. See Fannie Lafontaine, 'The Unbearable Lightness of International Obligations: When and How to

Exercise Jurisdiction under Canada's Crimes Against Humanity and War Crimes Act' (2010) 23(2) Quebec Journal of International Law 1, 7.

24 Crimes Against Humanity and War Crimes Act 2000, s 6(3) and Canadian Charter of Rights and Freedoms 1982, s 11(g).

25 Crimes Against Humanity and War Crimes Act 2000, s 7(2).

26 ibid, s 7(2.01).

27 ibid, s 7(3.1).

28 This was because the doctrine of "Command Responsibility" as delineated in the Rome Statute contains a disjunctive *mens rea* test, allowing for either an objective *or* subjective test for mental culpability. However, the Canadian constitutional practice required strict subjectivity for a crime that would reflect the high degree of moral stigma society subscribes to those convicted of such crimes. To address this concern while also including the ICC Statute principle of command responsibility, the Canadian Parliament included it as a separate offence. See Michael Hatchell, 'Closing the Gaps in the United States Law and Implementing the Rome Statute: A Comparative Approach' (2005) 12(1) ILSA Journal of International & Comparative Law 183, 192–194.

29 Crimes Against Humanity and War Crimes Act 2000, s 8. See William A Schabas, 'Canada', in Ben Brandon and Max du Plessis (eds), *The Prosecution of International Crimes: A Practical Guide to Prosecuting ICC Crimes in Commonwealth States* (Commonwealth Secretariat 2005) 153.

30 Crimes Against Humanity and War Crimes Act 2000, s 9(3).

31 Lafontaine (n 23) 27.

32 *R v Munyaneza,* 2009 QCCS 2201, [2009] RJQ 1432; *Sa Majesté la Reine v Jacques Mungwarere*, 2011 CSON 1254 [2011]; see Robert Currie and Ion Stancu, 'R v. Munyaneza: Pondering Canada's First Core Crimes Conviction' (2010) 10 International Criminal Law Review 829.

33 Canada, Department of Justice, Crimes Against Humanity and War Crimes Program – Summative Evaluation: Final Report (Evaluation Division, Office of Strategic Planning and Performance Management 2008).

34 Act no 65 of 15 June 2001 relating to the implementation of the Statute of the International Criminal Court of 17 July 1998 (the Rome Statute) in Norwegian law 2001.

35 Human Rights Watch, *Universal Jurisdiction in Europe: The State of the Art*, 18(5D) (2006).

36 *The Prosecutor v Michel Bagaragaza*, Case no ICTR-2005-86-S, 'Decision on the Prosecution Motion for Referral to the Kingdom of Norway' (Trial Chamber) 19 May 2006.

37 *The Prosecutor v Michel Bagaragaza*, 'Decision on Rule 11 bis Appeal' (Appeals Chamber) 30 August 2006, para 17.

38 Lov om endringer i straffeloven 20. mai 2005 nr. 28 mv. (Unofficial translation: Act on Amendments to the Criminal Code 20 May 2005 No 28 etc.), published in I 2008 hefte 3 s 443, Journal no 2008-0181, 7 March 2008, available at <https://lovdata.no/dokument/LTI/lov/2008-03-07-4>

39 Norwegian Criminal Code 2005, ch 16.

40 Julia Selman-Ayetey, 'Universal Jurisdiction: Conflict and Controversy in Norway', in Kevin Heller and Gerry Simpson (eds), *The Hidden Histories of War Crimes Trials* (OUP 2013) 267–285.

41 Norwegian Penal Code 2005, s 5(1)–(3).

42 ibid, ss 5(7) and 6(2).

43 Recommendations from the Ministry of Justice and the Police of 9 November 2007 on the Act on Amendments to the Penal Code of 20 May 2005 no 28, Ot prp no 8 (2007–2008) (hereinafter, Preparatory Documents 2005), ch 12.2.1.3, p 279, available at <www.regjeringen.no/contentassets/380dda240b3f47a0a2d8e4151d4f4ca9/no/pdfs/otp200720080008000dddpdfs.pdf> ch 30.1, 404.

44 Norwegian Penal Code 2005, s 27.

45 Preparatory Documents 2005, ch 30.1, 402.

46 See generally, Selman-Ayetey (n 40) 267–285.

47 *Public Prosecuting Authority v Misrad Repak*, Case no HR-201-2057-P, Supreme Court of Norway, 12 March 2010; *Prosecuting National Authority v Sadi Bugingo*, Case no 13-041556ASTBORG/02, Borgating Court of Appeal, 16 January 2015, para 25.

48 See Gerhard Kemp, 'South Africa's (Possible) Withdrawal from the ICC and the Future of the Criminalization and Prosecution of Crimes Against Humanity, War Crimes and Genocide Under Domestic Law: A Submission Informed by Historical, Normative and Policy Considerations' (2017) 16 Washington University Global Studies Law Review 411.

49 Constitution of the Republic of South Africa, s 232.

50 The Implementation of the Rome Statute of the International Criminal Court Act 27 of 2002 (hereinafter, South Africa, ICC Act) entered into force on 16 August 2002.

51 Florian Jeßberger and Cathleen Powell, 'Prosecuting Pinochets in South Africa – Implementing the Rome Statute of the International Criminal Court' (2001) 14 South African Journal of Criminal Justice 344, 361.

52 South Africa, ICC Act, s 5(1).

53 South Africa, ICC Act, s 4(3). See Max du Plessis, 'South Africa's Implementation of the ICC Statute: An African Example' (2007) 5 Journal of International Criminal Justice 460, 462–463.

54 *National Commissioner of the South African Police Service v Southern African Human Rights Litigation Centre & Another* 2015 (1) SA (CC) (S Afr) (Torture Docket Case), para 47. See Max Du Plessis and Christopher Gevers, 'Civil Society, "Positive Complementarity" and the "Torture Docket" Case' (2016) 1 Acta Juridica 158.

55 In October 2016, the South African government gave notice of its withdrawal from the ICC Statute. In a case before the High Court of South Africa, the Democratic Alliance (DA), a political party, challenged the government's decision to withdraw from the Rome Statute. The court delivered its final judgment annulling the notice delivered to the UN Secretary-General. *Democratic Alliance v Minister of International Relations and Cooperation and Others* (Council for the Advancement of the South African Constitution Intervening) 2017 (3) SA 212 (GP) (S Afr). See Ntombizozuko Dyani-Mhango, 'Reflecting on South Africa's Attempt to Withdraw from the Rome Statute in Favour of Immunities for Sitting Heads of State: An Analysis of the International Crimes Bill 2017' (2020) 28(2) African Journal of International and Comparative Law 319.

56 International Criminal Court Act 2001 (c 17) ("UK ICC Act").

57 Robert Cryer and Olympia Bekou, 'International Crimes and ICC Cooperation in England and Wales' (2007) 5(2) Journal of International Criminal Justice 441, 444.

58 UK ICC Act, s 50(2) .

59 ibid, s 50(5).
60 ibid, s 50(4).
61 ibid, s 51(2).
62 ibid, s 68(1)–(2).
63 ibid, s 51(2)(b); see Kate Grady, 'International Crimes in the Courts of England and Wales' (2014) 10 Criminal Law Review 693.
64 UK ICC Act, s 65.
65 Cryer and Bekou (n 57) 446.
66 Nathan Rasiah, 'The Court-Martial of Corporal Payne and Others and the Future Landscape of International Criminal Justice' (2009) 7(1) Journal of International Criminal Justice 177.
67 See ICC – Preliminary Examination: Iraq/UK available at <www.icc-cpi.int/iraq>.

Selected Bibliography

Alvarez A, 'The Implementation of the ICC Statute in Argentina' (2007) 5(2) *Journal of International Criminal Justice* 480

Burke-White W, 'Proactive Complementarity: The International Criminal Court and National Courts in the Rome System of International Justice' (2008) 49 *Harvard International Law Journal* 53

Cryer R and Bekou O, 'International Crimes and ICC Cooperation in England and Wales' (2007) 2 *Journal of International Criminal Justice* 441

Currie R and Stancu I, 'R. v. Munyaneza: Pondering Canada's First Core Crimes Conviction' (2010) 10 *International Criminal Law Review* 829

Du Plessis M, 'South Africa's Implementation of the ICC Statute: An African Example' (2007) 5 *Journal of International Criminal Justice* 460

Dyani-Mhango N, 'Reflecting on South Africa's Attempt to Withdraw from the Rome Statute in Favour of Immunities for Sitting Heads of State: An Analysis of the International Crimes Bill 2017' (2020) 28(2) *African Journal of International and Comparative Law* 319

Garcia A L, 'Overview of the Argentine Lawsuit against the Crimes of the Franco Regime: Outcomes and Challenges' (2021) 9 *Journal of Political Sciences & Public Affairs* 110

Grady K, 'International Crimes in the Courts of England and Wales' (2014) 10 *Criminal Law Review* 693

Hage R, 'Implementing the Rome Statute: Canada's Experience', in Thomas Lee (ed), *Responses to Issues Arising from the ICC Statute (*Brill Nijhoff 2005) 47

Human Rights Watch, *Universal Jurisdiction in Europe: The State of the Art, 18(5D)* (2006)

Jeßberger F and Powell C, 'Prosecuting Pinochets in South Africa-Implementing the Rome Statute of the International Criminal Court' (2001) 14 *South African Journal of Criminal Justice* 344

Kemp G, 'South Africa's (Possible) Withdrawal from the ICC and the Future of the Criminalization and Prosecution of Crimes Against Humanity, War Crimes and Genocide Under Domestic Law: A Submission Informed by Historical, Normative and Policy Considerations' (2017) 16 *Washington University Global Studies Law Review* 411

Kreß C and others (eds), *The Rome Statute and Domestic Legal Orders: Constitutional Issues, Cooperation and Enforcement,* vol 2 (Nomos 2005)

Lafontaine F, *Prosecuting Genocide, Crimes Against Humanity and War Crimes in Canadian Courts* (Carswell 2012)

Lafontaine F, 'The Unbearable Lightness of International Obligations: When and How to Exercise Jurisdiction under Canada's Crimes Against Humanity and War Crimes Act' (2010) 23(2) *Quebec Journal of International Law* 1

Langer M and Mackenzie E, 'The Quiet Expansion of Universal Jurisdiction' (2019) 30(3) *European Journal of International Law* 779

Luterstein N, 'A Historical Approach to International Criminal Law through the lenses of Domestic Prosecutions: Judging Massive Human Rights Violations in Argentina', in Morten Bergsmo and others (eds), *Historical Origins of International Criminal Law,* vol 4 (Torkel Opsahl Academic EPublisher 2015)

Parenti P, 'The Prosecution of International Crimes in Argentina' (2010) 10 *International Criminal Law Review* 491

Rasiah N, 'The Court-Martial of Corporal Payne and Others and the Future Landscape of International Criminal Justice' (2009) 7(1) *Journal of International Criminal Justice* 177

Schabas WA, 'Canada', in Ben Brandon and Max du Plessis (eds), *The Prosecution of International Crimes: A Practical Guide to Prosecuting ICC Crimes in Commonwealth States* (Commonwealth Secretariat 2005)

Selman-Ayetey J, 'Universal Jurisdiction: Conflict and Controversy in Norway', in Kevin Heller and Gerry Simpson (eds), *The Hidden Histories of War Crimes Trials* (Oxford University Press 2013)

Terracino J, *'National Implementation of ICC Crimes: Impact on National Jurisdictions and the ICC'* (2007) 5(2) *Journal of International Criminal Justice* 421

Thun K and Ojea Quintana T, 'Symposium on the Current Crisis in Myanmar: Inching Closer to a Historic Universal Jurisdiction Case in Argentina on the Rohingya Genocide', Opinio Juris, 30 September 2021, available at <http://opiniojuris.org/2021/09/30/symposium-on-the-current-crisis-in-myanmar-inching-closer-to-a-historic-universal-jurisdiction-case-in-argentina-on-the-rohingya-genocide/>

Werle G and Jeßberger F, 'Domestic Implementation', in *Principles of International Criminal Law* (Oxford University Press 2020)

Part IV

Defining International Crimes in the Domestic Legislation

4.1 How to Implement Crimes Against Humanity and Genocide in the Italian System

Maria Crippa

1 Introduction: The Extent of International Obligations to Adopt Domestic Provisions on Genocide and Crimes Against Humanity

The Italian legal system represents a particularly significant field of investigation when assessing the scope of domestic implementation of international crimes. Despite the decisive role played by the Italian delegation during the United Nations Diplomatic Conference of Plenipotentiaries on the Establishment of an International Criminal Court (ICC) in 1998 and the prompt ratification and execution of the treaty, Italian legislation still lacks substantive provisions on international crimes. Law no 962/1967 – implementing the obligations arising from the ratification of the Convention on the Prevention and Punishment of the Crime of Genocide (Genocide Convention)[1] – is to various extents inadequate. Furthermore, in the absence of domestic provisions, crimes against humanity can be prosecuted by Italian courts only through recourse to corresponding ordinary offences and the general discipline therewith applicable.[2]

Notwithstanding the lack of direct obligations under the Rome Statute of the ICC (Rome Statute) to criminalise genocide, crimes against humanity, war crimes and aggression, States are generally bound by other international conventions that, to various extents, require the adoption of domestic provisions incorporating such offences. For instance, Article 5 of the Genocide Convention imposes on States Parties an explicit obligation to adopt the necessary legislation to implement its provisions, and specifically to provide effective sanctions, commensurate with the seriousness of the conduct. Crimes against humanity, conversely, are currently still not enshrined in a specific international treaty, but remain to a large extent relevant under customary international law.[3] Only some of the offences listed under Article 7 of the Rome Statute (such as torture and other cruel, inhuman and degrading treatment, apartheid, and forced disappearances) are already included in specific conventions. At the same time, however, most scholars agree that an indirect obligation to enact domestic legislation on crimes falling under the jurisdiction of the ICC descends from the enforcement system established under the principle of complementarity (Rome Statute, Articles 1 and 17).[4] The lack of domestic provisions on international crimes may indeed not only

DOI: 10.4324/9781003320951-16

in theory threaten the judicial intervention of the ICC, but also result in the impossibility for Italian legal judicial authorities "to comply with some of its obligations of cooperation under Part 9 of the Statute".[5] The belated adoption of norms on international crimes would thus represent a most needed step and an unprecedented opportunity for the Italian legislator to comply with international obligations, at the same time ensuring the highest standards of international criminal law. The current moment is indeed particularly noteworthy: on 22 March 2022, the Ministry of Justice appointed the Ministerial Commission Palazzo–Pocar on International Crimes (the "Commission"), tasked with drafting a code of international crimes. The Commission issued its Final Report on 24 June 2022.[6]

Against this backdrop, this chapter aims at assessing the coherence of Italian provisions currently in force with Articles 6 and 7 of the Rome Statute and at envisaging possible solutions for the implementation of crimes against humanity (Section 2) and genocide (Section 3) into the domestic legal system.[7] Finally, some conclusions on the relevance of the issue and on future perspectives will be presented (Section 4).

2 The Lack of Domestic Provisions on Crimes Against Humanity: Shortcomings of Prosecuting International Crimes as Ordinary Offences

Unlike war crimes and genocide, crimes against humanity are still not foreseen in the Italian criminal or military criminal law system.[8] While it is true that most conducts are indeed already incriminated under domestic law,[9] prosecuting international crimes as ordinary offences has noteworthy consequences.[10] First, in the absence of derogatory provisions, general principles apply, even when they lead to solutions that are, at the very least, problematic under international law. This is the case, for instance, for statutes of limitations, whose applicability often leads to the result of impeding the prosecution of international crimes.[11]

Furthermore, domestic crimes lack the definition of the contextual element, which conveys the macro and systematic dimension of international crimes and acknowledges the violation of specific protected interests belonging to the international community. In this regard, various national legislations on crimes against humanity neglected the so-called "policy" element, which requires the commission of multiple acts "pursuant to or in furtherance of a State or organizational policy to commit such attack" (Rome Statute, Article 7), but did not appear in the statutes of international courts and tribunals until the adoption of the Rome Statute. Furthermore, recent ICC jurisprudence seems to downplay the strict interpretation of this element, entailing the formal adoption of such policy, and requires instead that acts amounting to crimes against humanity are "linked" to a State or organisation, thus excluding isolated episodes of violence.[12] For the same reason, the private initiative to draft an Italian code of international crimes (so-called "Progetto Cariplo" of 2015) chose to consider the policy element only as aggravating circumstance.[13] Adopting a different approach, the Articles on Crimes Against Humanity drafted by the Commission Palazzo-Pocar connected the attack to a State or organisation's "program", in order to "ensure legal certainty and procedural applicability" and to exclude "phenomena that do not seem to amount to international crimes, such as offences committed during spontaneous riots".[14]

Ordinary offences are also often not perfectly equivalent to the material elements required under Article 7 of the Rome Statute for crimes against humanity. Penal code provisions may in fact encompass a broader scope than the international norm. This consideration is, for instance, evident in the definition of "enslavement" under Articles 600 and 601 of the Italian Penal Code, which is not limited to the exercise of powers attaching to the right of ownership but extends to any conduct related to a status of continuous constraint. Again, ordinary norms are often conceived as "*reati propri*" – requiring a specific personal status (eg official capacity) – whilst under the Rome Statute they apply generally to common agents. This appears to be the case of the crime of "illegal arrest or arbitrary deprivation of personal liberty" under Articles 606 and 607 of the Italian Penal Code, which can only be committed by State agents, whilst Article 7(1)(e) of the Rome Statute incriminates the "imprisonment or other severe deprivation of physical liberty" regardless of official capacity.

The same consideration applies with regard to the discipline of sexual offences under Articles 609*bis* and following of the Italian Penal Code, which mainly attains to the exercise of violence, threats, or abuse of authority against the victim in order to force him or her to perform or suffer sexual acts. Conversely, the corresponding international offences encompass a wider range of conduct, such as sterilisation or forced pregnancy, as confirmed by recent ICC jurisprudence in the *Ongwen* case.[15] In light of the diversity of protected legal interests, the German legislator opted for a distinction between offences against sexual self-determination and offences against reproductive self-determination, as provided by Article 7(1) no 6 of the German Code of Crimes Against International Law (*Völkerstrafgesetzbuch*, VStGB).[16]

Although only recently introduced in Article 613*bis* of the Italian Penal Code, the domestic definition of torture is largely considered unsatisfactory when compared to international obligations binding Italy since the ratification of the Convention Against Torture and Other Cruel, Inhuman or Degrading Treatment or Punishment in 1988.[17] The issue has been extensively debated and exceeds the scope of this chapter. It is, however, worth highlighting that although torture has been characterised as a common offence, applicable to private agents, the second paragraph of the provision sets out harsher penalties for State agents abusing their official capacity. As emphasised by most scholars, international obligations and a systematic interpretation of the domestic criminal system require interpreting the provision as an autonomous offence, instead of a mere aggravating circumstance.[18] A different reading would in fact allow it to be potentially counterbalanced with mitigating circumstances, thus denying the core character of torture performed by State agents. Furthermore, the provision omitted the indeed common hypothesis of superior responsibility for negligent omission or facilitation of the crime of torture.

Other conducts amounting to crimes against humanity are still not foreseen under Italian criminal law and need therefore to be criminalised, even when they are already partially included in the definition of genocide under Law no 962/1967.[19] This is the case, for instance, for the crimes against humanity of deportation, forcible transfer of population, extermination, persecution, forced disappearance and apartheid.

As previously anticipated, the belated adoption of international crimes into the Italian domestic system represents an opportunity to ensure the highest standards of international law. At the same time, however, the "domestication" of international crimes needs to comply with the constitutional framework. In this regard, the criminal principle of strict legality led some national legislators to exclude from domestic provisions on crimes against humanity the residual hypothesis of "other inhumane acts of a similar character intentionally causing great suffering, or serious injury to body or to mental or physical health" under Article 7(1)(k) of the Rome Statute. This clause aimed at introducing more clarity than the analogous provisions of Article 5 of the ICTY Statute and Article 3 of the ICTR Statute. The ICC jurisprudence interprets it as a residual category, not intended to be "applicable without limits" but related to acts of great suffering or serious injury to body or to mental health, similar in nature and gravity to the other acts referred to in Article 7 of the Rome Statute.[20] Such interpretation would ensure the compliance of the provision with the Italian constitutional jurisprudence on the *ejusdem generis* principle, which forbids heterogeneous norms incriminating structurally similar conducts.[21]

3 Italian Law no 962/1967 on Genocide: Seizing the Opportunity of a Code of International Crimes to Expand the Scope of Domestic Provisions Already in Force

Unlike crimes against humanity, provisions on acts amounting to genocide are already included in the Italian criminal law system. In order to give effect to the Genocide Convention and to "provide effective penalties for persons guilty of genocide" (Genocide Convention, Article V), the Italian legislator adopted Law no 962 in 1967, which incriminates some of the offences listed under Article III of the Genocide Convention.[22] Although Articles 1 to 8 of Law no 962/1967 adopt *verbatim* Articles II and III of the Genocide Convention, the Italian framework shows some inconsistencies when compared to the internationally recognised definition of genocide.

Notwithstanding the broad discretion left upon States to criminalise acts of genocide set out in the Genocide Convention and the absence of a direct obligation descending from Article 6 of the Rome Statute,[23] the adoption of domestic legislation on international crimes may represent an opportunity to reflect on the extent of Italian provisions' adherence to the international norm.

Specifically, the adoption of domestic norms on international crimes requires consideration on the possible extension of the protected groups envisaged by the established definition of genocide. Several national legislations broadened their provisions on genocide in order to include political,[24] social (with reference to either economic status or sexual orientation),[25] and cultural groups.[26] In general, the jurisprudence of international criminal tribunals – albeit not extending the scope of genocide to such entities – seems to give relevance to the subjective attribution of the group character, which is therefore not limited to mere objective criteria.[27] The traditional listing (national, ethnical, racial or religious) would not, thus, be exhaustive, since Article II of the Genocide Convention represents a crystallisation, at a precise historical moment, of the generally accepted notion of genocide at the time. The adoption of subjective criteria in the interpretation of the group character would also allow to fully grasp the nature of collective entities, which "by their nature constitute social constructs, entities 'imagine' entirely dependent on variable and contingent perceptions, and not social facts, which are verifiable as natural phenomena or physical facts".[28]

An extensive notion of the contextual element of genocide is indeed not unknown to the Italian legal system, although not explicitly foreseen. Domestic courts confronted the political nature of genocide in the *Acosta Jorge Eduardo* case, when the Court of Assizes of Rome sentenced to life imprisonment four soldiers of the Argentinian military navy for the killing of three Italian citizens.[29] In assessing the defendants' criminal liability, the Court traced such conduct to the broader context of the "tragic genocide" committed by the Argentinian regime against political opponents.

Nonetheless, as explained in its *Final Report*, the Commission Palazzo–Pocar defined genocide by relying on the exact wording of Article II of the Genocide Convention and Article 6 of the Rome Statute, with the only extension to linguistic identity.[30]

Minor adjustments seem advisable, moreover, in regard to the material conducts amounting to genocide, such as the abduction and forcible transfer of minors under 18 years – instead of 14 years (Law 962/1967, Article 5)[31] – or the inclusion of serious mental harm in the definition of the violation of personal integrity, as required by both international and domestic provisions.[32]

The belated adoption of norms on genocide shall also encompass offences not included in Law no 962/1967, like the "deprivation of resources indispensable for the survival of the same [group], such as food or medical care, or [in] the systematic expulsion from their homes", as well as sexual violence and forced pregnancy aimed at modifying or altering the ethnic composition of the group or at determining in the victim the decision not to procreate.[33]

Finally, the scope of the crime shall not be unduly restricted to events perpetrated against more than one group member, as currently provided by Article 1(2) of Law no 962/1967. A broadened provision seems rather advisable in light of Article 6(1)(a), (b) and (e) of the Rome Statute, which encompasses the commission of relevant conducts against "one or more members of the group".[34]

4 Conclusions

The late implementation of the Rome Statute in the domestic legal system constitutes, as already anticipated, an opportunity to expand its provisions, overcoming those compromises imposed during the negotiations and complying with the most recent developments of international criminal law.

Furthermore, the long-awaited adoption of domestic norms on international crimes allows the exercise of domestic jurisdiction on such offences by national authorities, thus reinforcing the Italian position in the system of international criminal justice. In this sense, the implementation of the mechanism conceived under the principle of complementarity demands a reconsideration of the relationship between the ICC and Italian national authorities. The challenges that, as the current moment demonstrates, hinder the international community's goal to put "an end to impunity against the perpetrators of these crimes and thus contributing to their prevention",[35] require in fact a coordinated and harmonious enforcement of all mechanisms asserting responsibility for international crimes.

Against this backdrop, the Italian legislator seems to have finally seized the opportunity to reinforce the role of Italian judicial authorities, in light of their efforts in domestic proceedings and in the context of international organisations and agencies. The adoption of the most advanced Code of international crimes will thus allow the Italian legal system not only to fully comply with its international obligations, but also to pursue an effective and functioning system of international criminal justice.

As clarified in Section 2, the domestic adoption of provisions on crimes against humanity proves to be particularly crucial in light of the limited overlap between ordinary offences and the corresponding international crimes. On the one hand, the consideration is especially striking in relation to the absence under domestic criminal law of the contextual element, which expresses the typical disvalue and the macro-systematic dimension of international crimes. On the other hand, the recourse to ordinary offences is unsatisfactory in consideration of the conducts listed under Article 7 of the Rome Statute, as shown by recent investigations and proceedings conducted by Italian judicial authorities on crimes committed against migrants in Libyan detention camps or on their *routes* to European borders. Section 3 assessed that a new discipline on genocide would overcome the shortcomings of provisions already in force under Law no 962/1967, which proves to be largely outdated and does not fully reflect the international discipline of the crime.

In conclusion, the recent initiative undertaken by the Commission Palazzo–Pocar is therefore to be welcomed, as it aims at systematically overcoming the above-mentioned shortcomings of provisions already in force and at introducing the long-awaited domestic implementation of the Rome Statute. It remains, however, to be seen if the discipline and its future jurisprudential applications would constitute a reference model in the international scenario.

Notes

1 UN General Assembly, Convention on the Prevention and Punishment of the Crime of Genocide, 9 December 1948, United Nations, Treaty Series, vol. 78, p. 277.
2 See Marco Pedrazzi, Chapter 2.2, Previous Italian Legislative Drafts.
3 Draft articles on Prevention and Punishment of Crimes Against Humanity 2019, UN General Assembly (A/74/10), *Yearbook of the International Law Commission 2019*, vol II (part two).
4 Marco Longobardo, 'The Italian Legislature and International and EU Obligations of Domestic Criminalisation' (2021) 21 International Criminal Law Review 623, 628.
5 ibid. See also Gerhard Werle and Florian Jeßberger, *Principles of International Criminal Law* (OUP 2020) 34. On the relationship between implicit obligations to criminalise arising from the Rome Statute and the Italian legal system, *see* Luigi Prosperi, '"With or Without You": Why Italy Should Incorporate Crimes Against Humanity and Genocide Into Its National Legal System' (2021) 21 International Criminal Law Review 707.
6 Commission Palazzo–Pocar on International Crimes, *Final Report*, 24 June 2022: www.giustizia.it/giustizia/it/mg_1_36_0.page?contentId=COS372730.
7 See Luigi Prosperi, Chapter 4.3, Prosecuting Genocide and Crimes Against Humanity as Ordinary Offences: What Consequences?
8 On war crimes, see Giulio Bartolini and Marco Longobardo, Chapter 4.2, The Italian Legislation on War Crimes: Obligations to Implement and Principle of Legality.
9 Commission Palazzo–Pocar on International Crimes (n 5) 22.
10 On the extent of the obligation upon States to incriminate acts amounting to genocide and the consequences of prosecuting them as ordinary offences, see again Luigi Prosperi, Chapter 4.3.
11 Court of Cassation, Sect VI, 17 July 2014, 46634; Court of Assizes of Rome, 17 January 2017 (10 April 2017) no 31079; Emanuela Fronza, 'Il processo italiano al Plan Cóndor. Uno stress test superato dall'ordinamento italiano', in Roberto Acquaroli, Emanuela Fronza and Alessandro Gamberini (eds), La giustizia penale tra ragione e prevaricazione. Dialogando con Gaetano Insolera (Aracne 2021) 477.
12 ICC, Trial Chamber II, Situation in the Democratic Republic of the Congo, *The Prosecutor v Germain Katanga*, Judgment pursuant to article 74 of the Statute, 7 March 2014, ICC-01/04-01/07-3436-tENG, 1111ff; Pre-Trial Chamber III, Situation in the Central African Republic, *The Prosecutor v Jean-Pierre Bemba Gombo*, Decision on the Prosecutor's Application for a Warrant of Arrest against Jean-Pierre Bemba Gombo, 12 June 2008, ICC-01/05-01/08-14-tENG, 33ff.
13 See Fausto Pocar, Chapter 2.1, The Domestic Codification of International Crimes: the Private Initiative "Cariplo Project".
14 Commission Palazzo–Pocar on International Crimes (n 5) 22. Translation by the Author.
15 ICC, Trial Chamber IX, Situation in Uganda, *The Prosecutor v Dominic Ongwen*, Trial Judgement, 4 February 2021, ICC-02/04-01/15-1762-Red.

16 The recent proposals to reform the current formulation of VStGB, Art 7 are motivated by the need for a more effective prosecution of such crimes (ie sexual slavery, forced pregnancy and the residual clause of conduct of equal gravity), as well as by systematic reasons, imposed by recent amendment of the corresponding offences in the ordinary penal code (StGB, Art 177). Tanja Altunjan and Leonie Steinl, 'Zum Schutz der sexuellen und reproduktiven Selbstbestimmung – Aktuelle Entwicklungen und Reformbedarf im Völkerstrafgesetzbuch' (2021) 12(3) RW Rechtswissenschaft 335, 337.

17 UN General Assembly, Convention Against Torture and Other Cruel, Inhuman or Degrading Treatment or Punishment, 10 December 1984, United Nations, Treaty Series, vol. 1465, p. 85. Law of 3 November 1988, no 498, *Ratifica ed esecuzione della convenzione contro la tortura ed altre pene o trattamenti crudeli, disumani o degradanti, firmata a New York il 10 dicembre 1984*, *Gazzetta Ufficiale* Serie Generale no 271 of 18 November 1988.

18 Angela Colella, 'Il nuovo delitto di tortura', in Roberto Garofoli and Tiziano Treu, *Voce per "Il libro dell'anno del diritto Treccani 2018"* (Istituto della Enciclopedia Italiana 2018).

19 See below, Section 3.

20 Elements of Crimes, Art 7(1)(k); ICC, Pre-Trial Chamber I, *The Prosecutor v Germain Katanga*, Decision on the confirmation of charges, 30 September 2008, ICC-01/04-01/07-717, 445ff; Pre-Trial Chamber II, *The Prosecutor v Uhuru Muigai Kenyatta*, Decision on the confirmation of charges, 29 January 2012, ICC-01/09-02/11-382-Red, 267ff.

21 *Ex multis*, Italian Constitutional Court, 1 August 2008, no 327.

22 Law of 9 October 1967 no 962, *Prevenzione e repressione del delitto di genocidio*, *Gazzetta Ufficiale* no 272 of 30 October 1967. Italy ratified the Genocide Convention with Law of 11 March 1952, no 153, *Gazzetta Ufficiale* no 74 of 27 March 1952 (accession occurred on 4 June 1952, with publication in the *Gazzetta Ufficiale* no 161 of 14 July 1952 and entered into force on 2 August 1952).

23 Again, see Luigi Prosperi, Chapter 4.3.

24 Ethiopian Penal Code, Art 269; Bangladesh Act on Courts for International Crimes, Art 3(2)(c); Ivorian Penal Code, Art 137; Costa Rican Penal Code, Art 375; Colombian Penal Code, Art 101; Lithuanian Penal Code, Art 99; Swiss Penal Code, Art 264.

25 Estonian Penal Code, Art 90 ("a national, ethnic, racial or religious group, or a group that resists an occupation or another social group"); Latvian Penal Code, Art 71; Lithuanian Penal Code, Art 99; Paraguayan Penal Code, Art 319; Peruvian Penal Code, Art 319; Swiss Penal Code, Art 264.

26 Werle and Jeßberger (n 4) 347ff.

27 ICTR, ICTY and ICC jurisprudence departed from an objective determination of the protected groups under the Genocide Convention. Instead, the decisions by international tribunals increasingly rely on a subjective approach, with an emphasis on the perpetrator's perception of the victim group. William A Schabas, 'Part 2 Jurisdiction, Admissibility, and Applicable Law: Compétence, Recevabilité, Et Droit Applicable, Art.6 Genocide/Crime de génocide', in William A Schabas, *The International Criminal Court: A Commentary on the Rome Statute* (Oxford Scholarly Authorities on International Law 2016) 124ff.

28 Report of the International Commission of Inquiry on Darfur to the United Nations Secretary-General, Pursuant to Security Council Resolution 1564 of 18 September 2004, Geneva, 25 January 2005, para 494.

29 Court of Assizes of Rome, 17 January 2017 (10 April 2017) no 31079.
30 Commission Palazzo–Pocar on International Crimes (n 5) 22.
31 See Note 5 to Art 6(e) of the Elements of Crimes (EoC). Such age limit is, however, not provided for under Genocide Convention, Art II.
32 Genocide Convention, Art II; Rome Statute, Art 6(b); see also ICTR, *The Prosecutor v T Muvuni*, 11 February 2010, ICTR-2000-55A-T, par. 486. The ordinary offence of personal injury pursuant to the Italian Penal Code, Art 582 expressly criminalises the causation of a "disease in the body or mind", defined as an "anatomical or functional alteration of the organism, even if localized, destined to persist until the [...] alteration process is underway" (eg Court of Cassation, Sect V, 25 October 2012, no 8351; Sect V, 29 September 2010, no 43763; Sect V, 25 October 2012, no 8351; Sect V, 29 September 2010, no 43763). Translation by the Author.
33 Note 4 to Art 6(e) EoC.
34 VStGB, Art 6 and Spanish Penal Code, Art 607(1) require, according to the prevailing interpretation of Art 6 of the Rome Statute, the commission of at least one conduct constituting genocide against at least one member of the attacked group.
35 Preamble of the Rome Statute.

Selected Bibliography

Altunjan T and Steinl L, 'Zum Schutz der sexuellen und reproduktiven Selbstbestimmung – Aktuelle Entwicklungen und Reformbedarf im Völkerstrafgesetzbuch' (2021) 12(3) *RW Rechtswissenschaft* 335

Colella A, 'Il nuovo delitto di tortura', in Roberto Garofoli and Tiziano Treu, *Voce per "Il libro dell'anno del diritto Treccani 2018"* (Istituto della Enciclopedia Italiana 2018)

Commission Palazzo–Pocar on International Crimes, *Final Report*, 24 June 2022, www.giustizia.it/giustizia/it/mg_1_36_0.page?contentId=COS372730

Court of Assizes of Rome, 17 January 2017 (10 April 2017) no 31079

Court of Cassation, Sect V, 25 October 2012, no 8351

Court of Cassation, Sect V, 29 September 2010, no 43763

Court of Cassation, Sect VI, 17 July 2014, 46634

Draft articles on Prevention and Punishment of Crimes Against Humanity 2019, UN General Assembly (A/74/10), *Yearbook of the International Law Commission 2019*, vol II (part two)

Fronza E, 'Il processo italiano al Plan Cóndor. Uno stress test superato dall'ordinamento italiano', in Acquaroli R, Fronza E and Gamberini A (eds), *La giustizia penale tra ragione e prevaricazione. Dialogando con Gaetano Insolera* (Aracne 2021)

ICC, Pre-Trial Chamber I, *The Prosecutor v. Germain Katanga*, Decision on the confirmation of charges, 30 September 2008, ICC-01/04-01/07-717

ICC, Pre-Trial Chamber II, *The Prosecutor v. Uhuru Muigai Kenyatta*, Decision on the confirmation of charges, 29 January 2012, ICC-01/09-02/11-382-Red

ICC, Pre-Trial Chamber III, Situation in the Central African Republic, *The Prosecutor v. Jean-Pierre Bemba Gombo*, Decision on the Prosecutor's Application for a Warrant of Arrest against Jean-Pierre Bemba Gombo, 12 June 2008, ICC-01/05-01/08-14-tENG

ICC, Trial Chamber II, Situation in the Democratic Republic of the Congo, *The Prosecutor v. Germain Katanga*, Judgment pursuant to article 74 of the Statute,77 March 2014, ICC-01/04-01/07-3436-tENG

ICC, Trial Chamber IX, Situation in Uganda, *The Prosecutor v. Dominic Ongwen*, Trial Judgement, 4 February 2021, ICC-02/04-01/15-1762-Red

ICTR, *The Prosecutor v. T. Muvuni*, 11 February 2010, ICTR-2000-55A-T

Italian Constitutional Court, 1 August 2008, no 327

Law of 11 March 1952 no 153, GU no 74 of 27 March 1952

Law of 3 November 1988 no 498, *Ratifica ed esecuzione della convenzione contro la tortura ed altre pene o trattamenti crudeli, disumani o degradanti, firmata a New York il 10 dicembre 1984*, GU Serie Generale no 271 of 18 November 1988

Law of 9 October 1967 no 962, *Prevenzione e repressione del delitto di genocidio*, GU no 272 of 30 October 1967

Longobardo M, 'The Italian Legislature and International and EU Obligations of Domestic Criminalisation' (2021) 21 *International Criminal Law Review* 623

Prosperi L, '"With or Without You": Why Italy Should Incorporate Crimes Against Humanity and Genocide Into Its National Legal System' (2021) 21 *International Criminal Law Review* 707

Report of the International Commission of Inquiry on Darfur to the United Nations Secretary-General, Pursuant to Security Council Resolution 1564 of 18 September 2004, Geneva, 25 January 2005

Schabas WA, 'Part 2 Jurisdiction, Admissibility, and Applicable Law: Compétence, Recevabilité, Et Droit Applicable, Art.6 Genocide/Crime de génocide', in Schabas WA, *The International Criminal Court: A Commentary on the Rome Statute* (Oxford Scholarly Authorities on International Law 2016)

UN General Assembly, Convention Against Torture and Other Cruel, Inhuman or Degrading Treatment or Punishment, 10 December 1984, United Nations, Treaty Series, vol. 1465, p. 85

UN General Assembly, Convention on the Prevention and Punishment of the Crime of Genocide, 9 December 1948, United Nations, Treaty Series, vol. 78, p. 277

Werle G and Jeßberger F, *Principles of International Criminal Law, Oxford Public International Law* (Oxford University Press 2020)

4.2 The Italian Legislation on War Crimes

Obligations to Implement and the Principle of Legality

Giulio Bartolini and Marco Longobardo[1]

1 Introduction

This chapter analyses how Italy has implemented the duty to criminalise war crimes in the Italian domestic legal system.[2] The analysis addresses the obligations of domestic criminalisation incumbent upon Italy in the field of war crimes, the extant implementing legislations (with all its shortcomings), and the role of the constitutionally protected principle of legality in this matter. Other related issues – such as the rules governing the exercise of Italian jurisdiction over war crimes – are outside the purview of this study.

This chapter argues that the Italian domestic legal system related to war crimes is characterised by several shortcomings. The implementation of war crimes legislation is still largely centred on the provisions provided by the War Military Criminal Code (WMCC) adopted in 1941. Only marginal updating to its provisions has occurred since then, in particular as a result of military operations involving Italy in Afghanistan since 2001. As a consequence, Italy lags behind the overall evolution of international humanitarian law (IHL) in the field of the criminalisation of war crimes. The fact that Italy is bound by certain obligations of domestic criminalisation in the field of war crimes is not enough to make them applicable in the Italian domestic legal system because the principle of legality enshrined in the Italian Constitution,[3] as interpreted by the Italian Constitutional Court, demands that offences be adopted by the Italian Parliament.

Our analysis is structured as follows. Section 2 offers a brief overview on the principle of legality in the Italian Constitution, as interpreted and applied by the Italian Constitutional Court. Section 3 explores how war crimes are punished in the WMCC, which is the main Italian legislation implementing war crimes in the Italian domestic legal order, taking into account its peculiar scope of application. Section 4 assesses the lacunae in the implementation of war crimes that can be identified in light of the legislation embodied in the WMCC and other more recent acts. Finally, Section 5 provides the conclusions of this research, emphasising that Italy is not fully complying with its duty to criminalise war crimes.

DOI: 10.4324/9781003320951-17

2 The Italian Constitution, the Principle of Legality, and Obligations of Domestic Criminalisation

Before analysing the Italian implementation of war crimes, it is necessary to provide a brief overview on the role of the principle of legality enshrined in the Italian Constitution vis-à-vis obligations of domestic criminalisation. The rigidity of the Italian Constitutional Court's approach to this issue[4] should be taken into account when analysing war crimes legislation.

Article 25(2) of the Italian Constitution states that "[n]obody can be punished except by virtue of a law in force at the time the offence was committed". This rule is generally interpreted as requiring that criminal offences in the Italian domestic legal system must be embodied in a law adopted by the Italian Parliament.[5] This position has been confirmed by the Italian Constitutional Court, which emphasised that the filter of the parliament creates a link between the exercise of the State's *jus puniendi* and the Italian population which elects democratically the parliament.[6] Accordingly, not only does the Constitution demand that there is a previous criminal offence, but that criminal offence must be approved by the Italian democratically elected organ, the parliament.[7]

Which is the legal situation of war crimes provisions that are binding upon Italy? Following a strictly dualistic approach, treaties are usually incorporated by the so-called executive order (*ordine di esecuzione*), which reproduces a treaty in the Italian domestic legal system, turning it into Italian law.[8] However, for obligations of domestic criminalisation, this is not enough, since in the matter of criminal law Article 25(2) of the Italian Constitution is read as requiring a formal act of parliament.[9]

Contrary to what happens in international human rights law,[10] the principle of legality under the Italian Constitution is not satisfied by the existence of an international criminal offence. Rather, for the current interpretation of Article 25(2) offered by the Italian Constitution, it is not enough that international criminal offences exist in the Italian domestic legal system by virtue of the *ordine di esecuzione* pertaining to a specific treaty or due to the automatic incorporation of customary international law in the Italian domestic legal system. As affirmed by the Italian Constitutional Court, the main elements of the crimes must be embodied in an act of the Italian parliament, whereas references to international sources are only permissible if they integrate factual elements of an offence.[11] The doctrinal attempt to align Article 25(2) of the Italian Constitutional Court with the interpretation of the principle of legality enshrined in international human rights law, which allows recourse to international criminal law sources,[12] has so far received no approval from the Italian Constitutional Court. Article 25(2) of the Italian Constitution is seen as one of the fundamental principles of the Italian Constitution, and thus it also prevails over international rules,[13] which are usually considered to be hierarchically superior to ordinary legislation and – if enshrined in customary international law – over non-fundamental rules of the Italian Constitution itself.[14]

There are several different reasons behind this conservative approach to the principle of legality. Generally speaking, they are linked to the Illuminist tradition, which relied on the parliament as the main actor tasked with the production of criminal law in order to avoid abuses.[15] There are also some reasons that have been advanced with the specific discipline of war crimes in mind. For instance, it is possible that the structure of a war crime included in a treaty or the common understanding of a customary international law war crime is not detailed enough to be in line with the required detailed character of criminal offences.

However, the position of the Italian Constitutional Court on Article 25(2) would also bar the application of the most detailed rule because international obligations on war crimes, even when incorporated in the Italian domestic legal system, do not indicate with sufficient clarity the penalties that are applicable.[16] This is a result of the fact that in the Italian legal system, the parliament provides statutory penalties for each criminal offence, identifying the minimum and maximum amount of the penalty that the judges can apply. This is considered an intrinsic component of the principle of legality even though, at the international level, international criminal statutes do not embody specific penalties for each crime, but rather, they only provide a generic framework applicable for all crimes.[17] For instance, the ICC Statute provides that the ICC can sentence individuals up to 30 years of imprisonment and, for extremely grave cases, to life imprisonment, without providing more specific indications for each of the crimes under the Court's jurisdiction.[18] Such a generic framework would be unconstitutional from the standpoint of the Italian Constitutional Court, which has considered that a very wide framework of statutory framework for a crime leaves too much discretion to the judges in the application of the penalty and is, as a result, unconstitutional for lack of foreseeability.[19] It has been noted that the lack of a statutory penalty for war crimes is a procedural issue pertaining to the preparedness of the Italian legal system to implement its international obligations, rather than an issue concerning fundamental values of the Italian Constitution.[20] Nevertheless, it is a fact that the punishment of war crimes presented in the Italian domestic legal system can be paralysed by the need for purely Italian provisions on penalties adopted by the parliament.[21]

3 The Main Italian Legislation on War Crimes: The 1941 WMCC and Its Complex Scope of Application

The Italian legislation on war crimes is still centred around the 1941 WMCC, particularly its Book III, Title IV (Articles 165–230) devoted to "offences against the laws and customs of war". These offences are applicable by the military judicial system, which operates under guarantees of independence from the Ministry of Defence, through the involvement of military tribunals comprising both military judges (ie civilian judges specialised in this area) and officers of the armed forces.[22] However, the cases in which the WMCC applies are not easy to identify for two reasons: first, the application of the WMCC echoes an old understanding of the divide between peacetime and wartime embodied in the WMCC, which is no longer in line with contemporary international law;[23] and second, selective and disorganised legislative interventions have manipulated the application of the war crimes provision embodied in the WMCC in a confusing case-by-case way.

The original Article 9 of the WMCC, in force until 2001, stated that "the expeditionary forces operating abroad for military operations are subject to the wartime military criminal code, even in peacetime". Under its Article 3, the WMCC is applicable "from the moment when the state of war is declared to the moment of its cessation" (Article 3). However, until the 2001 military operations in Afghanistan, the application of the WMCC had always been barred by legislative interventions adopted by the government. Decree-laws enacted by the government and subsequently approved by the parliament had always provided that "the peacetime military criminal code applies to military personnel" participating in multinational missions abroad.[24] This solution, based on constitutional and political assessments,[25] barred the application of the WMCC (including its provisions dealing with war crimes) for operations implying the involvement in armed conflict scenarios, such as the air raids in Iraq in 1990–1991. In this, the application of the WMCC, which was enacted before the adoption of the UN Charter, appears to be influenced by the establishment of a state of war in the formal sense, a remnant of an outdated conception on the divide between wartime and peacetime in international law which is present in other provisions of the Italian Constitution as well (eg, Articles 78, 87(9)).[26]

Only at the time of Italy's participation in military operations in Afghanistan was the WMCC formally applied, for the first time, through Decree-Law 421/2001. This piece of legislation required the application of the WMCC on the basis of the nature of the mission, ie "a military operation, whose basic characteristics are essentially similar to proper armed activities",[27] and in light of the aim to give effect to WMCC's war crimes provisions. In this context a reform was made to Article 9 of the WMCC, which now reads that the WMCC applies in "armed military operations" abroad.

Moreover, Article 165 of the WMCC, namely the opening provision of Book III, Title IV of the WMCC regarding "offences against the laws and customs of war", was modified by Law no 6/2002. Now, Article 165 of the WMCC states that "[t]he provisions of this title apply to all cases of armed conflict, independently of the declaration of the state of war". This comprehensive wording implies that war crimes can now be of relevance to any armed conflict involving Italy, ie both international (IAC) and non-international (NIAC) ones.[28] This point has been further specified by Law no 15/2002, according to which "[f]or the purposes of wartime military criminal law, 'armed conflict' is taken to mean a conflict where at least one of the parties involved makes militarily organised and extended use of arms against another to carry out war operations". Accordingly, only war crimes committed during an armed conflict fulfilling the characteristics defined in Article 165 of the WMCC, as modified by Law no 15/2002. This solution is partly unsatisfactory for many reasons and, particularly, because it does not reflect the generally accepted definition of IACs in international law.[29] Furthermore, Article 165 of the WMCC was also modified to specify its application "to armed military operations carried out by Italian armed forces abroad", pending "an organic reform in this area".

Until 2006, legislation authorising missions in Afghanistan and Iraq expressly subjected the activities of the military personnel involved therein to the WMCC due to the active military operations carried out in such contexts. On the other hand, the application of the Peace Military Criminal Code (PMCC) was imposed on other missions, such as operations in the Balkans or Lebanon. Nevertheless, from 2006, the relevant decree-laws authorising missions abroad have expressly required application of the PMCC to those missions. This issue was finally addressed by Law no 145/2016 devoted to military missions abroad. In particular, Article 19(1), devoted to penal provisions, adopts a systematic solution, maintaining that the PMCC applies by default to personnel participating and supporting international missions, unless the government requests parliament to expressly apply the WMCC.

There is nevertheless a risk in applying the PMCC rather than the WMCC since the former does not provide for the criminalisation of the war crimes punished by the latter. Accordingly, constantly applying the PMCC would paradoxically prevent the application of provisions related to war crimes included in the WMCC. An interpretive solution to this issue can still be identified on the basis of the new wording of Article 165 of the WMCC, according to which Book III, Title IV applies in "all cases of armed conflict", and "to armed military operations carried out by Italian armed forces abroad [pending] an organic reform in this area". Accordingly, it could be maintained that this specific section of the WMCC has its own autonomous relevance in case of armed conflicts, regardless of any legislative/political choices imposing the use of the PMCC during missions abroad. This position has been taken by military courts,[30] judges writing in personal capacity,[31] and scholars,[32] as rendering the prosecution of war crimes possible in any case.

All in all, even if the above-mentioned solution could creatively allow for the application of war crimes provisions of the WMCC, it is unable to resolve existing shortcomings in its substantive content, as explored in the next section.

4 A Review of War Crimes Provided by the Italian Legal System

4.1 The Evolution of War Crimes Punished by the WMCC

When the WMCC was adopted in 1941, its section dealing with "offences against the laws and customs of war" (Articles 165–230) provided for the very comprehensive criminalisation of several violations of IHL treaties existing at the time. Its content drew inspiration from the 1929 Geneva Conventions and the regulations annexed to the 1907 IV Hague Convention, regardless of their lack of ratification by the Kingdom of Italy.

However, subsequent legislative choices relegated issues regarding war crimes to a realm of neglect, resulting in the current shortcomings. Italy is party to the main post-1941 international humanitarian law treaties which include obligations of domestic criminalisation of war crimes, such as the four 1949 Geneva Conventions, the 1954 Hague Convention, the two 1977 Additional Protocols, and the 1998 Statute of the International Criminal Court (ICC). Nevertheless, parliament limited itself to authorising the President of the Republic to ratify these treaties and order their execution in the domestic legal system (through a so-called *ordine di esecuzione*), but without introducing any substantial change to the latter.[33] A similar approach was most recently adopted for the Kampala amendments to the ICC Statute, namely those affecting Article 8(2)(e)(xiii), (xiv) and (xv).[34] Only on the occasion of the ratification of the 1999 Second Protocol to the 1954 Hague Convention did parliament also introduce new ad hoc criminal provisions through Law no 45/2009, which was detached from the WMCC.[35]

The implementation mechanism offered by the *ordine di esecuzione* is completely inadequate to provide for a proper repression of war crimes at the domestic level. As mentioned above, pursuant to the principle of strict legality in criminal matters embedded in the Italian Constitution, international provisions establishing new criminal offences cannot be directly applied by the Italian judiciary without an intervention of the parliament.[36] In particular, as these provisions do not provide for any regime of penalties their direct application would violate the corollary principles of specificity, certainty, foreseeability and accessibility.

More specifically, war crimes provisions in treaties ratified after 1941 could only be applicable within the Italian legal order under certain circumstances. This is the case where such crimes were already covered by the 1941 WMCC, which provided for the criminalisation of certain conducts subsequently qualified as war crimes by relevant treaties. It is also possible to make use of the openly formulated character of some WMCC provisions intended, for instance, to repress the use of weapons prohibited by "international conventions" (eg Articles 174–175 of the WMCC); provided that such unlawful conducts are accompanied by provisions regarding penalties, it is possible to integrate these offences with post-1941 conventions widening the number of prohibited weapons. Finally, sometimes it is possible to rely on the few amendments made to the WMCC in 2002, which have partly adapted its content to current paradigms.

This inertia has thus been particularly unfortunate in relation to the 1949 Geneva Conventions and the 1977 First Additional Protocol, as they provide explicit obligations for the domestic criminalisation of violations identified by these treaties as serious breaches.[37] The exercise of jurisdiction on these breaches is a duty for every State Party, on the basis of the *aut dedere aut iudicare* principle.[38]

A similar reasoning could be applied concerning the ICC Statute. Even if, formally speaking, there is no obligation for States Parties to include war crimes provided in the Statute in their domestic legal system,[39] States Parties are implicitly encouraged to harmonise their criminal provisions with this instrument because of the principle of complementarity expressed by Articles 1 and 17 of the Statute. Indeed, the principle of complementarity incentives States to align their domestic legal systems with core crimes present in the ICC Statute because existing deficiencies in the domestic legal system may potentially trigger the exercise of the ICC's jurisdiction.[40] Law no 232/1999 permitted a swift ratification of the Rome Statute by Italy but failed to introduce any substantial reform, limiting itself to requesting its implementation through the *ordine di esecuzione*. Beside this early action by the parliament, we can only report failed attempts by the parliament and the government to adapt the Italian legal system to the crimes provided for in the Rome Statute.[41] So far, only provisions addressing cooperation with the ICC have been introduced through Law no 237/2012.[42] Such cooperation, however, may experience potential obstacles because of a lack of incorporation of the relevant war crimes in the Italian domestic legal system.[43]

So far, only at the time of above-mentioned reforms of the WMCC, urgently imposed in 2002 by the decision to apply this code to the mission in Afghanistan, were some provisions of the WMCC modified to partly adapt its content to current IHL paradigms. Before that, war crimes under the IV Geneva Convention were outside the scope of the WMCC.[44] The first significant development occurred with Law no 6/2002, which added a new provision (Article 184*bis*) aimed at criminalising the taking of hostages in an IAC. Second, a new Article 185*bis* was introduced to include additional criminal offences related to the obligations of domestic criminalisation required by the grave breaches system of the 1949 Geneva Conventions and the 1977 First Additional Protocol. Article 185*bis* criminalises unlawful conducts carried out by a member of the armed forces "to the detriment of prisoners of war or civilians or other persons protected by international conventions" with a statutory penalty of between two and five years' imprisonment, making specific reference to torture, inhuman treatment, illegal transfers, biological experiments, unjustified medical treatment and "other acts prohibited to him by international conventions".

This openly formulated latter clause might eventually provide some flexibility in the criminalisation of conducts against protected persons not yet included in the WMCC. For instance, it could be relevant for some grave breaches such as the deportation or unlawful confinement of a protected person. However, doubts could be raised about its capacity to constitute a proper basis for domestic criminalisation, as clear parameters of reference are lacking. In particular, it is unclear whether this clause only applies to grave breaches or might be extended to further conducts contrary to IHL treaty provisions carried out against protected persons, thus confirming the need for more clarity in this area rather than this potential omnibus clause.

However, the urgency imposed by the mission in Afghanistan allowed for only a few random changes addressing some of the existing shortcomings and prevented a more comprehensive assessment of current lacunae. A comparison between the current WMCC, relevant IHL and international criminal law treaties highlights various shortcomings, which have already been examined elsewhere,[45] and which are examined in the following subsection.

4.2 Shortcoming of the War Crimes Punished by the WMCC with Particular Reference to the ICC Statute

Due to the limited length of this chapter, it is impossible to conduct an exhaustive analysis of all the shortcomings of the Italian implementation of war crimes. We will therefore focus on the main deficiencies of the system, considering in particular the list of war crimes provided by the ICC Statute.

In relation to Article 8(2)(a), regarding the grave breaches of the 1949 Geneva Conventions, the main shortcomings are due to outdated terminologies in the original drafting in 1941, which was unable to properly address the notion of protected persons. For instance, with regard to Article 8(2)(a)(i), on "wilful killing", Article 185 of the WMCC criminalises such acts against "enemy private citizens". This wording is inadequate with respect to several categories of protected persons. Concerning the hypothesis provided by Article 8(2)(a)(v), on "compelling a prisoner of war or other protected person to serve in the forces of a hostile Power", Article 182 of the WMCC criminalises this conduct only in relation to "enemy subjects". In other instances, extensive use of the omnibus clause introduced by Article 185*bis* through Law no 6/2002 would need to be made in order to criminalise "other acts prohibited by international conventions" and repress other grave breaches not expressly provided by the WMCC, as in Article 8(2)(a)(vi) and (vii). These examples are merely illustrative of a number of shortcomings of the Italian legislation in relation to grave breaches.[46]

Concerning the war crimes embodied in Article 8(2)(b), addressing "[o]ther serious violations of the laws and customs applicable in international armed conflict", similar shortcomings can be identified. On some occasions the potential use of Article 185*bis* of the WMCC could be relevant to address offences against protected persons not expressly included in the WMCC but prohibited by IHL treaties, such as in the hypotheses provided by Article (8)(2)(b)(vi), (x), and (xiv). The same reasoning could be applied regarding Articles 174 and 175 of the WMCC, which prohibit ordering or making use of "means and methods of warfare prohibited by laws and international conventions". These openly formulated provisions could be extended to hypotheses not expressly prohibited by the WMCC, such as those provided for by Article 8(2)(b)(vii), (xi), (xii), (xvii), (xviii), (xix), (xx), (xxiii) and (xxv). This integration looks problematic under the aforementioned case law of the

Italian Constitutional Court on the integration of domestic offences with international sources, which demands that the core elements of any offence must be provided by the Italian legislation, while only some factual elements of those offences can be identified through the reference to external sources.[47] Accordingly, to fully comply with Article 25(2) of the Italian Constitution, it would be preferable to introduce ad hoc offences as well as to differentiate among statutory penalties. More generally, the WMCC is totally or partly unfit to cover certain other offences related to specific conducts which are out of the scope of any provision of the WMCC, as for Article 8(2)(b)(iii) dealing with attacks against humanitarian assistance or peacekeeping missions, to mention just one example.[48]

Finally, it should be noted that the WMCC criminalises certain conducts in IACs that are not considered as war crimes by Article 8(a) and (b) of the ICC Statute.[49] This is in line with the request made to States to also "take measures necessary for the suppression of all acts contrary to the provisions of the present Convention other than the grave breaches",[50] possibly also through "a list of war crimes, which goes well beyond the list of grave breaches".[51] However, it would be opportune to conduct a coherent review of this possibility, currently provided for by certain random solutions adopted in 1941.

The implementation of the war crimes listed in Article 8(2)(c) to (f), addressing war crimes committed in NIACs, is even more problematic. As mentioned previously, the new wording of Article 165 of the WMCC, extending the application of Book III, Title IV of this code to "all cases of armed conflict", implies its application also to NIACs. However, not having been accompanied by a substantial restyling of the WMCC, this solution implies significant challenges for the prosecution of war crimes listed in Article 8(2)(c) to (f), particularly considering the unfit terminology used in relevant WMCC provisions. Indeed, such provisions, drafted with interstate hostilities in mind, criminalise conducts whether committed against "enemy private citizens" (Article 185), the "enemy" (Articles 174, 175, 192, 193) or "persons belonging to the enemy State" (Article 177), or they introduce territorial qualifiers to cover offences committed in the "territory of the enemy State occupied by the armed forces of the Italian State" (Article 182) or in an "enemy territory" (Articles 187, 224). Similar expressions are problematic in relation to a NIAC, where there is protracted violence between a State and an organised armed group or between two or more armed groups. Even though the decision to apply the war crimes provided by the WMCC to NIACs may be saluted as part of the trend that favours the unification between rules pertaining to IACs and NIACs,[52] nevertheless similar inaccuracies may be problematic in the field of criminal law.

To overcome these problems, some scholars have to set aside literal interpretation of this provision, for instance "qualifying as an 'enemy' an individual who is not strictly speaking an enemy, but, de facto, assumes the role that would be covered by the enemy, if it were a war".[53] However, a comprehensive reform of the WMCC would be required in this area. Furthermore, even if the above-mentioned creative interpretation could be maintained, a series of crimes included in the ICC Statute in relation to NIACs are not present in the WMCC at all, such as the taking of hostages in NIACs under Article 8(2)(c)(iii). In several other instances, it would be necessary to make reference to the omnibus provision provided by Article 185*bis* for the prosecution of "other conduct prohibited by international conventions" against protected persons in Articles 8(2)(c)(iv) or 8(2)(e)(vii), although the compatibility of this solution with constitutional case law on Article 25(2) of the Italian Constitution remains doubtful. Robust intervention by the parliament would be the correct solution.

4.3 Criminalisation of War Crimes Outside the WMCC

Even if the WMCC represents the main source for the prosecution for war crimes in Italy, some other relevant provisions are embodied in different pieces of legislation. For instance, at the occasion of the ratification of the 1999 Second Additional Protocol to the 1954 Hague Convention, the above-mentioned Law no 45/2009 introduced substantive criminal provisions through its Articles 7–13.[54] These articles implement the explicit obligation of domestic criminalisation provided by Article 15(2) of the Protocol. The prosecution of such crimes could occur "during an armed conflict or international missions", as provided by Article 6 of Law no 45/2009. Furthermore, criminal prosecutions for the use (as well as other prohibited conducts as production or transfer) or of certain prohibited weapons were included at the time of the implementation of the Ottawa and Oslo Conventions in the Italian legal order, respectively Law no 374 of 29 October 1997[55] and Law no 95 of 14 June 2011.[56]

5 Conclusions

Italy has not implemented its duty to criminalise war crimes in an adequate way, notwithstanding the fact that the lack of full implementation can be a source of State responsibility.[57] The main responsibility to overcome this delay rests on the Italian Parliament because the principle of legality embodied in the Italian constitution, as interpreted by the Italian Constitutional Court, prevents the direct application of criminal offences embodied in international treaties into the Italian legal order. As a result, several war crimes could not be prosecuted in the Italian legal order, but rather, the extant legislation is still largely based on the 1941 WMCC as slightly modified subsequently. For all these reasons, the Italian implementation of international obligations of domestic criminalisation pertaining to war crimes is currently unsatisfactory and requires substantive reforms. Therefore, the recent establishment by the Ministry of Justice of a Commission charged to elaborate a code for international crimes should be welcomed in light of the possibility to systematically address above-mentioned shortcomings.[58] However the project finally elaborated by this Commission did not have the chance to be approved due to the end of the legislature.[59] Its results might nonetheless be the starting point for further efforts in the near future.

Notes

1 The texts of all the Italian documents cited in this chapter have been translated by the authors, except for where otherwise provided. Internet references were last accessed on 15 June 2022, when this chapter was completed. Giulio Bartolini is author of Sections 3 and 4, Marco Longobardo of Section 2. The introduction and conclusions have been jointly elaborated.

2 On this topic, see generally Guido Acquaviva, *La repressione dei crimini di guerra nel diritto internazionale e nel diritto italiano* (Giuffrè 2014); Giulio Bartolini, 'The Criminalization of War Crimes in Italy and the Shortcomings of the Domestic Legal Framework' (2021) 21 International Criminal Law Review 679.

3 Constitution of the Italian Republic (Italian Constitution), 1947, English text available at www.senato.it/documenti/repository/istituzione/costituzione_inglese.pdf.

4 See, generally, Beatrice I Bonafè, 'Constitutional Judicial Review and International Obligations of Criminalization' (2021) 21 International Criminal Law Review 660.

5 Carlo Federico Grosso and others, *Manuale di Diritto Penale: Parte Generale* (3rd edn, Giuffrè 2017) 88; Ferrando Mantovani, *Diritto Penale: Parte Generale* (11th edn, CEDAM 2020) 45.

6 Italian Constitutional Court, Decision no 487/1989, para 3.

7 Grosso (n 5) 88; Mantovani (n 5) 45.

8 Generally, on the Italian implementation of international law, see Carlo Focarelli, *International Law* (Edward Elgar 2019) 247–266.

9 Luigi Condorelli, *Il giudice italiano e i trattati internazionali. Gli accordi* self-executing *e non* self-executing *nell'ottica della giurisprudenza* (Cedam 1974) 62; Bonafè (n 4) 672. For a comparative analysis, see Andrea Caligiuri, 'Limiti alla efficacia di norme internazionali generali in materia penale nell'ordinamento italiano', in Giuseppe Puma (ed), *Diritto internazionale e sistema delle fonti* (Cacucci 2020) 53, 58–64.

10 See European Convention on Human Rights, Art 7(1): "No one shall be held guilty of any criminal offence on account of any act or omission which did not constitute a criminal offence under national or *international law* at the time when it was committed" (emphasis added); and International Covenant on Civil and Political Rights, Article 15(1): "No one shall be held guilty of any criminal offence on account of any act or omission which did not constitute a criminal offence, under national or *international law*, at the time when it was committed" (emphasis added).

11 See, eg, Italian Constitutional Court, decision no 21/2009, para 4. For more analysis of the relevant case law, see Daniele Amoroso, 'The Duties of Criminalization under International Law in the Practice of Italian Judges: An Overview' (2021) 21 International Criminal Law Review 641, 652–655; Bonafè (n 4) 669–673.

12 Francesco Salerno, 'Il limite—non il contro-limite—della riserva di legge all'attuazione diretta della norma internazionale "generalmente riconosciuta" in materia penale', in Umberto Leanza and others (eds), *Studi in onore di Giuseppe Tesauro* (Editoriale Scientifica 2014) 2861, 2876–2882.

13 Italian Constitutional Court, decision no 238/2014, para 2.1.
14 See the case law discussed in Focarelli (n 8) 249–252, 256–257.
15 Italian Constitutional Court, decision no 487/1989, para 3.
16 Natalino Ronzitti, 'Intervention', in Michael Bothe (ed), *National Implementation of International Humanitarian Law* (Martinus Nijhoff 1990) 56, 56.
17 See generally Silvia D'Ascoli, *Sentencing in International Criminal Law: The UN Ad Hoc Tribunals and Future Perspectives for the ICC* (Hart 2011).
18 ICC Statute, Art 77. See generally Alessandra Lanciotti, 'Le pene comminabili dalla Corte penale internazionale', in Gaetano Carlizzi and others (eds), *La Corte Penale Internazionale: problemi e prospettive* (Vivarium 2003) 405.
19 See, eg, Italian Constitutional Court, decision no 299/1992, para 4; decision no 230/2012, para 7.
20 Salerno (n 12) 2885–2887.
21 Other penal effects of the relevant war crimes provisions, even in the absence of implementation legislation, are outside the purview of this chapter. See, generally, Salerno (n 12) 2887–2891; Amoroso (n 11) 644–651, 655–657; Bonafè (n 4) 673–677.
22 David Brunelli and Giuseppe Mazzi, *Diritto penale militare* (Giuffrè 2007) 425–473; Pierpaolo Rivello, *Manuale del diritto penale militare e dell'ordinamento giudiziario militare* (Giappichelli 2019) 427–461.
23 See Natalino Ronzitti, 'Intervention', in Bothe (n 16) 36. On the demise of the relevance of the state of war, see generally Andrew Clapham, *War* (OUP 2021).
24 Decree-Law no 13/1998, Art 1(2) in Official Gazette no 18, 23 January 1988.
25 Maurizio Block, 'Introduzione', in Ida Caracciolo and Umberto Montuoro (eds), *Ricostruzione della pace, giustizia e tutela dei diritti umani* (Giappichelli 2021) xi, xii-xiii.
26 This is just an echo, since there is no legal correspondence between the establishment of the state of war and/or the issuance of a declaration of war, and the application of the WMCC. See ibid xi.
27 See Senate of the Republic, *Relazione al disegno di legge S.914*, 4 December 2013, www.senato.it/service/PDF/PDFServer/BGT/00009807.pdf.
28 Natalino Ronzitti, 'Una legge organica per l'invio di corpi di spedizione all'estero?' (2002) 85 Rivista di diritto internazionale 139, 142–143; Giulio Bartolini, 'Le modifiche al codice penale militare di guerra a seguito della missione italiana in Afghanistan' (2002) 57 La Comunità internazionale 171, 185–186.
29 See ICTY, *Prosecutor v D Tadić*, Decision on the Defence Motion for Interlocutory Appeal on Jurisdiction, 2 October 1995, para 70: "[A]n armed conflict exists whenever there is a resort to armed force between States".
30 Military Tribunal in Rome, *Stival and Allocca*, no 33/2007, Judgment, 9 May 2007, www.difesa.it/Giustizia_Militare/rassegna/Bimestrale/2008/Pagine/Sent-GUP-Trib-mil-Roma-9maggio2007-allocca-stival.aspx
31 Brunelli and Mazzi (n 22) 513, Marco De Paolis, 'Sull'applicazione dei codici penali militari di guerra e di pace nelle operazioni militari all'estero' (2017) Il Filangieri. Quaderno 125, 129–142; Rivello (n 22) 419.
32 Natalino Ronzitti, 'La legge italiana sulle missioni internazionali' (2017) 100 Rivista di diritto internazionale 474, 492–493; Bartolini, 'The Criminalization of War Crimes' (n 2) 688.
33 For the 1949 Geneva Conventions see Law 27 October 1951, no 1739, in Official Gazette, Ordinary Supplement no 53, 1 March 1952, while for the

1977 Additional Protocols see Law 11 December 1985, no 762, in Official Gazette, Ordinary Supplement no 303, 27 December 1985. The ICC Statute was implemented through Law 12 July 1999, no 232, in Official Gazette no 167, Ordinary Supplement no 135.

34 See Law 10 November 2021, no 202, in Official Gazette, Ordinary Supplement no 287, 2 December 2021. The amendments extend the jurisdiction of the Court to the war crimes of employing certain weapons and substances in armed conflicts not of an international character, particularly with regard to poison or poisoned weapons, asphyxiating, poisonous or other gases, and bullets which expand or flatten easily in the human body.

35 See below, Subsection 4.3.

36 See above, Section 2.

37 See in particular obligations of criminalisation provided by I Geneva Convention, Art 50; II Geneva Convention, Art 51; III Geneva Convention, Art 130; IV Geneva Conventions, Art 147; I Additional Protocol, Arts 11 and 85.

38 Various shortcomings in their implementation are identified as analysed below, Subsection 4.2.

39 William A Schabas, *An Introduction to the International Criminal Court* (6th edn, Cambridge University Press 2020) 190–192.

40 Marco Roscini, 'Great Expectations: The Implementation of the Rome Statute in Italy' (2007) 5 Journal of International Criminal Justice 493, 496–497.

41 Roberto Belelli, 'Come adattare l'ordinamento giuridico italiano allo Statuto della Corte dell'Aja' (2003) 9 Diritto penale e processo 1299.

42 Flavia Lattanzi, 'Un piccolo passo sulla via dell'adeguamento allo Statuto della Corte Penale Internazionale' (2013) 96 Rivista di diritto internazionale 492.

43 Limited space in this chapter does not allow for more analysis on this. See, generally, Luigi Prosperi, 'L'applicazione giudiziale delle norme dello Statuto di Roma sulla cooperazione con la Corte penale internazionale', in Giuseppe Palmisano (ed), *Il diritto internazionale ed europeo nei giudizi interni* (Editoriale Scientifica 2020) 209.

44 Mario Pisani, 'La penetrazione del diritto penale internazionale nel diritto penale sostanziale italiano (genocidio, pirateria e pirateria aerea, reati di guerra, droga ecc.)' (1979) Il Consiglio Superiore della Magistratura – Supplmento: Diritto Penale Internazionale 45, 57; Paolo Benvenuti, 'Il ritardo della legislazione italiana nell'adeguamento al diritto internazionale umanitario, con particolare riferimento alla disciplina dei conflitti armati non internazionali', in Pierluigi Lamberti Zanardi and Gabriella Venturini (eds), *Crimini di guerra e competenza delle giurisdizioni nazionali* (Giuffrè 1998) 107.

45 Report for Amnesty International Italy on 'L'Italia e l'adeguamento allo Statuto della Corte penale internazionale', drafted by Brando Ranalli under the supervision of Giulio Bartolini and Alice Riccardi in the framework of the Roma Tre IHL Legal Clinic (July 2019, on file with the author) 16–30; Bartolini (n 2).

46 See Bartolini (n 2).

47 See above, Section 2.

48 For similar shortcomings see for instance Art 8(2)(b), (iv), (v), and (xxvi).

49 See for example crimes affecting prisoners of war provided at Arts 213 of the WMCC (violations of the freedom of religion) and 214 of the WMCC (stealing of personal belongings).

50 See 1949 First Geneva Convention, Art 49.

51 Eve La Haye, 'Art. 49: Penal Sanctions', in ICRC (ed), *Commentary on the First Geneva Convention* (Cambridge University Press 2016), para 2897, https://ihl-databases.icrc.org/applic/ihl/ihl.nsf/Comment.xsp?action=openDocument&documentId=3ED0B7D33BF425F3C1257F7D00589C84.

52 See generally the analysis by Marco Sassòli, 'The Convergence of the International Humanitarian Law of Non-International and International Armed Conflicts: The Dark Side of a Good Idea', in Giovanni Biaggini, Oliver Diggelmann and Christine Kaufmann (eds), *Polis und Kosmopolis – Festschrift für Daniel Thürer* (Nomos 2015) 679.

53 Tullio Padovani, 'La legge penale militare di guerra, i conflitti armati e le operazioni militari all'estero', in Alberto Gargani (ed), *Il diritto penale militare tra passato e futuro* (Giappichelli 2009) 66.

54 Anna Maria Maugeri, 'La tutela dei beni culturali nell'ambito di conflitti armati: la l. 16.4.2009, n. 45' (2010) 30(1) La legislazione penale 5.

55 Law 26 March 1999, no 106, in Official Gazette, Ordinary Supplement no 94, 23 April 1999.

56 Law 14 June 2011, no 95, in Official Gazette, Ordinary Supplement no 153, 4 July 2011.

57 See generally Marco Longobardo, 'The Italian Legislature and International and EU Obligations of Domestic Criminalisation' (2021) 21 International Criminal Law Review 623.

58 Italian Ministry of Justice, Decree, 22 March 2022, www.giustizia.it/giustizia/it/mg_1_36_0.page?contentId=COS372730#.

59 For the text containing the main results of activities carried out by the Commission see www.giustizia.it/cmsresources/cms/documents/commissione_PALAZZO_POCAR_relazione_finale_31mag22.pdf.

Selected Bibliography

Acquaviva G, *La repressione dei crimini di guerra nel diritto internazionale e nel diritto italiano* (Giuffrè 2014);

Bartolini G, 'The Criminalization of War Crimes in Italy and the Shortcomings of the Domestic Legal Framework' (2021) 21 *International Criminal Law Review* 679;

Lamberti Zanardi P and Venturini G (eds), *Crimini di guerra e competenza delle giurisdizioni nazionali* (Giuffrè 1998);

Lattanzi F, 'Un piccolo passo sulla via dell'adeguamento allo Statuto della Corte Penale Internazionale' (2013) 96 *Rivista di diritto internazionale* 492;

Salerno F, 'Il limite—non il contro-limite—della riserva di legge all'attuazione diretta della norma internazionale «generalmente riconosciuta» in materia penale', in Umberto Leanza and others (eds), *Studi in onore di Giuseppe Tesauro* (Editoriale Scientifica 2014) 2861

4.3 Prosecuting genocide and crimes against humanity as ordinary offences

What consequences?

Luigi Prosperi

1 Introduction: circumscribing the scope of the analysis

In order to answer the main question this chapter aims to address – *what consequences follow from the prosecution of genocide and crimes against humanity as "ordinary offences" at the domestic level?* – one needs to also entertain two sub-questions:

1. are States under an obligation to prosecute conducts amounting to genocide and/or crimes against humanity (CAH)[1] pursuant to international law?
2. Are States under an obligation to prosecute conducts amounting to genocide and/or CAH *as such*?

In the next sections, I will therefore examine whether and to what extent international law dictates to States how to address genocide and CAH at the domestic level,[2] and discuss the consequences of the prosecution of such conducts as ordinary offences: (1) within the system of the Rome Statute of the International Criminal Court (ICC Statute, Rome Statute, ICCSt, ICC, the Court); and (2) within the international legal order.

In doing so, in each section I will consider two different scenarios: (a) the conduct can be prosecuted as an ordinary offence at the domestic level; and (b) domestic courts cannot exercise their jurisdiction over the conduct because the statute of limitations has expired in relation to such ordinary offence.

In Section 2 I will consider whether, by prosecuting conducts amounting to genocide or CAH as ordinary offences, the authorities of a State Party might violate *indirect* obligations to (criminalise and) prosecute stemming from the ICC Statute. To this end, I will analyse provisions setting out the principle of complementarity and introducing an exception to the *ne bis in idem* principle. By ratifying the Statute, Italy may have undertaken "implicit obligations"[3] to criminalise and prosecute crimes falling under the jurisdiction of the ICC.

In Section 3 I will focus on the specific obligations to criminalise and prosecute acts of genocide arising from the Convention on the Prevention and

DOI: 10.4324/9781003320951-18

Punishment of the Crime of Genocide (Genocide Convention, GenConv).[4] I will thus assess whether following the ratification of this convention on the part of Italy, and also in light of the legislation enacted in 1967 to implement it, the prosecution of acts of genocide as ordinary offences might violate such obligations.

Pending the adoption of a "Convention on the prevention and punishment of crimes against humanity", in Section 4 I will investigate whether explicit or implicit obligations to (criminalise and) prosecute conducts amounting to CAH may arise from treaties that Italy has ratified or from customary international law (CIL). A caveat is needed in this respect. For the purpose of this analysis I will not take into account conventions addressing "crimes against international law" which might *also* amount to CAH. Besides the fact that they do not require that the crime is committed as part of a widespread or systematic attack directed against any civilian population (in accordance with Article 7 of the ICCSt), such "suppression conventions" provide definitions of the underlying crimes that are not consistent with those enshrined in the Rome Statute. This is the case of the UN Convention Against Torture and Other Cruel, Inhuman or Degrading Treatment or Punishment (that Italy ratified in January 1989)[5] as well as the International Convention for the Protection of All Persons from Enforced Disappearance (that Italy ratified in October 2015).[6]

I will instead focus on the European Convention for the Protection of Human Rights and Fundamental Freedoms (European Convention on Human Rights, ECHR),[7] on the Convention on the Non-Applicability of Statutory Limitations to War Crimes and Crimes Against Humanity (Convention on the Non-Applicability of Statutory Limitations),[8] and on rules of CIL.

In sum, this chapter aims to shed a light on the consequences of the prosecution of acts of genocide and conducts amounting to CAH as ordinary offences vis-à-vis both the ICC system and the international legal order.

2 Prosecuting genocide and CAH as ordinary offences: what consequences in respect to *implicit* obligations to prosecute pursuant to the ICC Statute?

In a recent article, Longobardo argued that by ratifying the ICC Statute, States Parties do not undertake an obligation to enact domestic criminal legislation in relation to the crimes falling under the jurisdiction of the Court. If States decided not to enact such legislation, the only consequence would be "that the resulting lack of domestic prosecution may trigger the exercise of the Court's jurisdiction under the principle of complementarity".[9] On the other hand, Longobardo warned that "the lack of incorporation of the crimes in the Italian legal system may make it difficult for Italy to comply with some of its obligations of cooperation under Part 9 of the Statute, which may require … that the charges are criminalised at domestic level".[10] In other words: by ratifying the Statute, Italy may have undertaken "implicit" obligations to criminalise and prosecute conducts falling under the jurisdiction of the Court.

In this section, I will examine whether violations of implicit obligations to (criminalise and) prosecute genocide and CAH might follow from the decision to prosecute such conducts as ordinary offences. In particular, I will focus on situations where this decision may conflict with the rules on complementarity (Section 2.1) or on the *ne bis in idem* principle (Section 2.2).

2.1 The complementarity framework

According to Article 17(1)(a) of the Statute, the Court shall determine that a case is inadmissible (and thus recognise the primacy of national courts in accordance with Article 1) where it is "being investigated or prosecuted by a State which has jurisdiction over it, unless the State is unwilling or unable genuinely to carry out the investigation or prosecution".

As to the first requirement, the State must demonstrate that it is investigating or prosecuting, or has investigated or prosecuted "the same individual and substantially the same conduct as alleged in the proceedings before the Court".[11] For the purpose of this test, "same conduct" does not imply that the crime must be prosecuted as an international crime domestically. Conversely, it is sufficient that "the crimes prosecuted at the domestic level cover 'substantially the same conduct' as those charged by the Court".[12]

In practice, this means that domestic authorities *can* charge suspects with ordinary offences. Such prosecutions may nevertheless be barred on a different ground – such as the expiration of the statute of limitations. With respect to Italy, the latter scenario is not at all foreign. Pursuant to Article 157 of the Criminal Code, statutes of limitations are in fact applicable to most domestic offences "corresponding to" the underlying CAH enumerated in Article 7(1) ICC Statute. In addition, some of these statutes of limitations expire in a rather short time, particularly in relation to the offences of illegal arrest and unlawful deprivation of liberty[13] (time barred after 6 years), kidnapping[14] (8 or 10 years, depending on the existence of certain aggravating circumstances), and torture[15] (10 or 12 years, unless the conduct has resulted in a "very serious injury" to the victim[16]). Regrettable as this may be, the fact that such provisions could bar the prosecution of genocide or CAH at the domestic level does not amount to a violation of an obligation arising from the Statute.

In light of the above, Articles 1 and 17 do not entail any explicit or implicit obligation to criminalise and/or prosecute conducts falling under the jurisdiction of the ICC. In theory, ICC judges may invoke statutory rules on complementarity to claim jurisdiction where a "corresponding" ordinary offence is *not available* at the domestic level. The only consequence of the lack of criminalisation or prosecution at the national level would be to trigger the exercise of the Court's jurisdiction over the alleged crimes.

In practice, the problem lies in the relationship between the two legal systems. Where the alleged conduct did not amount to a crime under the applicable domestic legislation or the statute of limitations expired in relation to the corresponding offence, national authorities might not authorise the transfer of the suspect to the Court. With respect to the Italian legal system, judges may turn down the arrest and transfer because it would entail a violation of a fundamental principle of the domestic legal system (the principle of legality). A violation of the duty to cooperate with the ICC in accordance with Part IX of the Statute would ensue.[17]

2.2 The exception to the **ne bis in idem** *principle*

Pursuant to Article 20(3)(a) ICCSt., the Court may exercise its jurisdiction over a person that has already been tried at the domestic level and with respect to the same conduct when the national proceedings were "for the purpose of shielding the person concerned from criminal responsibility for crimes within the jurisdiction of the Court". In such circumstances, the ICC can overrule the presumption of the application of the *ne bis in idem* principle.

Interestingly, a first draft of this provision was rejected during the negotiations of the Statute, according to which the ICC would be allowed to overrule the *ne bis in idem* principle where the other court characterised the conduct falling under the jurisdiction of the ICC as an ordinary crime. At the time, States delegates argued that this would infringe on the other court's prerogative to evaluate facts differently. A second draft of the exception, based on the fact that the sentence imposed in the first trial had not been severe enough, would also be turned down.[18]

The fundamental principle enshrined in the final version of Article 20 of the ICC Statute is that when a person has already been tried by another (international or domestic) court in relation to a conduct falling under the scope of Articles 6, 7, 8, or 8*bis* of the Statute, "a subsequent trial [before the ICC] for a different qualification based on the same historical facts would be prohibited".[19] Considering that the premise of this contribution is that prosecutions have been initiated at the national level, I will assume that a suspect has indeed been tried, and focus on whether and under which conditions the ICC may find that an exception to the *ne bis in idem* applies. Two situations shall be considered. First, the domestic proceeding might fail the "same conduct" test. Second, domestic authorities might have had the purpose of shielding the suspect. Since so far the ICC has not had the opportunity to rule on any of these scenarios, the analysis will centre on the academic debate.

As to the "same conduct" test, commentaries have argued that the ICC should follow the same rationale as in the decisions on the admissibility of a case and get to the same conclusion that crimes prosecuted at the domestic level must cover substantially the same conduct as those charged by the Court.[20]

Concerning the purpose of shielding the suspect, scholars noted that while "[i]t is difficult to decipher what kind of situations fall under this clause", one may assume that an example would be a case "where an atrocity amounting to genocide is charged as an evidently disproportionate ordinary crime, such as an assault".[21] Based on the letter of the statutory provision, in the specific circumstances of the case this disproportion must be so evident as to demonstrate the intention, on the part of the judicial organ involved, to shield the perpetrator. The threshold would be quite high.

As a result, I believe that the prosecution of a conduct falling under the jurisdiction of the Court as an ordinary offence might only give rise to exceptions to the *ne bis in idem* principle where at the domestic level the perpetrator has been sentenced to an extremely lenient penalty, disproportionate to the seriousness of his/her conducts. In such circumstances, the State Party would not violate any – explicit or implicit – obligation to criminalise or prosecute. The only consequence would be to trigger the exercise of the ICC's jurisdiction. Similarly to requests based on Articles 1 and 17, however, in this scenario domestic authorities might as well conclude that they *cannot* authorise the transfer of the convicted person, as it would in turn result in a violation of the fundamental principle of (domestic) *ne bis in idem* as interpreted by the European Court of Human Rights (Strasbourg Court, ECtHR).[22]

3 Prosecuting acts of genocide as ordinary offences: what consequences under the Genocide Convention?

With respect to acts amounting to genocide, specific obligations arise from the Genocide Convention – which Italy ratified through Law no 153/1952 adopted on 11 March 1952. As a result of the ratification, Italy undertook obligations to criminalise and prosecute acts of genocide and other prohibited conducts in accordance with the convention.

First, pursuant to Article I of the Genocide Convention Italy undertook "to prevent and punish" the crime of genocide "whether committed in time of peace or in time of war".

Article VI circumscribes the scope of the obligation to punish genocide by establishing that persons charged with a conduct enumerated in Articles II and III "shall be tried by a competent tribunal of the State in the territory of which the act was committed" or by a competent "international penal tribunal". As concerns the former duty, the International Court of Justice held that it is "subject to an express territorial limit".[23] As to the latter, it highlighted that Article VI "obliges the Contracting Parties to cooperate with such international criminal tribunal", and that this obligation "implies that they will arrest persons accused of genocide who are in their territory ... and, failing prosecution of them in the parties' own courts, that they will hand them over for trial by the competent international tribunal".[24] Where a Contracting Party – such as Italy – has also ratified the ICC Statute, the execution of this obligation requires that domestic authorities are put in the position to execute cooperation requests submitted by the Court in relation to acts of genocide falling within the scope of Article 6 ICCSt.

Pursuant to Article VI, the duty to exercise jurisdiction at the domestic level seems to bind only the territorial State. However, according to Schiffbauer Article IV would establish "a prohibition of impunity for genocide and related acts", and impose on States Parties a "subsidiary" duty "to contribute to the final aim of punishment" by taking all possible measures so that punishment can finally be applied.[25]

As to the obligation to criminalise, pursuant to Article V States Parties undertake a duty to enact "the necessary legislation to give effect to the provisions of the present Convention, and, in particular, to provide effective penalties for persons guilty of genocide or any of the other acts enumerated in article III" – namely, acts of genocide, conspiracy to commit genocide, direct and public incitement to commit genocide, attempt to commit genocide, and complicity in genocide. While Article IV sets out a duty to punish perpetrators of conducts enumerated in Articles II and III, it is Article V that identifies the "means of punishment" – that is, *effective penalties*.[26] The Genocide Convention provides neither a definition of "effective" penalty nor any guidance concerning the minimum or maximum penalties to be associated with the prohibited conducts. Schiffbauer has argued in this regard that "it may be assumed that in order to be 'effective', penalties for genocide must meet a minimum threshold of 'severity'" and "have to reflect the gravity of the crime".[27]

Although the above-mentioned provisions do not expressly require that States Parties prosecute conducts enumerated in Articles II and III of the convention *as such*, scholars have argued that this would follow from Article V. In this regard, Schiffbauer claimed that "[t]he verdict of guilt of genocide and a subsequent penalty are only available if a corresponding provision criminalising genocide exists in municipal law".[28]

It took almost 15 years for Italy to implement the Genocide Convention. To this aim, the legislator adopted Constitutional Law no 1/1967 (ConstLaw 1/1967) and Law no 962/1967 (Law 962/1967). The former consisted of a single article, according to which the "political offence exception" to the extradition of foreigners – as provided under Article 10(4) of the Constitution of Italy – would not apply with regard to acts of genocide. Law 962/1967 consisted of nine articles criminalising acts of genocide (Articles 2–8) and establishing that the Court of Assize would exercise jurisdiction over such offences (Article 9).

Concerning the obligation to enact domestic legislation to give effect to the provisions of the Genocide Convention, not only did Law 962/1967 criminalise all conducts enumerated in Articles II and III, but it also introduced two additional offences: the deportation of members of the protected group (Article 2), and the application of "badges" on members of the protected group (Article 6). Accordingly, domestic authorities can prosecute conducts falling under the scope of the Genocide Convention as well as hand suspects over to competent international tribunals – including the ICC.

It is therefore unlikely that domestic authorities may decide to prosecute an act of genocide as an ordinary offence. If that was the case, a violation of the obligation to punish as arising from Articles IV and V of the Genocide Convention would only ensue where an "ineffective" (that is, not severe enough) penalty was attached to such offence. Moreover, the domestic legal system provides an additional safeguard in this respect. Where a domestic prosecutor decided to charge a suspect with an ordinary offence instead of one of the offences criminalised pursuant to Law 962/1967, judges would be in a position to reverse this decision. In fact, Articles 292, 309, 310, and 521 of the Code of Criminal Procedure provide criminal judges with the power to unilaterally modify the legal characterisation of the facts at different phases of a criminal proceeding.

On the other hand, a violation of the duty to punish or transfer the suspect may result from the *unavailability* of domestic offences due to the expiration of statutes of limitations. All offences introduced in Articles 2 to 8 of Law 962/1967 are subjected to the general principles on statutory limitations. In light of Article 157 of the Criminal Code, prosecutions would only be time barred in respect to conducts not resulting in the death of any person – such as causing serious bodily or mental harm to members of the group (18 years), incitement to commit genocide (12 years), and complicity in genocide not resulting in the commission of an act of genocide (6 years). In principle, these rules seem to be compatible with Articles IV and V GenConv. On the other hand, where the statute of limitations expired in relation to the domestic offence, it would bar not only the prosecution of a suspect at the domestic level, but also his/her extradition to a third State Party or his/her transfer to an "international penal tribunal" such as the ICC – and *thus* result in the violation of the duty to punish, as arising from Articles I and VI GenConv.

4 Prosecuting CAH as ordinary offences: "residual" obligations to punish under conventional and customary law

No analogous obligations to criminalise and/or punish as those analysed in Section 3 have been undertaken by Italy with regard to CAH. Pending the adoption of a "Convention on the prevention and punishment of crimes against humanity", and considering that no such duties stemmed from the statutes of the international criminal tribunals so far established by the international community, Italy seems to be under no obligation to criminalise and prosecute CAH *as such*.[29] Nevertheless, "residual" obligations may arise from other conventional and customary rules of international law.

First, States Parties to the European Convention on Human Rights undertake implicit obligations to criminalise and punish grave violations of human rights which may also amount to CAH. As underlined by Karavias, the Strasbourg Court has acknowledged a duty to prosecute grave violations of human rights affecting the life, physical integrity, and freedom of the victims, which is incumbent "upon the contracting state in the territory of which the violation has occurred".[30]

In *Cestaro*, the ECtHR has provided three important clarifications regarding the implications of this duty. First, it entails that "national courts should not under any circumstances be prepared to allow assaults on individuals' physical and moral integrity to go unpunished".[31] Second, the Strasbourg Court may intervene "in cases of manifest disproportion between the gravity of the act and the punishment imposed".[32] Third, the State must enact provisions "capable of preventing and effectively punishing the perpetrators", and must guarantee that no measures are in place which can "prevent the authorities from prosecuting violations" and "imposing adequate penalties" or "weaken the penalty excessively" – such as a short limitation period, amnesties, or pardons.[33] In other words: by ratifying the ECHR, States Parties undertake implicit obligations to criminalise and punish grave violations of human rights affecting the life, physical integrity, and freedom of the victims. In the specific circumstances of the case, such violations might also amount to CAH pursuant to Article 7 ICCSt.[34]

In consequence, provided that the conduct under scrutiny falls within the scope of Articles 2 or 3 ECHR, the European Court of Human Rights would be entitled to intervene where domestic authorities did not identify and prosecute those responsible for the violations as well as in cases where they did not impose adequate penalties on them. Therefore, not only would Italy violate this implicit obligation to prosecute where the legislator did not enact the necessary criminal provisions, but also where the statute of limitations expired in relation to the offence "corresponding" to such grave violations and where the penalty associated with the offence was too lenient.

An obligation to criminalise and punish CAH may also arise from the Convention on the Non-Applicability of Statutory Limitations. Pursuant to Article IV, States Parties "undertake to adopt … any legislative or other measures necessary to ensure that statutory or other limitations shall not apply to the prosecution and punishment" of war crimes and CAH and that "where they exist, such limitations shall be abolished". In order to fully implement this provision, one might argue that Italy would need to make sure that the prosecution of conducts amounting to CAH is not time barred, and *thus* introduce legislation criminalising CAH as such. Unfortunately, this argument has no merit with respect to Italy since it has not (yet) ratified the convention – nor the similarly worded European Convention on the Non-Applicability of Statutory Limitation to Crimes Against Humanity and War Crimes.[35] On the other hand, there is support for the view that the rule on the non-applicability of statutory limitations to core international crimes may have crystallised into CIL.[36] In practice, such a rule would imply that domestic authorities must be capable of prosecuting persons for conducts amounting to CAH – including as ordinary offences. Thus the expiration of the statutory time limit in relation to the "corresponding" ordinary offence would result in the breach of the CIL rule.

Similar considerations may be shared regarding another emerging CIL rule, according to which "the state in which a crime under international law is committed has a duty to prosecute".[37] Provided that there are differing views concerning this rule,[38] it seems to me that the only implication of the said duty would be that the territorial State shall make sure that its domestic authorities can prosecute the conduct amounting to CAH – including as an ordinary offence. On the other hand, where a statute of limitations had expired in relation to the "corresponding" ordinary offence the State would incur in a violation of the CIL rule.

5 Conclusions

In this chapter, I argued that the decision to prosecute genocide and CAH as ordinary offences may result, in the specific circumstances of the case, in violations of explicit and implicit obligations Italy has undertaken under international law.

By ratifying the Rome Statute Italy has *not* undertaken an obligation to punish genocide or CAH – either as ordinary offences or as such. However, in Section 2 I argued that it may be under an implicit obligation to do so. This would follow from the duty to cooperate with the ICC.

Problems would arise where in the specific circumstances of the case, conducts falling under the jurisdiction of the ICC were not prosecutable at the domestic level, including due to the expiration of statutes of limitations. In such scenarios, not only would perpetrators evade justice at the national level, but domestic courts may have to turn down cooperation requests submitted by the Court. In fact, the execution of a request to transfer a suspect would entail the violation of fundamental principles of the Italian legal system. Therefore the prosecution of genocide and CAH as ordinary offences might result in a violation of the statutory duty to cooperate with the ICC – and lead to the ICC's decision to refer the matter to the Assembly of States Parties or the UN Security Council.

In Section 3, I argued that although Italy has fully implemented the obligations to (criminalise and) punish prohibited conducts in accordance with the Genocide Convention, there is a potential "blind spot" with regard to Article VI. Where conducts within the scope of the Genocide Convention were prosecuted as ordinary offences, the prosecution of a suspect as well as his/her extradition/transfer to a third State or an international criminal tribunal (particularly the ICC) would be subjected to the expiration of time limits set under statutes of limitations. Although Italy is under no explicit obligation to prosecute acts of genocide *as such*, in such circumstances the decision to prosecute them as ordinary offences might therefore result in a violation of the obligations stemming from Article VI GenConv.

In Section 4 I focused on "residual" obligations to punish CAH, as arising from conventional and customary norms of international law.

As to the former, I argued that by ratifying the ECHR, Italy undertook an obligation to punish grave violations of human rights affecting the life, physical integrity, and freedom of the victims. According to the practice of the

European Court of Human Rights, domestic authorities would violate the convention not only where they did not prosecute perpetrators but also if they did not impose adequate penalties on them. The Strasbourg Court may thus find that Italy violated the convention because in the specific circumstances of the case, the penalties associated with the ordinary offences "corresponding to" such violations – and also amounting to CAH – were not adequate.

The decision to prosecute CAH as ordinary offences may also result in the violation of obligations arising from customary international law norms, particularly where in the specific circumstances of the case the prosecution was time barred. First, the expiration of a statute of limitations in relation to the offence "corresponding to" a CAH would violate the rule on the non-applicability of statutory limitations to core international crimes. In addition, it might also result, if the crime had been committed in Italy, in the violation of the customary duty to prosecute CAH on the part of the State on the territory of which such crimes have been committed.

Notes

1 For the purpose of this chapter, I will follow the definition of crimes against humanity as provided in the Rome Statute of the International Criminal Court.

2 On matters relating to war crimes, see Giulio Bartolini and Marco Longobardo, Chapter 4.2, The Italian Legislation on War Crimes: Obligations to Implement and Principle of Legality.

3 On the concept of "implicit" obligations, *see* Marco Longobardo, 'The Italian Legislature and International and EU Obligations of Domestic Criminalisation' (2021) 21 International Criminal Law Review 623, 628–632.

4 Convention on the Prevention and Punishment of the Crime of Genocide (adopted 9 December 1948, entered into force 12 January 1951) 78 UNTS 277.

5 According to CAT, Art 1, torture consists in "any act by which severe pain or suffering, whether physical or mental, is intentionally inflicted on a person for such purposes as obtaining from him or a third person information or a confession, punishing him for an act he or a third person has committed or is suspected of having committed, or intimidating or coercing him or a third person, or for any reason based on discrimination of any kind, when such pain or suffering is inflicted by or at the instigation of or with the consent or acquiescence of a public official or other person acting in an official capacity". However, ICCSt, Art 7(2)(e) does not incorporate the purpose element nor the official capacity requirement.

6 According to the Convention, Art 2, enforced disappearance means "the arrest, detention, abduction or any other form of deprivation of liberty by agents of the State or by persons or groups of persons acting with the authorization, support or acquiescence of the State, followed by a refusal to acknowledge the deprivation of liberty or by concealment of the fate or whereabouts of the disappeared person, which place such a person outside the protection of the law". Conversely, while ICCSt, Art 7(2)(i) does not require that the crime is committed by a State agent or with the acquiescence of the State, it introduces a "purpose element" (that the crime is committed "with the intention of removing them from the protection of the law for a prolonged period of time").

7 European Convention for the Protection of Human Rights and Fundamental Freedoms (adopted 4 November 1950, entered into force 3 September 1953) ETS 005.

8 Convention on the non-applicability of statutory limitations to war crimes and crimes against humanity (adopted 26 November 1968, entered into force 11 November 1970) 754 UNTS 73.

9 *Longobardo* (n 3) 637. On this issue, see also Maria Crippa, Chapter 4.1, How to Implement Crimes Against Humanity and Genocide in the Italian System.

10 *Longobardo* (n 3) 637. On the relationship between the implicit obligations to criminalise arising from the ICC Statute and the Italian legal system, *see* Luigi Prosperi, '"With or Without You": Why Italy Should Incorporate Crimes Against Humanity and Genocide Into Its National Legal System' (2021) 21 International Criminal Law Review 707–714.

11 *Prosecutor v Muthaura, Kenyatta, and Ali* (Judgment on the appeal of the Republic of Kenya against the decision of Pre-Trial Chamber II of 30 May 2011 entitled 'Decision on the Application by the Government of Kenya Challenging the Admissibility of the Case Pursuant to Article 19(2)(b) of the Statute') ICC-01/09-02/11, Appeals Chamber (30 August 2011), [39].

12 *Prosecutor v Gaddafi and Al-Senussi* (Judgment on the appeal of Mr Abdullah Al-Senussi against the decision of Pre-Trial Chamber I of 11 October 2013 entitled 'Decision on the admissibility of the case against Abdullah Al-Senussi') ICC-01/11-01/11, Appeals Chamber (24 July 2014), [119]. *See* also *Prosecutor v Simone Gbagbo* (Judgment on the Appeal of Côte d'Ivoire against the Decision of Pre-Trial Chamber I of 11 December 2014 entitled 'Decision on Côte d'Ivoire's Challenge to the Admissibility of the Case against Simone Gbagbo') ICC-02/11-01/12, Appeals Chamber (27 May 2015), [99] (finding that a domestic prosecution for ordinary domestic crimes was not based on substantially the same conduct as alleged before the ICC).

13 Criminal Code, Arts 606 and 607, corresponding to "imprisonment or other severe deprivation of physical liberty" (ICCSt, Article 7(1)(e)).

14 ibid, Art 605, corresponding to "enforced disappearance of persons" (ICCSt, Art 7(1)(i)).

15 As criminalised through Art 613*bis*. Since this provision only entered into force in July 2017, the "corresponding" ordinary offence in relation to conducts committed before then would be "personal injury" pursuant to Arts 582 and 583 (time barred after 6, 7 or 12 years, depending on the gravity of such injury).

16 In such circumstance, pursuant to Arts 157 and 613*bis* of the Criminal Code the statute of limitations would expire in 15 or 18 years (depending on whether the suspect is a public official).

17 On this matter, see *Prosperi* (n 10) 706–709.

18 On the negotiations, *see* Immi Tallgren and Astrid Reisinger Coracini, 'Article 20', in Otto Triffterer and Kai Ambos (eds), *The Rome Statute of the International Criminal Court. A Commentary* (3rd edn, CH Beck/Hart/Nomos 2016) 899, mns 32–34, pp 918–920.

19 ibid mn 22, p 914.

20 *See* Tijana Surlan, '*Ne bis in idem* in Conjunction with the Principle of Complementarity in the Rome Statute' (2005) European Society of International Law, 5–6 < www.esil-sedi.eu/sites/default/files/Surlan_0.PDF> (accessed 25 April 2022); and *Tallgren Coracini* (n 18) mn 41, p 923.

21 *Tallgren Coracini* (n 18) mn 46, p 926.

22 *See Zolotukhin v Russia* App no 14939/03 (ECtHR, 10 February 2009) [82] ("Article 4 of Protocol No 7 must be understood as prohibiting the prosecution or trial of a second 'offence' in so far as it arises from identical facts or facts which are substantially the same").
23 *Application of the Convention on the Prevention and Punishment of the Crime of Genocide (Bosnia and Herzegovina v Serbia and Montenegro)* (Merits) [2007] ICJ Reports 43, 81.
24 ibid 227.
25 Bjorn Schiffbauer, 'Article IV', in Christian J Tams and others (eds), *Convention on the Prevention and Punishment of the Crime of Genocide: A Commentary* (CH Beck/Hart/Nomos 2014), mns 25 and 30, pp 197–198.
26 ibid mn 22, p 196.
27 Bjorn Schiffbauer, 'Article V', in *Tams* (n 25) mn 41, p 230.
28 ibid mn 19, p 223.
29 On the obligations arising from the statutes of international criminal tribunals and from the Draft articles on the prevention and punishment of CAH, see *Prosperi* (n 10) 704–706.
30 Markos Karavias, 'Duty to Punish', in Antonio Cassese (ed), *The Oxford Companion to International Criminal Justice* (OUP 2009) 305.
31 *See Cestaro v Italy* App no 6884/11 (ECtHR, 7 April 2015) [206].
32 ibid [207].
33 ibid [209].
34 However, the competent judge should first determine whether the underlying CAH under scrutiny fell within the scope of those grave violations of human rights.
35 European Convention on the Non-Applicability of Statutory Limitation to Crimes Against Humanity and War Crimes (adopted 25 January 1974, entered into force 27 June 2003) ETS 082.
36 On this matter, *see* Christine Van den Wyngaert and John Dugard, 'Non-Applicability of Statute of Limitations', in Antonio Cassese and others (eds), *The Rome Statute of the International Criminal Court: A Commentary*, vol I (OUP 2002) 873–888.
37 Gerhard Werle and Florian Jeßberger, *Principles of International Criminal Law* (4th edn, OUP 2020) 104.
38 *See* Michael P Scharf, 'The Amnesty Exception to the Jurisdiction of the International Criminal Court' (1999) 32 Cornell International Law Journal 507, 519–521; and Anja Seibert-Fohr, *Prosecuting Serious Human Rights Violations* (OUP 2009) 250–254.

Selected bibliography

Application of the Convention on the Prevention and Punishment of the Crime of Genocide (Bosnia and Herzegovina v Serbia and Montenegro) (Merits) [2007] ICJ Reports 43, 81

Bjorn Schiffbauer, 'Article V', in Tams CJ and others (eds), *Convention on the Prevention and Punishment of the Crime of Genocide: A Commentary* (CH Beck/Hart/Nomos 2014)

Cestaro v Italy App no 6884/11 (ECtHR, 7 April 2015)

Karavias M, 'Duty to Punish', in Antonio Cassese (ed), *The Oxford Companion to International Criminal Justice* (Oxford University Press 2009)

Longobardo M, 'The Italian Legislature and International and EU Obligations of Domestic Criminalisation' (2021) 21 *International Criminal Law Review* 628

Prosecutor v Gaddafi and Al-Senussi (Judgment on the appeal of Mr Abdullah Al-Senussi against the decision of Pre-Trial Chamber I of 11 October 2013 entitled 'Decision on the admissibility of the case against Abdullah Al-Senussi') ICC-01/11-01/11, Appeals Chamber (24 July 2014)

Prosecutor v Muthaura, Kenyatta, and Ali (Judgment on the appeal of the Republic of Kenya against the decision of Pre-Trial Chamber II of 30 May 2011 entitled 'Decision on the Application by the Government of Kenya Challenging the Admissibility of the Case Pursuant to Article 19(2)(b) of the Statute') ICC-01/09-02/11, Appeals Chamber (30 August 2011)

Prosecutor v Simone Gbagbo (Judgment on the Appeal of Côte d'Ivoire against the Decision of Pre-Trial Chamber I of 11 December 2014 entitled 'Decision on Côte d'Ivoire's Challenge to the Admissibility of the Case against Simone Gbagbo') ICC-02/11-01/12, Appeals Chamber (27 May 2015)

Prosperi L, '"With or Without You": Why Italy Should Incorporate Crimes Against Humanity and Genocide Into Its National Legal System' (2021) 21 International Criminal Law Review 707

Scharf MP, 'The Amnesty Exception to the Jurisdiction of the International Criminal Court' (1999) 32 *Cornell International Law Journal* 519

Schiffbauer B, 'Article IV', in Tams CJ and others (eds), *Convention on the Prevention and Punishment of the Crime of Genocide: A Commentary* (CH Beck/Hart/Nomos, 2014)

Seibert-Fohr A, *Prosecuting Serious Human Rights Violations* (Oxford University Press 2009)

Surlan T, 'Ne bis in idem in Conjunction with the Principle of Complementarity in the Rome Statute' (2005) *European Society of International Law* 5–6 <www.esil-sedi.eu/sites/default/files/Surlan_0.PDF> (accessed 25 April 2022)

Tallgren I and Reisinger Coracini A, 'Article 20', in Triffterer O and Ambos K (eds), *The Rome Statute of the International Criminal Court. A Commentary* (3rd edn, CH Beck/Hart/Nomos 2016)

Van den Wyngaert C and Dugard J, 'Non-Applicability of Statute of Limitations', in Cassese A and others (eds), *The Rome Statute of the International Criminal Court: A Commentary,* vol I (Oxford University Press 2002)

Werle G and Jeßberger F, *Principles of International Criminal Law* (4th edn, Oxford University Press 2020)

Zolotukhin v Russia App no 14939/03 (ECtHR, 10 February 2009)

4.4 Domesticating the Sidelined Crime of Aggression

Annegret Hartig

1 Introduction

Since the end of World War II, interstate war has declined precipitously.[1] This period of unprecedented peace between States[2] made it easy to sideline the crime of aggression. Efforts were directed towards more common crimes and conflicts. This tendency is reflected in State practice and debates concerning the domestic implementation of crimes under international law. The crime of aggression has been domesticated in approximately 40 States.[3] Crimes against humanity, in contrast, have been incorporated into the domestic law of over 100 States.[4] Undefined in the early 2000s, the crime of aggression was largely omitted when scholars debated the legislative implementation of the newly adopted Statute of the International Criminal Court (ICC).[5]

The Russian invasion of Ukraine in 2022 showed that the 21st century is not free from brutal exceptions to the rule of unprecedented peace. It makes it imperative to catch up with previous debates. It requires assessing the main legal questions that arise for the domestic legislative branch when implementing the formerly sidelined crime of aggression. This includes the questions of whether there is an obligation or at least a need to criminalise aggression. It also includes the operationalisation of domestic implementation. This questions how to incorporate the definition of the ICC Statute into domestic law and how to specify the geographical ambit of domestic jurisdiction. The latter may be affected by potential prohibitive rules on the exercise of jurisdiction by domestic courts, such as immunities.

2 No Hard Legal Obligation to Criminalize Aggression Under Domestic Law

Most scholars agree that the ICC Statute does not oblige States to criminalise genocide, crimes against humanity, war crimes and the crime of aggression under domestic law.[6] This lack of an obligation under the ICC Statute is normally compensated by the innovative enforcement system it establishes.[7] Based on the principle of complementarity, this system helps to achieve the desired result of domestic criminalisation by the threat of judicial interventions. If a

DOI: 10.4324/9781003320951-19

State is legally "unable"[8] to prosecute due to the lack of a substantive norm, the ICC may take over cases the State had a prosecutorial interest in. The complementary jurisdiction of the ICC creates a sovereignty-driven incentive to implementation.

Due to the restricted aggression jurisdiction of the ICC, however, the coercive potential of complementarity on States is reduced.[9] States do not need to proactively enact anti-aggression legislation to avoid an intervention by the ICC. They can simply refrain from ratifying the Aggression Amendments. The lacking ratification seems to prevent the ICC from exercising jurisdiction over the nationals and the territory of the State in question.[10] This is a departure from the regime applicable to other ICC Statute crimes. They can be prosecuted on the basis of a territorial link to a State Party even if the national State of the defendant has not accepted the jurisdiction of the ICC.[11] Nonetheless, States vulnerable to being the victim of aggression may still have a strong self-interest to legislatively earmark their territory as one in which aggressors risk prosecution.[12]

Domestic fundamental rights and international human rights are a more promising source for an obligation to criminalise aggression. Due to the traditional overemphasis of aggression as a crime against State sovereignty,[13] it seems counterintuitive to infer an obligation to criminalise aggression from obligations States have towards individuals. Domestic constitutions tend to oblige States to protect fundamental rights of individuals.[14] The ICCPR obliges each State Party "to ensure to all individuals within its territory and subject to its jurisdiction the rights recognized in the present Covenant".[15] The situation in Ukraine shows that the existence of peace and the absence of war is a prerequisite for the enjoyment of fundamental rights and human rights.[16] Moreover, the UN Human Rights Committee recently confirmed that aggression has relevance under human rights law. Whenever States engage in acts of aggression that result in the deprivation of life, they violate the right to life *ipso facto*, meaning irrespective of any additional violation of the laws of armed conflict.[17] Even if one accepts that aggression can affect the rights of individuals, the inference of an obligation to criminalise aggression requires additional interpretative steps.[18] One of these steps is related to the transboundary nature of the crime of aggression. This raises the thorny question of the extraterritorial applicability of constitutional law[19] and human rights law.[20]

Due to the limited aggression-specific State practice, customary international law does not seem to oblige States to domesticate the crime of aggression. However, the prohibition of aggression undoubtedly forms part of *ius cogens*. What would be the added value of having a *ius cogens* basis, if the obligation to criminalise aggression required the same burdensome way of establishing general practice accepted as law as any other crime based on a non-peremptory norm? A semi-deductive approach may provide a compromise. This consists of "empirically proving that a certain *jus cogens* effect is produced in one legal context and … inferring a different effect in another context, again without apparently any need to specifically test the effect thus inferred against international practice".[21] An obligation to criminalise could then be inferred from the accepted consequences of *ius cogens* under the law of State responsibility. The general obligation of the responsible State to make reparations[22] could be interpreted in a way that included the obligation to prosecute its agents once aggression occurs.[23] To ensure their general ability to fulfil this obligation, States would be required to criminalise aggression in an anticipatory manner.

Overall, however, controversies about the existence of an obligation render any obligation "legally soft".[24] Controversies lower the reputational costs of legislative inaction.[25] If the law is open to radically different interpretations, States can easily justify non-criminalisation.[26] This is why the claimed "soft legal obligations" stemming from domestic fundamental rights, international human rights or *ius cogens* will not necessarily convince States to criminalise aggression.

3 Need for Criminalizing Aggression Under Domestic Law

Irrespective of an obligation, there is a need for implementation on the part of States that wish to have the core wrong of the crime of aggression adequately reflected under their domestic law. States are otherwise mostly unable to hold aggressors responsible for their wrong. The core wrong of the crime of aggression[27] can be perceived in the manifestly unlawful and serious use of armed force by a State against another State that affects State sovereignty, international peace and, arguably, individual interests.[28] It can only be triggered by persons from the leadership circle of a State.[29] Existing types of criminal offences under domestic law are mostly unable to cover this wrong.[30]

Normally, the non-implementation of other ICC Statute crimes leaves States with the alternative of covering aspects of these crimes by relying on ordinary criminal offences.[31] The crime of aggression, however, would often lack a counterpart under ordinary criminal offences. Relying on ordinary criminal offences would also send a distortive message about the core wrong of the crime of aggression. Its protection of individual interests is less pronounced and integrated into the context of macro criminality committed against the collective interests of State sovereignty and international peace. Moreover, prosecuting the aggressive bombardment against the territory of a State,[32] for example, as ordinary offences against the property[33] and against the person[34] would typically be barred: if the bombardment is in compliance with the law of armed conflict, aggressors enjoy the combatant's privilege. Although it is not alien to domestic law that previous unlawful conduct can negatively affect the invocation of a defence,[35] it is far from being a general principle that provides an exception to the combatant's privilege due to the previous unlawful use of armed force.

Normative gaps also persist under the law of States which have criminalised genocide, crimes against humanity and war crimes. Their courts can focus on these core crimes that are committed cumulatively with, or subsequently to, the crime of aggression. This would emphasise the common description of aggression as being the "mother of all crimes".[36] It also emphasises the "gravity" of an act of aggression punishable under Article 8*bis* of the ICC Statute, which is understood as referring to the effects of the act.[37] The scepticism expressed towards establishing a special aggression tribunal for Ukraine suggests that there is an alarming tendency to be content with holding aggressors responsible for other core crimes.[38] Focusing on the subsequent or cumulative commission of genocide, crimes against humanity and war crimes, however, fails to acknowledge that aggressors violate State sovereignty and international peace by the unlawful use of armed force. Such a focus fails to condemn the violation of the prohibition of the use of force, which is described as the "cornerstone"[39] of the UN Charter and prerequisite of a "true legal system".[40] It also fails to condemn all effects that result from the act of aggression. Combatants and civilians who were lawfully killed in the conflict between Ukraine and Russia would be a forgotten cost of war. Their deaths, however, ultimately result from the initial unlawful use of armed force which triggered the law of armed conflict. Convicting aggressors for the commission of other core crimes may still serve the purpose of "somehow" punishing them. With respect to crimes under international law, however, it is generally questionable whether the length of any prison sentence can adequately reflect the enormous level of wrongdoing.[41] This is why the proper label for the committed wrong of aggressors matters. Their exclusive conviction of any other core crime appears unsatisfactory and provokes substantive selectivity in international criminal justice.[42]

The violation of *ius ad bellum* can also not be covered by prosecuting aggressors on the basis of the implemented war crime of "excessive attack" or the crime against humanity of an "other inhumane act". There are creative proposals which inject *ius ad bellum* considerations into the assessment of the vague terms "excessive attack"[43] and "other inhumane act".[44] However, they face interpretative obstacles. These obstacles are related to the function of these vague terms. Like the underlying principle of proportionality, the term "excessive attack" has the function to provide a flexible rule.[45] It would be a fixed rule with a predetermined balance of interests, however, if the aggressive use of armed force was automatically considered as an "excessive attack".[46] The function of "other inhumane acts" is to provide a residual clause for those acts which States were unable to think of when drafting the ICC Statute.[47] The crime of aggression, however, was a wrong known during the drafting as expressed in the placeholder of former Article 5(2) of the ICC Statute.

Minor normative gaps exist in States, such as Ukraine[48] and Russia,[49] that have the "crime of aggressive war" under domestic law. They can cover most aspects of the crime of aggression as defined by the ICC Statute. The Nuremberg and Tokyo version of the "crime of aggressive war" only leaves minor gaps by requiring an *animus aggressionis*. It offers a surplus in terms of the personal scope of application.[50] The "preliminary offenses"[51] of "incitement to war" and "propaganda for war",[52] in contrast, fail to reflect the wrong of the execution phase. They only have some overlap with the preparation or planning of an act of aggression.[53]

4 Options for Incorporating the Definition of Article 8*bis* of the ICC

States that acknowledge the need for implementing the crime of aggression can choose among three options of how to incorporate the definition into domestic law. These options are implementation by copying the definition, implementation by reference to Article 8*bis* of the ICC Statute, and the modified implementation of the definition.[54]

Implementations by copying or by reference are economic options without risking gaps in the complementary jurisdiction of the ICC. Among the 16 implementers as of 2022,[55] two States opted for an implementation by copying.[56] Merely copying Article 8*bis* of the ICC Statute, however, does not suffice to make domestic law consistent with the ICC Statute. Only the additional implementation of the absolute leadership clause of Article 25(3*bis*) of the ICC Statute excludes accessorial responsibility for non-leaders. As expected, the implementation by reference was chosen by States that are influenced by common law.[57] Its understanding of the principle of legality tends to be less opposed to the technique of using references. Despite the reluctance of civil law countries to use references, static references to Article 8*bis* of the ICC Statute do not seem to impair the understanding of a crime that is committed by persons from the leadership circle of a State.[58] These persons are typically legally trained or legally advised.

States that opt for modified implementation take advantage of the flexible functioning of complementarity.[59] To prevent the ICC from exercising complementary jurisdiction, it suffices that States exercise jurisdiction over "substantially the same conduct".[60] This allows implementing States to adopt modifications that take into account their domestic legal culture, such as the usually stricter domestic principle of legality.[61] As of 2022, most States opted for a modified implementation.[62] The enacted domestic definitions of the crime of aggression, however, do not seem to leave gaps to the parent norm. In cases where substantive modifications occurred, they rather led to over-inclusive implementations which render domestic courts "all too able" to prosecute.[63] Most of the modifications, in contrast, were of a technical or conceptual nature without changing the definition in substance. This suggests that States closely mirror the ICC Statute definition even if the disciplinary effect of complementarity is reduced due to the restricted jurisdiction of the ICC over the crime of aggression. Among the elements mostly left unchanged was the "manifest" threshold.[64] It is noteworthy that the stricter domestic principle of legality did not prevent most implementers from including the allegedly vague[65] "manifest" threshold without modifications. This seems to confirm that States Parties did their best to describe with sufficient clarity a crime which is based on violations of a field of law that is known for its ambiguities.

5 Specifying the Geographical Ambit of Domestic Criminal Jurisdiction

The second part of the operationalisation of implementation requires States to specify the geographical ambit of domestic jurisdiction. To avoid State responsibility or corrective interpretations by domestic courts, the legislative specification of domestic jurisdiction needs to respect international law. In contrast to the traditional reading of the *Lotus* case, international law nowadays requires a "permissive rule".[66] Such a rule serves to rebut the presumed general prohibition under international law to extend jurisdiction to matters with a foreign element.

The principle of nationality is the most uncontroversial one with respect to the crime of aggression. It gives States a right to exercise prescriptive jurisdiction over the aggressive conduct of their own nationals.

The principle of territoriality allows States to exercise prescriptive jurisdiction to cover situations in which they either aggress or are aggressed. This is due to the constituent elements of the crime of aggression which typically occur in the aggressor State and the victim State. The place of commission is the only relevant factor for the principle of territoriality to apply.[67] This is why the right to exercise territorial jurisdiction to prescribe is not challenged by the nationality of the perpetrator or the nature of the crime.

Like the principle of territoriality, the protective principle allows States to criminalise aggression committed against them. Aggression affects the core sovereign interests of a State and even allows a technical form of self-defence. The practice after World War II and after the Russian invasion also suggests an extension to allied or third States whose vital interests are threatened.[68] Poland, for example, initiated criminal investigations with respect to the crime of aggression allegedly committed against Ukraine in 2022 on the basis of the protective principle.[69]

The applicability of the passive personality principle depends on whether the crime of aggression can be understood as a crime committed against individuals. Establishing a jurisdictional link merely by an attack on nationals abroad, however, could be criticised as a "narrow and nationalistic standard"[70] for bringing those to justice who violated the fundamental interests of the international community.

This is why universal jurisdiction would be better suited to enable third States to exercise jurisdiction. Its applicability to the crime of aggression, however, is controversial. It could be claimed under an inductive approach by emphasising the practice of the International Military Tribunal (IMT) in Nuremberg. The inductive approach argues that the practice of the IMT, together with the IMT Charter and the subsequent endorsement by the international community, led to an accelerated formation of a customary rule.[71] This rule also applies at the domestic level and has since not been rebutted by contrary general practice.[72] If sceptics doubt the stretch from Nuremberg to the same right of States at the domestic level, the limited affirmative State practice at the domestic level[73] only gives rise to a customary right by using deductive reasoning "as an aid".[74] The authority to exercise universal jurisdiction can deductively be inferred from the nature of "crimes under international law".[75] International criminal law and universal jurisdiction are claimed to be two sides of the same coin.[76] Crimes under international law are directed against the fundamental interests of the international community.[77] Their prosecution cannot be an interference in the internal affairs of the territorial State or national State.[78] This builds a bridge to the perception of Nuremberg under the inductive approach as the birthplace of a right to exercise universal jurisdiction over the crime of aggression. It claims that international criminal law never existed without universal jurisdiction.

6 Immunities

It would be quite ironic to claim the right of a State to exercise prescriptive jurisdiction if domestic courts do not have the congruent right to exercise adjudicative jurisdiction. A realistic legislature may prefer creating laws that reflect the limits of domestic courts to avoid the impression of overly symbolic legislation.

There is indeed a presumption of congruency between prescriptive and adjudicative jurisdiction.[79] Hence, a State which has the right to exercise prescriptive jurisdiction over the crime of aggression is presumed to have the congruent authority to entertain legal proceedings. This presumption, however, can be rebutted by a prohibitive rule under international law, such as immunities.

As demonstrated by the recent discussions on how to prosecute those responsible for the alleged crime of aggression against Ukraine, the issue of immunities is likely to arise in aggression proceedings. This crime can only be committed by persons from the leadership circle of a State[80] and requires them to plan, prepare, initiate or execute a State act. Immunities are linked to a specific status of the person within the State (personal immunity) and to acts on behalf of the State (functional immunity).

Personal immunity precludes States from exercising adjudicative criminal jurisdiction against foreign heads of State, heads of government and ministers of foreign affairs while they are in office.[81] Considering that this troika is only a small, albeit important, circle of potential aggressors, personal immunity would not bar all imaginable criminal proceedings. Even under the "Führerprinzip" of Hitler, the crime of aggression was not committed by a single State leader. Moreover, personal immunity ceases after the term in office.

The more delicate question is related to functional immunity. This conduct-based prohibitive rule is temporally unlimited. If applicable, it bars all aggression proceedings of domestic courts against foreign State officials, even after they have left office. The International Law Commission (ILC) did not reject its applicability to the crime of aggression. It adopted a Draft Article in 2017 which stipulates that functional immunity shall not apply in respect of a closed list of "crimes under international law". This list includes genocide, crimes against humanity and war crimes, but excludes the crime of aggression.[82] The omission, however, received criticism from members of the ILC,[83] scholars[84] and some States.[85] Moreover, it should be kept in mind that whatever the ILC adopts is not black letter law.

It is thus still possible, albeit not uncontroversial, to assume the inapplicability of functional immunity in domestic aggression proceedings. The inapplicability can be claimed inductively if particular weight is placed on the aggression-specific practice generated and endorsed in the aftermath of World War II.[86] This practice does not explicitly limit the claimed inapplicability of functional immunity to international courts. The IMT used general language and explained the inapplicability based on the foundational logic of international criminal law instead of its nature as an international tribunal. In the famous passage, it states *inter alia* "The principle of International Law, which under certain circumstances protects the representatives of a State, cannot be applied to acts which are condemned as criminal by International Law".[87] The subsequent reference of the IMT to the substantive defence of irrelevance of official position in Article 7 of the IMT Charter and to the absence of functional immunity suggests that these concepts were not systematically distinguished at that time.[88] The judgment's rejection of functional immunities and the irrelevance of official position in Article 7 of the IMT Charter were soon endorsed by the UN General Assembly in Resolution 95(I). It was followed by an endorsement by the ILC in Principle III of the formulated "Nuremberg Principles"; by the International Military Tribunal for the Far East (IMFTE) in its "unqualified adherence" to the Nuremberg paradigm; and by Article 6 of the IMTFE Charter. Due to these numerous endorsements of the generally phrased Nuremberg claim, it can be assumed that a rule crystallised into customary international law which renders functional immunities inapplicable in international and domestic aggression proceedings.

Sceptics may argue that the general claim made in Nuremberg by an international tribunal requires additional affirmation at the domestic level. Such affirmative State practice, however, is limited. There are domestic aggression trials and investigations in response to World War II or the Russian-Ukrainian conflict.[89] Moreover, there are approximately 40 domestic legislative acts[90] and a few verbal acts of States in support of the inapplicability of functional immunity to the crime of aggression.[91] The inapplicability of functional immunity in domestic aggression proceedings could still be claimed in combination with deductive reasoning "as an aid". According to one of the most prominent deductive reasonings, the inapplicability of functional immunity depends on the categorisation of the crime as a "crime under international law" and the recognition of universal, or at least extraterritorial jurisdiction for the crime.[92] As to the first requirement, the crime of aggression has been described as a "crime under international law", or even "supreme international crime"[93] in various international documents.[94] Given that the crime of aggression stretches over the territory of at least two States, it can automatically rely on the principle of territoriality to fulfil the second requirement for deductively explaining the inapplicability of functional immunity. Whether functional immunity is also inapplicable in proceedings in third States depends on the acceptance of universal jurisdiction. The controversy about the right to exercise universal jurisdiction over the crime of aggression can logically not affect the inapplicability of functional immunity in proceedings in the victim State. Those assuming that functional immunities bar any domestic aggression proceedings, even those in the victim State, would ignore the indifference of territorial jurisdiction with respect to the nature of the crime. They would also favour protection of the sovereignty of the aggressor State over the sovereignty of the victim State. The sovereignty of the latter stands behind functional immunity. The sovereignty of the former stands behind territorial jurisdiction. The applicability of functional immunity would favour the sovereignty of the aggressor State although it has fundamentally disrespected the sovereignty of another State.

7 Conclusion

The Russian invasion of Ukraine in 2022 made it imperative to thoroughly explore the legal questions that arise for States that contemplate the legislative implementation of the crime of aggression. There is no hard legal obligation but a need to criminalise aggression to adequately reflect the core wrong of aggression under domestic law. Although the principle of complementarity allows States some flexibility to modify the definition, the existing implementations show that States did their best to describe in Article 8*bis* of the ICC Statute with sufficient clarity a crime which is based on violations of a field of law that is known for its ambiguities. The most controversial questions concern the right of States to establish universal jurisdiction and the inapplicability of functional immunity in domestic aggression proceedings. Both can be assumed inductively if particular weight is placed on the aggression-specific practice generated and endorsed in the aftermath of World War II.

Admittedly, the existence of the crime of aggressive war under Ukrainian[95] and Russian law[96] did not prevent the Russian President Putin from ordering the invasion of Ukraine. Nonetheless, the punishability of aggression under the domestic law of the warring parties as well as under international law may facilitate discussions about how to prosecute those responsible once the fog of war has cleared. It offers a bargaining chip and a safety net for Ukraine. If

Ukraine fails to convince the international community to put those responsible before an international criminal court, they could still prosecute the aggressors before Ukrainian criminal courts. To have a similar safety net, States are advised to take stock of their domestic criminal law and its potential to address future aggressors.

Notes

1 Oona A Hathaway and Scott J Shapiro, *The Internationalists* (Simon & Schuster 2017) 418.

2 ibid xxi.

3 Astrid Reisinger Coracini, '(Extended) Synopsis: The Crime of Aggression under Domestic Criminal Law', in Claus Kreß and Stefan Barriga (eds), *The Crime of Aggression: A Commentary* (Cambridge University Press 2017) 1038.

4 See ILC Special Rapporteur Murphy, *Second Report on Crimes against Humanity, A/CN.4/690* (2016), para 18.

5 See in particular, Claus Kreß, *Vom Nutzen eines deutschen Völkerstrafgesetzbuchs* (*On the Benefits of Having a German Code of Crimes Against International Law*) (Nomos 2000); Helmut Satzger, 'Das neue Völkerstrafgesetzbuch – Eine kritische Würdigung' ('The New Code of Crimes Against International Law – A Critical Appraisal') [2002] Neue Zeitschrift für Strafrecht 125; Gerhard Werle, 'Konturen eines deutschen Völkerstrafrechts' ('The Contours of German International Criminal Law') (2001) 56(18) Juristenzeitung 885; Gerhard Werle, 'Völkerstrafrecht und geltendes deutsches Strafrecht' ('International Criminal Law and German Criminal Law') [2000] Juristenzeitung 755.

6 Kai Ambos, *Internationales Strafrecht: Strafanwendungsrecht, Völkerstrafrecht, Europäisches Strafrecht, Rechtshilfe* (*International Criminal Law*) (5th edn, CH Beck 2018) §6, mn 36ff; Robert Cryer, Darryl Robinson and Sergey Vasiliev, *An Introduction to International Criminal Law and Procedure* (4th edn, Cambridge University Press 2019) 80ff; Carsten Stahn, *A Critical Introduction to International Criminal Law* (Cambridge University Press 2019) 225; Gerhard Werle and Florian Jeßberger, *Principles of International Criminal Law* (4th edn, OUP 2020) para 465.

7 See in detail, Annegret Hartig, *Making Aggression a Crime Under Domestic Law* (TMC Asser Press 2023) ch 2.

8 See ICC Statute, Art 17(1).

9 See, in detail, Hartig (n 7) ch 2.

10 See the exclusion of Non-States Parties in ICC Statute, Art 15*bis*(5). The exclusion of States Parties that have not ratified the Aggression Amendments is more controversial, see Resolution ICC-ASP/16/Res.5 of 14 December 2017 Resolution. For an interpretation, see Jennifer Trahan, 'From Kampala to New York – The Final Negotiations to Activate the Jurisdiction of the International Criminal Court over the Crime of Aggression' (2018) 18(2) International Criminal Law Review 197.

11 See ICC Statute, Art 12(2)(a).

12 For this view, see in general Frédéric Mégret, 'Why Would States Want to Join the ICC? A Theoretical Exploration Based on the Legal Nature of Complementarity', in Jann K Kleffner and Gerben Kor (eds), *Complementary Views on Complementarity: Proceedings of the International Roundtable on the*

Complementary Nature of the International Criminal Court, Amsterdam, 25/26 June 2004 (TMC Asser 2006) 30.

13 For a discussion of the traditional view, see Tom Dannenbaum, 'Why Have We Criminalized Aggressive War?' (2017) 126 The Yale Law Journal 1242, 1254ff; Frédéric Mégret, 'What is the Specific Evil of Aggression?', in Claus Kreß and Stefan Barriga (eds), *The Crime of Aggression: A Commentary* (Cambridge University Press 2017) 1402ff.

14 See, eg, Samantha Besson, 'Les obligations positives de protection des droits fondamentaux – Un essai en dogmatique comparative' (2003) 1 Revue de droit suisse 49.

15 See ICCPR, Art 2(1).

16 Similarly, Djacoba L Tehindrazanarivelo and Robert Kolb, 'Peace, Right to, International Protection', in Rüdiger Wolfrum (ed), *Max Planck Encyclopedias of Public International Law (online edn)* (2006) para 13.

17 See UN Human Rights Committee, General Comment No 36: Article 6 (Right to Life), 3 September 2019, para 70.

18 See in detail, Hartig (n 7) ch 2.

19 See, eg, Rainer Hofmann, *Grundrechte und grenzüberschreitende Sachverhalte* (*Fundamental Laws and Cases with an Transboundary Element*) (Springer-Verlag Berlin Heidelberg 1994).

20 On the latter, see Marko Milanovic, *Extraterritorial Application of Human Rights Treaties: Law, Principles, and Policy* (OUP 2011).

21 Carlo Focarelli, 'Promotional Jus Cogens: A Critical Appraisal of Jus Cogens' Legal Effects' (2008) 77(4) Nordic Journal of International Law 429, 447.

22 See Art 31 in International Law Commission, 'Draft Articles on Responsibility of States for Internationally Wrongful Acts with Commentaries', *Yearbook of the International Law Commission 2001*, vol II (part two). This obligation arises generally and does not require a serious breach of an obligation under a *ius cogens* norm.

23 In case of crimes that are based on a *ius cogens* norm, one could suppose that the caused injury can hardly be made good by restitution or compensation only and that it always requires the third form of reparation, namely satisfaction. Satisfaction includes "disciplinary or penal action against the individuals whose conduct caused the internationally wrongful act", see Commentary to Draft Article 37 in ibid, para 5.

24 See Christine Chinkin, 'Normative Development in the International Legal System', in Dinah Shelton (ed), *Commitment and Compliance: The Role of Non-Binding Norms in the International Legal System* (OUP 2003) 26, whereby "legal soft law" fuses legal form with soft obligations.

25 See Andrew T Guzman, 'A Compliance-Based Theory of International Law' (2002) 90(6) California Law Review 1823, 1863.

26 See also Thomas M Franck, *Fairness in International Law and Institutions* (reprinted, OUP 2002) 31.

27 As defined in ICC Statute, Art 8*bis*.

28 See, in detail, Hartig (n 7) ch 3.

29 See, in detail, ibid.

30 See, in detail, ibid ch 4.

31 See, eg, for the practice in Germany before the implementation of crimes against humanity and war crimes, Julia Geneuss, *Völkerrechtsverbrechen und*

Verfolgungsermessen (*Crimes under International Law and Prosecutorial Discretion*) (Nomos 2013) 198ff.

32 See ICC Statute, Art 8*bis*(2)(b).

33 For example criminal damage and mischief.

34 For example homicide and offences against physical integrity.

35 For an overview in English, see Joachim Herrmann, 'Causing the Conditions of One's Own Defense: The Multifaceted Approach of German Law' [1986] Brigham Young University Law Review 747; Jens D Ohlin, 'The Crime of Bootstrapping', in Kreß and Barriga (eds) (n 13) 1456ff. For an overview of the related concepts under American law, see Paul H Robinson, 'Causing the Conditions of One's Own Defense: A Study in the Limits of Theory in Criminal Law Doctrine' (1985) 71 Virginia Law Review 1.

36 Cryer, Robinson and Vasiliev (n 6) 302ff.

37 Claus Kreß, 'The State Conduct Element', in Kreß and Barriga (eds) (n 13) 520.

38 They can be prosecuted by the ICC, see www.icc-cpi.int/ukraine.

39 Albrecht Randelzhofer and Oliver Dörr, 'Article 2 (4)', in Bruno Simma and others (eds), *The Charter of the United Nations: A Commentary* (3rd edn, OUP 2012) para 1.

40 Mary E O'Connell, 'The Prohibition of the Use of Force', in Nigel D White and Christian Henderson (eds), *Research Handbook on International Conflict and Security Law* (Edward Elgar Publishing 2013) 89.

41 Cryer, Robinson and Vasiliev (n 6) 31.

42 Annegret Hartig, 'Ein internationales Aggressionstribunal für die Ukraine? Ein Mittel gegen die materielle Selektivität in der strafrechtlichen Aufarbeitung des Ukrainekonflikts' [2022] Zeitschrift für Internationale Strafrechtsdogmatik 642.

43 See, eg, Rachel E VanLandingham, 'Criminally Disproportionate Warfare: Aggression as a Contextual War Crime' (2016) 48 Case Western Reserve Journal of International Law 215.

44 Benjamin B Ferencz, 'The Illegal Use Of Armed Force As A Crime Against Humanity' (2015) 2(2) Journal on the Use of Force and International Law 187, 195ff; Manuel J Ventura and Matthew Gillett, 'The Fog of War: Prosecuting Illegal Uses of Force as Crimes Against Humanity' (2013) 12 Wash U Global Stud L Rev 523.

45 See Enzo Cannizzaro, 'Proportionality in the Law of Armed Conflict', in Andrew Clapham and Paola Gaeta (eds), *The Oxford Handbook of International Law in Armed Conflict* (1st edn, OUP 2015) 332.

46 Hartig (n 7) ch 4.

47 Christopher K Hall and Carsten Stahn, 'Article 7', in Otto Triffterer and Kai Ambos (eds), *Rome Statute of the International Criminal Court: A Commentary* (3rd edn, CH Beck 2016) para 95.

48 See Ukrainian Criminal Code, Art 437.

49 See Russian Criminal Code, Art 353.

50 See in detail, Carrie McDougall, 'The Crimes Against Peace Precedent', in Kreß and Barriga (eds) (n 13).

51 For an understanding of preliminary offences under English law, see J W C Turner and Courtney S Kenny, *Kenny's Outlines of Criminal Law* (18th edn, Cambridge University Press 2013) 94ff.

52 Modelled after ICCPR, Art 20(1).

53 They only cover communicative planning and preparation in the sense of "psychological armament". See Claus D Classen, '§ 80', in Wolfgang Joecks and Klaus Miebach (eds), *Münchener Kommentar zum Strafgesetzbuch* (3rd edn, CH Beck 2017) para 8. See also John B Whitton and Arthur Larson, *Propaganda – Towards Disarmament in the War of Words* (Oceana Publications 1964) 39.

54 For the different options for implementation, see in detail Werle and Jeßberger (n 6) paras 467ff.

55 Afghanistan, Austria, Croatia, Cyprus, Czech Republic, Ecuador, Estonia, Finland, Georgia, Germany, Liechtenstein, Luxembourg, the Netherlands, North Macedonia, Samoa and Slovenia.

56 Luxembourg and the Netherlands.

57 Cyprus and Samoa.

58 For an attenuated standard of the principle of legality in case of expert criminal law, see Gerhard Werle and Florian Jeßberger, 'Das Völkerstrafgesetzbuch' ('The German Code of Crimes Against International Law') [2002] Juristenzeitung 725, 730.

59 Werle and Jeßberger (n 6) para 464.

60 On the interpretation, see Rod Rastan, 'What is "Substantially the Same Conduct"?' (2017) 15(1) Journal of International Criminal Justice 1 (accessed 18 February 2019).

61 Werle and Jeßberger (n 6) para 474.

62 See Afghanistan, Austria, Croatia, Czech Republic, Ecuador, Estonia, Finland, Georgia, Germany, Liechtenstein, North Macedonia and Slovenia.

63 They primarily occurred with respect to the "manifest" threshold and the leadership clause. See Hartig (n 7) ch 6.

64 Afghanistan, Austria, Cyprus, Czech Republic, Finland, Georgia, Germany, Liechtenstein, Luxembourg, the Netherlands, North Macedonia, Samoa and Slovenia.

65 Andreas Paulus, 'Second Thoughts on the Crime of Aggression' (2009) 20(4) European Journal of International Law 1117, 1121 (accessed 28 January 2019).

66 See Florian Jeßberger, *Der transnationale Geltungsbereich des deutschen Strafrechts: Grundlagen und Grenzen der Geltung des deutschen Strafrechts für Taten mit Auslandsberührung* (*The Transnational Applicability of German Criminal Law*) (Mohr Siebeck 2011) 203ff.

67 See Roger O'Keefe, *International Criminal Law* (OUP 2015) para 1.26.

68 On the former, see Michael Akehurst, 'Jurisdiction in International Law' (1972–1973) 46 British Yearbook of International Law 145, 159; Kevin J Heller, *The Nuremberg Military Tribunals and the Origins of International Criminal Law* (OUP 2011); Jeßberger (n 66) 256, fn 201.

69 The communiqué of the Polish Ministry of Justice emphasised that when the violations of the legal rights of the "country directly neighboring Poland harm European and international security", these acts are "directed against the interests of the international community, including the Republic of Poland". See www.gov.pl/web/sprawiedliwosc/dzialania-ministerstwa-sprawiedliwosci-i-polskiej-prokuratury-wobec-wojny-na-ukrainie (last visited April 2022).

70 With respect to other crimes under international law, see Antonio Cassese and others, *Cassese's International Criminal Law* (3rd edn, OUP 2013) 277.

71 Michael P Scharf, 'Universal Jurisdiction and the Crime of Aggression' (2012) 53 Harv Int'l LJ 357 <http://heinonline.org/hol-cgi-bin/get_pdf.cgi?handle=hein.journals/hilj53&section=12> (accessed 15 December 2016); Pal Wrange, 'The

Crime of Aggression, Domestic Prosecutions and Complementarity', in Kreß and Barriga (eds) (n 13) 719.

72 ibid.

73 See in detail Hartig (n 7) ch 7

74 See Commentary to Draft Conclusion 2, International Law Commission, 'Draft Conclusions on Identification of Customary International Law with Commentaries', *Yearbook of the International Law Commission 2018*, vol II (part two) para 5.

75 See, eg, Luis Benavides, 'The Universal Jurisdiction Principle: Nature and Scope' (2001) 1 Anuario Mexicano de Derecho Internacional 19, 86; Geneuss (n 31) 122; Claus Kreß, 'War Crimes Committed in Non-International Armed Conflict and the Emerging System of International Criminal Justice' (2000) 30 Israel Yearbook on Human Rights 103, 169.

76 Geneuss (n 31) 122.

77 Werle and Jeßberger (n 6) para 107.

78 Kai Ambos, *Treatise on International Criminal Law: International Criminal Procedure*, vol III (OUP 2013) 226; Benavides (n 75) 87; Werle and Jeßberger (n 6) para 259.

79 Jeßberger (n 66) 9ff.

80 See ICC Statute, Article 8*bis*(1).

81 See Chiara Ragni, Chapter 6.1, Prosecuting International Crimes Before Domestic Courts and the Question of Immunities.

82 See Draft Article 7(1) in International Law Commission, *Report on the Work of its Sixty-Ninth Session* (2017) UN Doc A/72/10, 176ff.

83 Nine members in total: Mr Hassouna: Egypt; Mr Hmoud: Jordan; Mr Jalloh: Sierra Leone; Mr Murase: Japan; Mr Nguyen: Vietnam; Mr Ouazzani Chahdi: Morocco; Mr Park: Republic of Korea; Mr Tladi: South Africa; Mr Valencia-Ospina: Colombia. See International Law Commission, 'Summary Record of the 3361st Meeting', A/CN.4/SR.3361, pp 6, 11, 14; 'Summary Record of the 3362nd Meeting', A/CN.4/SR.3362, p 4; 'Summary Record of the 3364th Meeting', A/CN.4/SR.3364, p 16.

84 See, eg, Hervé Ascensio and Beatrice I Bonafè, 'L'absence d'immunité des agents de l'État en cas de crime international: Pourquoi en débattre encore?' (2018) 122 Revue Générale de Droit International Public 821, 845; Roger S Clark, 'Complementarity and the Crime of Aggression', in Carsten Stahn and Mohamed M El Zeidy (eds), *The International Criminal Court and Complementarity: From Theory to Practice* (Cambridge University Press forthcoming); Claus Kreß, 'Article 98', in Kai Ambos (ed), *Rome Statute of the International Criminal Court* (4th edn, CH Beck 2021) para 49.

85 See, eg, the statements made at the Sixth Committee of the 72nd session of the UN General Assembly in 2017 and its 73rd session in 2018 by: Germany, Ukraine, Portugal, Slovenia, Estonia and Nicaragua. Available at www.un.org/en/ga/sixth.

86 Wrange (n 71) 723.

87 IMT, Judgment of 1 October 1946, in *The Trial of German Major War Criminals. Proceedings of the International Military Tribunal sitting at Nuremberg, Germany*, Part 22 (22 August 1946 to 1 October 1946), p 447.

88 For this view, see Kreß, 'Article 98' (n 84) paras 48, 62; International Law Commission, *Special Rapporteur Escobar Hernández, Fifth Report on the Immunity of State Officials from Foreign Criminal Jurisdiction* (2016) UN Doc A/CN.4/701, para 150.

89 Hartig (n 7) ch 8, Sect 8.4.5.3.
90 Reisinger Coracini (n 3) 1038.
91 Namely by Estonia, Portugal, Slovenia, Ukraine, Germany and Nicaragua at the Sixth Committee, see Hartig (n 7) ch 8, Sect 8.4.5.5.
92 See, for example, Dapo Akande and Sangeeta Shah, 'Immunities of State Officials, International Crimes, and Foreign Domestic Courts' (2010) 21(4) European Journal of International Law 815; Pavel Caban, 'Immunity of State Officials from Foreign Criminal Jurisdiction – Exceptions to Immunity Ratione Materiae' [2016] Czech Yearbook of Public & Private International Law 306, 317; Kreß, 'Article 98' (n 84) para 37; Rosanne van Alebeek, 'Functional Immunity of State Officials from the Criminal Jurisdiction of Foreign National Courts', in Tom Ruys (ed), *The Cambridge Handbook of Immunities and International Law* (2019) 509; Stahn (n 6) 253.
93 See IMT, Judgment of 1 October 1946, in *The Trial of German Major War Criminals. Proceedings of the International Military Tribunal sitting at Nuremberg, Germany*, Part 22 (22 August 1946 to 1 October 1946), p 421.
94 Principle VI of International Law Commission, 'Principles of International Law Recognized in the Charter of the Nürnberg Tribunal and in the Judgment of the Tribunal, with Commentaries', *Yearbook of the International Law Commission 1950*, vol II, 374; Article 2 of the 1954 'Draft Code of Offences against the Peace and Security of Mankind'; Article 16 of the International Law Commission, 'Draft Code of Crimes Against the Peace and Security of Mankind with Commentaries', *Yearbook of the International Law Commission 1996*, vol II (part two); Article 20(b) of the 1994 Draft Statute for an International Criminal Code; Article 5 of the ICC Statute.
95 See Ukrainian Criminal Code, Art 437.
96 See Russian Criminal Code, Art 353.

Selected Bibliography

Akande D and Shah S, 'Immunities of State Officials, International Crimes, and Foreign Domestic Courts' (2010) 21(4) *European Journal of International Law* 815

Akehurst M, 'Jurisdiction in International Law' (1972–1973) 46 *British Yearbook of International Law* 145

Ambos K, *Treatise on International Criminal Law: International Criminal Procedure,* vol III (1st edn, Oxford University Press 2013)

Ambos K, *Internationales Strafrecht: Strafanwendungsrecht, Völkerstrafrecht, Europäisches Strafrecht, Rechtshilfe [International Criminal Law]* (5th edn, *CH* Beck 2018)

Ascensio H and Bonafè BI, 'L'absence d'immunité des agents de l'État en cas de crime international: Pourquoi en débattre encore?' (2018) 122 *Revue Générale de Droit International Public* 821

Benavides L, 'The Universal Jurisdiction Principle: Nature and Scope' (2001) 1 *Anuario Mexicano de Derecho Internacional* 19

Besson S, 'Les obligations positives de protection des droits fondamentaux – Un essai en dogmatique comparative' (2003) 1 *Revue de droit suisse* 49

Caban P, 'Immunity of State Officials from Foreign Criminal Jurisdiction – Exceptions to Immunity Ratione Materiae' [2016] *Czech Yearbook of Public & Private International Law* 306

Cannizzaro E, 'Proportionality in the Law of Armed Conflict', in Andrew Clapham and Paola Gaeta (eds), *The Oxford Handbook of International Law in Armed Conflict* (1st edn, Oxford University Press 2015)

Cassese A and others, *Cassese's International Criminal Law* (3rd edn, Oxford University Press 2013)

Chinkin C, 'Normative Development in the International Legal System', in Dinah Shelton (ed), *Commitment and Compliance: The Role of Non-Binding Norms in the International Legal System* (Oxford University Press 2003)

Clark RS, 'Complementarity and the Crime of Aggression', in Carsten Stahn and Mohamed M El Zeidy (eds), *The International Criminal Court and Complementarity: From Theory to Practice* (Cambridge University Press forthcoming)

Classen CD, '§ 80', in Wolfgang Joecks and Klaus Miebach (eds), *Münchener Kommentar zum Strafgesetzbuch* (3rd edn, CH Beck 2017)

Cryer R, Robinson D and Vasiliev S, *An Introduction to International Criminal Law and Procedure* (4th edn, Cambridge University Press 2019)

Dannenbaum T, 'Why Have We Criminalized Aggressive War?' (2017) 126 *The Yale Law Journal* 1242

Ferencz BB, 'The Illegal Use Of Armed Force As A Crime Against Humanity' (2015) 2(2) *Journal on the Use of Force and International Law* 187

Focarelli C, 'Promotional Jus Cogens: A Critical Appraisal of Jus Cogens' Legal Effects' (2008) 77(4) *Nordic Journal of International Law* 429

Franck TM, *Fairness in International Law and Institutions* (Reprinted, Oxford University Press 2002)

Geneuss J, *Völkerrechtsverbrechen und Verfolgungsermessen [Crimes under International Law and Prosecutorial Discretion]* (Nomos 2013)

Guzman AT, 'A Compliance-Based Theory of International Law' (2002) 90(6) *California Law Review* 1823

Hall CK and Stahn C, 'Article 7', in Otto Triffterer and Kai Ambos (eds), *Rome Statute of the International Criminal Court:: A Commentary* (3rd edn, CH Beck 2016)

Hartig A, 'Ein internationales Aggressionstribunal für die Ukraine? Ein Mittel gegen die materielle Selektivität in der strafrechtlichen Aufarbeitung des Ukrainekonflikts' [2022] *Zeitschrift für Internationale Strafrechtsdogmatik* 642.

Hartig A, *Making Aggression a Crime Under Domestic Law* (TMC Asser Press 2023)

Heller KJ, *The Nuremberg Military Tribunals and the Origins of International Criminal Law* (Oxford University Press 2011)

Herrmann J, 'Causing the Conditions of One's Own Defense: The Multifaceted Approach of German Law' [1986] Brigham Young University Law Review 747

Hofmann R, *Grundrechte und grenzüberschreitende Sachverhalte [Fundamental Laws and Cases with an Transboundary Element]* (Springer-Verlag Berlin Heidelberg 1994)

International Law Commission, 'Principles of International Law Recognized in the Charter of the Nürnberg Tribunal and in the Judgment of the Tribunal, with Commentaries', *Yearbook of the International Law Commission 1950,* vol II, 374

International Law Commission, 'Draft Code of Crimes Against the Peace and Security of Mankind with Commentaries', *Yearbook of the International Law Commission 1996*, vol II *(part two)*

International Law Commission, 'Draft Articles on Responsibility of States for Internationally Wrongful Acts with Commentaries', *Yearbook of the International Law Commission 2001*, vol II *(part two)*

International Law Commission, *Special Rapporteur Escobar Hernández, Fifth Report on the Immunity of State Officials from Foreign Criminal Jurisdiction* (2016) UN Doc A/CN.4/701

International Law Commission, *Report on the Work of its Sixty-Ninth Session* (2017) UN Doc A/72/10

International Law Commission, 'Draft Conclusions on Identification of Customary International Law with Commentaries', *Yearbook of the International Law Commission 2018*, vol II *(part two)*

Jeßberger F, *Der transnationale Geltungsbereich des deutschen Strafrechts: Grundlagen und Grenzen der Geltung des deutschen Strafrechts für Taten mit Auslandsberührung [The Transnational Applicability of German Criminal Law]* (Mohr Siebeck 2011)

Kreß C, *Vom Nutzen eines deutschen Völkerstrafgesetzbuchs [On the Benefits of Having a German Code of Crimes Against International Law]* (Nomos 2000)

Kreß C, 'War Crimes Committed in Non-International Armed Conflict and the Emerging System of International Criminal Justice' (2000) 30 *Israel Yearbook on Human Rights* 103

Kreß C, 'The State Conduct Element', in Claus Kreß and Stefan Barriga (eds), *The Crime of Aggression: A Commentary* (Cambridge University Press 2017)

Kreß C, 'Article 98', in Kai Ambos (ed), *Rome Statute of the International Criminal Court (4th edn*, CH Beck 2021)

McDougall C, 'The Crimes Against Peace Precedent', in Claus Kreß and Stefan Barriga (eds), *The Crime of Aggression: A Commentary* (Cambridge University Press 2017)

Mégret F, 'Why Would States Want to Join the ICC? A Theoretical Exploration Based on the Legal Nature of Complementarity', in Jann K Kleffner and Gerben Kor (eds), *Complementary Views on Complementarity: Proceedings of the International Roundtable on the Complementary Nature of the International Criminal Court, Amsterdam, 25/26 June 2004* (TMC Asser 2006)

Mégret F, 'What is the Specific Evil of Aggression?', in Claus Kreß and Stefan Barriga (eds), *The Crime of Aggression: A Commentary* (Cambridge University Press 2017)

Milanovic M, *Extraterritorial Application of Human Rights Treaties: Law, Principles, and Policy* (Oxford University Press 2011)

O'Connell ME, 'The Prohibition of the Use of Force', in Nigel D White and Christian Henderson (eds), *Research Handbook on International Conflict and Security Law* (Edward Elgar Publishing 2013)

O'Keefe R, *International Criminal Law* (Oxford University Press 2015)

Ohlin JD, 'The Crime of Bootstrapping', in Claus Kreß and Stefan Barriga (eds), *The Crime of Aggression: A Commentary* (Cambridge University Press 2017)

Paulus A, 'Second Thoughts on the Crime of Aggression' (2009) 20(4) *European Journal of International Law* 1117

Randelzhofer A and Dörr O, 'Article 2 (4)', in Bruno Simma and others (eds), *The Charter of the United Nations: A Commentary (3rd edn*, Oxford University Press 2012)

Rastan R, 'What is 'Substantially the Same Conduct'?' (2017) 15(1) *Journal of International Criminal Justice* 1

Reisinger Coracini A, '(Extended) Synopsis: The Crime of Aggression under Domestic Criminal Law', in Claus Kreß and Stefan Barriga (eds), *The Crime of Aggression: A Commentary* (Cambridge University Press 2017)

Robinson PH, 'Causing the Conditions of One's Own Defense: A Study in the Limits of Theory in Criminal Law Doctrine' (1985) 71 *Virginia Law Review* 1

Satzger H, 'Das neue Völkerstrafgesetzbuch – Eine kritische Würdigung [The New Code of Crimes Against International Law – A Critical Appraisal]' [2002] *Neue Zeitschrift für Strafrecht* 125

Scharf MP, 'Universal Jurisdiction and the Crime of Aggression' (2012) 53 *Harv Int'l LJ* 357

Stahn C, *A Critical Introduction to International Criminal Law* (Cambridge University Press 2019)

Tehindrazanarivelo DL and Kolb R, 'Peace, Right to, International Protection', in Rüdiger Wolfrum (ed), *Max Planck Encyclopedias of Public International Law (online edn)* (2006)

Trahan J, 'From Kampala to New York—The Final Negotiations to Activate the Jurisdiction of the International Criminal Court over the Crime of Aggression' (2018) 18(2) *International Criminal Law Review 197*

Turner JWC and Kenny CS, *Kenny's Outlines of Criminal Law* (18th edn, Cambridge University Press 2013)

van Alebeek R, 'Functional Immunity of State Officials from the Criminal Jurisdiction of Foreign National Courts', in Tom Ruys (ed), *The Cambridge Handbook of Immunities and International Law* (2019)

VanLandingham RE, 'Criminally Disproportionate Warfare: Aggression as a Contextual War Crime' (*2016*) 48 *Case Western Reserve Journal of International Law 215*

Ventura MJ and Gillett M, 'The Fog of War: Prosecuting Illegal Uses of Force as Crimes Against Humanity' (2013) 12 *Wash U Global Stud L Rev 523*

Werle G, 'Völkerstrafrecht und geltendes deutsches Strafrecht [International Criminal Law and German Criminal Law]' [2000] *Juristenzeitung 755*

Werle G, 'Konturen eines deutschen Völkerstrafrechts [The Contours of German International Criminal Law]' (2001) 56(18) *Juristenzeitung* 885

Werle G and Jeßberger F, 'Das Völkerstrafgesetzbuch [The German Code of Crimes Against International Law]' [2002] *Juristenzeitung* 725

Werle G and Jeßberger F, *Principles of International Criminal Law (4th edn*, OUP 2020)

Whitton JB and Larson A, *Propaganda – Towards Disarmament in the War of Words* (Oceana Publications 1964)

Wrange P, 'The Crime of Aggression, Domestic Prosecutions and Complementarity', in Claus Kreß and Stefan Barriga (eds), *The Crime of Aggression: A Commentary* (Cambridge University Press 2017)

Part V

Individual criminal responsibility, sanctions and sentencing in the domestic legislation

5.1 How to domesticate the modes of liability for international crimes in the Italian system

Chantal Meloni

1 Implementing the general part of international criminal law in the domestic legal order

Moving into the discussion on the general part of international criminal law, and how to best implement it at the domestic level, there are relevant differences compared to the implementation of the special part to be considered. In particular, the different provisions' respective origins and sources, when dealing with the general rather than the special part's norms of international criminal law, shall not be forgotten. While the special part, the crimes, are the core, the original "*Kern*" of international criminal law, which finds its sources directly in international law, the same is not true for the general part, which provisions – with a few exceptions – find their sources in domestic criminal law, including the common/general principles of criminal law.[1]

It is well known that the 1998 Rome Statute for the first time included a comprehensive set of principles that were absent in the statutes of previous international criminal tribunals. Thus, the question is, to what extent does this general part, as defined in Articles 22–33 of the Rome Statute, need to be implemented at the domestic level? Looking at other implementation processes, the preferred option at the domestic level is not to duplicate the general part but rather to clarify that already existing criminal law principles and rules apply also to the newly introduced international crimes. Thus, in hypothesis, the "General Part" of the Italian Penal Code would remain applicable also to the new provisions regulating international crimes.

The same approach has been adopted by other countries, including Germany. The 2002 German Code of Crimes under international law (*Völkerstrafgesetzbuch* – VStGB), at § 2, states that the general criminal law shall apply as far as not decided otherwise.[2] Accordingly, the VStGB contains no special provisions regarding most of the "general principles" contained in the Rome Statute, including the principle of legality (Articles 22 to 24), the minimum age of criminal responsibility (Article 26), the irrelevance of official capacity (Article 27), the mental element (Article 30), and grounds to exclude liability, like insanity, duress and self-defence (Article 31) and mistake (Article

DOI: 10.4324/9781003320951-21

32). In relation to these issues, the provisions of the German Penal Code (*Strafgesetzbuch* – StGB) remain applicable as well as general criminal law provisions. In the end, a few special provisions were included in the VStGB with regard to the general part of international criminal law. They relate to the responsibility of military commanders and other superiors, the absence of statutory limitation for crimes against international law, and obedience to superior orders. These are the cases where, according to § 2 of the VStGB, it "is decided otherwise" and thus the special provisions of the VStGB prevail over the general ones.

The challenge of the implementation process is to determine when a rethinking, and thus a special provision – an exception – is actually warranted in the particular domestic legal order.[3] This process happens *vis-à-vis* specific provisions of the general part but in light of the specificity of the crimes at stake (thus of the special part). The need for a departure from the general principles can occur when, either (1) some principles or rules of international criminal law are not yet regulated under the general criminal law of that specific legal system, or (2) deviations to the general principles are necessary to meet the standards of international criminal law.

One example could be the need to expressly regulate the defence of superior orders or acting upon orders: in international criminal law the superior order can exclude culpability for the commission of war crimes only if a) the order was binding; b) the defendant did not know that the order was unlawful; and c) the order was not manifestly unlawful. Moreover, the question of a necessary ad hoc regulation arises in particular with regard to the rules on attribution, as we shall see in the following paragraphs.

2 The need for specific modes of liability for international crimes

The debate around the need to develop specific modes of liability for international crimes is still intense and presents not irrelevant challenges both at the domestic and at the international level.[4] The Rome Statute for the first time provided for a detailed set of rules on attribution in international criminal law. During the first 20 years of activity of the Court, the judges have refined the theories and now we can benefit from a fairly rich case law on, at least some, modes of liability. I am thinking, in particular, of the mode of liability of perpetration (which in turn includes the co-perpetration, indirect perpetration and even indirect co-perpetration) pursuant to Article 25(3)(a) of the Rome Statute, which was thoroughly analysed and interpreted during the first trial conducted at the International Criminal Court, the case against Thomas Lubanga Dyilo (as well as during the following cases in the DRC situation).[5] Aiding and abetting and other forms of participation contained in the Statute, however, have received less attention so far. And certainly, there is still much confusion about Article 28 of the Rome Statute, command responsibility, as we shall see further, also following extensive judgments that are of difficult interpretation.[6]

So, going back to Article 25(3)(a), containing what are considered to be the gravest mode of liability, perpetration or commission in its three forms, the ICC judges, from the *Lubanga* case onwards, have elaborated and specified the details of these modes of liability, also picking from and referring to the famous doctrine of "Täterschaft und Tatherrschaft" of renowned German law professor Claus Roxin.[7]

There can be no doubt that the legal theories at the basis of the "control over the crime" approach have been derived by the judges from domestic criminal law principles. The judges observed in this regard that "the control over the crime approach has been applied in a number of legal systems and is widely recognised in legal doctrine".[8] The "control over the crime" approach adopted by the ICC judges in *Lubanga* and in later cases of course departed to some extent from the original version. Professor Roxin himself intervened in the debate to clarify some aspects of his doctrine that he felt had been misrepresented in the ICC judgments.[9]

It is beyond the scope of this paper to go into this debate. The bottom line is that the way Article 25(3) of the Rome Statute is interpreted at the ICC and the way it was drafted at the time of the negotiation of the Statute, is strongly influenced by the German doctrine on criminal participation, which follows a differentiated approach. Through the "domination over an organizational apparatus" (*Organisationsherrschaft*), and Roxin's dogmatic on indirect perpetration through control over the apparatus, it is possible to establish the parallel responsibility of the two levels, namely the leader and the subordinate respectively, as indirect and direct perpetrator of the crime. Clearly this is coherent with an understanding of criminal participation based on a very distinct and sharply differentiated model.[10]

There have been pushbacks on this, both in scholarship and at the Court. I am referring in particular to Judge Fulford, a former British judge at the ICC, who signed interesting dissenting opinions, making the point that the differentiated model of participation was over-complicating things and that an alternative reading of the Rome Statute was possible, based on a unified perpetrator model.[11] Professor James Stewart, as well, raised pointed questions at the academic level, on the feasibility and desirability of such a complex system of attribution of responsibility in an interesting article with the iconic title "The End of Modes of Liability".[12]

Indeed, the unified perpetrator model presents some immediate advantages, at least at the attribution level, simplifying the burden of proof with regard to the elements of criminal participation. As has been clear since the first international tribunals were established after the Second World War, and as became particularly evident during the years of activity of the International Criminal Tribunal for the former Yugoslavia and the International Criminal Tribunal for Rwanda, the judges have had to deal with the need to broaden the scope of individual attribution and alleviate the burden posed on the prosecution by a strict interpretation of the principle of causality and criminal participation (for instance through the doctrine of joint criminal enterprise at the ICTY).[13] However, we must be aware that the same problems – and ultimately the need to differentiate among the various criminal contributions to the commission of the crime – normally resurface at the sentencing level, where the gravity of the single conduct and the individual culpability need to be established.

In Italy, where the Penal Code ("*Codice Rocco*", dating 1930!) adopted the unified perpetrator model of criminal participation, under Articles 110ff (pursuant to which everyone who participates in the crimes is responsible for the crime itself), there is nevertheless a vivid debate among criminal law scholars and practitioners on the elements of the various forms of participation.

2.1 A proposal for modes of liability for international crimes in the Italian system

With an eye on the project of domestic implementation of the Rome Statute in Italy, the specific question regarding the rules on attribution is whether a system, like the Italian one, that includes a very broad clause of participation pursuant to Article 110 of the Penal Code would be appropriate and able to encompass the provisions of the Rome Statute.

With regards to letters a) and b) and c) of Article 25(3), I do not see obstacles in this sense, for the reasons better explained below. Less clear is the situation with regard to letter d) of the same article, which in some way resembles the "joint criminal enterprise" (JCE) of the ad hoc tribunals. Yet, it must be clear that we are talking about a different mode of liability and that the JCE as such was not accepted by the ICC judges who found it not to be part of customary law.[14]

As far as the Italian system is concerned, we can also note that these scenarios are also punished through distinct offences of criminal association ("associazione criminale"), rather than in application of general rules on criminal participation. Therefore, one possibility is also to consider whether it would be appropriate to provide for the introduction of specific offences of criminal association for the commission of international crimes.[15]

In the context of the draft Italian Code of International Crimes,[16] with regards to the modes of liability, the draft legislation does not provide for any changes or additions to the existing rules on criminal participation as contained in the general Italian Penal Code, except for command responsibility (*infra*). This means that Articles 110ff of the Italian Penal Code will also apply to the international crimes, as defined in the new Code.

Regardless of the fact that, as explained above, Article 25(3)(a)–(d) of the Rome Statute is formulated following a differentiated model of imputation of responsibility (inspired by the German model), the Italian rules on criminal participation appear to be able to encompass the different modes of liability under the Rome Statute. While the Rome Statute typifies the different modes of liability, identifying distinct *actus reus* and *mens rea* standards, which can result in different degrees of criminal liability, the Italian Penal Code adopts a unitary model of criminal participation pursuant to which all contributions that have a causal or facilitative effect on the commission of the crime can be punished for the same crime. In this sense the law overcomes the distinction between principal perpetrators and accessory/participants. The area punishable as criminal participation according to the Italian Penal Code is ultimately broader than that defined by the Statute.

Also, from a political-criminal rationale, the Italian unitary-model doctrine is consistent with the perpetrators-complex structures that normally are a feature of international crimes. The unitary model is a solution that ultimately mirrors the difficulty of predetermining in abstract which responsibility should be the gravest. This means that the law does not postulate a necessarily heavier punishment for the material perpetrator of the criminal conduct than for an accomplice or participant. The attribution of responsibility to co-perpetrators and participants, and the related sentence, is not rigidly predetermined but depends on the contribution made by each individual to the commission of the crime. For the purpose of sentencing, of course, differentiations of the gravity of the various contributions can and must be introduced, as the Italian case law shows. Also, scholars have long since elaborated theories to frame individual contributions and their gravity into categories, aimed at guiding the work of the judges at sentencing, according to the criteria set forth by Articles 133ff of the Italian Penal Code. An important role is also played at the sentencing level by the circumstances of the crime, that can result in aggravating (Italian Penal Code, Articles 111 and 112) or mitigating (Italian Penal Code, Article 114) factors.

This flexibility of the Italian model of criminal participation appears to be particularly suitable precisely in relation to macro-crimes such as those under the jurisdiction of the ICC: international crimes typically imply a great deal of responsibility on the apical subjects, who are often removed from the material commission of the crime and, therefore, are not the material perpetrators, in the sense that they are not committing the *actus reus*. This is particularly evident with regard to the crime of aggression.[17]

3 Implementing the doctrine of command responsibility

Against this backdrop, the doctrine of command responsibility is a different issue. This is actually unsurprising, if we consider the origins of this mode of liability, which is an original creation of international criminal law. The doctrine, which was derived from the military field, then became a rule of international humanitarian law and finally, with the ad hoc tribunals in the 1990s, it was expanded and made applicable to the non-military, thus civilian, hierarchical relationships: therefore, regardless of the common language in use, it is more correct to speak of "superior responsibility", to include not only the military commanders but also the civilian superior.[18]

Indeed, it was the Rome Statute (Article 28) that for the first time made clear that this form of liability applies both to military and to civilian superiors. This clarification was of course welcomed, but the fact is that it continues to be exceptionally difficult to bring charges against non-military commanders under Article 28 of the Rome Statute, especially with regard to civilian superiors. There is in fact no case law on the point; moreover, also with regard to military commanders, it has proven extremely difficult not only to charge them under Article 28, but also to successfully try an accused, as evidenced by the ICC *Bemba* judgment.[19]

Already back in 2010, when closing my book on this topic, it was possible to observe an "erosion" of command responsibility, in the sense that this mode of liability was not "used" anymore by the prosecutors at the ad hoc tribunals, eroded by the JCE and other easier-to-prove modes of liability. At the ICC the situation is even worse, as it became too complicated to establish the responsibility of superiors based on Article 28 of the Statute. It is a regretful result, as command responsibility has an important role to play in international criminal law, not only at the stage of punishment, but already at the preventive level.

The reasons for this complexity are to a certain extent obvious and are related to the difficult assessment of individual criminal liability for omission. In Italian criminal law, commission by omission is a well-accepted principle pursuant to the general clause of equivalence contained in Article 40(2) of the Italian Penal Code. In a similar vein, §13 of the German Penal Code provides for the criminal relevance of the failure to act. However, this is not the case in many other jurisdictions, including European counties, that do not recognise this principle and do not have a general clause of equivalence for omission in criminal law.

But there is more than that: the problem with command responsibility, as defined in Article 28 of the Rome Statute, is that it conflated in one single provision different types of liability that cannot be treated in the same way. A thorough analysis shows that there are at least four forms of command/superior responsibility that can be outlined according to their different objective and subjective elements:

1 Intentional failure to prevent.
2 Negligent failure to prevent.
3 Intentional failure to punish.
4 Negligent failure to punish.[20]

Not all of them are modes of liability; while the intentional failure to prevent can integrate a commission by omission and the negligent failure to prevent can amount to participation in the crime of the subordinate, the failure to punish forms, which are responsibility ex post, can be more properly framed as a dereliction of duty offence in domestic law.

In this regard the VStGB can be considered a very good model for the domestic implementation of the doctrine.[21] The German legislator split Article 28 of the Rome Statute into three separate provisions: the first one has been introduced as §4, in Part 1 of the VStGB and provides that a superior who is vested with the appropriate supervisory powers and who does not hinder a subordinate from the commission of genocide, a crime against humanity or a war crime shall be punished like a perpetrator of the offence committed by the subordinate. Then §13 of the VStGB provides for a separate crime of dereliction of duty, namely the infringement of supervisory duties, taking into account the varying grades of guilt in cases where the superior did not know about the impending commission of the crime by the subordinate. Finally, §14 of the VStGB provides for the punishment of a superior for the non-reporting of a crime against international law committed by a subordinate.[22]

3.1 A proposal for implementing command responsibility in the Italian system

Similar to the solution adopted by the German legislator, the draft Italian Code of International Crimes includes a few specific provisions implementing command and superior responsibility, pursuant to Article 28 of the Rome Statute. The effort to regulate this form of responsibility, which was unknown in the domestic system, was very significant. Most importantly, the Italian criminal law system is well familiar with the positions of guarantee, including those aimed at preventing the crime of others. As already anticipated, Article 40(2) of the Italian Penal Code contains an equivalence clause, which equates omission to commission in case of dereliction of a legally binding duty to act.

The draft legislation introduces three provisions breaking down the different hypotheses of command responsibility contained in Article 28 of the Rome Statute. Thus, pursuant to the principles of culpability, legality and proportionality of punishment, the draft modulates the various forms of command responsibility according to their structural differences.[23]

1 Under Article 8, the draft Code regulates the "Intentional failure to prevent", pursuant to which the superior answers to the same crime as that committed by the subordinate as if he/she had committed it.
2 Article 9 regulates the "Negligent failure to prevent", pursuant to which the superior answers to the same crime as that committed by the subordinate but with a diminished sentence.
3 Finally, Article 63A of the draft Code provides a separate offence for the superior for cases of intentional failure to punish and intentional failure to report the subordinate's crime.

The Italian proposal is partly based on the German model adopted by the VStGB, which as we have seen also encompasses three separate provisions; but it also contains significant departures, due to the different approaches to criminal participation of the respective systems.

The first hypothesis, the "intentional failure to prevent", determines the responsibility of military commanders and civilian superiors for failure to prevent their subordinate's crime. This responsibility stems from the superior's position of guarantee, which is based on the existence of a corresponding position of guarantee in international law, aimed at preventing the subordinate's crime, in combination with the underlying crime by the subordinate. This is not strict liability or a position-liability, but rather the subordinate's crime must be covered by the superior's intent, in accordance with constitutional principles. This also implies that the superior had not only a legal obligation but also the power to prevent the crime.

The second provision, which also punishes the superior's failure to prevent the crimes of the subordinate, but on the basis of negligence, is built as a form of culpable facilitation of the subordinate's crime, modelled on an existing form of liability provided for in the Italian Penal Code with regard to the editor of a press.[24] The superior answers to the same crime as committed by the subordinate, but a decreased punishment, of one-third to one-half, is provided for the superior.

With regard to the "intentional failure to punish" and "failure to report" the subordinate's crime, they are provided as separate offences of the commander/superior and not as modes of liability. Notably, in fact, the provision is not included under the general part of the draft Code, but rather at the end of its special part (Article 63). The superior in these cases is not responsible for the crime committed by the subordinate, but rather for a distinct offence integrated by dereliction of his duty, which consisted in the punishment or reporting of the subordinate's crime, and independently of the crime committed by the subordinate. This offence is punishable only if committed intentionally.

Article 10 of the draft Code clarifies the concepts of military commander and civilian superior for the purposes of the law itself. While the former is based on command and control and extends to the *de facto* commander, in line with the international provisions, the civilian superior must possess powers of authority and control over the subordinates to be held accountable.

4 Corporate liability for international crimes

During the Rome Statute negotiations the possibility of introducing a criminal liability for legal persons was discussed but ultimately excluded. The main difficulty was to identify clear models for the attribution of criminal liability and sanctioning of corporate actors for the commission of international crimes and the lack of harmonisation of the domestic legislations on this form of responsibility. Although, thus, the Rome Statute does not provide for the criminal liability of corporate actors, the debate is still well present in international criminal law and some countries have implemented legislation that permits corporate actors to be charged for the commission of international crimes.[25]

Not only has corporate criminal liability been accepted at the legislative level in several countries, but corporate complicity in international crimes has also become a heated topic among scholars and practitioners, both nationally and internationally.[26] Some egregious cases of criminal responsibility of organisations had already been litigated during the trials conducted in Nuremberg.[27] In recent times, there have been some prominent cases of domestic prosecutions of international crimes, such as the *Lafarge* case in France, where a cement factory was charged with complicity in the commission of crimes against humanity (besides terrorism charges) for its conducts in Syria.[28]

Given growing awareness regarding the role of corporate actors in the commission of international crimes,[29] the question arises at this stage, whether current projects of domestication of international criminal law can provide the opportunity for an advancement of the law in this direction, thus expanding criminal liability *to corporate actors and organisations* for the commission of and participation in international crimes. Indeed, even if the Rome Statute only provides for the criminal responsibility of natural persons, this exclusion is only relevant before the ICC. In other words, the Rome Statute's provision is without prejudice to making entities, companies or corporations responsible for such violations at the domestic level.

Moreover, regardless of the nature of the responsibility, it is the substance that is at stake: it can thus be that domestic laws provide a possibility to hold corporations accountable for the commission of crimes even if the liability is not formally of a criminal but rather of an administrative nature.

4.1 A proposal for corporate responsibility in the Italian system

In this sense, one of the most significant proposals contained in the Italian draft Code of International Crimes is the provision of an administrative corporate responsibility. Already in 2001, Italy has adopted a legislation on the responsibility of legal persons for the commission of crimes: according to the Italian Legislative Decree no 231 of 8 June 2001, entities, companies and associations may be held liable for crimes committed in the interest or to the benefit of the organisation. There is a debate over the nature of corporate liability under such decree, partly resolved by the Italian Supreme Court, which described the liability as a *tertium genus*, between the criminal and administrative ones.[30]

The law distinguishes between two kinds of situations, namely when: (i) the offence is committed by individuals who hold executive/managerial positions; and (ii) the violation is perpetrated by employees "managed or supervised" by the former. In the first scenario, the corporation can be acquitted if it proves the absence of an "organizational fault". Such concept is central to the law's rationale, which, in the first place, is aimed at preventing the commission of crimes rather than punishing them. It refers to the failure to adopt and effectively implement organisational models. The compliance system also establishes controls mechanisms through an external independent body. The responsibility of the corporation can be established when the commission of a criminal offence can be linked to an organisational fault, while the corporation can be exempted from responsibility if it is able to prove that it has complied with, and effectively implemented, such organisational models and that, nevertheless, the manager bypassed said controls. The law also provides for a vast array of fines, disqualification sanctions and confiscation of crime proceeds.

Article 15 of the draft Code of International Crimes now extends this form of liability to the commission of international crimes, by expanding the range of application the law. Such proposal should be strongly supported as the *opinio* is growing that limiting punishment for individuals addresses only a part of the complex series of responsibilities for international crimes, which are increasingly committed through, with the support of, or with the benefit of corporations.

The Italian legal framework on corporate liability is well developed, but needs some amendments in this specific context in consideration of the special features of international crimes and their contextual elements. In this sense, the draft Code limits the corporation's liability to those cases when the crime is due to "severe organizational shortcomings" (see Article 67 of the draft Code, which refers to paragraph 1 of Article 25 *septiesdecies* of Legislative Decree 231/2002).

In terms of sanctions, fines range from 200 shares to 1,000 shares depending on the gravity of the sanction provided for by the Penal Code for the offence committed and the presence of aggravating factors, such as having gained a significant profit or having caused particularly serious damage, may lead to exceptionally high sanctions. The draft Code imposes, inter alia, the sanction of disqualification from exercising the activity to the so-called "illegal enterprise". On the other side, with the intent to preserve those business activities that are legal but that intrinsically present risk dimensions, a provision was introduced to exempt legal persons from responsibility when the corporate conduct is authorised by State authorities, introducing a ground for exclusion of liability. The question can be asked whether such a clause is advisable, in particular with regard to these opaque business activities – such as the supply of dual-use goods, software and technology, as well as the export of arms – which typically happen with the formal authorisation of State authorities, though not necessarily granted according to the appropriate standards of due diligence on behalf of the actors involved.[31]

Notes

1 See Kai Ambos, *Der Allgemeine Teil des Vòlkerstrafrechts* (Dunker & Humboldt 2002) 40ff.

2 See Volker Nerlich, Chapter 5.2, The Implementation of International Criminal Law in Germany: the Approach to Modes of Liability.

3 See Chantal Meloni and Florian Jeßberger, Chapter 1.1, Obligations, Options and Obstacles: Implementing the Rome Statute Revisited.
4 See chapters by J De Hemptinne, R Roth, E Van Sliedregt, T Gal, D Roseen and T Van Poecke in M Cupido, M Ventura and L Yanev (eds), *Modes of Liability in International Criminal Law* (Cambridge University Press 2019).
5 *The Prosecutor v Thomas Lubanga Dyilo* (ICC-01/04-01/06) was the first case tried at the ICC. Its judgments can be consulted on the ICC website www.icc-cpi.int/drc/lubanga.
6 See for instance, the proceedings regarding *The Prosecutor v Jean-Pierre Bemba Gombo* (ICC-01/05-01/08), including in particular the final Appeals Chamber acquittal judgment. They can be consulted on the ICC website www.icc-cpi.int/car/bemba
7 See Claus Roxin, 'Straftaten Im Rahmen Organisatorischer Machtapparate' [1963] GA 193.
8 See Stefano Manacorda and Chantal Meloni, 'Indirect Perpetration *versus* Joint Criminal Enterprise: Concurring Approaches in the Practice of International Criminal Law' (2011) 9 J Int Crim Justice 159.
9 See Claus Roxin, 'Crimes as Part of Organised Power Structures' (2011) 9 J Int Criminal Justice 193.
10 cf Ambos (n 1) 518ff.
11 See Judge Fulford, Separate and Dissenting Opinion, *The Prosecutor v Thomas Lubanga Dyilo*, Judgment Pursuant to Article 74 of the Statute, Trial Chamber I, 2012. On the topic, also see Jens Ohlin, 'Lubanga Decision Roundtable: Lubanga and the Control Theory', Opinio Juris, 15 March 2012.
12 James G Stewart, 'The End of Modes of Liability for International Crimes' [2012] Leiden Journal of International Law 165ff.
13 See Elinor Fry and Elies van Sliedregt, 'Conspiracy/Joint Criminal Enterprise', in *Oxford Bibliography of International Law* (2021), available at www.oxfordbibliographies.com/display/document/obo-9780199796953/obo-9780199796953-0096.xml
14 ibid.
15 This solution has been adopted by the draft Italian Code of International Crimes, at Art 64 (see the Annex in this volume, containing the English translation of the Draft Code).
16 See the English translation of the Project, which has been included as an Annex in this Volume.
17 See Annegret Hartig, Chapter 4.4, Domesticating the Sidelined Crime of Aggression.
18 See Ilias Bantekas, 'The Contemporary Law of Superior Responsibility' (1999) 93 The American Journal of International Law 573.
19 *Bemba* (n 6).
20 I have elaborated quite extensively on the point in Chantal Meloni, *Command Responsibility in International Criminal Law* (TMC Asser 2010).
21 Gerhard Werle and Florian Jeßberger, 'International Criminal Justice is Coming Home: The New German Code of Crimes Against International Law' (2002) 13 Criminal Law Forum 191.
22 See VStGB, §4 ("liability of military commanders and other superiors"), §13 ("breach of the duty of supervision") and §14 ("failure to report a crime").
23 In detail, Meloni (n 20) 139ff.

24 Italian Penal Code, Art 57 provides that the editor of a newspaper is responsible for his/her own negligent omission, consisting in a failure to exercise the control necessary to prevent crimes being committed through the press; the editor is punished with the same punishment established for the crime committed through the press, decreased by up to one third.

25 See Stefano Manacorda, '"Fragments" of International Economic Criminal Law: Short Notes on Corporate and Individual Liability for Business Involvement in International Crimes', in Jeßberger and others (eds), *Strafrecht und Systemunrecht* (Mohr Siebeck 2022) 193ff.

26 *Report of the Working Group on the issue of human rights and transnational corporations and other business enterprises* (June 2022) UN Doc A/HRC/50/40/Add.4.

27 Florian Jeßberger, 'On the Origins of Individual Criminal Responsibility under International Law for Business Activity: IG Farben on Trial' (2010) 8 J Int Crim Justice 783.

28 See *European Center for Constitutional and Human Rights et Sherpa c. Lafarge SA, Cour de Cassation*, Pourvoi no 19-87.367, 2 September 2021.

29 Also significant in this sense is the EU Commission's 2022 proposal for a Directive on corporate sustainability due diligence. cf A Nieto, 'Towards a European Economic Criminal Law of Human Rights' (2021) 21 European Criminal Law Review 6.

30 *Thyssenkrupp, Italian Court of Cassation*, Judgment of 24 April 2014, no 38343, paras 60–63.

31 See the pioneer case brought in Italy in 2018 by ECCHR against RWM, for its involvement in war crimes in Yemen through arms exports: www.ecchr.eu/en/case/european-responsibility-for-war-crimes-in-yemen/. The case is currently ongoing in the investigation stage.

Selected bibliography

Burghardt B, *Die Vorgesetztenverantwortlichkeit im völkerrechtlichen Straftatsystem: Eine Untersuchung zur Rechtsprechung der Internationalen Strafgerichtshöfe für das ehemalige Jugoslawien und Ruanda* (Berliner Juristische Universitätsschriften 2008)

Fronza E and Meloni C, 'The Draft Italian Code of International Crimes?' (2022) 20 *J Int Crim Justice* 1027

Jeßberger F and Geneuss J, 'On the Application of a Theory of Indirect Perpetration in Al Bashir: German Doctrine at The Hague?' (2008) 6 *J Int Crim Justice* 853

Manacorda S and Meloni C, 'Indirect Perpetration *versus* Joint Criminal Enterprise: Concurring Approaches in the Practice of International Criminal Law' (2011) 9 *J Int Crim Justice* 159

Meloni C, *Command Responsibility in International Criminal Law* (TMC Asser Press 2010)

Nerlich V, 'Superior Responsibility under Article 28 ICC Statute: For What Exactly is the Superior Held Responsible?' (2007) 5 *J Int Crim Justice* 665

Roxin C, 'Straftaten Im Rahmen Organisatorischer Machtapparate' [1963] *GA* 193

Roxin C, 'Crimes as Part of Organized Power Structures' (2011) 9 *J Int Crim Justice* 193

Werle G and Jeßberger F, 'International Criminal Justice is Coming Home: The New German Code of Crimes Against International Law' (2002) 13 *Criminal Law Forum* 191

Werle G and Jeßberger F, 'Einleitung VStGB', in *Münchener Kommentar zum Strafgesetzbuch, Band 9 Nebenstrafrecht II Völkerstrafgesetzbuch* (4th edn, CH Beck 2021)

Werle G and Nerlich V, 'Die Strafbarkeit von Kriegsverbrechen nach deutschem Recht' [2002] *Humanitäres Völkerrecht-Informationsschriften* 124

5.2 The implementation of international criminal law in Germany

The approach to modes of liability

Volker Nerlich[1]

1 Introduction

When States decide to domesticate international criminal law, the focus usually is on transposing the definitions of international crimes, as set out in the Rome Statute of the International Criminal Court ("ICC Statute" and "ICC", respectively) and in other international instruments, into the domestic legal order. Without doubt, this is the most important aspect of any attempt to harmonise international criminal law and a State's domestic legal order: if a given crime recognised at the international level does not exist under a State's criminal law, that State will often not be able to prosecute conduct amounting to international crimes.[2]

Yet, the question of domestication also arises with regard to the "general part" of international criminal law, including modes of liability. This is because, whenever a definition of a crime is applied, the attendant rules of the "general part" – concerning matters such as the mental element, potential justifications or defences – will need to be considered too. Modes of liability play a particularly important role in this regard, not least because international crimes are typically complex, involving a plurality of persons who contribute in different ways and at different levels to the commission of atrocities. It is the modes of liability that delineate what type of conduct that does not in itself fulfil the material elements of a given crime nevertheless gives rise to criminal liability.

This chapter surveys how Germany dealt with modes of liability when it transposed international criminal law into its domestic legal order in 2002. I will first set out the provisions concerning superior responsibility in the German Code of Crimes Against International Law ("CCAIL").[3] I will then turn to the approach concerning other modes of liability and assess the overall German implementation concerning modes of liability.

2 Domesticating superior responsibility – untangling Article 28 of the ICC Statute

Article 28 of the ICC Statute provides that military commanders and civilian superiors incur under certain conditions criminal responsibility for

DOI: 10.4324/9781003320951-22

international crimes committed by their subordinates.[4] Article 28 is a complex provision, recognising several different scenarios that lead to the criminal liability of the commander or superior.[5] The jurisprudence of the ICC has sought to elucidate the meaning of the provision in several judgments and decisions. When enacting the CCAIL in 2002, however, the German legislator could not rely on any such guidance from jurisprudence. There was also no domestic equivalent available in German criminal law.

Article 28 of the ICC Statute covers, for commanders and superiors separately, four different scenarios that give rise to criminal liability:

a Failure of the commander/superior to take measures to prevent or repress international crimes committed by subordinates in the knowledge that these crimes were being, or were about to be, committed.
b Failure of the commander/superior to take measures to prevent or repress international crimes by subordinates, in circumstances where the commander should have known or the superior consciously disregarded information clearly indicating that the crimes were being, or were about to be, committed.
c Failure of the commander/superior to take measures to punish international crimes of subordinates, in the knowledge that such crimes had been committed.
d Failure of the commander/superior to take measures to punish subordinates for international crimes, in circumstances where the commander should have known/the superior had consciously disregarded information clearly indicating that such crimes had been committed.

These four scenarios can be grouped along two dimensions. The first dimension concerns the *point in time* at which the commander's/superior's failure to act occurred, relative to the commission of the subordinates' crimes, namely whether the commander/superior failed to act *before or while* the crimes were being committed (scenarios a. and b., above – hereinafter: "superior responsibility before the fact"), or whether the commander's/superior's failure to act occurred *after* the crimes had been committed (scenarios c. and d. – hereinafter: "superior responsibility after the fact").

The second dimension concerns the commander's/superior's knowledge of the subordinates' crimes. In scenarios a. and c., the commander/superior had such knowledge (hereinafter: "intentional[6] superior responsibility"), whereas in scenarios b. and d., the commander/superior did not have such knowledge, but *should have known* of the crimes or *consciously disregarded* information that clearly indicated the commission of crimes (hereinafter: "non-intentional superior responsibility").

Thus, scenario a. may be labelled "intentional superior responsibility before the fact", scenario b. "non-intentional superior responsibility before the fact", scenario c. "intentional superior responsibility after the fact" and, finally, scenario d. "non-intentional superior responsibility after the fact".

Article 28 of the ICC Statute provides that, in all four scenarios, the commander/superior is "criminally responsible" for the crimes committed by their subordinates. This suggests that the crimes themselves are imputed on the commander/superior. For the German legislator, this imputation of the subordinates' crimes on the commander/superior was, as far as scenarios b. to d. are concerned, in tension with the culpability principle, which enjoys constitutional status in Germany. As far as superior responsibility after the fact is concerned (scenarios c. and d.), the legislator considered that a commander/superior could not be held responsible for crimes that were committed before the commander's/superior's failure to act occurred. This is because failure to act after the fact cannot, as a matter of logic, have had any influence on the commission of the crimes. It is therefore, so the argument goes, not possible to impute the crimes on the commander/superior. Further, as far as non-intentional superior responsibility is concerned (scenarios b. and d.), the German legislator considered that commanders/superiors could not be held responsible for intentional crimes committed by their subordinates if the commanders/superiors themselves lacked such intent.[7]

The solution adopted by the German legislator to address this dilemma was to break up Article 28 of the ICC Statute into separate sections: section 4(1) CCAIL provides for the responsibility of commanders/superiors who intentionally failed to prevent their subordinates' crimes.[8] They shall be punished "in the same way as a perpetrator of the offence committed by that subordinate". This corresponds to above scenario a.; the commander/superior is held responsible for the subordinates' crimes. Interestingly, section 4(1) CCAIL does not actually lead to an extension of criminal liability under German law. This is because even without it, conduct of this type would be covered by liability based on commission by omission (German Criminal Code, s 13) or for aiding and abetting by omission (German Criminal Code, s 27).[9] However, the second sentence of section 4(1) CCAIL removes the possibility of a mitigated sentence that is otherwise available pursuant to section 13(2) of the German Criminal Code for cases of commission by omission.

As regards the remaining scenarios b. to d., the German legislator opted for the adoption of separate offences or for the non-transposition into German law. Section 14 CCAIL[10] criminalises the failure to properly supervise subordinates who commit crimes under the CCAIL in circumstances where the commander/superior did not have knowledge of these crimes – scenario b. in the list above. In line with Article 28 of the ICC Statute, section 14 CCAIL makes a distinction in respect of the requisite mental element for commanders on the one hand and superiors on the other: for the former, the imminent commission of the subordinates' crimes must have been "discernible" (section 14(1) CCAIL), whereas for the latter, the imminent commission of crimes must have been "discernible … without more".

Section 14 CCAIL introduces another distinction in respect of the mental element. If the failure to properly supervise the subordinates was intentional, the punishment is up to five years of imprisonment, whereas punishment in case of only negligent failure to supervise the subordinates is limited to three years of imprisonment. By also allowing for punishment in cases of negligent failure to exercise proper control over subordinates, section 14 CCAIL arguably goes beyond what is criminalised under Article 28 of the ICC Statute. This is because, according to Article 30(1) of the ICC Statute and unless otherwise provided, "intent and knowledge" are required with respect to *all* material elements of a crime, and pursuant to Article 30(2)(a) of the ICC Statute, "intent" regarding "conduct" – such as the failure to exercise control properly – requires that the perpetrator "means to engage in the conduct". While Article 28 ICC Statute, in scenario b., provides for a lowered mental element, this applies only to the knowledge of the subordinates' crimes, but not the rest of the material elements of superior responsibility, including the failure to exercise control properly.

While section 14 CCAIL deals with the failure to prevent or repress crimes of which the commander/superior was not, but should have been, aware, section 15 CCAIL deals with scenario c. above – intentional superior responsibility after the fact. Such failure may be punished by imprisonment of up to five years. What is missing, however, is a provision that would criminalise scenario d., ie non-intentional superior responsibility after the fact. Thus, under the CCAIL, commanders and superiors cannot be held responsible for the failure to ensure the punishment of their subordinates' crimes if they had no actual knowledge of these crimes. The official commentary on the bill introducing the CCAIL does not contain any explanation as to why this form of superior responsibility should not be transposed into German law.[11]

Overall, the German approach to the domestic implementation of Article 28 of the ICC Statute is a complex one. As was the case with the implementation of provisions on war crimes,[12] the German legislator did not shy away from deconstructing Article 28 of the ICC Statute and adopting provisions that, in the legislator's view, fit more easily into the German legal order than the provision in the ICC Statute, even if this was at the expense of full congruence between the notions of superior responsibility at the international and the domestic levels.

3 The approach to other modes of liability – application of general rules

While Germany thus chose an innovative approach to the implementation of superior responsibility into domestic law, the approach to the transposition other modes of liability was one of inaction. In the absence of any specific provision in this regard in the CCAIL, general German criminal law applies.[13] Accordingly, the modes of liability provided for in sections 25 to 27 of the German Criminal Code also apply to crimes under the CCAIL.

This was a conscious decision of the drafters of the CCAIL. The official commentary on the draft CCAIL noted that there was no need to transpose the modes of liability recognised in Article 25(3) of the ICC Statute into German law because they corresponded in substance to the existing modes of liability set out in the German Criminal Code.[14] Such an approach is not without downsides. As noted above, international crimes are typically committed by a plurality of individuals – dozens or hundreds – who fulfil different functions, roles and responsibilities in the commission of the crimes. It is all but inconceivable that a crime of genocide or a crime against humanity should be committed by a single person.[15] Over the years, international jurisprudence – both of the ICC and of the ad hoc international criminal tribunals ICTY and ICTR – has developed and identified concepts that seek to capture such forms of criminal group behaviour and to clearly delineate the border between conduct that – although not itself fulfilling the material elements of an international crime – gives rise to criminal liability and behaviour that – although somehow related to such a crime – does not. Of particular note are the notion of "joint criminal enterprise", developed by the ICTY and ICTR,[16] and the ICC's interpretation of Article 25(3)(a) ICC Statute, according to which those who have control over a crime have "committed" it in terms of that provision, even if the control takes the form of organisational control.[17] There is also extensive jurisprudence of the ICC and of the ad hoc tribunals regarding other modes of liability, notably aiding and abetting the commission of an international crime.

It is beyond the scope of this paper to assess whether the scope of liability arising from these "international" modes of liability is broader – or indeed more limited – than that arising from the application of "domestic" modes of liability. Such an endeavour might even be impossible, given that judicial determinations concerning modes of liability will always depend on the specific facts. Still, given that the elements differ to some extent, it stands to reason to assume that international and domestic modes of liability are not fully congruent. This means that the German approach of non-transposition of "international" modes of liability and the application of "German" modes of liability instead could lead to situations where certain conduct will give rise to punishment before the ICC, but not in Germany, or *vice versa*.[18]

Nevertheless, the German approach of applying "domestic" modes of liability to the crimes set out in the CCAIL is understandable. Modes of liability constitute a complex subject and it most certainly would have led to confusion and ambiguity had German courts been required to apply a different set of modes of liability to crimes under the CCAIL than those applicable to "common" crimes under the German Criminal Code.[19] In addition, German criminal law should be well prepared to deal with mass atrocities, given that German courts had to grapple with the challenge of appropriately capturing criminal behaviour in the context of mass and State criminality of Nazi Germany and of State crimes of the German Democratic Republic (GDR) – and developed its own doctrinal responses.

As concerns the criminal liability of the State leadership, the German Federal Supreme Court (*Bundesgerichtshof*, BGH) found in 1994 that the members of the GDR's National Defence Council were criminally responsible as principal perpetrators for the killings at the German–German border.[20] The BGH based this finding on the notion of control over crimes through hierarchically structured organisations – which initially had been developed by Claus Roxin in response to the crimes of the Nazis.[21] The BGH applied the same notion a few years later to the members of the East German Politburo.[22] It should provide a powerful tool in the prosecution of crimes under the CCAIL.[23]

Similarly, existing jurisprudence concerning aiding and abetting liability for crimes committed in German extermination camps during World War II could potentially be relied upon in the prosecution of crimes under the CCAIL. In particular the more recent jurisprudence could be of great significance. In 2016, the BGH determined in the case against Oskar Gröning that working in an administrative function in the Auschwitz-Birkenau extermination camp could be considered a form of psychological support to the leadership of Nazi Germany and the SS with regard to the so-called "Hungary-Action" – the systematic deportation and murder of Hungarian Jews in spring 1942, thus giving rise to Gröning's aiding and abetting liability for murder.[24] This decision of the BGH marked an important departure from previous jurisprudence, which initially required a showing of a more direct contribution to the crimes committed in Nazi concentration camps.[25] Again, this doctrinal approach can potentially be utilised for the effective prosecution of crimes under the CCAIL too.

When adjudicating crimes under the CCAIL, however, German courts have shown some reluctance to rely on either the notion of control over crimes through hierarchically structured organisations or the broader notion of aiding and abetting accepted in the *Gröning* case. Two recent cases may serve to exemplify this reluctance.

In the case of *Anwar R.*, who in January 2022 was found guilty by the Koblenz Higher Regional Court of crimes against humanity committed in the Section 251 prison of the Syrian secret service,[26] the BGH had found in 2019 that there were significant grounds to believe that he was responsible as a principal perpetrator for the crimes committed at Section 251 because he had assumed, as head of the investigations subsection, a central role similar to that of gang leader.[27] According to the BGH, it was therefore not necessary to resort to the notion of control over crimes through hierarchically structured organisations.[28] Even if the BGH's decision, which concerned the suspect's continued detention, was not binding on the Higher Regional Court's decision on Anwar R's guilt, it may nevertheless be assumed that, when determining the accused's guilt, the court will not have ignored the BGH's view of Anwar R's criminal responsibility.

Similarly, in the case of *Eyad A.*, another person accused of being responsible for crimes against humanity in Section 251,[29] the Koblenz Higher Regional Court found that the accused was criminally responsible as an aider and abettor in respect of 30 victims because he had been involved in their arrest and transport to the prison. The court, however, acquitted him of the charge of being responsible as an aider and abettor for other crimes that may have been committed by the security service of which he was a member, finding that there was no evidence that he had supported such crimes.[30] In doing so, the Higher Regional Court followed an earlier finding of the BGH in that case, which had overturned in part a decision concerning Eyad A's detention. Notably, the BGH had concluded that there was no strong suspicion that Eyad A was criminally responsible for two cases of murder and one thousand other cases of torture at Section 251 prison, noting the lack of evidence that Eyad A had directly participated in these victims' arrest and transport.[31] The BGH declined to rely on the principles established in the *Gröning* case. According to the BGH, there was no indication that, at the time the Syrian leadership decided to violently quell the protests in Syria, Eyad A had been a member of Section 251; that, unlike the "Hungary action" that was the subject of the *Gröning* case, the cases of torture at issue did not amount to a "clearly defined complex"; and that there were no clear indications that Eyad A had been permanent part of the organisation of mass torture.[32] The BGH declined to determine whether any of the three criteria would be dispensable for finding Eyad A liable based on the *Gröning* principle.[33] While this may be seen as an indication that the BGH deliberately left some room for further development and clarification of the jurisprudence, the hesitance of the court to rely on *Gröning* is palpable.[34]

4 Conclusion

In sum, the German approach to the implementation of "international" modes of liability may best be described as robust. As far as the implementation of superior responsibility is concerned – the only genuinely international mode of liability – the German legislator opted for an implementation that, as far as the form is concerned, deviates significantly from Article 28 of the ICC Statute. As to the substance, there are some areas that lead to criminal responsibility under Article 28 of the ICC Statute, but that have no equivalent under German law.

As for other modes of liability, the German legislator decided simply to apply general German criminal law. Undoubtedly, this facilitates the application of the CCAIL by German courts, even if it means that certain conduct that may give rise to criminal liability at the international level may not be covered in Germany and *vice versa*.

It should be noted that how a State implements international criminal law, including modes of liability, into its own legal system has repercussions not only for that legal system. The legislative and jurisprudential decisions concerning modes of liability for international crimes are expressions of how the State in question understands the law at the international level, too. This, in turn, may influence and inform the interpretation of international criminal law by the ICC or by other States. Particularly in the field of modes of liability, where international jurisprudence is relatively recent and far from consolidated, such continued dialogue across jurisdictions can only be welcomed.

Notes

1 Judge, Appeals Chamber, Special Criminal Court, Bangui; honorary professor, Humboldt-University of Berlin. The views expressed are those of the author alone and cannot be attributed to any institution the author is or was associated with.

2 While in some situations it may be possible to revert to "ordinary" crimes to punish international crimes, several of these crimes – such as the recruitment and use of child soldiers, a war crime – do not have any domestic equivalent.

3 *Völkerstrafgesetzbuch* adopted on 26 June 2002, as amended on 22 December 2016; an English translation of the CCAIL is available at: www.gesetze-im-internet.de/englisch_vstgb/englisch_vstgb.html (last visited on 6 July 2022).

4 In what follows, military commanders will simply be referred to as "commanders", while civilian superiors will be referred to as "superiors". The term "superior responsibility" will be used to refer to the responsibility of commanders and superiors alike.

5 See, for instance, Boris Burghardt, *Die Vorgesetztenverantwortlichkeit im völkerrechtlichen Straftatsystem: Eine Untersuchung zur Rechtsprechung der Internationalen Strafgerichtshöfe für das ehemalige Jugoslawien und Ruanda* (Berliner Juristische Universitätsschriften 2008); Chantal Meloni, *Command Responsibility in International Criminal Law* (TMC Asser Press 2010); Volker Nerlich, 'Superior Responsibility under Article 28 ICC Statute: For What Exactly is the Superior Held Responsible?' (2007) 5 J Int Crim Justice 665.

6 In Nerlich (n 5), I proposed to label this type of superior responsibility "knowledge superior responsibility". I now prefer the more plastic term "intentional superior responsibility" and to oppose it to "non-intentional superior responsibility" (as opposed to "lack-of-knowledge superior responsibility"). This change in terminology is not meant to denote a change in meaning. Of course, the terms "intentional" and "non-intentional" could also be delusive, given that ICC Statute, Art 30 uses "intent" and "knowledge" to describe separate, yet related concepts. In the present paper, I use "intent" in the sense of the German concept of "*Vorsatz*", which comprises both a volitional and a cognitive element.

7 See *Entwurf eines Gesetzes zur Einführung des Völkerstrafgesetzbuches of 2002* Drs 14/8524, 18–19, 36 (Germany 2002). See also Thomas Weigend and Milan Kuhli, '§ 4 VStGB', in *Münchener Kommentar zum Strafgesetzbuch, Band 9 Nebenstrafrecht II Völkerstrafgesetzbuch* (4th edn, CH Beck 2021) paras 7–8.

8 CCAIL, s 4(1) does not expressly define the mental element of the commander/superior. However, in accordance with general German criminal law, the lack of mention of a mental element means that only acts with intent (*Vorsatz*) are punished (see s 15 of the German Criminal Code [*Strafgesetzbuch*] of 15 May 1871, last amended on 22 November 2021; an English translation of the German Criminal Code is available at: www.gesetze-im-internet.de/englisch_stgb/index.html [last accessed on 20 June 2022]).

9 See Weigend and Kuhli, '§ 4 VStGB' (n 7) para 12.

10 Note that in the initial version of the CCAIL, this was s 13. With the inclusion of a provision on the crime of aggression as s 12 of the CCAIL in December 2016, the numbering of the subsequent sections of the CCAIL changed.

11 Thomas Weigend and Milan Kuhli, '§ 15 VStGB', in *Münchener Kommentar zum Strafgesetzbuch, Band 9 Nebenstrafrecht II Völkerstrafgesetzbuch* (4th edn, CH Beck 2021) paras 17, footnote 30, consider that providing for non-intentional superior responsibility after the fact would have led to over-criminalisation; non-implementation of this aspect of ICC Statute, Art 28 was therefore preferable.
12 See CCAIL, ss 8–12. On this, see Gerhard Werle and Volker Nerlich, 'Die Strafbarkeit von Kriegsverbrechen nach deutschem Recht' [2002] Humanitäres Völkerrecht-Informationsschriften 124.
13 See CCAIL, s 2.
14 See *Entwurf eines Gesetzes zur Einführung des Völkerstrafgesetzbuches of 2002* Drs 14/8524, 17 (Germany 2002).
15 The matter may be different as far as war crimes are concerned, as violations of humanitarian law may amount to war crimes even if they were not widespread or committed as part of a plan or policy.
16 See *Prosecutor v Tadic* (Judgement) IT-94-1-A (15 July 1999) (ICTY, Appeals Chamber), paras 185–228.
17 The ICC Appeals Chamber adopted the "control over the crime" approach in its first judgment on a final appeal. See *Prosecutor v Lubanga* (Judgment) ICC-01/04-01/06-3121-Red (1 December 2014), para 473.
18 See in this regard also Thomas Weigend and Milan Kuhli, '§ 2 VStGB', in *Münchener Kommentar zum Strafgesetzbuch, Band 9 Nebenstrafrecht II Völkerstrafgesetzbuch* (4th edn, CH Beck 2021) paras 15–16, who consider that, generally speaking, the German rules concerning modes of liability correspond to those at the international level.
19 See also Gerhard Werle and Florian Jeßberger, 'Einleitung VStGB', in *Münchener Kommentar zum Strafgesetzbuch, Band 9 Nebenstrafrecht II Völkerstrafgesetzbuch* (4th edn, CH Beck 2021) para 45; Weigend and Kuhli, '§ 2 VStGB' (n 18) paras 1–3.
20 Bundesgerichtshof, 26 July 1994, 5 StR 98/94.
21 Claus Roxin, 'Straftaten im Rahmen organisatorischer Machtapparate' [1963] GA 193. For an English translation of excerpts of this article, see Claus Roxin, 'Crimes as Part of Organized Power Structures' (2011) 9 J Int Crim Justice 193.
22 Bundesgerichtshof, 8 November 1999, 5 StR 632/98.
23 Interestingly, the ICC's jurisprudence on the interpretation of Art 25(3)(a) of the ICC Statute was also heavily influenced by *Roxin's* theories. See Florian Jeßberger and Julia Geneuss, 'On the Application of a Theory of Indirect Perpetration in Al-Bashir: German Doctrine at The Hague?' (2008) 6 J Int Crim Justice 853. This could lead to more congruence of the application of modes of liability at the (German) domestic and the international level.
24 Bundesgerichtshof, 20 September 2016, 3 StR 49/16, paras 21–26.
25 See Boris Burghardt, 'Die Strafsache "Oskar Gröning" vor dem Bundesgerichtshof' [2019] ZIS 21. The BGH's jurisprudence built on jurisprudence in the *Demanjuk*-case, which, however, had never reached the level of the BGH.
26 Higher Regional Court Koblenz, 13 January 2022, 1 StE 9/19. See 'Life imprisonment due to crimes committed against humanity and murder – sentencing of a suspected member of the Syrian secret service' (17 January 2022) <https://olgko.justiz.rlp.de/de/startseite/detail/news/News/detail/life-imprisonment-due-to-crimes-committed-against-humanity-and-murder-sentencing-of-a-suspected-me/> (accessed 27 May 2022).
27 See Bundesgerichtshof, 5 September 2019, AK 47/19, paras 47–48.

28 ibid. The full reasoning of the Higher Regional Court's judgment convicting R is not yet available. It is therefore not clear whether, in convicting R, the Higher Regional Court followed the BGH's lead, or whether it did apply the notion of control over crimes through hierarchically organised structures.

29 The cases of *Anwar R* and *Eyad A* were initially tried together. Since the case against the latter was significantly smaller, the court decided during the trial to separate the two cases and to issue a judgment on *Eyad A's* responsibility first.

30 Higher Regional Court Koblenz, 24 February 2021, 1 StE 3/21, para 580.

31 Bundesgerichtshof, 6 June 2019, StB 14/19, para 75.

32 ibid para 79.

33 ibid para 80.

34 The BGH also declined to apply the *Gröning* jurisprudence in the case of a member of the Rwandan FDLR militia. See Bundesgerichtshof, 20 December 2018, 3 StR 236/17, paras 94–108.

Selected bibliography

Burghardt B, *Die Vorgesetztenverantwortlichkeit im völkerrechtlichen Straftatsystem: Eine Untersuchung zur Rechtsprechung der Internationalen Strafgerichtshöfe für das ehemalige Jugoslawien und Ruanda* (Berliner Juristische Universitätsschriften 2008)

Burghardt B, 'Die Strafsache "Oskar Gröning" vor dem Bundesgerichtshof' [2019] *ZIS* 21

Jeßberger F and Geneuss J, 'On the Application of a Theory of Indirect Perpetration in Al Bashir: German Doctrine at The Hague?' (2008) 6 *J Int Crim Justice* 853

Meloni C, *Command Responsibility in International Criminal Law* (TMC Asser Press 2010)

Nerlich V, 'Superior Responsibility under Article 28 ICC Statute: For What Exactly is the Superior Held Responsible?' (2007) 5 *J Int Crim Justice* 665

Roxin C, 'Straftaten im Rahmen organisatorischer Machtapparate' [1963] GA 193

Roxin C, 'Crimes as Part of Organized Power Structures' (2011) 9 *J Int Crim Justice* 193

Weigend T and Kuhli M, '§ 2 VStGB', in *Münchener Kommentar zum Strafgesetzbuch, Band 9 Nebenstrafrecht II Völkerstrafgesetzbuch* (4th edn, CH Beck 2021)

Weigend T and Kuhli M, '§ 4 VStGB', in *Münchener Kommentar zum Strafgesetzbuch, Band 9 Nebenstrafrecht II Völkerstrafgesetzbuch* (4th edn, CH Beck 2021)

Weigend T and Kuhli M, '§ 15 VStGB', in *Münchener Kommentar zum Strafgesetzbuch, Band 9 Nebenstrafrecht II Völkerstrafgesetzbuch* (4th edn, CH Beck 2021)

Werle G and Jeßberger F, 'Einleitung VStGB', in *Münchener Kommentar zum Strafgesetzbuch, Band 9 Nebenstrafrecht II Völkerstrafgesetzbuch* (4th edn, CH Beck 2021)

Werle G and Nerlich V, 'Die Strafbarkeit von Kriegsverbrechen nach deutschem Recht' [2002] *Humanitäres Völkerrecht-Informationsschriften* 124

5.3 Sanctions and Sentencing for International Crimes in Domestic Legal Systems

Aziz Epik[1]

1 Introduction

The implementation of international criminal law into domestic legislation raises various difficult questions. One issue that is occasionally considered as a mere afterthought, but is of central importance to the defendant, concerns sanctions and sentencing. In the following, I will focus on two questions: does the specific character of crimes under international law warrant a fundamentally different regime of sanctions and sentencing?; and are there particular issues that should be considered by a domestic legislator when determining the applicable penalties and sentencing ranges for crimes under international law?

In order to give some tentative answers to these questions, I will first provide a cursory overview of the sentencing framework of the Rome Statute, and then discuss the challenges in providing a domestic framework for sanctions and sentencing for international crimes.

2 The Sentencing Framework of the Rome Statute

2.1 Purposes of Punishment

At the outset it is necessary to consider the purposes of punishment as they influence the process and outcome of sentencing.[2] Interestingly, neither the ICC Statute nor the Rules of Procedure and Evidence (RPE) contain provisions explicitly outlining the sentencing objectives. An analysis of the relevant provisions of the Statute and Rules as well as the ICC sentencing decisions to date reveals, however, that the traditional purposes of punishment, on which most domestic criminal justice systems rely, apply – with some adjustments – regardless of the macro-criminal character of international crimes and the inherent shortcomings of each purpose. As in the domestic context, it is not a single theory of punishment that justifies and defines international punishment, but a combination of retributive and preventive considerations.[3] The ICC itself has repeatedly identified retribution and deterrence as primary sentencing objectives, which is in line with the law and practice of other international courts and tribunals. In addition, positive general

DOI: 10.4324/9781003320951-23

prevention as well as rehabilitation are relevant objectives even though less weight is attached to them. With regard to the two main sentencing objectives, the ICC judges clearly view retribution as closely linked to the expressive capacity of punishment on the one hand and as demanding proportionate sentences on the other, while the term deterrence refers to both general and special deterrence.[4]

2.2 Applicable Penalties

Let us turn to the applicable penalties. In this regard, the Rome Statute includes a single provision determining the penalties that apply uniformly to all four core crimes and their respective individual acts: Article 77. According to this provision, the ICC may impose either "imprisonment for a specified number of years, which may not exceed a maximum of 30 years" or "a term of life imprisonment". In addition, but not instead of imprisonment, Article 77(2) of the ICC Statute allows the Court to order a fine or a forfeiture of proceeds, property and assets derived directly or indirectly from the crime. Thus, the principal penalty is imprisonment. Interestingly, the Statute establishes a clear relationship of rule and exception in favour of fixed-term imprisonment as a sentence of life imprisonment is only admissible "when justified by the extreme gravity of the crime and the individual circumstances of the convicted person".[5] This is confirmed by Rule 145(3) RPE, according to which life imprisonment will generally only be justified if at least one aggravating circumstance under Rule 145(2)(b) exists. By not imposing any *mandatory* life sentences for particular crimes, Article 77(1) of the ICC Statute ensures that the Court is always able to impose a sentence that actually fits the crime *and* the perpetrator.

2.3 Determination of the Sentence

The determination of the sentence in a particular case is governed by a number of provisions in the Statute and Rules of Procedure and Evidence. Read together, these provisions establish a rather comprehensive sentencing framework.[6] First, any sentencing decision of the ICC has to comply with the overarching principle of proportionality. This follows from Articles 81 and 83 of the Statute, according to which a sentence may only be successfully appealed if the sentence is disproportionate to the crime. In addition, Rule 145 of the Rules of Procedure and Evidence provides that the totality of any sentence must reflect the culpability of the convicted person; the degree of culpability thus sets the frame for any sentencing considerations and bars sentences that are detached from the individual responsibility of the perpetrator for the harm caused by his or her crimes. In *Lubanga* the Appeals Chamber explained that "proportionality is generally measured by the degree of harm caused by the crime and the culpability of the perpetrator and, in this regard, relates to the determination of the length of the sentence".[7]

With a view to the specific sentencing factors, Article 78(1) of the ICC Statute lists the "gravity of the crime" and the "individual circumstances of the convicted person" as the primary sentencing factors, while Rule 145 lists further relevant sentencing factors and provides a list of mitigating and aggravating circumstances that the Court "shall take into account, as appropriate".

a **Gravity:** Corresponding with the overarching importance of the proportionality principle, the gravity of the crime must be classified as the principal sentencing factor.[8] However, neither the Statute nor the Rules of Procedure and Evidence provide a definition of the gravity concept.[9] The Trial Chamber in *Ongwen* has recently stated that "gravity is generally measured *in abstracto*, by analysing the constituent elements of the crime, and *in concreto*, in light of the particular circumstances of the case, and by considering both qualitative and quantitative aspects. The assessment of the gravity must take into account both the gravity of the crime and also the gravity of the convicted person's culpable conduct".[10] Thus, the gravity of the crime is understood as a rather broad concept that includes abstract and concrete, objective and subjective criteria.[11]

b **Individual circumstances:** In addition to the gravity of the crime, Article 78 refers to the individual circumstances of the convicted person as the second main sentencing factor. This reference should be interpreted as to allowing the Court to consider circumstances that relate to the personal situation of the offender, such as his age and his socio-economic background, as well as his (general) conduct so long as such circumstances are not already considered in the determination of the gravity of the crime.[12] Circumstances relating to the preventive objectives of sentencing can be considered in this context as well, such as the risk of recidivism or the prospect of his or her reintegration into society.

c **Sentencing factors:** Rule 145 of the Rules of Procedure and Evidence then provides a non-exhaustive list of sentencing factors that have to be considered "in addition" to the factors already mentioned in Article 78 of the ICC Statute. The relationship between these sentencing factors and those already included in Article 78 remains dubious.[13] In my view the factors mentioned in Rule 145 can be considered as relevant either with regard to the gravity of the crime or the individual circumstances of the convicted person so that they concretise these rather broad categories. The ICC has not taken a definitive stance on the interpretation so far; the sentencing decisions to date rather stress that "what is of importance is not so much in which category a given factor is placed, but that the Trial Chamber identifies all relevant factors and attaches reasonable weight to them in its determination of the sentence, carefully avoiding that the same factor is relied upon more than once".[14]

d **Mitigating/aggravating circumstances:** Finally, the Court has to take into account mitigating and aggravating circumstances as appropriate. Again, the ICC is of the view that it is not so much a question under which category these factors are considered but that they are identified and taken into account at all. This view might facilitate the judge's task but is problematic with a view to Rule 145(3) that links the presence of an aggravating circumstance with the possibility to impose a sentence of life imprisonment. It remains to be seen how such issues if they arrive in the future will be dealt with.

e **Weighing up:** Once the judges have identified all relevant factors, they have to determine the weight that should be attached to each of the factors and balance them against each other in an effort to determine a sentence that is proportionate and reflective of the offender's culpability. The judges then have to pronounce a sentence for each crime of which the accused has been convicted and a joint sentence specifying the total period of imprisonment where the accused is convicted of more than one crime.[15]

3 Key Elements of a Domestic Sentencing Framework for Crimes under International Law

Let me now turn to possible issues that can arise when discussing a domestic legal framework for sanctions and sentencing for international crimes.

3.1 Purposes of Punishment

With regard to the purposes of punishment, I would argue that, in general, the traditional purposes of punishment remain relevant.[16] As Italian courts already have to consider a variety of sentencing objectives and as Italian law also demands proportionality between the crime and the sentence and stresses the principle of personal culpability,[17] major adjustments do not seem necessary. However, it might merit consideration whether the weight attached to the respective sentencing objectives domestically needs to be reviewed given that retribution and deterrence are seen as primary sentencing objectives while rehabilitation and other purposes of punishment have been given less weight at the international level.

3.2 Applicable Penalties

With a view to the applicable penalties, the general gravity of crimes under international law is a strong argument in favour of custodial sentences. Imprisonment should therefore be the primary penalty for all core crimes. Pecuniary sanctions could be considered as additional sanctions but will rarely be adequate on their own. The Italian Penal Code also includes provisions on civil sanctions (*Delle sanzioni civili*). It seems sensible to apply these provisions to crimes under international law as well. As the reparations regime of the Rome Statute demonstrates, the compensation of victims is an important element of the overall legal reaction to such crimes.[18]

3.3 Sentencing Ranges

The principle of legal certainty demands that the form and scope of possible penalties is determined by law. While this principle is construed less strictly in international criminal law so that the general sentencing range provided in the Rome Statute is not considered problematic,[19] most domestic legal systems – including the Italian – are much stricter in this regard.[20] Therefore, the legislator is obliged to provide specific sentencing ranges for every crime. But how should such ranges be determined?

a First, I would argue that, as a general rule, it does not seem appropriate to classify the core crimes or their underlying acts merely as contraventions in the Italian criminal law categories. This follows from a comparison between the underlying acts of the core crimes and corresponding ordinary crimes. Even war crimes against property – supposedly the least grave crimes in the Rome Statute as the relatively low sentences for pillaging in the *Ongwen* sentencing judgment have confirmed once again[21] – would equate at least to a delict under Article 635 of the Italian Penal Code. Given the international dimension of crimes under international law, it would therefore be inconsistent to classify such crimes as contraventions rather than delicts.

b Second, when considering appropriate sentencing ranges for crimes under international law, it should be kept in mind that there will rarely be a case where the perpetrator's actions do not simultaneously fulfil the elements of ordinary crimes or where he or she will not have committed ordinary crimes in addition to crimes under international law. Against this backdrop, it could be useful to take the sentencing ranges of relevant ordinary crimes as reference points when deciding on the ranges for crimes under international law.

c Third, the sentencing ranges should reflect that there exists, in my view, a hierarchy of crimes between the core crimes as well as a gradation between the underlying acts within each core crime. Even though all core crimes can be described as the "most serious crimes of concern to the international community as a whole",[22] a gradation of the core crimes of genocide, crimes against humanity, and war crimes,[23] based on the wrongfulness of these crimes, can be established by analysing the objective and subjective elements of each crime and by taking into account their respective contextual elements. Such an analysis reveals that the crime encompassing the highest degree of wrongfulness is genocide, followed by crimes against humanity and war crimes, all else being equal.[24]

d Fourth, the principle of personal culpability requires a careful consideration of the appropriate lower and upper limits of the respective sentencing ranges as the principle demands that the punishment adequately reflects the guilt of the offender as defined by his or her individual responsibility for the harm done.[25]

The most important consequence of this principle is that the courts must be in a position to meet out sentences that are reflective of the perpetrator's individual guilt. In this regard, mandatory life sentences tend to be problematic.[26] This might sound contra-intuitive as we regard these crimes as the "most serious crimes of concern to the international community as a whole".[27] However, it is of the utmost importance that the seriousness of these crimes is not automatically equated with the individual guilt of the offender given the macro-criminal context in which the individuals act.[28] In particular, international crimes are often committed by a collective of perpetrators that includes perpetrators of different hierarchical ranks: while they might all be considered as principal perpetrators from a doctrinal point of view, the varying degrees of responsibility that can be attributed to them need to be considered.[29] Therefore it must be taken into account what role an individual had in the commission of the crime, to what extent he or she is responsible for the overall harm and to what extent he or she acted under circumstances that reduce his or her guilt, such as a duress-like situation, acting under the impact of massive propaganda and neutralising mechanisms or under the pressure of superior orders. To this end, a certain degree of judicial discretion is indispensable.[30]

We do not need to look far for an example that demonstrates that mandatory life sentences could lead to problematic outcomes: just recently the ICC pronounced its sentencing decision in the *Ongwen* case.[31] Had the ICC Statute prescribed mandatory life sentences for the crimes Ongwen was convicted for, as for example the German Code of Crimes Against International Law does for intentional killing as a crime against humanity or war crime, the judges would have had no legal path to consider the special circumstances of his case (which are not so special in some conflict regions of the world). A legal framework that bars judges from taking such circumstances that clearly influence a defendant's individual guilt into account collides with the principle of personal culpability and should not be promoted.[32]

In the domestic context it is even more important to keep these considerations in mind given that mostly lower- or mid-rank defendants will be prosecuted before national courts.

e Finally, the principle of complementarity is of relevance. It has been argued in the literature that the unwillingness of a State genuinely to carry out an investigation or prosecution, which would trigger the ICC's jurisdiction, can be assumed if perpetrators of international crimes systematically receive disproportionately lenient sentences.[33] Sentencing ranges therefore need to reflect the seriousness of such crimes. At the same time, States do have a large margin of appreciation in their legislative decisions given the vastly different sentencing traditions and cultures that exist at the domestic level. In particular, the Rome Statute does not demand the implementation of its provisions into domestic law.[34] A State's unwillingness can therefore not be determined based on the numerical difference between the maximum terms of imprisonment provided for in the Rome Statute and the domestic law respectively. Rather, the emphasis should be placed on the relation between the sentencing ranges provided for crimes under international law on the one and ordinary crimes on the other hand. Whether the domestic law provides for appropriate sentencing ranges is therefore a question that can only be answered by relative comparison within the same legal system.[35]

3.4 Sentencing Factors

My remarks on the sentencing factors that should be included in a provision on sentencing for international crimes will be very short. According to Article 133 of the Italian Penal Code, the gravity of the crime and the offender's capacity to commit the crime are the two central sentencing criteria. The factors that judges need consider in determining the two criteria are, based on a plain reading of the text, quite similar to those referred to in Article 78 and Rule 145. Without going into any detail, it appears to me that Article 133 of the Penal Code would therefore generally be a suitable provision in order to determine appropriate sentences for crimes under international law. At least, the factors included in the provision are very similar to those that need to be considered by the ICC's judges in their determination of an appropriate sentence. So long as the provision does not limit the judges in their consideration of other relevant factors, I do not see an urgent need to change it for the purposes of sentencing for international crimes.

4 Concluding Remarks

In conclusion, the most intricate issue for the Italian legislator will be the determination of appropriate sentencing ranges. A proper gradation which also takes into account sentencing ranges provided for ordinary crimes needs to be developed. In contrast, the definition of the relevant sentencing criteria is much less intricate: it is conceivable that a reference to the existing provision will be sufficient as they allow for the consideration of most factors identified as relevant in determining a proper sentence for crimes under international by the ICC.

Notes

1 This paper is a lightly edited and referenced version of the author's input presentation to Panel VII of the Conference 'Domesticating International Criminal Justice' held on 1 October 2021 in Milan.

2 See Gerhard Werle and Aziz Epik, 'Theories of Punishment in Sentencing Decisions of the International Criminal Court', in Florian Jeßberger and Julia Geneuss (eds), *Why Punish Perpetrators of Mass Atrocities* (CUP 2020) 323ff with further references.

3 See Silvia D'Ascoli, *Sentencing in International Criminal Law* (Hart 2011) 295; Werle and Epik (n 2) 323, 325. However, caution is warranted when transferring the purposes of punishment from the domestic to the international level as pointed out by the ICTY, see *Prosecutor v Erdemović* (IT-96-22-T) ICTY (Judgment of 29 November 1996), [62].
4 For an overview of the early sentencing case law of the ICC until 2020 see Werle and Epik (n 2) 323, 332ff.
5 See ICC Statute, Art 77(1)(b); on the relationship of rule and exception see Rolf Einar Fife, 'Article 77: Applicable Penalties', in Kai Ambos (ed), *The Rome Statute of the International Criminal Court* (4th edn, CH Beck/Hart/Nomos 2022) paras 2, 23f.
6 *The Prosecutor v Lubanga Dyilo* (ICC-01/04-01/06-3122) ICC (Judgment of 1 December 2014), [32].
7 *The Prosecutor v Lubanga Dyilo* (ICC-01/04-01/06-3122) ICC (Judgment of 1 December 2014), [40].
8 *The Prosecutor v Bemba Gombo* (ICC-01/05-01/08-3399) ICC (Decision of 21 June 2016), [15].
9 On this see Kai Ambos, *Treatise on International Criminal Law*, vol II (OUP 2014) 291.
10 *The Prosecutor v Ongwen* (ICC-02/04-01/15-1819-Red) ICC (decision of 6 May 2021), [52].
11 Ambos (n 9) 293; D'Ascoli (n 3) 145ff; Aziz Epik, *Die Strafzumessung bei Taten nach dem Völkerstrafgesetzbuch* (Mohr Siebeck 2017) 304. For a more detailed discussion of the gravity concept see Werle and Epik (n 2) 323, 338ff.
12 *The Prosecutor v Bemba Gombo* (ICC-01/05-01/08-3399) ICC (Decision of 21 June 2016), [68]; *The Prosecutor v Al Mahdi* (ICC-01/12-01/15-171) ICC (Judgment of 27 September 2016), [94]; see Werle and Epik (n 2) 323, 349.
13 Werle and Epik (n 2) 323, 347 fn 131.
14 *The Prosecutor v Bemba et al* (ICC-01/05-01/13-2275) ICC (Judgment of 8 March 2018), [4].
15 ICC Statute, Art 78(3). Compared with the practice of other international courts and tribunals, the provision in ICC Statute, Art 78(3) contributes to a higher degree of transparency as the Chamber cannot simply meet out a final sentence but has to specify the sentences it deemed appropriate for each crime.
16 That is my position on the German Code of Crimes Against International Law, see Epik (n 11) 163ff.
17 Manfred Maiwald, *Einführung in das italienische Strafrecht und Strafprozessrecht* (Peter Lang 2009) 29f.
18 See for an overview David Donat-Cattin, 'Article 75: Reparations to victims', in Kai Ambos (ed) (n 5) paras 1f.
19 See Gerhard Werle and Florian Jeßberger, *Principles of International Criminal Law* (4th edn, OUP 2020) para 135.
20 Maiwald (n 17) 39f.
21 See the disposition in *The Prosecutor v Ongwen* (ICC-02/04-01/15-1819-Red.) ICC (Decision of 6 May 2021), 133ff.
22 Preamble of the ICC Statute, para 4.
23 The crime of aggression will not be considered in this context as (i) its structure is not comparable with those of genocide, crimes against humanity and war crimes and (ii) it does not aim to protect individual interests and cannot therefore be

compared with the other core crimes. Seen in the abstract, the commission of a crime of aggression is, however, likely to trigger high sentences, not least because it can only be committed by State leaders and threatens the peace of the world as a whole.

24 See Werle and Epik (n 2) 323, 342f. with further references. For a thorough analysis see Marlen Vesper-Gräske, *Zur Hierarchie der Völkerrechtsverbrechen nach dem Statut des Internationalen Strafgerichtshofs* (Nomos 2016) 323ff. See also Ambos (n 9) 252f; D'Ascoli (n 3) 303ff; Epik (n 11) 461ff.

25 See Werle and Jeßberger (n 19) para 141.

26 See Epik (n 11) 472ff regarding the German Code of Crimes Against International Law.

27 Preamble of the ICC Statute, para 4.

28 See Epik (n 11) 95ff.

29 See ibid 477ff.

30 See ibid 477.

31 *The Prosecutor v Ongwen* (ICC-02/04-01/15-1819-Red.) ICC (Decision of 6 May 2021), [65ff.].

32 For the German Code of Crimes Against International Law see Epik (n 11) 482.

33 See Kevin Jon Heller, 'A Sentence-Based Theory of Complementarity', in William A Schabas, Yvonne McDermott and Niamh Hayes (eds), *The Ashgate Research Companion to International Criminal Law* (Routledge 2013) 335, 337, 340.

34 Werle and Jeßberger (n 19) para 90.

35 See Epik (n 11) 456f.

Selected Bibliography

Ambos K, *Treatise on International Criminal Law, vol II* (Oxford University Press 2014)

D'Ascoli S, *Sentencing in International Criminal Law* (Hart Publishing 2011)

Donat-Cattin D, 'Article 75: Reparations to Victims', in Kai Ambos (ed), *The Rome Statute of the International Criminal Court* (4th edn, CH Beck/Hart/Nomos 2022)

Epik A, *Die Strafzumessung bei Taten nach dem Völkerstrafgesetzbuch* (Mohr Siebeck 2017)

Fife RE, 'Article 77: Applicable Penalties', in Kai Ambos (ed), *The Rome Statute of the International Criminal Court* (4th edn, CH Beck/Hart/Nomos 2022)

Heller KJ, 'A Sentence-Based Theory of Complementarity', in W Schabas, Y McDermott and N Hayes (eds), *The Ashgate Research Companion to International Criminal Law* (Routledge 2013)

Maiwald M, *Einführung in das italienische Strafrecht und Strafprozessrecht* (Peter Lang 2009)

Vesper-Gräske M, *Zur Hierarchie der Völkerrechtsverbrechen nach dem Statut des Internationalen Strafgerichtshofs* (Nomos 2016)

Werle G and Epik A, 'Theories of Punishment in Sentencing Decisions of the International Criminal Court', in F Jeßberger and J Geneuss (eds), *Why Punish Perpetrators of Mass Atrocities* (Cambridge University Press 2020)

Werle G and Jeßberger F, *Principles of International Criminal Law* (4th edn, OUP 2020)

5.4 Applying the "international" rationales of sentencing into the domestic criminal systems

Alice Riccardi

1 Introduction

The possibility to transplant domestic sentencing rationales into international criminal proceedings has been explored since the establishment of ad hoc tribunals.[1] No attention has been paid so far to the opposite idea: that of an "international sentencing analogy". In other terms, it has never been investigated whether it would be feasible to transplant sentencing rationales elaborated by international criminal courts and tribunals (ICTs) into domestic legal systems, and according to which methodology. However, should it be demonstrated that one or more general principles of international criminal law concerning sentencing exist, then a non-mechanical importation or transposition of such principles into domestic law may be imagined.

In the following pages I will attempt to answer the question of whether an "international sentencing analogy" would work in three steps. First, I will briefly delve into the question of the "uniqueness" of international criminal proceedings when it comes to sentencing. Second, I will argue that this uniqueness may be explained by the existence of general principle(s) of sentencing law that formed within the international criminal legal system. These principles emerged as opposed to municipal sentencing rationales, which do not entirely fit international criminal proceedings. Third, I will try to understand whether such principle(s) may be transposed domestically and how. I will answer this question in the positive and argue that such cross-fertilisation may safeguard the coherence of the international criminal system of law. I will use one example to illustrate the case for an "international sentencing analogy": ie, that of the sentencing rationale of "internationalised" rehabilitation, which I will define in the next paragraph. The selection of this example does not imply that other general sentencing principles do not exist.

2 On the uniqueness of international sentencing practice: the emergence of the rationale of "internationalised" rehabilitation

The idea that an "international sentencing analogy" may work logically rests on the assumption that international sentencing law is unique – *ergo*,

DOI: 10.4324/9781003320951-24

that there are areas where international sentencing practice on core crimes is uniform enough to be identified as distinctive vis-à-vis the domestic sentencing practice on "ordinary" crimes. It is here held that at the current stage of development of international criminal law as interpreted and applied by ICTs it is hard to rebut that, in some selected areas, trends have emerged and even crystallised into a consistent practice. This is due to the inherent characteristics of international criminal law. Namely, ICTs' sentencing practice was shaped by the fact that international criminal law is a branch of international law which is both horizontally and vertically hybrid; created in order to answer to the macro-criminal; vocationally universal;[2] and by the fact that ICTs exercise their jurisdiction on crimes under international law on behalf of the international community as a whole.[3] These characteristics have prompted international judges to formulate a sentencing theory of their own – at least, as mentioned above, in some selected areas. This particularly includes the sentencing rationale of rehabilitation, as follows.

Back in 2003, Trial Chamber II of the International Criminal Tribunal for the former Yugoslavia (ICTY) in the *Nikolić* case accepted that a general principle of law *in foro domestico* may be said to exist whereby the mitigating effect of a guilty plea is limited to non-serious crimes.[4] Nonetheless, "in contrast to national legal systems",[5] it decided to accept Dragan Nikolić's guilty plea in mitigation with respect to the crimes against humanity of persecution, murder, rape, and torture. Indeed, the Trial Chamber felt that the said general principle of law *in foro domestico*, although common to the principal legal systems of the world, was not capable of operating in international law due to the latter unique features vis-à-vis municipal law. Subsequently, also other Trial Chambers of both the ICTY and the International Criminal Tribunal for Rwanda (ICTR) accepted guilty pleas in mitigation. They all embraced the idea that in international criminal proceedings guilty pleas shall be accepted in mitigation since by pleading guilty accused persons "take an important step in the rehabilitation and reintegration process … [hence] contribute to reconciliation".[6] Notably, the 70% of ICTY trial judgments pronounced following the entering of a guilty plea by the accused affirmed that in international criminal proceedings the sentencing rationale of rehabilitation requires a guilty plea to be accepted in mitigation – no matter how serious the crimes committed; indeed, by pleading guilty the accused persons concretely demonstrate the highest potential for rehabilitation, as they show their willingness to appease the consequences of the crimes, to attain reconciliation in the affected community, to establish the truth, and to promote the international rule of law. The same reasoning was shared by the 75% of guilty plea judgments at the ICTR.[7]

This interpretation of rehabilitation may be defined as "internationalised", in the sense that the two ad hoc tribunals deduced from the international criminal legal system an understanding of the sentencing rationale of rehabilitation consonant with the specificities of international criminal proceedings and international criminality. Generally speaking, rehabilitation rests on the idea that everyone can, if treated, be reintegrated into the society as a crime-free actor. Accordingly, offenders shall not be treated alike; sentences shall be rather individualised taking into consideration the circumstances of the offender.[8] Elements typical to evaluate the offenders' potential for reintegration into the society in "ordinary" cases include their age, family situation, manner in detention and demeanour during trial, and absence of previous criminal records. According to the notion of "internationalised" rehabilitation, instead, little weight shall be accorded to those elements that usually matter in "ordinary" cases. Rather, what matters for "internationalised" rehabilitation is that the offender demonstrates the willingness to contribute to placate the effects of the crimes committed, to reconcile the communities affected by them and to uphold the international rule of law.[9] This rationale was gradually translated by ad hoc tribunals into a number of different *rules*, including the rule on guilty pleas – but not only. The same rationale underpinned, for instance, the progressive abandonment by the ICTY and the ICTR of "ordinary" rehabilitative elements in mitigation (eg, age, family situation and health), which were eventually assigned merely "little", "limited", "minimal" weight;[10] and the progressive expansion of the catalogue of mitigating circumstances as to include elements more consonant with the aim to "contribute to the restoration and maintenance of peace", including:[11] expression of sincere remorse towards the victims,[12] regret for the suffering caused to them, and even partial acceptance of responsibility by the accused person.[13] Increasingly, the two ad hoc tribunals insisted even more on the "restorative" connotation of the rationale of "internationalised" rehabilitation, and looked in mitigation at circumstances such as: acts of assistance towards the victims, the conduct generally maintained by the accused during the conflict, their efforts towards the dissemination of a culture of respect for the international rule of law, participation in peace processes, surrender, and prevention of others from committing crimes.[14]

The notion of "internationalised" rehabilitation has also been embraced by the International Criminal Court (ICC or the Court). This stems from both the Court's founding treaty and its case law.

By way of example, Rule 145(2)(ii) of the Rules of Procedure and Evidence (ICC RPE) establishes a broad category of mitigating circumstances which comprises the convicted person's conduct after the act, including any efforts to compensate the victims and any cooperation with the Court. It has been held that this allows the permeation of transitional justice elements into the process of sentencing determination; this may for instance include "a display of remorse during a truth and reconciliation process" or a surrender "in the light of an amnesty-peace deal".[15] In concrete cases, Rule 145(2)(ii) has allowed ICC Chambers to evaluate in mitigation elements similar to those taken into account by the ad hoc tribunals, including the accused persons' disposition towards civilians in an armed conflict, their willingness and ability to engage in reconciliatory actions, their support for disarmament and demobilisation processes,[16] and their contribution to peacebuilding.[17]

Moreover, the ICC Statute expressly provides for accused persons to enter guilty pleas (see Article 65) and the Court practice demonstrates that high value is assigned to situations in which the accused persons publicly apologise for their wrong. In the *Lubanga* sentencing hearing, for instance, the Prosecutor even affirmed to be ready to accept a reduced sentence of imprisonment had the accused offered a (late) apology and used "his leadership and position of respect to promote peace, advocate for measures to unify and heal and improve injured communities"[18] – an offer that Mr Lubanga, however, did not accept.

A further example is represented by Article 110(4) of the Statute and Rule 223 ICC RPE, which provide for a non-exhaustive list of factors to be taken into consideration by the Court in reviewing sentences and granting early release to convicted persons, including: cooperation with the Court, voluntary assistance in enabling the enforcement of judgments, whether the early release would give rise to significant social instability, and any significant action taken for the benefits of the victims. The principle of "internationalised" rehabilitation undoubtedly underpins these criteria, which not only focus on the person of the accused but consider the broader impact of their post-trial conduct on the community affected by the crimes. It is held that this rationale also underpinned the decision of the three-judge panel who reduced the sentence against Mr Katanga under Article 110 of the Statute by taking into high consideration the fact that the convicted person decided to withdraw his appeal against the trial judgement, by choosing "not to exercise this right as a result of acknowledging that he … is guilty of the crimes committed and publicly apologise[d] thereof".[19]

3 On the existence of general principles of international criminal law on sentencing

Against this background, it may be asked whether a general principle of law formed within the international criminal legal system[20] whereby vis-à-vis international crimes rehabilitation shall be read through "internationalised" lenses. The main characteristics of general principles of international law suggest that this question may be answered in the positive.

First, "internationalised" rehabilitation fits the commonly accepted definition of general principles of international law as "general proposition[s] considered to be expressive of the ratio of a series of more detailed rules".[21] In the context of international criminal law, general principles are defined as those "consonant with the fundamental features and the basic requirements of international criminal justice".[22] As mentioned above, "internationalised" rehabilitation appears to be the idea behind a number of rules applied by ICTs, including for instance rules dictating the selection of relevant mitigating circumstances in international criminal proceedings. Moreover, it is consonant with and derives from the very aims of international criminal justice.

Second, akin to general principles of international law, "internationalised" rehabilitation has been inferred by ICTs' judges from a process of deduction from existing conventional and customary international law which it underlies.[23] In fact, it has been deducted from the general tenor of ICTs' founding instruments[24] or from their sentencing provisions since, as it is well known, said instruments do not provide for penological rationales of sentencing.

Third, the general principle of "internationalised" rehabilitation has not been used to deduce "primary", but rather "secondary" rules, which do not impact the merit of the case.[25] This aligns "internationalised" rehabilitation to most general principles of international law, which are procedural in nature (eg, *res iudicata*, sound administration of justice) or concern issues of interpretation and responsibility for internationally wrongful acts.

Lastly, "internationalised" rehabilitation has always been invoked to fulfil the auxiliary functions of producing new rules (as in the above-mentioned example of the rule concerning guilty pleas) or interpreting existing rules (as in the mentioned example of the interpretation of the catalogue of mitigating circumstances at the ICC), as generally required from general principles of international law.[26]

Conclusively, it may be affirmed that "internationalised" rehabilitation is a general principle of international criminal sentencing law. It shall now be verified whether it can be translated into a domestic legal principle.

4 Conclusion: on transposing general principles of international criminal law on sentencing into domestic legal systems

International criminal law sources do not bind States to implement into their own legal orders specific sentencing rationales (or a sentencing determination framework) on international crimes. Article 80 of the ICC Statute even provides for a non-prejudice clause to the application by States of penalties for crimes under the Court jurisdiction other than those established by the ICC Statute. This does not mean, however, that international criminal sentencing *principles* should not be transposed by States into domestic law. First, Article 80 was included in the Statute *in extremis*, with the mere aim to achieving a consensus on Part 7 of the Statute among retentionist States who feared that statutory provisions on penalties might be understood as an instance of practice towards the prohibition under customary law of the death penalty.[27] Therefore, this provision shall not be interpreted as barring States from importing ICC sentencing practice into their own legal orders. Second, as to the absence of treaties binding States to implement a sentencing framework on international crimes, this simply means that there is a lacuna in the applicable positive law, which judges have indeed filled by resorting to general principles of international law, including the general principle of "internationalised" rehabilitation, which therefore formed within the international criminal legal system.

Domestic transposition of general principles of international law happens in accordance with municipal laws determining how international law penetrates in the given internal legal order. Therefore, States may receive into their own legal order the general principle of "internationalised" rehabilitation either through legislation (eg, by adopting specific sentencing provisions on international crimes) or through judicial interpretation of "ordinary" sentencing provisions when applied to persons guilty of international crimes, if this is possible in the given domestic legal framework, also in the light of the principle of legality of penalties. In any event, transposition shall never be mechanical. Rather, some sort of "reverse" *Furundžija* test shall be implemented. As is well known, in the *Furundžija* case the ICTY refused a "mechanical importation or transposition" of general principles *in foro domestico* into international law, due to the "unique traits" of international criminal proceedings which differentiate them from national criminal proceedings.[28] A "reverse" *Furundžija* test would require shaping or revisiting a general principle of international law in order for it to fit the characteristics of the municipal legal order of importation. This is in perfect harmony with the nature of general principles, which are adaptable to the features of the system in which they are imported. Indeed, general principles work as tools to ensure *conformity* between their interpretation in the legal order of origin and the manner in which the given issue is regulated in the legal order of importation.

I will now use the example of the criminal legal order of Italy (as a State that has not, at the time of writing, implemented the ICC Statute yet but may be in the process of doing so, following the appointment of an ad hoc drafting commission on a law on international crimes in early 2022),[29] as a test-case for the possibility to import the general principle of "internationalised" rehabilitation into the domestic. In the Italian context it may be noted that, first, this general principle does not contrast with the fundamental values underpinning the Italian Constitution; rather, it is in complete accord with Article 27 of the Constitution, which establishes that sentences must have an overarching rehabilitative aim. Second, there is a lacuna in the applicable law. Third, and as a consequence, the importation of this general principle should entail the inclusion into the (future, at the time of writing) law on international crimes of a set of sentencing determinants and of provisions on the execution of sentences consonant with it. For instance, this may include the provision of mitigating circumstances specific for international crimes (eg, dissemination of a culture of respect for international law, specific acts of assistance to victims in a context of violence/armed conflict or reparation towards the victims). The provision of specific mitigating circumstances with respect to serious crimes is not new in the Italian legal order. Especially in the 1970s and 1980s, Italy knew a season of internal terrorism. In this context, new legislation on terrorism offences was introduced. Notably, special laws were adopted which provided for penalties reduction or even exemption from criminal liability had the offender dissociated from the offence, strived to avoid further such acts, eliminated or attenuated its criminal consequences, prevented the commission of connected offences, helped the police in gathering evidence, and fully confessed before the pronouncement of the judgment.[30] Also, other possible rules to be implemented domestically deriving from the general principle of "internationalised" rehabilitation may include: the assignment to prosecutors of a margin of appreciation to decide whether to open/discontinue an investigation on international crimes if for instance a peace process is ongoing; and the provision of alternative forms of punishment with a clear restorative aim.[31]

In conclusion, it cannot be refuted that the status of international sentencing law is no longer as embryonic as it was back in the 1990s and early 2000s. Rather, it is at present a developed branch of international criminal procedure and in some areas consistent practices have emerged, including on the general principle of "internationalised" rehabilitation. National legislatures should take this into account when drafting codes on international crimes by formulating rules consonant with it; also, municipal judges should interpret domestic laws in accordance with it. Indeed, by ensuring conformity between its interpretation in the international criminal legal system and the manner in which a legislation on international crimes is enacted domestically or interpreted by domestic judges, the general principle of "internationalised" rehabilitation would "smoothen tensions inherent to legal pluralism by ensuring a minimum openness and conversation between legal orders ... [thus] precluding them from living in clinical isolation".[32] In turn, this may even contribute to a broader and faster process towards the internalisation of the norms prohibiting the commission of international crimes. Indeed, the implementation of a common and coherent, albeit adapted to each legal system, sentencing policy may allow the spectators of trials on international crimes (whether held domestically or internationally) to understand their outcomes more easily.

Notes

1 Doctrine is abundant on this point. Recently see Elies van Sliedregt, 'Punishment and the Domestic Analogy. Why It Can and Cannot Work', in Florian Jeßberger and Julia Geneuss (eds), *Why Punish Perpetrators of Mass Atrocities?* (CUP 2020) 81ff.

2 Among many see Frédéric Mégret, 'In Search of the "Vertical": An Exploration of What Makes International Criminal Tribunals Different (and Why)', in Carsten Stahn and Larissa van den Herik (eds), *Future Perspectives on International Criminal Justice* (Springer 2010) 182ff.

3 *Al-Bashir* (Joint Concurring Opinion of Judges Eboe-Osuji, Morrison, Hofmański and Bossa) ICC-02/05-01/09-397-Anx1 (6 May 2019) para 445.

4 *Nikolić D* (Sentencing Judgment) IT-94-2-S (18 December 2003) para 57ff.

5 ibid para 233.

6 *Češić* (Sentencing Judgment) IT-95-10/1 (11 March 2004) para 28.

7 cf Alice Riccardi, *Sentencing at the International Criminal Court: From Nuremberg to the Hague* (Giappichelli/Eleven 2016) 97.

8 Scholarship on rehabilitation is massive. Among others see Francis T Cullen and Paul Gendreau, 'Assessing Correctional Rehabilitation: Policy, Practice, and Prospects', in July Horney (eds), *Criminal Justice 2000. Policies, Processes and Decisions of the Criminal Justice System*, vol 3 (US Department of Justice 2000).

9 cf Alice Riccardi, 'Sulla disciplina delle circostanze attenuanti in diritto internazionale penale alla luce delle sentenze nei confronti di Karadžić e Mladić' (2018) 2 Diritto Penale Contemporaneo, Rivista trimestrale 296, 306.

10 At the ICTY, above all see *Limaj et al* (Judgment) IT-03-66-T (30 November 2005) para 372. See also the trial judgments against Perišić, Tolimir, Brđanin, Banović, Nikolić M, Jelisić, Haradinaj et al, Orić, Rajić, Jokić, Zelenović, Popović et al and Delić.

11 cf the text of ICTR (UNSC Res 955 (8 November 1994) UN Doc S/RES/ 955, preamble para 7) and ICTY (UNSC Res 827 (25 May 1993) UN Doc S/RES/827, preamble para 6) establishing resolution; see also *Tadić* (Judgment) ICTY-94-1-T bis R117 (11 November 1999) para 7.

12 Inter alia see *Serugendo* (Sentencing Judgment) ICTR-2005-84-I (12 June 2006) para 33.

13 *Popović et al* (Judgment) IT-05-88-T (10 June 2010) para 2178.

14 cf Riccardi, 'Sulla disciplina delle circostanze attenuanti' (n 9) 306–309.

15 Carsten Stahn, 'Complementarity, Amnesties and Alternatives Forms of Justice: Interpretative Guidelines for the International Criminal Court' (2005) 3 *Journal of International Criminal Justice* 695, 704.

16 *Katanga* (Decision on the Sentence pursuant to Article 76 of the Statute) ICC-01/ 04-01/07-3484 (25 May 2014) paras 188, 92, 115.

17 *Bemba* (Decision on the Sentence pursuant to Article 76 of the Statute) ICC-01/ 05-01/08-3399 (21 June 2016) paras 71, 82ff.

18 *Lubanga* (Transcript of the Hearing pursuant to Article 76(2)) ICC-01/04-01/06-T-360-Red2-ENG (13 June 2012) 35.

19 *Katanga* (Decision on the Review concerning Reduction of Sentence of Mr Germain Katanga) ICC-01/04-01/07-3615 (13 November 2015) para 3, 34.

20 The doctrinal debate on the nature of general principles of international law is gargantuan. Among many see: Michael N Shaw, *International Law* (CUP 2003) 94; Giorgio Gaja, 'General Principles of Law', in Rüdiger Wolfrum (ed), *Max Planck Encyclopedia of Public International Law* (OUP 2020).

21 Robert Kolb, 'General Principles of Procedural Law', in Andreas Zimmerman, Christian Tomuschat and Karin Oellers-Frahm (eds), *The Statute of the International Court of Justice: A Commentary* (OUP 2006) 794.

22 International Law Commission, *Second Report on General Principles of Law by Marcelo Vázquez-Bermúdez, Special Rapporteur* (9 April 2020) UN Doc A/CN.4/ 741, para 155 quoting *Kupreškić et al* (Judgment) ICTY-95-14/2 (17 December 2004) para 738.

23 Beatrice I Bonafè and Paolo Palchetti, 'Relying on General Principles in International Law', in Catherine Brolmann and Yannick Radi (eds), *Research Handbook on the Theory and Practice of International Lawmaking* (Elgar 2016) 160, 162ff.

24 Inter alia see *Kupreškić et al* (n 22) para 1233; *Babić* (Sentencing Judgment) IT-03-72-S (29 June 2004) para 47; *Katanga* (n 16) para 38.

25 Bonafè and Palchetti (n 23) 173.

26 Massimo Iovane, 'Metodo costituzionalistico e ruolo dei giudici nella formulazione dei principi generali del diritto internazionale' (2008) 1 Ars interpretandi 103, 116ff.
27 Rolf E Fife, 'Article 80', in Otto Triffterer (ed), *Commentary on the Rome Statute of the International Criminal Court* (2nd edn, CH Beck/Hart/Nomos 2010) 1444.
28 *Furundžija* (Judgment) IT-95-17/1-T (10 December 1998) para 178. More recently International Law Commission (n 22) paras 75ff, explaining the necessity for a 'compatibility test' to ascertain whether an identified general principle *in foro domestico* would work within the broader framework of international law.
29 Italian Ministry of Justice, *Commissione per l'elaborazione di un Progetto di Codice di Crimini internazionali*, Ministerial Decree of 22 March 2022, available at <www.giustizia.it/giustizia/it/mg_1_8_1.page?contentId=SDC372746&previsiousPage=mg_1_36_0#>.
30 cf Law 29 May 1982, no 304, *Misure per la difesa dell'ordinamento costituzionale*, available at <www.gazzettaufficiale.it/eli/id/1982/06/02/082U0304/sg>.
31 See the opinions of Emanuela Fronza and Paolo Caroli in Maria Crippa and Lavinia Parsi, 'Report del Convegno Domesticating International Criminal Justice – Current Challenges' (2021) 20–21 Sistema penale, available at <www.sistemapenale.it/pdf_contenuti/1637747684_report-domesticating-international-criminal-justice-current-challenges-milano-30-settembre-1-2-ottobre-2021.pdf>.
32 Jan Wouters, 'Conclusions: The Role of General Principles in a Multi-layered Legal Setting', in Mads Andenas and others (eds), *General Principles and the Coherence of International Law* (Brill Nijhoff 2019) 196, 197.

Selected bibliography

Andenas M and others (eds), *General Principles and the Coherence of International Law* (Brill Nijhoff 2019)

Bonafè BI and Palchetti P, 'Relying on General Principles in International Law', in Brolmann C and Radi Y (eds), *Research Handbook on the Theory and Practice of International Lawmaking* (Elgar 2016)

Cullen FT and Gendreau P, 'Assessing Correctional Rehabilitation: Policy, Practice, and Prospects', in Horney J (eds), *Criminal Justice 2000. Policies, processes and decisions of the criminal justice system*, vol 3 (US Department of Justice 2000)

Fife RE, 'Article 80', in Otto Triffterer (ed), *Commentary on the Rome Statute of the International Criminal Court* (2nd edn, CH Beck/Hart/Nomos 2010)

Iovane M, 'Metodo costituzionalistico e ruolo dei giudici nella formulazione dei principi generali del diritto internazionale' (2008) 1 *Ars interpretandi* 103

Kolb R, 'General of Procedural Law', in Zimmerman A, Tomuschat C and Oellers-Frahm K (eds), *The Statute of the International Court of Justice: A Commentary* (OUP 2006)

Mégret F, 'In Search of the "Vertical": An Exploration of What Makes International Criminal Tribunals Different (and Why)', in Stahn C and van den Herik L (eds), *Future Perspectives on International Criminal Justice* (Springer 2010)

Riccardi A, *Sentencing at the International Criminal Court: From Nuremberg to the Hague* (Giappichelli/Eleven 2016)

Riccardi A, 'Sulla disciplina delle circostanze attenuanti in diritto internazionale penale alla luce delle sentenze nei confronti di Karadžić e Mladić' (2018) 2 *Diritto Penale Contemporaneo, Rivista trimestrale* 296

Shaw MN, *International Law* (CUP 2003)
Stahn C, 'Complementarity, Amnesties and Alternatives Forms of Justice: Interpretative Guidelines for the International Criminal Court' (2005) 3 *Journal of International Criminal Justice* 695
Van Sliedregt E, 'Punishment and the Domestic Analogy. Why It Can and Cannot Work', in Florian Jeßberger and Julia Geneuss (eds), *Why Punish Perpetrators of Mass Atrocities?* (CUP 2020)

Part VI

Immunities, Jurisdiction and Prosecutorial Discretion

6.1 Prosecuting International Crimes Before Domestic Courts and the Question of Immunities

Chiara Ragni

1 The Immunity of State Officials from Foreign Criminal Jurisdiction: Does It Also Apply to International Crimes?

The question of whether the immunity of State officials from jurisdiction applies in domestic criminal proceedings regarding international crimes has long been debated by States and scholars. A problem arises as to how to ensure a fair balance between the need to provide the greatest possible protection of fundamental rights against mass atrocities and the interests of States in preserving their sovereignty from potential interference from other States.

In addressing the matter, a distinction must be drawn between personal and functional immunities. As for personal immunity, although the irrelevance of the official role of individuals accused of international crimes before competent international courts seems to be a well-established rule found in the statutes of all international courts, the possibility of extending its application to domestic proceedings is still highly controversial. Personal immunities permit State agents to carry out their functions abroad without hindrance from the host State; they may be enjoyed only while the person is in office unless the sending State decides to waive them beforehand. Thus, the ratification of the ICC Statute, whose Article 27 states that personal immunities cannot be invoked to provide exemption from prosecution for criminal activity falling within the jurisdiction of the Court, may be read, according to Article 32 of the 1961 Vienna Convention on Diplomatic Relations, as an expression of the waiver of immunity in proceedings before it.

It is, however, still questionable whether the norm also reflects a customary rule establishing the irrelevance of immunities before international courts, which would thus be binding on States regardless of their express acceptance of the jurisdiction of the ICC. The issue is germane not only to the question of whether the ICC and other international tribunals established by international agreement may issue a warrant for the arrest of diplomatic agents or Heads of States from non-signatory States and conduct proceedings against them but also – and above all – to the horizontal relationship between States. By assuming that Article 27, rather than reflecting the will of the Parties, stems from custom, ICC members should not encounter difficulties, as used

DOI: 10.4324/9781003320951-26

to happen in the past when they were requested to arrest and surrender public officials by a non-Party State.

The problem was broadly addressed in the Al-Bashir case[1] since some ICC Member States, such as South Africa and Jordan, failed to arrest the incumbent Sudanese Head of State when he was found in their territories, notwithstanding the warrant of arrest pending on him issued by the Court. They justified their decision by holding that the arrest would violate the international customary rule on diplomatic immunity: derogation from the rule, they claimed, was not supported by sufficient *opinio juris* or practice. In both cases, regarding South Africa and Jordan respectively, the Pre-Trial Chamber determined that it was "unable to identify a rule in customary international law that would exclude immunity for Heads of State when their arrest is sought for international crimes by another State, even when the arrest is sought on behalf of an international court".[2] It held, however, that the applicability of the exception under Article 27 of the ICC to a non-member State, namely Sudan, was a consequence of Resolution 1593 (2005), whereby the Security Council, acting under Chapter VII of the Charter and in accordance with Article 13(b) of the Statute, referred the situation to the Court. The Chamber affirmed that the effect of this Resolution is that "the legal framework of the Statute applies, in its entirety, with respect to the situation referred".[3]

This conclusion was recently reversed by the Appeals Chamber of the ICC, which overturned the traditional perspective on the matter by stating that rather than focusing on the customary exception to the rule of immunity, it would be more appropriate to question the existence of the rule in relation to international tribunals.[4] According to the judges, the absence of a rule in customary international law recognising the immunity of the head of State vis-à-vis an international court is justified on the ground of "the different character of international courts when compared with domestic jurisdictions. Although the latter are essentially an expression of a State's sovereign power, which is necessarily limited by the sovereign power of the other States, the former, when adjudicating international crimes, do not act on behalf of a particular State or States. Rather, international courts act on behalf of the international community as a whole".[5]

While the contribution of the Chamber's decision to the development of international law is very important, it, however, indirectly takes for granted that personal immunity may still be invoked in domestic proceedings regarding international crimes. Hence, what matters is whether the court in question is a domestic or an international one rather than the characteristics or gravity of the crime.[6] Consequently, even assuming that a customary norm exists, it only impinges on international courts. Notwithstanding that, the importance of the Appeals' Chamber decision should not be underestimated since it implies that States can hand over to justice a person if a warrant of arrest has been issued against them by a competent international court, even in the case where the accused person is an incumbent diplomatic agent of a State that did not ratify the Rome Statute.[7]

It is worth noting that, in line with the above conclusion, the drafters of the recent Italian Draft Code of International Crimes inserted an interim rule whereby personal immunity cannot be invoked before international courts. Interestingly, the explanatory report clarifies that Article 27 amounts to a rule of customary international law.[8] It therefore specifies that personal immunities do not preclude Italy's cooperation with the ICC, should the State be called upon to surrender persons accused of international crimes before the Court even if they are diplomatic agents (or other State officials entitled to personal immunity) from States not a party to the Rome Statute.

On the other hand, functional immunity may be invoked by anyone who has acted officially on behalf of their State. It attaches to the act and is grounded on the assumption that acts committed by State agents acting in their official capacity pertain to the State rather than to the individuals acting on their behalf. But since States enjoy immunity from foreign jurisdictions as a means of ensuring their sovereign independence and equality, foreign domestic courts cannot judge the official conduct of State agents. They may, however, pronounce on acts performed in a private capacity, with the proviso that those entitled to *ratione personae* immunities can only be charged once they cease to hold office or in the case of a waiver of the immunity by the entitled State.

The question of whether functional immunities also apply to international crimes is still debated and has recently been addressed by the International Law Commission (ILC). Its work will be examined here to assess whether it can only be regarded as the mere codification of customary international law or whether it represents a legislative development, or if, it may even be, as some have suggested, a step backwards in the protection of human rights. In the light of this reasoning, we will offer some considerations on the recent Italian Draft Code of International Crimes to establish whether – and to what extent – it takes into account the resolutions of the ILC or somehow reflects a different stance on the part of the State on the matter.

2 The "International Crime" exception in the ILC Draft Articles on the Immunity of State Officials from Foreign Criminal Jurisdiction: a Step Forward or Two Steps Back?

The work on the Immunity of State Officials from Criminal Jurisdiction was included in the ILC's agenda in 2007. Still, approval of the Draft Article in 2017 took ten years due to its complexity and controversial nature. One of the most contentious issues was precisely the inclusion, in Draft Article 7, of an exception to the rule of functional immunity. The norm states that "Immunity *ratione materiae* from the exercise of foreign criminal jurisdiction shall not apply in respect of the following crimes under international law: (a) crime of genocide; (b) crimes against humanity; (c) war crimes; (d) the crime of apartheid; (e) torture; (f) enforced disappearance".[9] The adoption of this Draft Article was based on a recorded vote, with 21 members voting in favour, eight voting against, and one member abstaining. According to those who voted against the provision, the Article reflects the ILC's legislative policy more than the codifying of a customary rule, not backed up by sufficient State practice.[10]

Other ILC members held that it failed to reach the objective of striking a balance between the sovereign equality of States and the need for stability in international relations on the one hand and, on the other, the interest of the international community as a whole in preventing and prosecuting the most serious crimes under international law. It was stressed that, as a fundamental principle of international law, the domestic courts of one State should not exercise their jurisdiction over official acts performed by agents of another State. Thus, one of the principal arguments put forward to exclude the application of this kind of immunity to international crimes is that they amount to private acts.[11] However, this reasoning is not persuasive, as State agents often commit international crimes as part of State policy. In some cases, such as torture or enforced disappearance, the participation of State officials in committing a crime is a constitutive element of the crime itself.

A more persuasive argument is grounded in the principle of individual criminal responsibility for international crimes; it lies at the core of international criminal law and dates back to the Nuremberg trials, where it was stated that: "Crimes against international law are committed by men, not by abstract entities, and only by punishing individuals who commit such crimes can the provisions of international law be enforced".[12] This implies that, as far as international crimes are concerned, the traditional rule of attribution, postulating that official acts of individuals acting on behalf of a State pertain only to that State, cannot apply. Neither, then, can functional immunity, which is, according to the proposed perspective, a necessary corollary of that rule.[13] Yet, States are not exonerated from all responsibility concerning international crimes. Indeed, they are under pressing and imperative obligations to prosecute most serious violations of peremptory human rights rules. Such obligations are not bilateral and fall outside the system of State-to-State relationships as they are beholden upon the international community as a whole. Prosecuting international crimes, which is essential to achieving global peace and justice, reflects a shared interest and should equally result in shared efforts by States.

Consequently, the elimination of functional immunity for international crimes before national courts aims to ensure this obligation is fulfilled. Nothwithstanding the importance of the role played by international tribunals, jurisdictional and material constraints prevent them from addressing all possible violations of international criminal law. As the adoption of the complementarity principle to coordinate the work of the ICC and domestic courts suggests, the latter should be, at least on paper, the most appropriate place to judge international crimes: they are close to the victims, they have easier access to evidence, and are less expensive than international courts. Occasionally, however, there may be legal obstacles that make it difficult for national courts to judge officials in their own States (suffice it to recall Italian constitutional rules on the immunity of high-ranking State officials), or there may be political impediments, especially in States emerging from war or otherwise affected by political instability and tensions. This is especially true if one considers that international crimes are often committed by State agents implementing State policy. In these situations, allowing foreign courts to prosecute international crimes may be viewed as a possible means of overcoming obstacles that both international and domestic courts encounter and guaranteeing justice is done, provided that standards of due process are strictly applied.

The same idea underlies the principle of universal criminal jurisdiction, which is intended to ensure the prosecution of international crimes to the utmost by allowing competent domestic courts to pronounce, regardless of the location of the crime and the nationality of the perpetrator or the victim and provided that some additional conditions required by both international and domestic rules are met.[14] Concerning the former, it should be recalled that, in the light of the prevailing practice, as stated above, universal jurisdiction cannot, however, overrule the procedural bar of personal immunities;[15] as for the latter, it is worth noting that domestic rules generally impose some limitations, the most important and widespread one being the presence of the accused person in the territory of the State.

In the light of the above considerations, Article 7 would appear to reflect the correct balance between State sovereignty and the quest to protect individuals from the most serious human rights violations. Moreover, the fact that it coincides with customary law is testified by a significant practice in this regard.[16] It is worth mentioning, by way of example, the decision rendered on 28 January 2021 by Germany's Federal Court of Justice, which substantially endorsed the ILC position by rejecting the functional immunity of low-ranking foreign State officials in a case regarding war crimes.[17] A further example may be traced in the Italian Draft Code, which provides for the irrelevance of *rationae materiae* immunities in domestic proceedings regarding international crimes.

3 Concluding Remarks

Although domestic courts on the territory where the offence has been committed are the best judicial forum for prosecuting international crimes,[18] their proper functioning is, however, subject to certain obstacles. Immunity from jurisdiction represents a considerable obstruction to domestic courts exercising jurisdiction; it is grounded in the principle of the sovereign equality of States and seeks to prevent interference in internal affairs and facilitate the maintenance of stable international relations. If this is the case, the question that this chapter has addressed is whether immunities should also apply in criminal proceedings regarding international crimes. The domestic prosecution of international crimes is, in fact, a fundamental means of protecting human rights from their most flagrant and large-scale violations, counteracting impunity in situations that do not fall within the limited jurisdiction of international criminal tribunals, and ultimately ensuring justice for the victims.

Notwithstanding the question is still a matter of debate in terms of both personal and functional immunities, a consensus as regards the existence of an exception as regards international crimes is emerging. Concerning the latter, the recent adoption of Article 7 of the ILC Draft Articles on Immunity of State Officials from Criminal Jurisdiction may be read in this vein, as may, with regard to the former, the recognition not only by the ICC but also by some States (eg, Italy if the legislator adopts the proposal for a code of international crimes) of a rule precluding the possibility to invoke personal immunities before international criminal tribunals.

Notwithstanding the significant steps taken towards ending impunity for international crimes, a criticism of how the question has been approached thus far regards considering the prosecution of international crimes as an exception to immunity rather than a rule, which requires the commitment of all States towards all others if the maximum protection of human rights is to be achieved.

The fight against international crime is not merely a response to the needs of one State or another; it reflects a shared interest in combating the most serious human rights violations. If conceived as an exception to the paramount obligation of States to prosecute international crime, the application of immunities should therefore be limited to the bare minimum necessary to maintain international peace in situations where the prosecution of international crimes by domestic courts may well not contribute to this end so much as thwart it.

Notes

1 ICC, *The Prosecutor v Omar Hassan Ahmad Al-Bashir*, ICC-02/05-01/09.

2 ICC (Pre-Trial Chamber II), Decision under Article 87(7) of the Rome Statute on the non-compliance by Jordan with the request by the Court for the arrest and surrender or Omar Al-Bashir, 11 December 2017, ICC-02/05-01/09, para 27; Decision under Article 87(7) of the Rome Statute on the non-compliance by South Africa with the request by the Court for the arrest and surrender of Omar Al-Bashir, 6 July 2017, ICC-02/05-01/09-302, para 68.

3 South Africa Decision, para 87; Jordan Decision, para 37.

4 ICC (Appeals Chamber), *The Prosecutor v Omar Hassan Ahmad Al-Bashir*, Judgment in the Jordan Referral re Al-Bashir Appeal, ICC-02/05-01/09-397-Corr, 06 May 2019.

5 ibid, para 115.

6 The existence of a special customary international law exception to international law immunities with respect to proceedings before international criminal courts against an incumbent Head of State, Head of Government, foreign minister, or other holders of high-ranking office has also been postulated by scholars. See for example Claus Kreß, 'The International Criminal Court and Immunities under International Law for States Not Party to the Court's Statute', in Morten Bergsmo and Ling Yan (eds), *State Sovereignty and International Criminal Law* (EICHL Publication Series No 15, Beijing 2012) 234; Paola Gaeta, 'Does President Al-Bashir Enjoy Immunity

from Arrest?' (2009) 7 JICJ 315. For a critical analysis of the reasoning see Nerina Boschiero, 'The ICC Judicial Finding on non-Cooperation against the DRC and No Immunity for Al-Bashir based on UNSC Resolution 1593' (2015) 13(3) JICJ 625; Chiara Ragni, 'Immunity of Heads of State: Some Critical Remarks on the Decision of the Special Court for Sierra Leone in the *Charles Taylor* case' (2004) 14(1) The Italian Yearbook of International Law 273.

7 As the Appeals Chamber explains, "[t]he absence of a rule of customary international law recognising Head of State immunity vis-à-vis international courts is relevant not only to the question of whether an international court may issue a warrant for the arrest of a Head of State and conduct proceedings against him or her, but also for the horizontal relationship between States when a State is requested by an international court to arrest and surrender the Head of State of another State" ICC (Appeals Chamber), Jordan Judgment, para 114.

8 The Commissione del "Codice dei Crimini internazionali", established by Decree 22 March 2022, *Final Report*, para 4.5, which makes reference to the obiter dictum of the International Court of Justice in the *Arrest Warrant* case (ICJ, Arrest Warrant of 11 April 2000 (*Democratic Republic of the Congo v Belgium*), Judgment, ICJ Reports 2002, p 3, para 58).

9 See International Law Commission, *Report on the Work of Its Sixty-Ninth Session* (11 September 2017) UN Doc A/72/10, 176–177.

10 For an analysis of the debate that accompanied the adoption of Draft Articles, cf 'Symposium on the Present and Future of Foreign Official Immunity' [2018] AJIL.

11 This is the reading proposed by Judges Higgins, Kooijmans and Buergenthal (*Arrest Warrant case, Joint Separate Opinion of Judges Higgins, Kooijmans, and Buergenthal, para* 88); Claus Kreß, 'Cooperation with Respect to Waiver of Immunity and Consent to Surrender', in Kai Ambos (ed), *The Rome Statute of the International Criminal Court* (4th edn, CH Beck/Hart/Nomos 2021) Art 98, para 36.7.

12 International Military Tribunal (Nuremberg), 1947, p 221.

13 In this regard, it is worth recalling the opinion expressed by Micaela Frulli. She rightly suggested that the irrelevance of official capacity where there are allegations of international crimes must be regarded not so much as an exception to immunity as a necessary consequence of the statement of individual responsibility for international crimes. If an exception exists, it therefore relates to the rule on the attribution of conduct. Micaela Frulli, 'The Draft Articles on Crimes Against Humanity and Immunities of State Officials Unfinished Business?' (2018) 16 JICJ 775.

14 According to some scholars, universal criminal jurisdiction may be read as an application in international law of Scelle's theory of "Role Splitting" (*dédoublement fonctionnel*). Domestic courts would act as organs of the entire international community in order to promote and protect fundamental shared values from unlawful acts that would remain otherwise unpunished. See on this point the particularly interesting contribution of Antonio Cassese, 'Remarks on Scelle's Theory of "Role Splitting" (*dédoublement fonctionnel*) in International Law' (1990) 1(1) European Journal of International Law 210, 228ff.

15 cf ICJ, *Arrest Warrant* case (n 8), para 59.

16 For a critical survey of the practice, see Micaela Frulli, 'On the Existence of a Customary Rule Granting Functional Immunity to State Officials and Its Exceptions: Back to Square One' [2016] Duke Journal of Comparative and International Law 479.

17 Bundesgerichtshof (Federal Court of Justice), Judgment of 28 January 2021 – 3 StR 564/19 [2021] Neue Juristische Wochenschrift 1326. See Andreas Zimmermann and John Schabedoth, Chapter 3.1, Domestic and International Criminal Justice: Challenges Ahead.

18 Antonio Cassese, 'The Rationale for International Criminal Justice', in A Cassese (ed), *The Oxford Companion to International Criminal Justice* (OUP 2009) 123–130.

Selected Bibliography

Boschiero N, 'The ICC Judicial Finding on non-Cooperation against the DRC and No Immunity for Al-Bashir based on UNSC Resolution 1593' (2015) JICJ 625Cassese A, 'Remarks on Scelle's Theory of "Role Splitting" (*dédoublement fonctionnel*) in International Law' (1990) 1(1) *European Journal of International Law* 210

Cassese A, 'The Rationale for International Criminal Justice', in Cassese A (ed), *The Oxford Companion to International Criminal Justice* (Oxford University Press 2009) 123

Frulli M, 'On the Existence of a Customary Rule Granting Functional Immunity to State Officials and Its Exceptions: Back to Square One', [2016] *Duke Journal of Comparative and International Law* 479

Frulli M, 'The Draft Articles on Crimes Against Humanity and Immunities of State Officials Unfinished Business?' (2018) 16 *JICJ* 775

Gaeta P, 'Does President Al-Bashir Enjoy Immunity from Arrest?' (2009) 7 *JICJ* 315

Kreß C, 'The International Criminal Court and Immunities under International Law for States not Party to the Court's Statute', in M Bergamo and L Yan (eds), *State Sovereignty and International Criminal Law (EICHL Publication Series* no 15, 2012)

Kreß C, 'Cooperation with Respect to Waiver of Immunity and Consent to Surrender', in K Ambos (ed), *The Rome Statute of the International Criminal Court* (4th edn, CH Beck/Hart/Nomos 2021)

Ragni C, 'Immunity of Heads of State: Some Critical Remarks on the Decision of the Special Court for Sierra Leone in the *Charles Taylor* case' (2004) 14(1) *The Italian Yearbook of International Law* 273

'Symposium on the Present and Future of Foreign Official Immunity' (2018) *AJIL*

6.2 The rejection of immunities for international crimes

A solution for the survival of the International Criminal Justice Project?

Valeria Vegh Weis[1]

1 Introduction

To approach the complex topic of immunities within the broader project of domestication of the Rome Statute, two particularly sensitive inquiries can be raised: (1) the (mis)use of neocolonial narratives to ensure immunity of heads of State, and (2) the symbolic nature of immunities as a privileged example of how international criminal law (ICL) targets individuals but fails to expose the eventual criminogenic nature of the State.

To dig into the first inquiry, the chapter will explore the case of Kenya where those accused of perpetrating crimes codified in the Rome Statute soak immunity by denouncing ICL as a neocolonial tool. The analysis will be based on secondary literature and my working experience at the International Center for Transitional Justice and the ICL Research Project at Strathmore University in Nairobi from 2016 to 2017. This analysis will be linked to brief reflections related to the second inquiry as a structural problem in ICL.

2 The misuse of neocolonial narratives to legitimise the immunity of heads of State

The transitional justice process in the country followed the 2007 massive violence when Kenyans voted in general elections. Before the balloting began, opinion polls suggested that Raila Odinga – presidential candidate for the opposition group known as Orange Democratic Movement (ODM) and member of the Luo community – had a considerable lead over then-president Mwai Kibaki, who was a Kikuyu and represented the Party of National Unity (PNU). After the elections, there were delays in announcing the results which led to deep frustration and suspicion among citizens. Security forces, informal militias and ordinary civilians initiated violence against people from the opposite party and other ethnic groups, all of which was encouraged by their political and ethnic leaders, the media and businessmen. Supporters of the PNU, a party that is mostly comprised of people from the Kikuyu, Kisii and Kamba ethnic communities, experienced ongoing confrontations with

DOI: 10.4324/9781003320951-27

ODM supporters who were mostly from the Kalenjin, Luo and Luhya ethnic communities. This situation continued for several months in six of the eight Kenyan Provinces.[2] Overall, more than 1,000 people were murdered, at least 900 suffered sexual violence and almost 700,000 were displaced.[3] This aforementioned violence included torture, abduction, severe ill-treatment, forced disappearances and violations of socio-economic rights including but not limited to the burning of houses, theft or killing of cattle, looting of property and destruction of crops. These events as a whole became infamously known as the 2007 post-election violence (PEV).

Considering the continuity of violence that dates back to Kenya's independence, the transitional justice process that formally commenced immediately following the PEV of 2007 was not influenced by just that singular – although dramatic – episode. Instead, the transitional process was designed in response to the entire history of Kenya as an independent country from 1963 to 2007. As stated in the report of the Commission of Inquiry into Post-Election Violence (known as CIPEV or Waki Commission because it was led by former Kenya Court of Appeal Judge, Philip Waki): "Kenya has an extremely troubled past. Its history of ethnic violence has been papered over for years until it exploded in horror during and after the 2007 elections".[4]

Finally, the breaking point and the start of the formal transitional justice process took place in 2008, when – amid the PEV – the two main political parties agreed to seek mediation by a Panel of Eminent African Personalities under the Chairmanship of former UN Secretary-General, Kofi Annan. Through this mediation process, the "Kenya National Dialogue and Reconciliation Agreements" were signed. These agreements included four agenda items, opening the path towards transitional justice that, as mentioned before, would include the human rights violations that occurred from 1963 to 2007.[5]

However, a problem arose concerning the crimes for which a perpetrator could be indicted. The Kenyan parliament enacted the International Crimes Act in 2009 to incorporate the Rome Statute – already ratified in 2005 – in their domestic law defining crimes against humanity and other crimes under international law as crimes in national law.[6] The problem was that the offences committed before the enactment of the law could not be judged as international crimes, frustrating the basis of a hybrid special tribunal.[7] As an alternative, civil society organisations, including Kenyans for Peace with Truth and Justice (KPTJ) proposed to create an International Crimes Division within the Kenyan High Court with international legal experts and Kenyan judges with a background in international criminal law. They also proposed that the Kenyan parliament adopt legislation to appoint prosecutors and investigators independent from the existing (and allegedly biased) Director of Public Prosecutions. However, the parliament rejected the proposal three times.[8] Presumably, many parliamentarians from the two leading political parties were implicated in the crimes but were not among the "big fish" – such as Ruto or Kenyatta – and thus had little to fear considering that the

ICC would only be able to judge a few high-ranking members of the government. Therefore, these parliamentarians obstructed the civil society's proposal and, instead, joined those who were truly sceptical of any Kenya-based court, trying to bring prosecutions to an international arena, under the slogan "don't be vague, let's go to The Hague".[9]

As the negotiations did not advance at the domestic level, by July 2009, Kofi Annan did hand over the Waki envelope and evidence to the ICC-Chief Prosecutor, Luis Moreno-Ocampo. On 26 November 2009, under Article 15 of the Rome Statute, the Prosecutor requested authorisation from Pre-Trial Chamber II to proceed with an investigation. Following a four-month review of the Prosecutor's application, Pre-Trial Chamber II granted Moreno-Ocampo's request.[10] There were two main cases involving six individuals who had been accused. Case I was carried out against the ODM members William Ruto and Henry Kiprono Kosgey, as well as the radio producer and journalist Joshua Arap Sang related to violence committed against perceived supporters of the PNU (as said, mostly from the Kikuyu, Kisii and Kamba ethnic communities living in and around Eldoret). Case II was against Uhuru Kenyatta from the PNU, former Police Commissioner Mohammad Hussein Ali and former Head of the Civil Service Francis Muthaura, who was in charge of coordinating all public servants on behalf of the president. The accusations they were facing were related to violence committed against perceived supporters of the ODM (as said, predominantly from the Kalenjin, Luo and Luhya communities living in Nakuru and Naivasha).

After the ICC initiated investigations, the government tried to undermine the process, completely disregarding Article 5 of the International Crimes Bill (2005), which obliges Kenya to cooperate with the Court. In December 2010, the parliament passed a non-binding motion urging the government to withdraw from the Rome Statute, repeal the International Crimes Act and establish a domestic accountability process to act instead of the ICC.[11] In February and March 2011, the government also tried to make the UN Security Council postpone the ICC's involvement arguing that the trials would endanger peace and security. The government also invoked Article 19 of the Rome Statute and challenged the admissibility of the cases in court. The basis of their argument was that the constitutional reform of 2010 (see next section of this chapter) was definitive proof of the government's willingness to deal with such criminal cases at the national level. However, the ICC resolved that the Rome Statute requires clear evidence of the initiation of a credible criminal process against the same alleged perpetrators and for the same crimes as the ones before the ICC. As this was not happening in the Kenyan case, the majority of the ICC Appeals Chamber rejected the government appeal.[12]

Indeed, at the domestic level, the efforts to ensure accountability were, at least, mild. A Multi-Agency Task Force created ad hoc under the supervision of the (presumably biased) Director of Public Prosecutions was established, but not until 2012.[13] The mandate of the Task Force included "reviewing, re-evaluating and re-examining all Post-Election Violence pending investigations, pending trials and concluded cases".[14] However, the Task Force has not yet published clear information about its work.[15] So far, only 24 low-level suspects were convicted out of the 6,081 cases presented by the police to the Task Force.[16] In terms of sexual violence, there were only 23 convictions out of 900 cases.[17] Moreover, the details surrounding these few convictions and the sentences issued remains unclear. The Task Force report has been "compiled hastily, with little concern for accuracy" and "a number of cases included in the report have nothing to do with the election violence" or are concerning extremely minor offences within the PEV such as "handling stolen property".[18] The Task Force concluded that most of the remaining cases were unsuitable for prosecution due to a lack of credible evidence, particularly enough witness statements.[19] Notably, evidence gathering was particularly undermined because those who were supposed to protect the witnesses were the ones the witnesses were likely to testify against.[20] This means that many civilians who were initially willing to testify were later afraid to do so because people from the military forces and the government were still in positions of power and could retaliate. In this regard, CSOs insisted on the need to strengthen witness protection because, even though there was a witnesses protection programme under the 2006 Witness Protection Act, it lacked funding and the capacity to implement its mandate.[21]

In what is the focus of the book, an interesting moment came up when, confronting the lack of accountability for mid- or high-ranking agents at the national level, the ICC continued investigating the cases. On 8 March 2011, the Pre-Trial Chamber II issued a summons requiring the six accused to appear before the Court. On 7–8 April 2011, all six individuals voluntarily appeared, and, between 1 September and 5 October, the hearings of the charges took place.

In this context, the Kenyan government initiated a new strategy: delegitimising the ICC as a neocolonial intervention[22] and a creature of an anti-Kenyan conspiracy.[23] Through this campaign, two of the defendants, Ruto and Kenyatta, efficaciously cast themselves as political victims of national and international plots against them and retained significant public support in their ethnic-regional communities.[24] Evidence of the positive results of the strategy was that, when returning after the initial hearings in The Hague, the accused were given a public heroes' welcome.[25] Moreover, the accused used this anti-imperialist and victimisation rhetoric not only to undermine the efforts of the ICC but also to gain more supporters for the upcoming election. Kenyatta and Ruto formed the Jubilee political party to compete in the 2013 elections while accusing the former Prime Minister and opposition leader, Odinga, of having engineered the submission of their names to the ICC. The neocolonial plot's discourse was involuntarily reinforced by US Assistant Secretary of State Johnnie Carson when saying that "choices would have consequences", about the possible victory of Kenyatta and Ruto.[26]

On top of that, the government also soaked up the support of the African Union.[27] The Union issued a resolution demanding that Kenyatta should not appear before the ICC "until such time as the concerns raised by the AU and its Member States have been adequately addressed by the UN Security Council and the ICC".[28] On 12 October 2013, in the Extraordinary Session of the Assembly of Heads of State and Government, the African Union issued a series of decisions, stating the need to "safeguard the constitutional order, stability and integrity of member states" by ensuring that "no charges shall be commenced or continued before any International Court or Tribunal against any serving AU Head of State or Government or anybody acting or entitled to act in such a capacity during their terms of office".[29] Therefore, it decided "that President Uhuru Kenyatta would not appear before the ICC until the concerns raised by the AU and its member states have been adequately addressed by the UN Security Council and the ICC".[30]

Overall, the scarce domestic criminal trials combined with intense anti-ICC propaganda and the undermining of the court's efforts to gather evidence[31] created a legal environment that made it extremely challenging to continue with the initial criminal proceedings. Even though the ICC Prosecutor first confirmed charges against Ruto, Sang and Kenyatta,[32] the newly appointed ICC Prosecutor, Fatou Bensouda, withdrew them because the available evidence was not sufficient to prove the alleged criminal responsibility beyond a reasonable doubt.[33]

The Kenyan case is crucial to discuss immunities as it raises relevant socio-normative questions around this fundamental topic, which demand a thorough discussion. Further discussion involves inquiring how ICL can regulate and enforce immunities without these being distorted as a neocolonial intervention in disrespect to the African countries' sovereignty. Moreover, might it be the case that a more even application of ICL can serve to overturn the neocolonial narrative and ensure that immunities are not an obstacle to accountability? Might it be the case that the inclusion of historical injustices and neocolonialism as a legitimate subject of ICL can make a difference in terms of its legitimation in the Global South?

3 The structural problem of ICL (or the paradox of immunities and ICL)

Micaela Frulli suggests that immunities hide a paradox. Even when it has often been said that *State officials* may not hide behind claims of *State sovereignty* to escape criminal accountability, she argues that the situation is exactly the opposite. Indeed, *States* may be the ones hiding behind *individuals*, because only the latter, at the end of the day, may be prosecuted before a domestic criminal court or, where available, an international criminal tribunal, while the State may not.[34]

There are some exceptions to this trend, such as the International Military Tribunal (IMT) in post-war Germany. In the final judgement, entire State agencies were framed as criminal organisations (the government, the leadership of the Nazi Party, the SS, the Gestapo, the Storm Detachment, and the General Staff and Supreme Command of the Wehrmacht).[35] However, this is not the rule. Generally, international crimes are framed as contextual based and target very specific perpetrators. The result of this phenomenon, as the Kenyan American scholar Makau wa Mutua explains,[36] is that once the "bad apples" are separated from the rest, the State remains a clean institution. This is particularly worrying when ICL fails to prosecute high-ranking perpetrators and focuses on the middle- or even low-ranking "bad apples", leaving the rest of the State agents and the State itself untouched. In this vein, double standards are not restricted to horizontal selectivity (which countries are targeted by ICL), but also include "vertical selectivity", "which refers to the decision as to which of the individuals involved in a situation should be singled out for prosecution".[37]

The question is then, how can we go beyond the individual features of ICL accusations to uncover the State's responsibility for international crimes? How can we address a full discussion about immunities without disregarding the broader picture of the State criminogenic structure? There might be two possible pathways. First, the holistic analysis of transitional justice – in which accountability and criminal justice *cannot* be isolated from reparations for the victims, the seeking of truth, and institutional, legal and cultural reforms to avoid repetition – might be a good path to explore.[38] Second, more innovative concepts, such as *transformative* justice being a necessary component of a truly engaging transitional justice, can also bring more comprehensive perspectives on ICL in general and on immunities in particular.[39]

Notes

1 This chapter is based on a former publication: Valeria Vegh Weis, 'The Effects of Seeking Justice *on Behalf of* the Victims: A Critical Analysis of Criminal Trials in the Kenyan Transitional Justice Process', in Ulrike Capdepón and Rosario Figari Layús (eds), *The Effects of Criminal Trials* (Leuven University Press 2020).

2 K Murphy, D Wray and C Ramírez-Barat, *Learning From Our Past: An Exploration of Truth, Justice, and Reconciliation in Kenya* (International Center for Transitional Justice 2015), www.ictj.org/publication/learning-our-past-exploration-truth-justice-and-reconciliation-kenya (accessed 9 March 2022)

3 Commission of Inquiry into the Post Election Violence (CIPEV), *Kenya: Final Report* (2008), available at: https://reliefweb.int/report/kenya/kenya-commission-inquiry-post-election-violence-cipev-final-report (accessed 9 March 2022); Human Rights Watch, *Reparations for Survivors of Kenya's 2007-2008 Post-Election Sexual Violence* (2015), available at: www.hrw.org/report/2016/02/15/i-just-sit-and-wait-die/reparations-survivors-kenyas-2007-2008-post-election (accessed 9 March 2022)

4 CIPEV (n 3) 15–16.

5 Amnesty International, *Police Reform in Kenya: "A Drop in the Ocean"* (2013) 7, available at: www.amnesty.org (accessed 9 March 2022).

6 S Brown, W Chandra and L Sriram, 'The Big Fish Won't Fry Themselves: Criminal Accountability for Post-Election Violence in Kenya' [2012] African Affairs 244.

7 LK Bosire and G Lynchy, 'Kenya's Search for Truth and Justice: The Role of Civil Society' (2014) 8(2) International Journal of Transitional Justice 256.

8 C Bjorkt and J Goebertustt, 'Note from the Field Complementarity in Action: The Role of Civil Society and the ICC in Rule of Law Strengthening in Kenya' (2011) 1 Yale Human Rights & Development Journal 205.

9 ibid.

10 A Senier, 'Introductory note to the International Criminal Court: Situation in the Republic of Kenya' (2011) 50(4) International Legal Materials 1. This was the first ruling by an ICC pre-trial chamber on a prosecutorial *proprio motu* request under the Rome Statute. The decision raised the discussion about how to interpret the contextual element of crimes against humanity in the Rome Statute, Art 7(2). In the absence of proof of a high-level State policy within the PEV, the question was whether the presence of an organisational policy required there to have been State intervention or whether an amorphous or private group of individuals infringing basic human values was enough (para 90; diss op, para 53). Ultimately, the majority determined that many of the PEV cases were planned, directed or organised by a concert of local leaders, businessmen and politicians affiliated with the two leading parties, and on that basis essentially disposed of the organisational policy requirement to ground a finding of crimes against humanity (paras 116–128): CC Jalloh, 'Situation in the Republic of Kenya' (2011) 105(3) American Journal of International Law 540.

11 Amnesty International, *Kenya: Crying for Justice: Victims' Perspectives on Justice for the Post-Election Violence in Kenya* (2014), available at: www.amnesty.org/en/documents/afr32/001/2014/en/ (accessed 9 March 2022)

12 The case *Prosecutor v Francis Kirimi Muthaura, Uhuru Muigai Kenyatta and Mohammed Hussein Ali* is the first ruling by the Appeals Chamber on whether national investigations must cover not only the same conduct but also the same person as a pending ICC case for the case to be declared inadmissible under the Rome Statute, Art 17(1)(a): E Stubbins Bates, 'The International Criminal Court Appeals Chamber: Prosecutor V. Francis Kirimi Muthaura, Uhuru Muigai Kenyatta and Mohammed Hussein Ali' (2012) 51(1) International Legal Materials 17.

13 Amnesty International, *Police Reform* (n 5).

14 ICC, *Situation in the Republic of Kenya in the Case of the Prosecutor v. William Samoei Ruto and Joshua Arap Sang*, submitted on 2 February 2017, para 13.

15 ibid para 14.

16 ibid para 16.

17 Human Rights Watch, *Reparations for Survivors of Kenya's 2007-2008 Post-Election Sexual Violence* (2015) 7, available at: www.hrw.org/report/2016/02/15/i-just-sit-and-wait-die/reparations-survivors-kenyas-2007-2008-post-election (accessed 9 March 2022)

18 KPTJ, *Securing justice. Establishing a Domestic Mechanism for the 2007/8 Post-Election Violence in Kenya* (2013) 9, available at: http://africog.org/new/wp-content/uploads/A%20Luxury%20Victims%20Cannot%20Afford%20-%20KPTJ%20JULY%202013.pdf (accessed 9 March 2022).

19 Amnesty International, *Kenya* (n 11).

20 High Court at Nakuru, *Republic v Stephen Kiprotich Leting & 3 others* [2009] eKLR.

21 M Cheptinga, Personal communication (2017).

22 LE Gissel, 'Justice Tides: How and When Levels of ICC Involvement Affect Peace Processes' (2015) 9(3) International Journal of Transitional Justice 428; G Lugano, 'Counter-shaming the International Criminal Court's Intervention

as Neocolonial: Lessons from Kenya' (2017) 11(1) International Journal of Transitional Justice 9.

23 G Lugano, 'Counter-Shaming the International Criminal Court's Intervention as Neocolonial: Lessons from Kenya' (2017) 11(1) International Journal of Transitional Justice 9.

24 Brown, Chandra and Sriram (n 6).

25 ibid.

26 U Capdepón and R Figari Layús, *The Impact of Human Rights Prosecutions* (Leuven University Press 2020).

27 ibid.

28 African Union, Decision on Africa's relationship with the International Criminal Court (2013), EXT/Assembly/AU/Dec.1, para 10xi.

29 ibid.

30 ibid.

31 Facing evidence challenges, the judgment in *Prosecutor v Ruto* is the first to determine that an ICC trial chamber may summon unwilling witnesses to testify and that the Court may request that a State Party to the Rome Statute compel the witnesses – if necessary by using compulsory means under its domestic law – to appear before the judges sitting in the territory of the State Party or through a video link to The Hague.

32 In 2012, the Pre-Trial Chamber II found that the ICC Prosecutor's evidence failed to satisfy the evidentiary threshold required in the case of Kosgey, Ali and Muthaura; the ICC Presidency constituted Trial Chamber V to conduct the Ruto, Sang and Kenyatta cases and, in a subsequent ruling, postponed Kenyatta's trial to April 2013 after the presidential election.

33 Notice of withdrawal of the charges against Uhuru Muigai Kenyatta, Office of the Prosecutor, *The Prosecutor v Uhuru Muigai Kenyatta*, 05 December 2014 ICC-01/09-02/11-983.

34 M Frulli, 'On the Existence of a Customary Rule Granting Functional Immunity to State Officials and Its Exceptions: Back to Square One' (2016) 26(3) Duke Journal of Comparative & International Law 479

35 S Romeike, *Transitional Justice in Germany after 1945 and after 1990* (2016), available at: www.nurembergacademy.org

36 M Mutua, 'Savages, Victims, and Saviors: The Metaphor of Human Rights' (2001) 42(1) Harvard International Law Journal.

37 W Kaleck, *Double Standards: International Criminal Law and the West* (Torkel Opsahl Academic Epublisher 2015) 14.

38 P de Greiff, 'Theorizing Transitional Justice', in Melissa S Williams and Jon Elster (eds), *Transitional Justice: NOMOS LI* (New York University Press 2012).

39 P Gready and S Robins, 'From Transitional to Transformative Justice: A New Agenda for Practice' (2014) 8(3) International Journal of Transitional Justice 339.

Selected bibliography

African Union, Decision on Africa's Relationship with the International Criminal Court (2013) EXT/Assembly/AU/Dec.1

Amnesty International, *Police Reform in Kenya: "A Drop in the Ocean"* (2013), available at: www.amnesty.org (accessed 9 March 2022)

Amnesty International, *Kenya: Crying for Justice: Victims' Perspectives on Justice for the Post-Election Violence in Kenya* (2014), available at: www.amnesty.org/en/documents/afr32/001/2014/en/ (accessed 9 March 2022)

Bjorkt C and Goebertustt J, 'Note from the Field Complementarity in Action: The Role of Civil Society and the ICC in Rule of Law Strengthening in Kenya' (2011) 1 *Yale Human Rights & Development Journal* 205

Bosire LK and Lynchy G, 'Kenya's Search for Truth and Justice: The Role of Civil Society' (2014) 8(2) *International Journal of Transitional Justice* 256 https://doi.org/10.1093/IJTJ/IJU002

Brown S, Chandra W and Sriram L, 'The Big Fish Won't Fry Themselves: Criminal Accountability for Post-Election Violence in Kenya' [2012] *African Affairs* 244 https://doi.org/10.1093/afraf/ads018

Capdepón U and Figari Layús R, *The Impact of Human Rights Prosecutions* (Leuven University Press 2020)

Cheptinga M, *Personal communication* (2017)

Commission of Inquiry into the Post Election Violence (CIPEV), *Kenya: Final Report* (2008), available at: https://reliefweb.int/report/kenya/kenya-commission-inquiry-post-election-violence-cipev-final-report (accessed 9 March 2022)

de Greiff P, 'Theorizing Transitional Justice', in Melissa S Williams and Jon Elster (eds), *Transitional Justice: NOMOS LI* (New York University Press 2012) 31

Frulli M, 'On the Existence of a Customary Rule Granting Functional Immunity to State Officials and Its Exceptions: Back to Square One' (2016) 26(3) *Duke Journal of Comparative & International Law* 479, available at: https://scholarship.law.duke.edu/djcil/vol26/iss3/2 (accessed 9 March 2022)

Gissel LE, 'Justice Tides: How and When Levels of ICC Involvement Affect Peace Processes' (2015) 9(3) *International Journal of Transitional Justice* 428 https://doi.org/10.1093/IJTJ/IJV021

Gready P and Robins S, 'From Transitional to Transformative Justice: A New Agenda for Practice' (2014) 8(3) *International Journal of Transitional Justice* 339 https://doi.org/10.1093/IJTJ/IJU013

Human Rights Watch, *Reparations for Survivors of Kenya's 2007-2008 Post-Election Sexual Violence* (2015), available at: www.hrw.org/report/2016/02/15/i-just-sit-and-wait-die/reparations-survivors-kenyas-2007-2008-post-election (accessed 9 March 2022)

ICC, *Situation in the Republic of Kenya in the Case of the Prosecutor v. William Samoei Ruto and Joshua Arap Sang*, submitted on 2 February 2017

Jalloh CC, 'Situation in the Republic of Kenya' (2011) 105(3) *American Journal of International Law* 540 https://doi.org/10.5305/AMERJINTELAW.105.3.0540

Kaleck W, *Double Standards: International Criminal Law and the West* (Torkel Opsahl Academic Epublisher 2015)

KPTJ, *Securing justice. Establishing a Domestic Mechanism for the 2007/8 Post-Election Violence in Kenya* (2013), available at: http://africog.org/new/wp-content/uploads/A%20Luxury%20Victims%20Cannot%20Afford%20-%20KPTJ%20JULY%202013.pdf (accessed 9 March 2022)

Lugano G, 'Counter-shaming the International Criminal Court's Intervention as Neocolonial: Lessons from Kenya' (2017) 11(1) *International Journal of Transitional Justice* 9 https://doi.org/10.1093/IJTJ/IJW026

Murphy K, Wray D and Ramírez-Barat C, *Learning From Our Past: An Exploration of Truth, Justice, and Reconciliation in Kenya* (International Center for Transitional

Justice 2015), available at: www.ictj.org/publication/learning-our-past-exploration-truth-justice-and-reconciliation-kenya (accessed 9 March 2022)

Mutua M, 'Savages, Victims, and Saviors: The Metaphor of Human Rights' (2001) 42(1) *Harvard International Law Journal*, available at: https://digitalcommons.law.buffalo.edu/journal_articles/570 (accessed 7 December 2021)

Romeike S, *Transitional Justice in Germany after 1945 and after 1990* (2016), available at: www.nurembergacademy.org

Senier A, Introductory Note to the International Criminal Court: Situation in the Republic of Kenya (2011) 50(4) *International Legal Materials* 1 https://doi.org/10.5305/INTELEGAMATE.50.4.FM

Stubbins Bates E, 'The International Criminal Court Appeals Chamber: Prosecutor V. Francis Kirimi Muthaura, Uhuru Muigai Kenyatta and Mohammed Hussein Ali' (2012) 51(1) *International Legal Materials* 17 https://doi.org/10.5305/INTELEGAMATE.51.1.0017

6.3 Justice of the Powerful

Abusing Prosecutorial Discretion in the Punishment of International Crimes?

Triestino Mariniello

1 Introduction

Discretionary powers of the Prosecutor constituted one of the most contentious issues among the participants of the United Nations Conference of Plenipotentiaries on the Establishment of an International Criminal Court (ICC).[1] In Rome, the idea of an independent Prosecutor able to initiate an investigation without the authorisation of a State Party or the Security Council was quite controversial. Still, the majority of the conference delegates agreed that denying the Prosecutor the power to open investigations *ex officio* would have deprived the international community of a significant tool for the prosecution of the most serious crimes.[2] According to the compromise reached by States in Rome, the Prosecutor may initiate a *proprio motu* investigation, but the judiciary is called to supervise the reasonableness of such decision.[3] Nonetheless, while conference delegates were mainly concerned with how to limit the Office of the Prosecutor (OTP)'s powers when it decides to start an investigation, they did not pay significant attention to the opposite scenario, ie when the Prosecutor decides *not to open an investigation*.[4]

Hence, the Rome Statute confers a wide scope of discretion on the Prosecutor to commence an investigation. It enables the Prosecutor not only to select cases to prosecute but also to identify "situations" to investigate. However, such prosecutorial discretion is generally not unfettered. The OTP decision to start a *proprio motu* investigation is indeed subject to judicial authorisation.[5] The Statute also grants Pre-Trial Chambers the authority to regulate the Prosecutor's decision *not* to start an investigation into referred situations.[6] The only circumstance in which the Rome Statute does not establish any form of judicial oversight is when the Prosecutor decides *not* to start a *proprio motu* investigation. Unless the decision not to proceed is based solely on the interests of justice,[7] a *negative decision* of the OTP under Article 15 cannot be subject to judicial review even if the Prosecutor's conclusions were the result of an abuse of his discretionary powers.

Scholars have placed emphasis on the significance of prosecutorial discretion in international criminal law. They have indeed labelled prosecutorial discretion as an essential element of international criminal courts that could

DOI: 10.4324/9781003320951-28

potentially have their jurisdiction over thousands of cases.[8] Academic literature has found that, because of the practical impossibility to deal with all crimes falling within the competence of international criminal tribunals, it is necessary that international prosecutors have the powers to select which cases to investigate.[9] Limited resources for international criminal tribunals would further justify the need of selectivity for international prosecutors.[10] As a means to shield the Prosecutor from political pressures of States, discretionary powers apparently constitute the cornerstone of prosecutorial independence.[11]

Nonetheless, while scholarship has strongly supported the recognition of discretionary powers for international prosecutors, the practice of international criminal tribunals shows how an improper exercise of prosecutorial discretion may have a significant impact on the legitimacy and credibility of such institutions. Thus far, the ICC's overall practice indicates that what is problematic in relation to the procedure under Article 15 is not when the Prosecutor uses his *proprio motu* powers, rather when, following a (generally long) preliminary investigation,[12] the OTP decides *not* to initiate an investigation on the basis of contrived legal arguments that give rise to concern about the Court's practice of selectivity and double standards.

The intent of this chapter is to critically assess the OTP's exercise of its discretionary powers at the pre-investigative stage of the proceedings in the situations in Iraq, Palestine and Afghanistan. A comprehensive analysis of the OTP's decisions in these three situations goes beyond the ambits of this research. In line with more detailed accounts, this chapter explores the (main) contradictions and ambiguities characterising the decisions not to open an investigation in Iraq (Section 2) and Palestine (Section 3), as well as the decision to de-prioritise aspects of the investigation in Afghanistan (Section 4). By way of conclusion, this paper reflects on the exceptionalism with which the Court treats alleged crimes committed by nationals of powerful Western States.

2 The Situation in Iraq and the Politics of Inadmissibility

In two different decisions, the OTP admitted that there was reasonable basis to believe that British troops had committed war crimes within the context of the armed conflict in Iraq.[13] However, in both the circumstances, it decided not to open an investigation by stating that potential cases against British troops would have been inadmissible.

2.1 Not Sufficiently Serious: The OTP's (Mis)Use of Gravity

In 2006, the OTP relied on an ambiguous interpretation of the concept of gravity to decline to start an investigation.[14] It decided that potential cases would not have been sufficiently serious because of the low number of victims of the war crimes allegedly perpetrated by British soldiers. The OTP argued that the standard of proof to open an investigation was satisfied, but it refused to open an investigation since the number of potential victims "was of a different order than the number of victims found in other situation under investigations".[15] In particular, the OTP compared the limited number of victims in Iraq with the situations in Uganda, Democratic Republic of Congo and Darfur, which involved hundreds or thousands of victims of international crimes. In so doing, the OTP relied on an improper comparison between the *specific case* concerning the British troops in Iraq and the *general situation* in Uganda and DRC.[16]

By placing the Iraq decision within the wider context of the OTP's practice, contradictions and ambiguities in the legal analysis of gravity appear even more manifest. At the time of writing, there is no other decision, by the Prosecutor or the judiciary, providing a purely quantitative analysis of gravity. In the evaluation of gravity in other situations, the OTP stresses the significance of qualitative factors such as the scale, nature, manner of commission and impact of the crimes. The exceptionalism of the Iraq (first) decision resides in the fact that it is the OTP's sole decision that relies *only* on the number of victims in the interpretation of gravity. The OTP's stance towards gravity solely on the basis of the number of victims has led to the misperception that the Court's mandate only extends to incidents with very significant numbers of casualties.[17]

Before the decision not to start the Iraq investigation, the same OTP had stated that the evaluation of gravity cannot be purely quantitative as "there are several factors that must be considered".[18] Then, it is again the OTP, in its working documents and practice, that places emphasis on the necessity to put in place a more comprehensive approach that is not confined to the number of victims.[19] Regulations of the OTP, adopted in 2009, clearly establish that, in the assessment of the gravity of the crimes, the OTP has to consider "various factors including their scale, nature, manner of commission, and impact".[20]

Scholarship has stressed how this fundamentally quantitative approach ignored important factors in the determination of sufficient gravity, such as the nature of the crimes and the involvement of State authorities. It has placed into question why other crimes under investigation, such as the conscription of children in the *Lubanga* case, would have been more serious than killing and rape allegedly perpetrated by British soldiers.[21] In deciding that the situation was inadmissible, according to Schabas, the OTP overlooked relevant factors for the determination of the gravity of the crimes, such as the context in which alleged crimes occurred, namely a war of aggression that has caused hundreds of thousands of victims.[22]

2.2 Persevering in Error: The Prosecutor's Second Rejection in the Iraq Situation

In 2020, the OTP found that there was reasonable basis to believe that British troops had committed war crimes of wilful killing, torture, inhuman/cruel treatment, outrages upon personal dignity, and rape and/or other forms of sexual violence within the context of the armed conflict in Iraq.[23] However, it declined to start an investigation since there was insufficient evidence that the UK was *unwilling* genuinely to investigate and prosecute the allegations. Therefore, according to the OTP, potential cases would have not been admissible under the complementarity principle.

Experts have immediately criticised this decision on several grounds. They have argued that this second rejection fails to take into account the political context in which domestic investigations took place as well as the actions of the British governments to prevent investigations and prosecutions of UK forces.[24] The Prosecutor's conclusion that the UK was not unwilling to investigate appears contradictory with respect to the same OTP's findings that stressed the reluctance and hostility of the British government to any attempt to investigate members of the armed forces.[25] In order to protect the armed forces from vexatious litigation, the Defence Minister had decided to close ahead of schedule the Iraq Historic Allegations Team that had been set up set up to investigate allegations of abuse of Iraqi civilians by the UK armed forces. As reported by the OTP, both the BBC and the *Sunday Times* newspaper had found that the British authorities "had attempted to cover up killings in Iraq, including through the obstruction of investigative steps, political pressure and the premature termination of cases".[26]

The Prosecutor's conclusion also fails to properly consider the very poor record of the UK's genuine willingness to investigate and prosecute war crimes independently. Despite the ample evidence of alleged war crimes perpetrated by British troops in Iraq, since 2001 there has been only one prosecution of a British member of the armed forces for war crimes abroad.[27] In particular, for the purposes of the complementarity principle, it is important to highlight that no single domestic prosecution has concerned senior military or political officers for alleged crimes committed overseas.[28] Nonetheless, the same OTP reported that "several levels of institutional civilian supervisory and military command failures contributed to the commission of crimes against detainees by UK soldiers in Iraq".[29] As stressed by Meloni, "the repeated and systematic occurrence of acts of torture and mistreatment of prisoners in Iraq implies various levels of criminal responsibility, from the ordinary soldier, direct perpetrator of the offences, up along the chain of command".[30] Still, when it comes to the conclusions in the Iraq second decision, the failure of domestic investigations to address the responsibility of higher military and political echelons did not play any role in the Prosecutor's evaluation of "unwillingness" under Article 17(2)(a) of the Statute.

Moreover, the Prosecutor's analysis of the complementarity principle is characterised by (basic) legal errors which concern both the applicable *standard of proof* as well as the *object* of the admissibility test. As regards the standard of proof, Articles 15(3) and 53(1)(b) require the Prosecutor to assess the admissibility conditions in light of the "reasonable basis" test. The very rationale for applying the lowest evidentiary threshold in the Rome Statute at this early stage of the proceedings is to avoid "unwarranted, frivolous, or politically motivated investigations".[31] Nonetheless, in the decision not start an investigation in Iraq, the Prosecutor applied to the complementarity principle a higher standard of proof by concluding that "the Office has not been able to substantiate, with evidence that it could rely upon in court". As noted by Heller, this "is not the legal standard – neither procedurally nor substantively".[32] At this stage of the proceedings, the OTP, indeed, does not need to collect "evidence that it could rely on in court", which proves the State is unwilling to genuinely investigate. According to Baldwin, the evidentiary threshold identified by the OTP is almost impossible to prove. This is due to the fact that, at this phase of the proceedings, the OTP Office is vested with very limited investigatory powers, which prevents it proving that in each individual case there was an active attempt to shield the perpetrators.[33]

The Prosecutor's conclusion also appears problematic in relation to the *object* of the evaluation of the complementarity principle. In the assessment of "unwillingness" under Article 17(2), indeed, the OTP focused on the entire situation and a multitude of potential cases and suspects. On the basis of this general analysis, it concluded that there is no "larger pattern of shielding".[34] However, in contrast to the Prosecutor's conclusion, Article 17(2) does not require that admissibility is assessed in relation to the whole situation. In other words, in the evaluation of complementarity, the Prosecutor does not have to act as an oversight body for the domestic authorities and their investigations in general. For the purposes of proving whether national authorities are unwilling, this provision refers specifically to a concrete case with a concrete suspect, rather than to the overall situation.[35]

3 Evading *Proprio Motu* Powers: The OTP's (First) Decision in the Palestine Situation[36]

In April 2012, the OTP decided not to open an investigation into the Palestine situation by arguing that it was unclear whether Palestine was a State under the Rome Statute.[37] Therefore, it delegated to the UN General Assembly and the ICC Assembly of States Parties the competence to determine whether Palestine qualified as a State under the Rome Statute, thereby enabling the exercise of jurisdiction by the Court.[38]

Palestine's formal engagement with the ICC had begun days after Israel ended "Operation Cast Lead", its military offensive in the Gaza Strip, in January 2009, with the submission of its first Article 12(3) declaration to the OTP. Neither that specific bout of hostilities nor the timing of the declaration's submission were central to this move to trigger the ad hoc jurisdiction of the Court retroactively from 1 July 2002. The OTP's deliberative process, which became a public free-for-all on the question of Palestine writ large, was procedurally flawed at the outset. If Palestine's ability to confer jurisdiction onto the Court was genuinely in doubt, the Prosecutor should have referred the question at once to the Pre-Trial Chamber.[39] Instead of *referring* questions of Palestine's status as a State to a proper forum, the brief "decision" issued by the OTP in April 2012 closed the deliberation process, while effectively *deferring* the questions to a host of *political bodies* such as the UN Assembly General and the ICC's Assembly of State Parties (ASP).

Numerous international experts identified flaws in the Prosecutor's 2012 decision.[40] Scholars argued that Palestine's 2009 declaration was validly lodged and could have been accepted by the ICC according to Article 12 of its Statute.[41] The OTP decided that acceptance of Palestine's declaration hinged on the formal recognition of Palestinian statehood by the UN or the ICC's ASP. Yet even if it had addressed the issue using the correct functional approach, the OTP erred by overlooking relevant UN practice, which confirmed Palestine's statehood status; namely, a vote by a majority of UN Member States in October 2011 that accepted Palestine's membership in UNESCO.[42] The OTP decision failed to acknowledge the relevant practice of the UN Secretary-General, which, as depositary for the Rome Statute, had accepted the Cook Islands' accession even though it – as with Palestine at the time of its submission of the 2009 declaration – was not listed as a UN "non-member State".[43]

Despite a lengthy and laborious process, the OTP issued a two-page deferral that was nothing short of anticlimactic: it was neither thorough nor well-reasoned; not commensurate with the institutional interests of the Court to remain seized of the matter; and marred by a lack of transparency. In November 2012, the UN General Assembly resolved any possible remaining questions the OTP may have had when it upgraded Palestine's observer status in the General Assembly to that of a non-member *State* (previously entity), *affirming* its status as a State. Given the dispositive (and not constitutive) nature of its contribution, the OTP could have used the opportunity to initiate a *proprio motu* preliminary examination, reconsider its previous decision and reopen its deliberations; instead, the Court proceeded with its previous course of action. The OTP singlehandedly insisted that Palestine must submit a new declaration to trigger jurisdiction, and insisted on the validity of its April 2012 decision. The OTP explicitly referred to these significant decisions only well after the fact, in its 2012 activities report.[44] A *proprio motu* investigation was, it appears, never contemplated as an option. In a May 2014 interview for the Israeli press, the former OTP Moreno-Ocampo was reportedly "eager to point out that joining the ICC could backfire for the Palestinians".[45] The apparent reason for the Court's reluctance to embark on an investigation of Israeli actions, as William Schabas remarked, is the likely impact of such an initiative on the Court's "cordial relationship" with the United States (US).[46]

4 Genuinely Unwilling to Investigate US Nationals: The Prosecutor's De-Prioritisation in the Afghanistan Situation

In 2021, the ICC Prosecutor announced a "de-prioritisation of war crimes" allegedly committed by the US members of the Central Intelligence Agency

(CIA) and armed forces, and by members of the former Afghan armed forces (funded by the US).[47] The Prosecutor argued that in light of the limited resources available to his office, he had to prioritise the investigation of potential cases against the Taliban and the Islamic State – Khorasan Province (IS-K). He explicitly mentioned that the criteria behind the prioritisation were the gravity, scale and continuing nature of alleged crimes by the Taliban and the IS-K.

Since 2006, the OTP had already found sufficient evidence to prosecute US nationals for war crimes including torture and cruel treatment, outrages upon personal dignity, rape and other forms of sexual violence.[48] The investigation, which had been authorised directly by the Appeals Chamber,[49] focused, inter alia, on the widely documented use by the US authorities of interrogation techniques that amount to torture, including sexual violence, severe isolation, suffocation by water or waterboarding, hooding under special conditions, threats of torture, the use of dogs to induce fear, imposition of stress positions, isolation and sensory deprivation, exposure to extreme temperatures, sensory overstimulation, prolonged sleep deprivation, food deprivation, and deliberately placing detainees in cramped conditions.[50]

Granting impunity for the institutionalised use of torture and other serious crimes committed during the military aggression towards Iraq and Afghanistan has been a shared policy of different US administrations.[51] As part of the detention and interrogation programmes, the CIA had set up prisons (black sites) in other countries, where detainees were systematically tortured for the purpose of extracting information.[52] The same black sites for the CIA's rendition programme of enforced disappearance, arbitrary detention and torture were established to avoid any scrutiny and accountability.[53] The former ICC Prosecutor had found that at least four black sites were situated on Afghan territory, while a number of other secret detention sites were located in other countries, including Lithuania, Poland and Romania.[54]

Civil society and legal representatives of victims immediately criticised the de-prioritisation decision since it carries the discriminatory effect of denying justice to certain victims of alleged war crimes.[55] The hibernation of the investigation against US nationals rewards uncooperative States and shows how the Court has surrendered to the strong political pressure of the US that had not only publicly threatened the Court in several circumstances,[56] but had also imposed severe economic sanctions and visa restrictions against the former Prosecutor and senior staff from her Office.[57]

The de-prioritisation decision appears particularly problematic since it oversteps the limits of the Prosecutor's (already wide) discretionary powers. Indeed, the applicable legal basis for the de-prioritisation under the Rome Statute and the Rules of Procedure and Evidence (RPE) remains obscure. That is arguably the reason why the same OTP does not mention any relevant provision, under the Rome Statute or the RPE, that would govern the "de-prioritisation" procedure.[58] At the same time, the use of "poor resources" to justify the decision to freeze the investigation is entirely arbitrary as the

Court's legal documents never mention financial resources as a condition to open an investigation or as a reason to cease it.

It is worth remembering that Article 18(2) requires the Prosecutor to "defer to the State's investigation where a State is investigating or has investigated its nationals with respect to criminal acts which may amount to international crimes under the Statute". However, according to the same Prosecutor, the authorities and entities in control of Afghanistan are not able to genuinely investigate and prosecute alleged crimes.[59] Moreover, Article 53(4) establishes that "the Prosecutor may, at any time, reconsider a decision whether to initiate an investigation or prosecution based on new facts or information". However, the Prosecutor did not invoke this provision in the de-prioritisation decision.

Therefore, having already determined that there is a reasonable basis to proceed, the only potential legal basis for not starting an investigation and a prosecution would be the "interests of justice" clause under Article 53(1)(c) and 53(2)(c) of the Statute. These are the only provisions that provide the Prosecutor with the discretion to decline an investigation once both the conditions of jurisdiction and admissibility are satisfied. However, the de-prioritisation decision does not make any references to the interests of justice. This is probably due to the fact that the use of the interests of justice would have triggered the *ex officio* judicial review under Article 53(3)(b). In other words, by deciding not to apply the interests of justice clause, the Prosecutor avoided any judicial oversight of the competent Pre-Trial Chamber.

Moreover, the Prosecutor argued that cases have been prioritised on the basis of their *gravity, scale and continuing nature*. One cannot fail to note that the Prosecutor's use of gravity presents contradictions and inconsistencies in light of the OTP's practice in Afghanistan as well as in other situations.

By maintaining that de-prioritised cases are less serious than those against the Taliban and the IS-K, the OTP appears to weaken the gravity of the alleged crimes committed by the members of the US defence forces and CIA. Attenuating the seriousness of alleged crimes, which include allegations of torture, appears in sharp contrast to the OTP's practice that has regularly placed significant emphasis on gravity of torture. In the evaluation of gravity in the same Afghanistan situation, the OTP had indeed stressed that the prohibition against torture represents a peremptory norm of international law (*jus cogens*).[60] In citing the International Court of Justice, the OTP had highlighted that the prohibition of torture is "grounded in a widespread international practice and on the opinio juris of States".[61] In stressing the gravity of torture as an international crime, the OTP had referred to the ICTY's words that the prohibition against torture "is absolute and non-derogable in any circumstances" and "applies at all times",[62] as well as to the United Nations Committee Against Torture, which, in its General Comment no 2, has similarly observed that "no exceptional circumstances whatsoever may be invoked by a State Party to justify acts of torture in any territory under its jurisdiction".[63]

5 Concluding Remarks

This chapter explored how the decisions not to open an investigation in the Iraq and Palestine situations, and to "de-prioritise" alleged war crimes in Afghanistan, do not appear extremely persuasive. The OTP indeed relied on motivations that either do not have any legal basis in the Rome Statute and the RPE, or stand in marked contrast to the OTP's actions in other situations. Admissibility conditions, statehood and "poor resources" seem to be used as a fig leaf to hide the political nature that drives the OTP to keep the Court far from disturbing investigations for powerful Western States. In doing so, the OTP's decisions raise concerns about its ability and willingness to act with integrity and in good faith in the face of overwhelming political forces.

The decisions in Iraq, Palestine and Afghanistan might be interpreted as the result of a pragmatic strategy that aims at normalising the Court's relationship with powerful States, particularly with the US.[64] For instance, the "de-prioritisation" reflects the views of some commentators, who have explicitly argued that the Court should avoid opening up investigations against powerful actors.[65] The rhetoric of "convenient pragmatism" guiding the Prosecutor's decisions resurfaces each time the Court is called to deal with powerful States or their allies, and it is generally used to hide the ICC's surrender to the strong political pressures of powerful States. However, the arguments on the necessity of a pragmatic Prosecutor rely on the unproven axiom that the Court may chart its successful path in the long term only avoiding those investigations that find the opposition of powerful States.[66]

Other experts have justified the "pragmatic" decision to redefine the Afghanistan investigation by placing emphasis on the fact that "international criminal justice is always and can only be selective".[67] It is beyond doubt that the enforcement of international criminal law will always be selective. Hence, it is not surprising that international criminal tribunals investigate only a few emblematic situations of international criminality. However, selectivity becomes problematic for the legitimacy of international criminal tribunals, when "international prosecutions are instituted mainly against citizens of States that are weak actors in the international arena or fail to enjoy the support of powerful nations".[68]

Therefore, those who justify the OTP's decisions in Iraq, Palestine and Afghanistan as being the result of a pragmatic stance ignore or underestimate the impact of these decisions on the already weak credibility and legitimacy of an institution that, while it claims universal aspirations, continues to discriminate among human rights abusers on the basis of their citizenship.

The Prosecutor's reluctance to investigate some of the most documented international violations in these three situations, indeed, continues to feed perceptions of the Court as a paradigm of a "justice of the powerful".[69] The unequal application of international criminal law by the Court, which has emphasised the criminality of some individuals while ignoring that of others, has been the main cause of the legitimacy crisis for the Court.[70]

In particular, the ICC's flawed and politically driven decisions, in the situations in Afghanistan, Iraq and Palestine, are the corollary of an institution that is unwilling (and most likely unable) to address situations (directly or indirectly) involving powerful Western States. The reality is that the Court has failed to render anyone accountable in situations that are (some of) the most documented (alleged) perpetrations of international crimes falling in the ICC's jurisdiction, such as the Israeli–Palestinian setting since the Gaza war 2008/09, the situation in Iraq since the invasion in 2003, and the war in Afghanistan.

It is almost certain that the curtain has fallen on international accountability for alleged crimes committed by nationals from the US and the UK, including torture within the context of the Afghanistan and Iraq armed conflicts.

It seems highly likely that the OTP decisions in Iraq and Afghanistan will lead to impunity for both UK and US nationals allegedly responsible for war crimes given the general unwillingness of national courts to hold those responsible for serious international law violations to account. The most likely effects of the decisions in these two situations will be that alleged crimes committed by the US and UK nationals slip quietly into oblivion.

To conclude, this strategy, aimed at keeping the Court far from investigations that would find opposition from powerful States, could appear as a way to protect the institution. However, in the long term, it is likely that it will completely deprive the Court of its credibility. In this context, the Court can still show its ability to withstand political pressures and interference with its work, by prosecuting alleged crimes in the Israeli–Palestinian setting. The ongoing investigation in this situation could be the final test bench for the legitimacy of this institution.

Notes

1 See Silvia A Fernandez de Gurmendi, 'The Role of the International Prosecutor', in Roy S Lee (ed), *The International Criminal Court: The Making of the Rome Statute: Issues, Negotiations, Results* (Kluwer Law International 1999) 175–188.
2 ibid 181.
3 Proposal by Argentina and Germany in UN Doc A/AC.249/1998/W.G.4/DP.35, 25 March 1998.
4 See Chantal Meloni, 'The ICC Preliminary Examination of the Flotilla Situation: an Opportunity to Contextualise Gravity' (2016) Questions of International Law 6, available at www.qil-qdi.org/icc-preliminary-examination-flotilla-situation-opportunity-contextualise-gravity/
5 See ICC Statute, Art 15(4).
6 See ICC Statute, Art 53(3)(a).
7 See ICC Statute, Art 53(3)(b).
8 Matthew R Brubacher, 'Prosecutorial Discretion within the International Criminal Court' (2004) Journal of International Criminal Justice 75.
9 ibid.

10 Allison M Danner, 'Enhancing the Legitimacy and Accountability of Prosecutorial Discretion at the International Criminal Court' (2003) American Journal of International Law 550.
11 Luc Cote, 'Reflections on the Exercise of Prosecutorial Discretion in International Criminal Law' (2005) Journal of International Criminal Justice 165.
12 Triestino Mariniello, 'Judicial Control over Prosecutorial Discretion in the Rome Statute' (2019) International Criminal Law Review 979–1013.
13 ICC, Situation in UK/Iraq: Final Report, OTP, 9 December 2020 (Iraq second decision); ICC, Letter concerning communication on the situation in Iraq, OTP, 9 February 2006, 8 (Iraq first decision).
14 ICC, Letter concerning communication on the situation in Iraq, OTP, 9 February 2006, 8–9.
15 OTP, Iraq first decision 2006.
16 William A Schabas, 'Prosecutorial Discretion v. Judicial Activism at the International Criminal Court' (2008) Journal of International Criminal Justice 741.
17 William A Schabas, 'The International Criminal Court at Ten' (2011) Criminal Law Forum 493.
18 Statement by Luis Moreno-Ocampo, Prosecutor of the International Criminal Court, Informal meeting of Legal Advisors of Ministries of Foreign Affairs, 24 October 2005, 6.
19 See, inter alia, (2013) Policy Paper on Preliminary Examinations, OTP, para 9.
20 See Regulation 29(2) Regulations of the Office of the Prosecutor.
21 Mohamed M El Zeidy, 'The Gravity Threshold under the Statute of the International Criminal Court' (2008) Criminal Law Forum 57.
22 Schabas, 'Prosecutorial Discretion v. Judicial Activism' (n 16) 742–748.
23 OTP, Iraq second decision (n 13) para 113.
24 See, inter alia, Clive Baldwin, 'The ICC Prosecutor Office's Cop-Out on UK Military Crimes in Iraq', Opinio Juris, 18 December 2020, at <https://opiniojuris.org/2020/12/18/the-icc-prosecutor-offices-cop-out-on-ukmilitary-crimes-in-iraq/>; Kevin J Heller, 'The Nine Words that (Wrongly) Doomed the Iraq Investigation', Opinio Juris, 10 December 2020, at https://opiniojuris.org/2020/12/10/the-nine-words-that-wrongly-doomed-the-iraqinvestigation/>; Andreas Schüller, 'The ICC, British War Crimes in Iraq and a Very British Tradition', Opinio Juris, 11 December 2020, at <https://opiniojuris.org/2020/12/11/the-icc-british-war-crimes-in-iraq-and-avery-british-tradition/>.
25 OTP, Iraq second decision (n 13) paras 372–385.
26 ibid para 373.
27 This case concerned the conviction for inhuman treatment of a Corporal, who was sentenced to one year's imprisonment. See Ceasefire Centre for Civilian Rights, 'Official Figures Reveal Only One Prosecution of UK Armed Forces Personnel for War Crimes Overseas Since 2001', 9 December 2020, at www.ceasefire.org/official-figures-reveal-only-one-prosecution-of-uk-armed-forces-personnel-for-war-crimes-overseas-since-2001/
28 www.hrw.org/news/2019/04/12/uk-century-after-amritsar-massacre-london-still-kicks-its-atrocities-under-rug
29 OTP, Iraq second decision (n 13) para 371.
30 See Chantal Meloni, 'Torture, Command Responsibility, and the Vicious Circle of Impunity: On the ICC's Failure to Investigate British Responsibilities for Their Crimes in Iraq', in Florian Jeßberger, Moritz Vormbaum and Boris Burghardt

(eds), *Strafrecht und Systemunrecht: Festschrift für Gerhard Werle zum 70. Geburtstag* (Mohr Siebeck, 2022) 207–220.

31 See ICC, Situation in the Republic of Kenya, Decision Pursuant to Article 15 of the Rome Statute on the Authorization of an Investigation into the Situation in the Republic of Kenya, 31 March 2010, ICC-01/09-19, para 32.

32 See Heller (n 24).

33 See Baldwin (n 24).

34 OTP, Iraq second decision (n 13) para 487.

35 ibid para 496.

36 This section elaborates on thoughts I have published earlier with Valentina Azarova, see Valentina Azarova and Triestino Mariniello, 'Why the ICC Needs a "Palestine Situation" (More Than Palestine Needs the ICC): On the Court's Potential Role(s) in the Israeli-Palestinian Context' (2017) Diritti umani e diritto internazionale 115–150.

37 See ICC, Situation in Palestine, OTP, 3 April 2012. At the time of writing, the OTP has opened a formal investigation into the Palestine situation. However, almost eight years after Palestine accepted the jurisdiction of the Court for the second time, the Prosecutor has not selected any case yet.

38 ibid para 5.

39 See ICC Rome Statute, Art 19(3).

40 See eg, Valentina Azarov and Chantal Meloni, 'Disentangling the Knots: A Comment on Ambos' "Palestine, 'Non-Member Observer' Status and ICC Jurisdiction"', EJIL: Talk!, 27 May 2014, at www.ejiltalk.org/disentangling-the-knots-a-comment-on-ambos-palestine-non-member-observer-status-and-icc-jurisdiction/.

41 See Alain Pellet, 'The Palestinian Declaration and the Jurisdiction of the International Criminal Court', (2010) Journal of International Criminal Justice 981ff; Vera Gowland-Debbas, 'Note on the Legal Effects of Palestine's Declaration under Article 12(3) of the ICC Statute', Office of the Prosecutor-NGO Roundtable Session on Palestine, 20 October 2010, at www.icc-cpi.int/NR/rdonlyres/56368E8B-2FBB-4CFB-88AB-98D105F2C56F/282610/PalestineGowllandDebbas.pdf.

42 Schabas notes that UNESCO's admission of Palestine in 2011 was of equivalent weight to a decision by the General Assembly; William A Schabas, 'Palestine Should Accede to the Rome Statute', 1 November 2011, at www.humanrightsdoctorate.blogspot.co.uk/2011/11/palestine-should-accede-to-rome-statute.html.

43 For discussion of the Cook Islands precedent, William A Schabas, 'The Prosecutor and Palestine: Deference to the Security Council', 8 April 2012, at www.humanrightsdoctorate.blogspot.co.uk/2012/04/prosecutor-and-palestine-deference-to.html.

44 ICC, 'Report on Preliminary Examination Activities 2013', OTP, November 2013, para 234ff.

45 Anshel Pfeffer, 'Israel Has Little to Fear from the International Criminal Court', Haaretz, 20 May 2014, at www.haaretz.com/blogs/jerusalem-babylon/1.591596.

46 William A Schabas, 'Out of Africa. Israel is Referred to the International Criminal Court', 15 May 2013, at www.humanrightsdoctorate.blogspot.co.uk/2013/05/out-of-africa-israel-is-referred-to.html

47 ICC, Statement of the Prosecutor of the International Criminal Court, Karim AA Khan QC, following the application for an expedited order under article 18(2) seeking authorisation to resume investigations in the Situation in Afghanistan,

27 September 2021, at www.icc-cpi.int/news/statement-prosecutor-international-criminal-court-karim-khan-qc-following-application
48 ICC, 'Public redacted version of "Request for authorisation of an investigation pursuant to article 15", 20 November 2017, ICC-02/17-7-Conf-Exp', OTP, 20 November 2017, ICC-02/17-7-Red 20-11-2017 (Afghanistan Request for Authorization).
49 See ICC, Judgment on the appeal against the decision on the authorisation of an investigation into the situation in the Islamic Republic of Afghanistan, Appeals Chamber, 5 March 2020, ICC-02/17 OA4.
50 See Afghanistan Request for Authorization (n 48) para 193.
51 See M Cherif Bassiouni, *The Institutionalization of Torture by the Bush Administration* (Intersentia 2010).
52 See Committee Study of the Central Intelligence Agency's Detention and Interrogation Program, 'Report of the Senate Select Committee on Intelligence', 9 December 2014, at www.intelligence.senate.gov/sites/default/files/publications/CRPT-113srpt288.pdf
53 Amnesty International, 'Afghanistan: ICC Prosecutor's Statement on Afghanistan Jeopardises His Office's Legitimacy and Future', 5 October 2021, at https://hrij.amnesty.nl/afghanistan-icc-prosecutors-statement-on-afghanistan-jeopardises-his-offices-legitimacy-and-future/
54 See Afghanistan Request for Authorization (n 48) para 189.
55 Alice Speri, 'How the US Derailed an Effort to Prosecute its Crimes in Afghanistan', 5 October 2021, at https://theintercept.com/2021/10/05/afghanistan-icc-war-crimes/
56 'Pompeo Slams International Criminal Court, Threatens to Deny, Revoke U.S. Visas', 16 March 2019, at www.rferl.org/a/pompeo-us-deny-visas-icc-investigators-afghanistan-/29824557.html; Human Rights Watch, 'US Threatens International Criminal Court', 15 March 2019, at www.hrw.org/news/2019/03/15/us-threatens-international-criminal-court; 'John Bolton Threatens ICC with US Sanctions', BBC, 11 September 2018, at www.bbc.com/news/world-us-canada-45474864.
57 Human Rights Watch, 'US Sanctions on the International Criminal Court', 14 December 2020, at www.hrw.org/news/2020/12/14/us-sanctions-international-criminal-court
58 See ICC, 'Victims' Request for Leave to Submit Observations Source: Legal', Legal Representative of Victims, 12 October 2021, ICC-02/17.
59 See Afghanistan Request for Authorization (n 48) paras 19 and 22.
60 ibid para 347.
61 ibid.
62 ibid para 348.
63 ibid.
64 Michael G Karnavas, 'The Big Pivot: ICC Prosecutor Khan's not so Slight, Afghan Slight Sleight of Hand', 4 October 2021, at https://michaelgkarnavas.net/blog/2021/10/04/icc-prosecutor-afghan-pivot/
65 Alex Whiting, 'Afghanistan Decision: Bending to U.S. or Focusing Court on Successful Investigations?', Just Security, 12 April 2019, at www.justsecurity.org/63613/the-iccs-afghanistan-decision-bending-to-u-s-or-focusing-court-on-successful-investigations/
66 ibid.

67 Janet Anderson, 'Afghanistan: A War of Positions at the ICC', Justice Info, 21 October 2021, at www.justiceinfo.net/en/83498-afghanistan-war-of-position-icc.html
68 See Mirjan Damaska, 'What is the Point of International Criminal Justice' (2008) Chicago-Kent Law Review 361.
69 See Frédéric Mégret and Nidal N Jurdi, 'The International Criminal Court, the Arab Spring and its Aftermath' (2016) Diritti umani e diritto internazionale 375;
70 Sarah MH Nouwen, 'Legal Equality on Trial: Sovereigns and Individuals before the International Criminal Court' (2012) Netherlands Yearbook of International Law 151–181.

Selected Bibliography

Amnesty International, *'Afghanistan: ICC Prosecutor's statement on Afghanistan jeopardises his Office's legitimacy and future'*, 5 October 2021, at https://hrij.amnesty.nl/afghanistan-icc-prosecutors-statement-on-afghanistan-jeopardises-his-offices-legitimacy-and-future/

Anderson J, 'Afghanistan: A War of Positions at the ICC', *Justice Info*, 21 October 2021, at www.justiceinfo.net/en/83498-afghanistan-war-of-position-icc.html

Azarova V and Meloni C, 'Disentangling the Knots: A Comment on Ambos' "Palestine, 'Non-Member Observer' Status and ICC Jurisdiction"', EJIL: Talk!, 27 May 2014, at www.ejiltalk.org/disentangling-the-knots-a-comment-on-ambos-palestine-non-member-observer-status-and-icc-jurisdiction/

Azarova V and Mariniello T, 'Why the ICC Needs a "Palestine Situation" (More Than Palestine Needs the ICC): On the Court's Potential Role(s) in the Israeli-Palestinian Context' [2017] *Diritti umani e diritto internazionale* 115

Baldwin C, 'UK: A Century After the Amritsar Massacre, London Still Kicks Its Atrocities Under the Rug', 12 April 2019, at www.hrw.org/news/2019/04/12/uk-century-after-amritsar-massacre-london-still-kicks-its-atrocities-under-rug

Baldwin C, 'The ICC Prosecutor Office's Cop-Out on UK Military Crimes in Iraq', Opinio Juris, 18 December 2020, at <https://opiniojuris.org/2020/12/18/the-icc-prosecutor-offices-cop-out-on-ukmilitary-crimes-in-iraq/>

Brubacher M R, 'Prosecutorial Discretion within the International Criminal Court' (2004) *Journal of International Criminal Justice* 71

Ceasefire Centre for Civilian Rights, 'Official Figures Reveal Only One Prosecution of UK Armed Forces Personnel for War Crimes Overseas Since 2001' 9 December 2020, at www.ceasefire.org/official-figures-reveal-only-one-prosecution-of-uk-armed-forces-personnel-for-war-crimes-overseas-since-2001/

Cherif Bassiouni M, *The Institutionalization of Torture by the Bush Administration* (Intersentia 2010)

Committee Study of the Central Intelligence Agency's Detention and Interrogation Program, 'Report of the Senate Select Committee on Intelligence', 9 December 2014, at www.intelligence.senate.gov/sites/default/files/publications/CRPT-113srpt288.pdf

Cote L, 'Reflections on the Exercise of Prosecutorial Discretion in International Criminal Law' [2005] *Journal of International Criminal Justice* 162

Damaska M, 'What is the Point of International Criminal Justice' [2008] *Chicago-Kent Law Review* 361

Danner A M, 'Enhancing the Legitimacy and Accountability of Prosecutorial Discretion at the International Criminal Court' [2003] *American Journal of International Law* 510

Fernandez de Gurmendi SA, 'The Role of the International Prosecutor', in Roy S Lee (ed), *The International Criminal Court: The Making of the Rome Statute: Issues, Negotiations, Results* (Kluwer Law International 1999) 175

Gowland-Debbas V, *'Note on the Legal Effects of Palestine's Declaration under Article 12(3) of the ICC Statute'*, Office of the Prosecutor-NGO Roundtable Session on Palestine, 20 October 2010, at www.icc-cpi.int/NR/rdonlyres/56368E8B-2FBB-4CFB-88AB-98D105F2C56F/282610/PalestineGowllandDebbas.pdf

Heller KJ, 'The Nine Words that (Wrongly) Doomed the Iraq Investigation', *Opinio Juris*, 10 December 2020, at https://opiniojuris.org/2020/12/10/the-nine-words-that-wrongly-doomed-the-iraqinvestigation/>

Human Rights Watch, 'US Sanctions on the International Criminal Court', 14 December 2020, at www.hrw.org/news/2020/12/14/us-sanctions-international-criminal-court

Human Rights Watch, 'US Threatens International Criminal Court', 15 March 2019, at www.hrw.org/news/2019/03/15/us-threatens-international-criminal-court;

Karnavas MG, 'The Big Pivot: ICC Prosecutor Khan's not so Slight, Afghan Slight Sleight of Hand', 4 October 2021, at https://michaelgkarnavas.net/blog/2021/10/04/icc-prosecutor-afghan-pivot/

Mariniello T, 'Judicial Control over Prosecutorial Discretion in the Rome Statute' (2019) *International Criminal Law Review* 979

Mégret F and Nidal NJ, 'The International Criminal Court, the Arab Spring and its Aftermath' [2016] *Diritti umani e diritto internazionale* 375

Meloni C, 'Torture, Command Responsibility, and the Vicious Circle of Impunity: On the ICC's Failure to Investigate British Responsibilities for Their Crimes in Iraq', in Florian Jeßberger, Moritz Vormbaum and Boris Burghardt (eds), *Strafrecht und Systemunrecht: Festschrift für Gerhard Werle zum 70. Geburtstag* 207

Meloni C, 'The ICC Preliminary Examination of the Flotilla Situation: an Opportunity to Contextualise Gravity' (2016) 6 *Questions of International Law*, available at www.qil-qdi.org/icc-preliminary-examination-flotilla-situation-opportunity-contextualise-gravity/

Nouwen SMH, 'Legal Equality on Trial: Sovereigns and Individuals before the International Criminal Court' [2012] *Netherlands Yearbook of International Law* 151

Pellet A, 'The Palestinian Declaration and the Jurisdiction of the International Criminal Court' [2010] *Journal of International Criminal Justice* 981

Pfeffer A, 'Israel Has Little to Fear from the International Criminal Court', *Haaretz*, 20 May 2014, at www.haaretz.com/blogs/jerusalem-babylon/1.591596

Schabas WA, 'The International Criminal Court at Ten' [2011] *Criminal Law Forum* 493

Schabas WA, 'Out of Africa. Israel is Referred to the International Criminal Court', 15 May 2013, at www.humanrightsdoctorate.blogspot.co.uk/2013/05/out-of-africa-israel-is-referred-to.html

Schabas WA, 'The Prosecutor and Palestine: Deference to the Security Council', 8 April 2012, at www.humanrightsdoctorate.blogspot.co.uk/2012/04/prosecutor-and-palestine-deference-to.html

Schabas WA, 'Palestine Should Accede to the Rome Statute', 1 November 2011, at www.humanrightsdoctorate.blogspot.co.uk/2011/11/palestine-should-accede-to-rome-statute.html

Schabas WA, 'Prosecutorial Discretion v. Judicial Activism at the International Criminal Court' [2008] *Journal of International Criminal Justice* 731

Schüller A, 'The ICC, British War Crimes in Iraq and a Very British Tradition', *Opinio Juris*, 11 December 2020, at <https://opiniojuris.org/2020/12/11/the-icc-british-war-crimes-in-iraq-and-avery-british-tradition/>

Speri A, 'How the US Derailed an Effort to Prosecute its Crimes in Afghanistan', 5 October 2021, at https://theintercept.com/2021/10/05/afghanistan-icc-war-crimes/

Whiting A, 'Afghanistan Decision: Bending to U.S. or Focusing Court on Successful Investigations?', *Just Security*, 12 April 2019, at www.justsecurity.org/63613/the-iccs-afghanistan-decision-bending-to-u-s-or-focusing-court-on-successful-investigations/

El Zeidy M, 'The Gravity Threshold under the Statute of the International Criminal Court' (2008) *Criminal Law Forum* 35

Annex: The Italian Ministry of Justice Proposal for a Code of International Crimes of 2022 ("Palazzo-Pocar Draft") (EN)[1]

TITLE I
GENERAL PROVISIONS

Article 1
(Nature of Crimes)

1 For all legal purposes, the crimes set forth in this Code are "delitti"[2] and the use of the term "crime", or "international crime", shall be construed as referring to "delitto".

Article 2
(International crimes committed in the territory of the State)

1 Article 6 of the Penal Code shall be applied to the crimes set forth in this Code committed in the territory of the State.

Article 3
(International crimes committed abroad)

1 The commission of a crime set forth in this Code by an Italian citizen abroad shall be punished according to the Italian law.

2 The commission of a crime set forth in this Code by a foreigner abroad against the Italian Republic or against an Italian citizen shall be punished according to the Italian law.

3 The commission of a crime set forth in this Code by a foreigner abroad, not directed against the Italian Republic or an Italian citizen, even in the case of complicity with an Italian citizen, shall be punished according to the Italian law, insofar as the perpetrator is on the Italian territory.

Article 4

Proposal 1

Art 4 (*Competence*)

1 The Corte d'Assise shall be competent for the crimes set forth in this Code. The Juvenile Court shall be competent for crimes committed by persons under the age of 18.[3]
2 The Corte d'Assise in Rome and the Juvenile Court in Rome are competent for crimes committed outside of national territory.
3 The functions of the Public Prosecutor shall be assigned to the Public Prosecutor's office attached to the Tribunal of the district capital in which the court with (territorial) competence sits.

Proposal 2

Art 4 (*Jurisdiction and competence*)

1 The Corte d'Assise shall be competent for the crimes set forth in this Code. The Juvenile Court shall be competent for crimes committed by persons under the age of 18.
2 The Corte d'Assise in Rome and the Juvenile Court in Rome shall be competent for crimes committed outside of national territory.
3 The functions of the Public Prosecutor shall be assigned to the Public Prosecutor's office attached to the Tribunal of the district capital in which the court with (territorial) competence sits.
4 The military judicial authority shall be competent for crimes committed by members of the Italian Armed Forces, and if they are committed abroad, the military court of Rome has competence. The provisions of book one of the Military Penal Code of Peace shall apply.

Proposal 3

Art 4 (*Jurisdiction and competence*)

1 The Corte d'Assise shall be competent for the crimes set forth in this Code. The Juvenile Court shall be competent for crimes committed by persons under the age of 18.

2 The Corte d'Assise in Rome and the Juvenile Court in Rome shall be competent for crimes committed abroad.

3 The functions of the Public Prosecutor shall be assigned to the Public Prosecutor's office attached to the Tribunal of the district capital in which the court with (territorial) competence sits.

4 The military judicial authority shall be competent for war crimes set forth in Title II, Chapter II of this Code committed by members of the Italian Armed Forces; if they are committed abroad, the military court of Rome has competence.

5 Whenever proceedings for war crimes, for which the military court is competent, are joined with other proceedings for war crimes or crimes against humanity or crimes of genocide under the competence of the ordinary court, the latter shall be competent for all of the proceedings.

Art 4 A (*Coordination Rule*)

1 The provisions of this Title shall also apply when the Military Penal Code of War is applicable.

Article 5

(Connected crimes / Joined proceedings)

Solution in accordance with Proposal 1

Art 5 (*Connected crimes / Joined proceedings*)

1 If a crime set forth in this Code is connected, pursuant to art. 12 of the Code of Criminal Procedure, or is joined, pursuant to art. 371, para. 2, letter b, of the Code of Criminal Procedure, to another offense falling within the competence of a different judge, whether ordinary or military, the ordinary judge with competence for the crime set forth in this Code shall be competent for all of the offenses.

Solutions in accordance with Proposal 2 and 3

Art 5 (*Connected crimes / Joined Proceedings*)

1 If a crime set forth in this Code falls within the competence of the ordinary judge and is connected, pursuant to art. 12 of the Code of Criminal Procedure, or is joined, pursuant to art. 371, para. 2, letter b, of the Code of Criminal Procedure, to a crime under this Code falling within the competence of the military judge, or to an offense within the

competence of another judge, whether ordinary or military, the ordinary judge with competence for the crime set forth in this Code shall be competent for all of the offenses.

Article 6

(Non-political nature for extradition and surrender purposes)

1 The crimes set forth in this Code do not constitute political offenses for the purposes of extradition or surrender to the International Criminal Court pursuant to articles 11 and 12 of Law n. 237 of 20 December 2012.

Article 7

(Immunity)

1 Functional immunity to the extent recognized under international law shall not apply in relation to the crimes set forth in this Code.

2 Personal immunity of Heads of State, Heads of Government and Ministers of Foreign Affairs during their term of office, as well as of other persons to whom international law expressly grants immunity in relation to their official capacity, shall apply with regard to national jurisdiction also with respect to the crimes set forth in this Code, without prejudice to the obligations to cooperate with the International Criminal Court, pursuant to Law no. 237 of 20 December 2012, and with other international criminal tribunals that may have jurisdiction.

Article 8

(Intentional omission to prevent the crime of the subordinate)

1 A military commander who, despite having the duty and power do so, omits to prevent the commission of a crime set forth in this Code by a subordinate under his command and effective control, shall be criminally responsible for the same crime.

2 A civilian superior who, despite having the duty and power to do so, fails to prevent the commission of a crime set forth in this Code by a subordinate under his authority and effective control, shall be criminally responsible for the same crime.

Article 9

(Culpable omission to prevent the crime of the subordinate)

1 A military commander who culpably omits to prevent the commission of a crime set forth in this Code by a subordinate under his command and effective control, in breach of his duty and despite the power at his

disposal, shall be punished as a perpetrator of the crime committed by the subordinate, with a reduced sentence by one-third up to one-half.

2 A civilian superior who culpably omits to prevent the commission of a crime set forth in this Code by a subordinate under his authority and effective control, in breach of his duty and despite the power at his disposal, shall be punished as a perpetrator of the crime committed by the subordinate, with a reduced sentence by one-third up to one-half.

Article 10

(*Subjective status*)

1 For the purposes of the provisions of this Code, any person exercising command and control, including de facto command and control, over a military organization shall be deemed equivalent to a military commander.

2 Any person exercising authority and control, including de facto authority and control, within a hierarchical structure of a non-military nature shall be deemed equivalent to a civilian superior.

Article 11

(*Superior orders*)

1 If a crime set forth in this Code is committed pursuant to an order of a superior, whether civilian or military, the person who gave the order shall always be criminally responsible for the crime. The person who executed the order shall also be criminally responsible for the crime, unless the person did not know that the binding order was unlawful and the order was not manifestly unlawful.

2 For the purposes of this article, orders to commit the crime of genocide or crimes against humanity set forth in this Code are always manifestly unlawful.

Article 12

(*Lawful use of weapons*)

1 The use of arms, or other means of physical coercion, which involves the commission of an international crime set forth by this Code shall never be considered as lawful (for the purpose of the defense envisaged by art. 51 of the Penal Code).

Article 13

(*Mitigating circumstances in case of cooperation*)

1 The penalty of life imprisonment is replaced by that of imprisonment for a term of 24 to 30 years and the other penalties are reduced by up to one-third for any defendant who, prior to the final judgement of conviction,

at any stage or level of the trial: distances himself from the criminal context and fully confesses to the commission of the crimes set forth in this Code; as well as, cooperates or has cooperated effectively to gather evidence for the identification or capture of one or more perpetrators of crimes committed in the same criminal context; or works or has worked effectively to remove or mitigate the harmful or dangerous consequences of the crime in favor of the victim.

2 Concurring aggravating circumstances shall not be deemed to prevail over the mitigating circumstance referred to in the first paragraph.

Article 14
(*Mandatory forfeiture*)

1 In the case of conviction, or application of the penalty upon request of the parties pursuant to art. 444 of the Code of Criminal Procedure, for one of the crimes set forth in this Code, it shall always be ordered the forfeiture of the things that were wholly or partially used or intended to be used to commit the crime and of the goods, money or other utilities that constitute its product, price or profit, unless they belong to a person not connected to the crime, as well as of anything that derives from the use of such product, price or profit.

2 When direct forfeiture is not possible, it shall be ordered the forfeiture of goods, money or other utilities which the defendant has at his disposal is ordered, for a value corresponding to that of the product, price or profit of the crime.

3 In the cases referred to in the previous paragraphs, the judge, with the judgement, determines the amount of money or identifies property or other assets subject to forfeiture, if possible.

Article 15
(*Liability of legal persons*)

1 The crimes set forth in this Code determine the administrative liability of legal persons regulated by Legislative Decree no. 231 of 8 June 2001, in accordance with the provisions of Articles x and y of the same legislative decree.

Article 16
(*Non-applicability of statute of limitations*)

1 The crimes set forth in Chapters I, II, III and IV of Title II of this Code are not subject to any statute of limitations.

TITLE II
CRIMES IN PARTICULAR

Chapter I
Genocide

Article 17
(Crimes of genocide)

1 Whoever, with the intent to destroy, in whole or in part, a national, ethnic, racial, religious or linguistic group as such, acting in a context of a pattern of conducts referred to in the following subparagraphs, intended to cause the destruction, even partial, of such group:

- a causes the death of a member of the group, shall be punished with life imprisonment;
- b causes a serious or very serious harm to a member of the group, shall be punished with imprisonment from twelve to twenty-four years;
- c inflicts on several members of the group conditions of life calculated to cause their death or serious or very serious injuries, shall be punished with imprisonment from twelve to twenty-four years;
- d forces, with violence or threats, or with the abuse of authority, a member of the group to perform or undergo sexual acts that constitute a serious offense to personal sexual freedom and dignity shall be punished with imprisonment from twelve to twenty-four years;
- e forces a member of the group to undergo mutilation of the genitals, sterilization, or measures intended to prevent or hinder births within the group, shall be punished with imprisonment from twelve to twenty-four years;
- f forcibly transfers a child of the group to another group, also by means of foster care measures however named, shall be punished with imprisonment from twelve to twenty-four years.

Article 18
(Cultural genocide)

1 Whoever, with the intent to destroy, in whole or in part, a national, ethnic, racial, religious or linguistic group as such, acting in a context of a pattern of conducts referred to in the following subparagraphs, intended to cause the destruction, even partial, of such group:

- a Forces members of the group to undergo deprivations of personal freedom or subjects them to deportation, tracking or mass surveillance measures, measures of forced indoctrination, or other measures or conditions of life calculated to remove the cultural, linguistic or religious features of the group, shall be punished with imprisonment from twelve to twenty-four years;

b subjects several members of the group to obligations or prohibitions concerning religious, spiritual or cultural practices, schooling or the use of language, suitable to remove the cultural, linguistic or religious features of the group, shall be punished with imprisonment from eight to twenty years.

Article 19

(Incitement to and condoning of genocide)

1 Whoever publicly incites to commit a crime described in this chapter shall, for the mere fact of incitement, be punished with imprisonment from three to twelve years.

2 The same punishment shall apply to any person who publicly condones a crime described in this chapter.

Chapter II
Crimes against humanity

Article 20

(Contextual element)

1 The conducts described in articles 21 to 31 of this Chapter shall constitute crimes against humanity if committed as part of a widespread or systematic attack directed against any civilian population pursuant to or in furtherance of a State or organizational policy.

Article 21

(Murder)

1 Whoever causes the death of a person shall be punished with life imprisonment.

Article 22

(Extermination)

1 Whoever imposes on more than one person conditions of life calculated to cause the total or partial destruction of a civilian population shall be punished with imprisonment from twelve to twenty-four years.

Article 23

(Serious or very serious bodily or mental harm)

1 Whoever causes serious harm to a person shall be punished with imprisonment from eight to sixteen years.

2 Whoever causes very serious harm to a person shall be punished with imprisonment from twelve to twenty-four years.

Article 24

(Enslavement)

1 Whoever exercises over a person the powers attaching to the right of ownership shall be punished with imprisonment from ten to twenty-four years.

2 The same penalty applies to anyone who reduces or maintains a person in a state of continuous subjection by means of violence, threats, deception, abuse of authority or taking advantage of a condition of vulnerability, physical or mental inferiority or necessity, trafficking the person or forcing the person to work or provide sexual services or to perform other activities that entail exploitation.

Article 25

(Rape and other crimes against sexual freedom and dignity)

1 Whoever forces a person:
  a to perform or be subjected to sexual acts that seriously offend sexual freedom and dignity;
  b into prostitution;
  c to terminate a pregnancy or become pregnant with the intent of affecting the ethnic composition of the targeted population;
  d to undergo sterilization, mutilation of the genital organs or other acts of deprivation of reproductive capacity, in the absence of therapeutic necessity; shall be punished by imprisonment from ten to twenty-four years.

Article 26

(Forced marriage)

1 Whoever forces a person to enter into marriage, or into a cohabitation analogous to that of marriage, shall be punished with imprisonment from five to twelve years.

2 Whoever forces a person under the age of eighteen years to enter into marriage, or in a cohabitation analogous to that of marriage, shall be punished with imprisonment from twelve to eighteen years.

Article 27

(Deportation or forcible transfer)

1 Whoever deports or forcibly transfers, in violation of international law, several persons from the territorial area in which they are lawfully located, by means of expulsion, or by acts of violence or threats, or by taking advantage of conditions of vulnerability, necessity or intimidation

resulting from the attack on the civilian population referred to in article 20 of this Code, shall be punished with imprisonment from ten to twenty-four years.

Article 28

(Unlawful or arbitrary detention)

1 Whoever, in violation of applicable international or domestic law, arrests or in any other manner deprives a person of physical liberty, shall be punished with imprisonment from five to twelve years.

Article 29

(Enforced disappearance)

1 Whoever arrests, even lawfully, or otherwise deprives a person of personal liberty, with the authorization, support or acquiescence of a State or an organization, and removes such person from the protection of the law for a prolonged period of time, refusing to give proper information as to the condition of the arrest or detention, the reasons for the measure or the whereabouts of such person, shall be punished with imprisonment from ten to twenty-four years.

2 Whoever, having custody of an arrested person, even lawfully, or otherwise deprived of personal liberty, removes the person from the protection of the law for a prolonged period of time, refusing to give proper information as to the condition of the arrest or detention, the reasons for the measure or the whereabouts of such person, with the authorization, support or acquiescence of a State or an organization, shall be punished with imprisonment from five to twelve years.

Article 30

(Torture and other inhuman or degrading treatment)

1 Whoever performs on a person subjected, even de facto, to his control or custody, authority, supervision, care or assistance, acts suitable to cause severe physical suffering or psychological trauma, or subjects such person to inhuman or degrading treatment, shall be punished with imprisonment from ten to twenty-four years.

2 This provision shall not apply in the case of physical suffering or psychological trauma resulting only from the execution of lawful restrictive measures under international law.

3 If the conduct referred to in the first paragraph is performed in order to obtain information or confessions from the victim or other persons or in order to punish, intimidate or coerce them or for any other purpose based on discriminatory grounds, the penalty is imprisonment from twelve to twenty-four years.

Article 31
(Persecution)

1 Whoever, by means of violence or threats, or in the exercise of legislative, judicial or administrative functions, prevents or seriously hinders one or more persons from exercising human rights by reasons of their membership to a group identified by political, racial, national, ethnic, linguistic, cultural, religious or gender features, or in any case of discriminatory grounds prohibited by international law, shall be punished with imprisonment from eight to fifteen years.

Article 32
(Apartheid)

1 Whoever commits one or more of the conducts set forth in Articles 21 to 31 of this Chapter in the context of an institutionalized regime of systematic oppression and domination by one racial or ethnic group over any other racial or ethnic group or groups, in order to maintain such regime or otherwise to implement its goals, shall be punished with the penalties set forth in those articles, increased by up to one-third, without prejudice to the limit indicated in article 64, para. 2, of the Penal Code.

Chapter III
War crimes

Section I
Scope and definitions

Article 33
(Contextual element)

1 The conducts described in this Chapter shall constitute war crimes if they are committed in the context an international armed conflict or of an armed conflict not of an international character and are connected to such conflict.

Article 34
(Definition of international armed conflict)

1 International armed conflicts are those between two or more States characterized by any contrast arising between them and leading to the intervention of the armed force of one State against another State, even in the absence of a formal declaration of war. International armed conflicts also include cases of total or partial occupation of the territory of a State

by the armed forces of another State, even if said occupation meets with no armed resistance.

2 Armed conflicts not of an international character are those occurring in the territory of a State between governmental forces and organized armed groups or between organized armed groups themselves characterized by the sustained use of arms. Internal situations of disorder and tension such as riots, isolated and sporadic acts of violence or other acts of a similar nature shall not be considered as armed conflicts.[4]

3 The provisions of this Chapter shall also apply to international missions established within the framework of international organizations or otherwise in accordance with international law providing for the use of armed force by the personnel employed.

Article 35

(Definition of protected persons)

1 For the purposes of this Chapter, protected persons are civilians, wounded, sick, shipwrecked persons, persons detained in connection with the conflict and persons otherwise under the power of the opposing party who have laid down arms or are otherwise defenseless, and any other person protected under the Geneva Conventions and their Additional Protocols.

Section II

Crimes against persons

Article 36

(Murder)

1 Whoever causes the death of a protected person shall be punished with life imprisonment.

Article 37

(Extermination)

1 Whoever imposes conditions of life calculated to cause the total or partial destruction of a population shall be punished with imprisonment for ten to twenty-four years.

Article 38

(Serious or very serious harm)

1 Whoever causes serious harm to a protected person shall be punished with imprisonment from eight to sixteen years.

2 Whoever causes very serious harm to a protected person or permanent deformation or disfigurement of the face shall be punished with imprisonment from twelve to twenty-four years.

Article 39

(Torture and other inhuman or degrading treatment)

1 Whoever performs on a protected person subjected, even de facto, to his control or custody, authority, supervision, care or assistance, acts suitable to cause serious physical suffering or psychological trauma, or subjects such person to inhuman or degrading treatment, shall be punished with imprisonment from ten to twenty-four years.

2 This provision shall not apply in the case of physical suffering or psychological trauma resulting only from the execution of lawful restrictive measures under international law.

3 If the conduct referred to in the first paragraph is performed in order to obtain information or confessions from the victim or other persons or in order to punish, intimidate or coerce them or for any other purpose based on discriminatory grounds, the penalty is imprisonment from twelve to twenty-four years.

Article 40

(Rape and other crimes against sexual freedom and dignity)

1 Whoever forces a person:
   a to perform or be subjected to sexual acts that seriously offend sexual freedom and dignity;
   b into prostitution;
   c to terminate a pregnancy or become pregnant with the intent of affecting the ethnic composition of the targeted population;
   d to undergo sterilization, mutilation of the genital organs or other acts of deprivation of reproductive capacity, in the absence of therapeutic necessity;
   e to be subjected to the exercise of the powers attaching to the right of ownership for the purpose of sexual exploitation, shall be punished with imprisonment from ten to twenty-four years.

Article 41

(Medical, scientific or biological experiments)

1 Whoever subjects a protected person to medical or scientific or biological experiments or other health treatments, suitable to cause death or serious or very serious harm, without valid consent or in any event in the absence of therapeutic needs, shall be punished with imprisonment from ten to twenty-four years.

Article 42
(Mutilation, abuse or abduction of a corpse)

1 Whoever interferes with the corpse or ashes of a protected person or destroys, suppresses or removes the corpse of a protected person, or a part of it, or removes or disperses the protected person's ashes, shall be punished with imprisonment from three to six years.

Article 43
(Taking hostages)

1 Whoever deprives one or more protected persons of their personal liberty by threatening to kill or injure them or to continue to detain them in order to compel a State, an international organization, a natural or legal person or a group of persons to act or to refrain from any act, shall be punished with imprisonment from eight to twenty years.

Article 44
(Deportation, transfer and illegal detention)[5]

1 Whoever unlawfully detains, deports or transfers several protected persons from the territorial area in which they are lawfully located, by means of expulsion, or by acts of violence or threats, or by taking advantage of conditions of vulnerability, necessity or intimidation resulting from the armed conflict, without the conduct being justified by the security needs of those persons or by imperative military necessity, shall be punished with imprisonment from ten to twenty-four years.

Article 45
(Transfer of the civilian population)

1 Whoever transfers in any manner part of the civilian population of a State or territory to another State or territory occupied by or under effective control of a Party to the conflict,[6] or otherwise facilitates such transfer, shall be punished with imprisonment from ten to twenty-four years.

Article 46
(Conscripting, enlisting and using children)[7]

1 Whoever conscripts or enlists persons under the age of eighteen years into the armed forces or armed groups shall be punished with imprisonment from five to twelve years.
2 Whoever uses minors under the age of eighteen years to participate actively in hostilities shall be punished with imprisonment from ten to twenty-four years.

3 The offender may not plead ignorance of the age of the victim as an excuse, unless it is inevitable ignorance.

Article 47

(Forced participation in hostilities)

1 Whoever coerces a protected person to serve in the armed forces of an adverse Party or to take part in military operations against his own country shall be punished with imprisonment from five to twelve years.

Article 48

(Deprivation of rights or actions)[8]

1 Whoever, in the exercise, including de facto exercise, of legislative, administrative or judicial functions, enforces the abolition, suspension or termination of admissibility in legal proceedings of certain rights or related actions of persons belonging to the opposing Party or of a group of them, shall be punished with imprisonment from five to twelve years.

Article 49

(Denial of due process)

1 Whoever deprives a protected person of the rights and guarantees of due process shall be punished with imprisonment from five to twelve years.

Section III

Crimes consisting in the use of prohibited methods of warfare

Article 50

(Destruction, pillaging and appropriation of property on a large scale)

1 Whoever commits acts of destruction or pillaging or, illegally and on a large scale, appropriates, requisitions, confiscates or destroys property belonging to subjects of the opposing Party, shall be punished with imprisonment from eight to fifteen years.

2 If the act is committed over protected cultural heritage, the penalty is imprisonment from ten to twenty-four years.

Article 51

(Attacks on the civilian population)

1 Whoever directs an attack against the civilian population or against civilians not taking direct part in hostilities shall be punished with imprisonment from ten to twenty-four years.

Article 52

(Attacks on civilian objects)[9]

1 Whoever directs an attack against civilian objects shall be punished with imprisonment from three to eight years.[10]

2 Whoever, outside the cases set forth in the following article, directs an attack against buildings dedicated to worship, education, art, science or humanitarian purposes, power plants or nuclear power plants, hospitals and places where the sick and wounded are collected, or against cities, towns or undefended locations or demilitarized zones, shall be punished with imprisonment from ten to twenty-four years.

Article 53

(Attacks on cultural property)[11]

1 Whoever directs an attack against protected cultural heritage shall be punished with imprisonment from four to twelve years.

2 If the act is committed against cultural heritage subject to special or reinforced protection, the penalty is imprisonment from ten to twenty years.

Article 54

(Attacks against personnel or objects involved in a humanitarian assistance or peacekeeping mission or protected by the distinctive emblem of international humanitarian law)[12]

1 Whoever directs an attack against personnel, installations, material, units or vehicles involved in humanitarian assistance or peacekeeping missions or buildings, equipment, assistance units, means of transport and medical personnel using the distinctive emblems of the Geneva Conventions and other international conventions shall be punished with imprisonment from ten to twenty-four years.

Article 55

(Excessive incidental damage)[13]

1 Whoever carries out an attack with the knowledge that it will incidental deaths or injuries to civilians or damage to civilian objects or widespread, long-term and severe damage to the natural environment, not proportional to the overall concrete and direct military advantage anticipated, shall be punished with imprisonment from ten to twenty-four years.

Article 56

(Use of prohibited methods of warfare)[14]

1 Whoever employs methods of warfare prohibited by customary international law or by international conventions or which for their nature are indiscriminate or which are able to cause unnecessary evil or unnecessary suffering shall be punished with imprisonment from ten to twenty-four years.

Article 57

(Deprivation of means of survival)[15]

1 Whoever as a method of warfare, leads civilians to starvation, prevents them from receiving the relief aid provided for in the Geneva Conventions or deprives them of other indispensable means of survival, shall be punished with imprisonment from ten to twenty-four years.

Article 58

(Human shields)[16]

1 Whoever uses civilians or other protected persons, or takes advantage of their location or movements, in order to shield from attack certain sites or zones or military objectives or to favor or impede military operations, shall be punished by imprisonment from ten to twenty-four years.

Article 59

(Denial of quarter)

1 Whoever, holding a position of command or effective control, denies quarter to the adversary, declaring that there will be no survivors, or conducts hostilities or threatens the adversary to conduct them on the basis of such a decision, shall be punished with imprisonment from five to fifteen years.

Article 60

(Spreading terror among the civilian population)[17]

1 Whoever commits acts of violence or threats directed and suitable to spread terror among the civilian population, shall be punished with imprisonment from six to twelve years.

Article 61

(Perfidy)[18]

1 Whoever causes harm to an adversary by fraudulently inducing him to believe that he is entitled to receive, or is obliged to accord, protection

under international law, shall be punished with imprisonment from ten to twenty-four years.

2 Whoever, engaging in the conduct described in the previous paragraph, causes the death of an adversary shall be punished with life imprisonment.

3 If the conducts described in the preceding paragraphs are carried out by means of the deceptive and arbitrary use of the white flag, the flag or military insignia and uniform of the hostile Party or of the United Nations or the distinctive emblems of the Geneva Conventions, the punishment shall be imprisonment from twelve to twenty-four years, when serious or very serious harm is caused to the adversary. When the conduct causes the death of the adversary, the penalty is life imprisonment.

Chapter IV
Crime of aggression

Article 62
(Aggression)

1 Whoever, in a position to effectively direct the political or military action of a State or to exercise control over it, plans, prepares, initiates or executes an act of aggression, that for its character, gravity and scale is such as to constitute a manifest violation of the Charter of the United Nations shall be punished with life imprisonment.

2 The use of armed force directed against the sovereignty, territorial integrity or political independence of another State or in any other manner inconsistent with the Charter of the United Nations shall constitute an act of aggression.

The following are acts of aggression, regardless of whether a declaration of war exists:

a the invasion or attack, by the armed forces of a State, of the territory of another State or any military occupation, however temporary, resulting from such invasion or attack, or any annexation by the use of force of the territory of another State or part thereof;

b bombardment by the armed forces of a State against the territory of another State, or the use of any other weapons by a State against the territory of another State;

c the blockade of the ports or coasts of a State by the armed forces of another State;

d an attack by the armed forces of a State on the land, sea or air forces, or marine or air fleets of another State;

e the use of the armed forces of a State which are within the territory of another State with the agreement of the receiving State, in contravention of the conditions of that agreement, or any extension of their presence in such territory beyond the termination of the agreement;

f the action of a State in allowing its territory, which it has placed at the disposal of another State, to be used by that other State for perpetrating an act of aggression against a third State;

g the sending by or on behalf of a State of armed bands, groups, irregulars or mercenaries, which carry out acts of armed force against another State of such gravity as to amount to the acts listed in letters a) and d), or its substantial involvement therein.

Chapter V
Other incriminating provisions

Article 63

(Omission to punish and intentional omission to report the subordinate's crime)

1 A military commander who omits to punish a subordinate, placed under his command and effective control, for the commission of a crime set forth in this Code, of which he has become aware in the exercise or because of his duties, shall be punished with imprisonment from two to seven years.

2 A military commander or a civilian superior who omits or delays the reporting to the judicial authority, or to another authority that is obliged to report to it, a crime set forth in this Code, committed by his subordinate, of which he has become aware in the exercise or because of his duties, shall be punished with imprisonment from one to five years.

Article 64

(Association for the commission of international crimes)

1 Anyone who promotes, establishes, organizes, manages or finances an association with the purpose to commit one or more of the international crimes set forth in this Code shall be punished with imprisonment from seven to fifteen years.

2 Anyone who participates in such association shall be punished with imprisonment from five to ten years.

TITLE III
LEGISLATIVE AMENDMENTS AND REPEALS

Article 65

(Amendment of Article 604 bis *of the Italian Penal Code)*

Omitted

Article 66

(Amendment of Article 344 bis *of the Code of Criminal Procedure)*

Omitted

Article 67

(Amendment to Legislative Decree no. 231 of 8 June 2001)

1 In Legislative Decree no. 231 of 8 June 2001, the following article is inserted after article 25 *sexiesdecies:*

Article 25 *septiesdecies. International crimes*

1 In relation to the commission of the crimes provided for by the law [. . .], when the offense has been caused by serious organizational failures, the following monetary sanctions are imposed to the entity:
   a if the crime is punishable by imprisonment of less than ten years, a fine of two hundred to seven hundred shares;
   b if the crime is punishable by imprisonment of not less than ten years or life imprisonment, a fine of four hundred to one thousand shares.
2 If, as a result of the commission of the offenses referred to in point 1, the entity has obtained a significant profit or has suffered damage of a particularly serious nature, monetary sanctions of between [. . .] and [. . .] shares are imposed.
3 In the cases referred to in paragraphs 1 and 2, the disqualification sanctions referred to in article 9, paragraph 2, are imposed for a duration of not less than [. . .] years and not more than [. . .] years, if the offense has been committed by one of the persons referred to in article 5, paragraph 1, letter a), and for a duration of not less than [. . .] years and not more than [. . .], if the offense has been committed by one of the persons referred to in article 5, paragraph 1, letter b).
4 If the entity or one of its organizational units is permanently used for the sole or prevalent purpose of allowing or facilitating the commission of the offenses indicated in point 1, the penalty of definitive disqualification from carrying out the activity is imposed in accordance with article 16, paragraph 3.
5 The entity is not liable when the conduct has been carried out in compliance with the directive of the authority.

Article 68

(Repeal of Law no. 962 of 9 October 1967)

Omitted

Article 69

(*Repeal of Article 4 of Law no. 145 of 21 July 2016*) Omitted

Article 70

(Repeals of provisions of the Military Penal Code of War)

Omitted

Notes

1 The translation of the draft Code has been curated by the Editors of this volume, who would like to thank Edoardo Bastianini for the kind support in carrying out this task. See https://www.giustizia.it/cmsresources/cms/documents/commissione_PALAZZO_POCAR_articolato_31mag22.pdf and also https://www.sistemapenale.it/it/documenti/codice-dei-crimini-internazionali-pubblicata-la-relazione-della-commissione-palazzo-pocar

2 Pursuant to Art 39 of the Penal Code, offences are classified into misdemeanours ("contravvenzioni") and felonies ("delitti"), according to the prescribed type of penalty (Editors' note).

3 Pursuant to Art 5 of the Code of Criminal Procedure, the Corte d'Assise ("Court of Assizes") is the tribunal with competence over the most serious crimes (Editors' note).

4 (Omitted).

5 The crime of unlawful detention is provided for in the ICC Statute only for international armed conflicts. Here it is set forth irrespective of the nature of the conflict. This also includes the failure to release prisoners of war, at the end of conflict, who have not been responsible for international or other crimes.

6 The proposed wording extends the scope of application of the provision, which the ICC Statute defines as limited to international conflicts and only as "the direct or indirect transfer, by the occupying power, of part of its civilian population into the occupied territories".

7 It should be kept in mind that Italy ratified in 2002 the Optional Protocol on the involvement of children in armed conflicts. This Protocol establishes the age limit of 18 years for compulsory enlistment and direct participation in hostilities, unlike the ICC Statute, which establishes a minimum age of 15 years. It was decided to draft the present article indicating the age provided for by the above-mentioned Protocol, since it is binding for Italy. An alternative would have been not to indicate the age, but to use the expression "in violation of international conventions" in view of the universal jurisdiction of the Code being drafted.

8 In this formulation, the case is also applicable to non-international conflicts. Replacing "nationals of the other Party" with "persons belonging to the other Party".

9 Civilian objects (including cultural and religious goods, hospital structures, etc.) are all those goods that do not constitute a military objective by nature, location, destination or use. A civil object, indeed, loses its "character" and therefore its protection if it has become a military objective (eg if a missile battery is placed inside the Colosseum, it loses its civil character and its protection, having become a military objective due to its particular use, even though a series of precautionary measures are taken to try to preserve it).

10 This crime is provided for in the ICC Statute only for international armed conflicts. Here it is provided for irrespective of the nature of the conflict.

11 (Omitted).

12 (Omitted).
13 (Omitted).
14 (Omitted).
15 This includes not only deprivation of food but also other means of survival (eg essential winter clothing). This crime is only provided for in the ICC Statute for international armed conflicts. Here it is provided for irrespective of the nature of the conflict.
16 This offence is provided for in the ICC Statute only for international armed conflicts. Here it is provided for irrespective of the nature of the conflict.
17 This provision is not present in the ICC Statute, even though the prohibition to perform such acts is set out in Article 33 IV of the GC and in Articles 51(2) and 13 of the I and II of the AP respectively.
18 In the present provision, the conduct relating to the misuse of white flag etc. is provided for as a war crime only in international conflicts. Here it is provided for irrespective of the nature of the conflict.

Index

Note: Endnotes are indicated by the page number followed by "n" and the note number e.g., 159n37 refers to note 159 on page 37.

FSC
www.fsc.org
MIX
Papier | Fördert gute Waldnutzung
FSC® C083411

Kolibri 360 GmbH
Ferdinand-Jühlke-Straße 7
99095 Erfurt, Deutschland
produktsicherheit@kolibri360.de